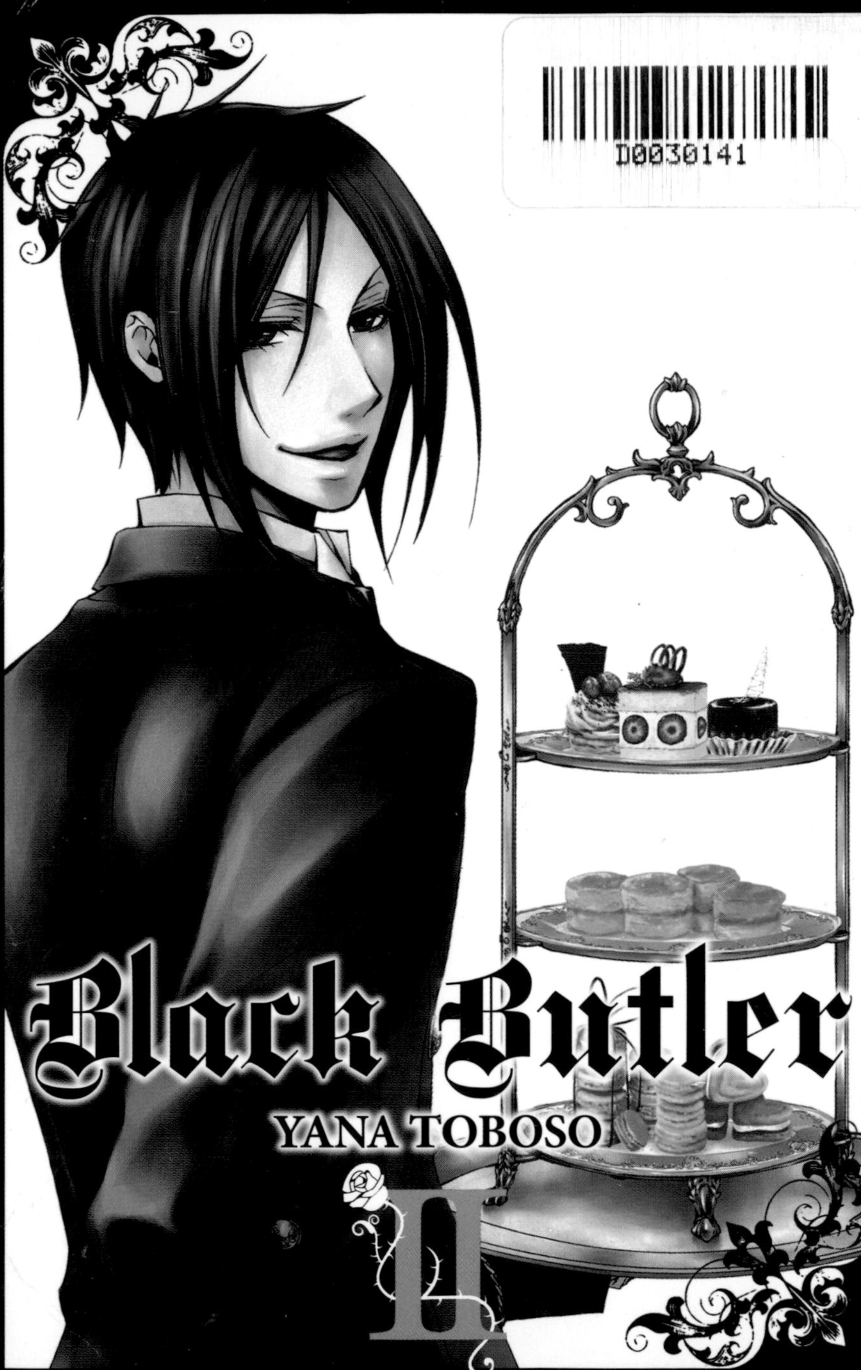
Black Butler
YANA TOBOSO
II

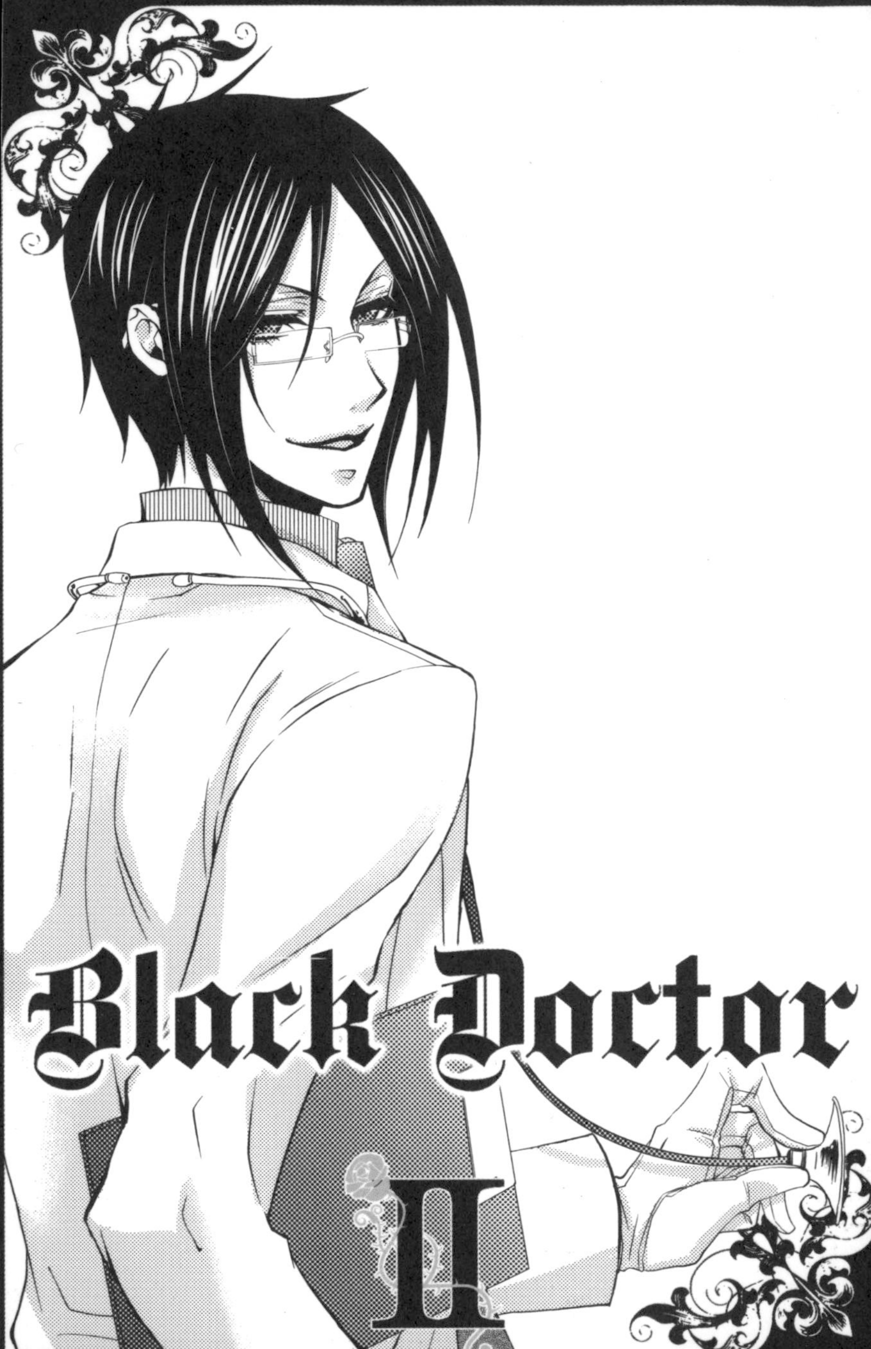
Black Doctor
II

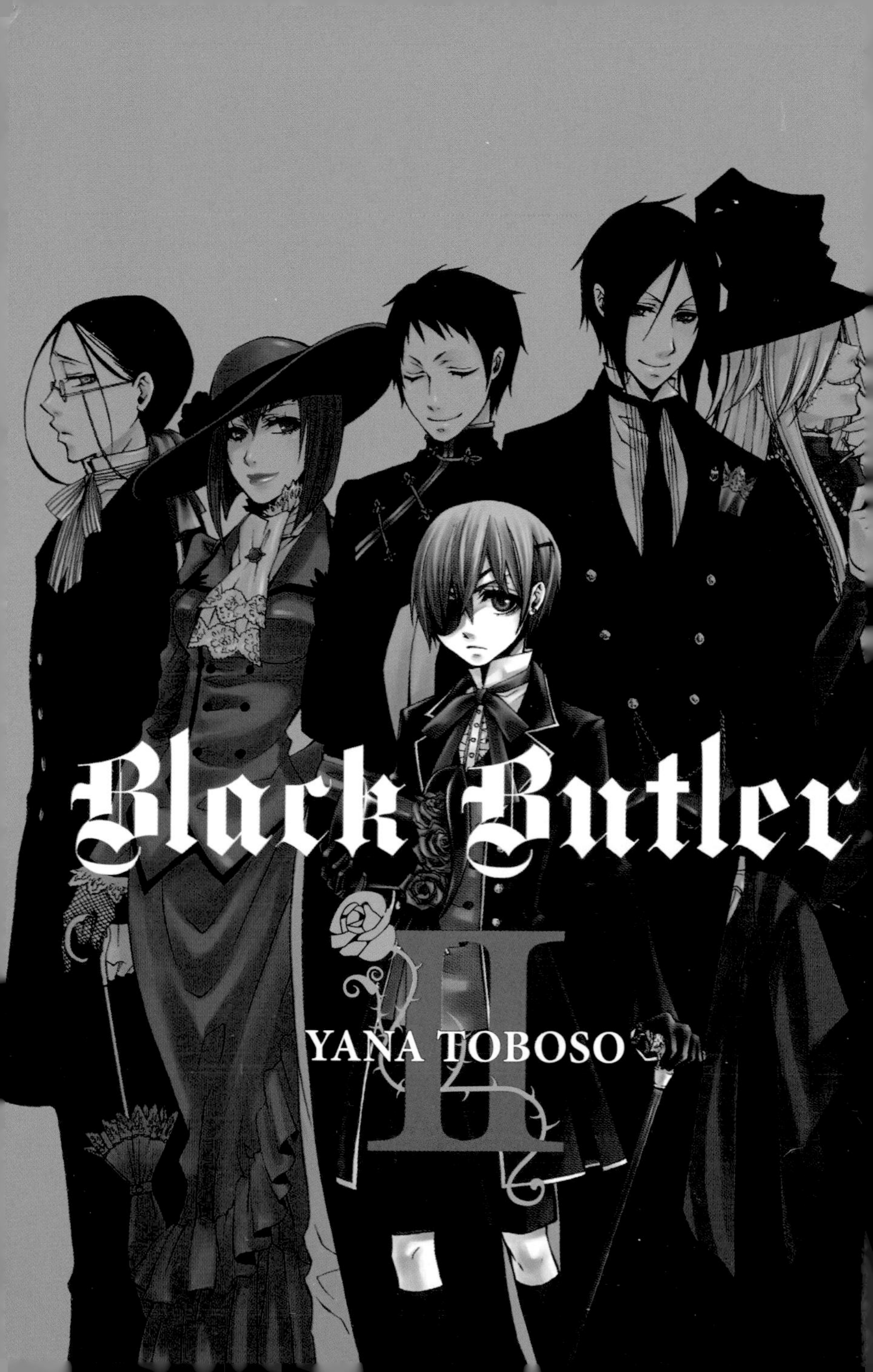
Black Butler
II
YANA TOBOSO

Contents

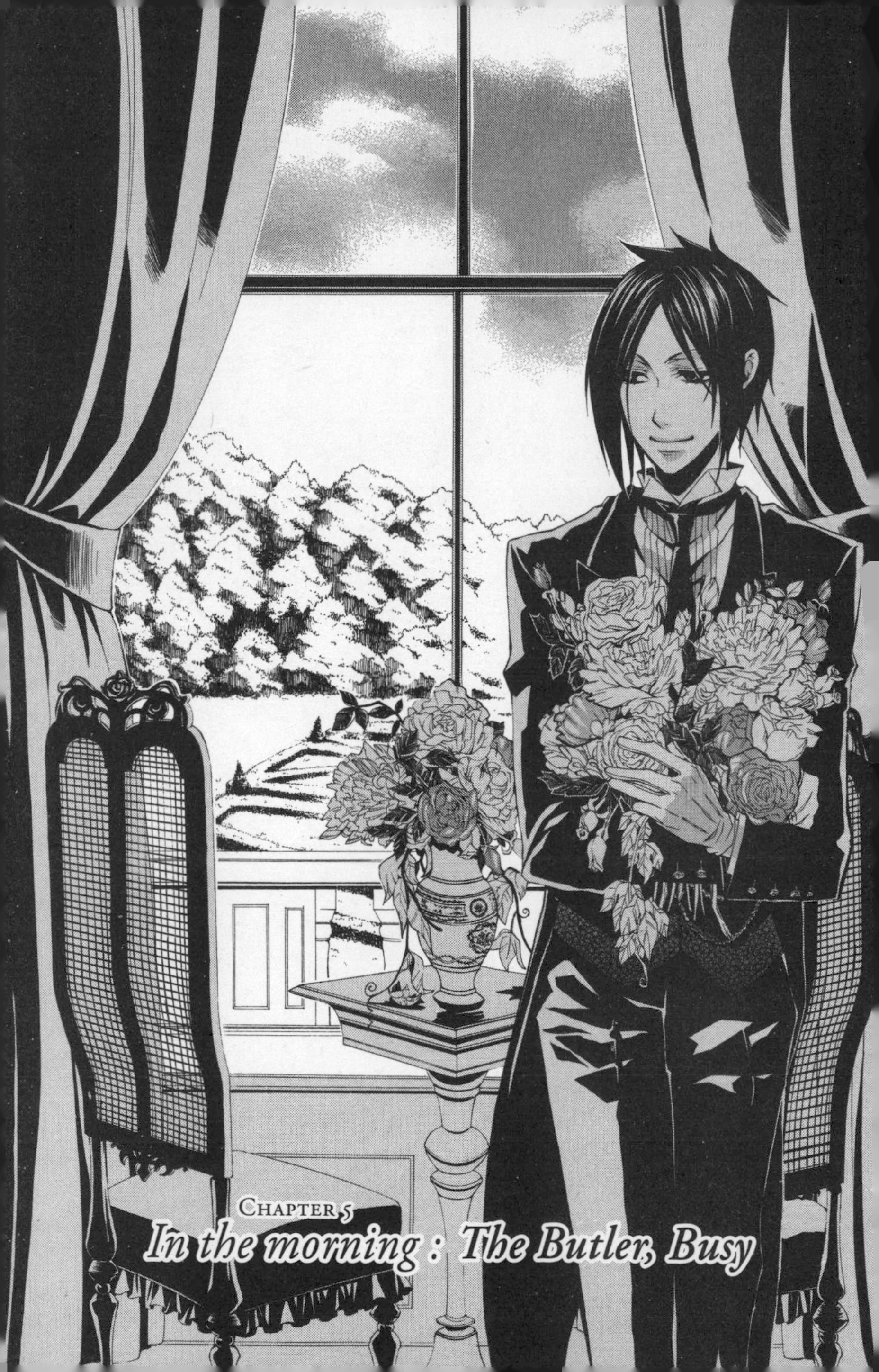
Chapter 5
In the morning : The Butler, Busy

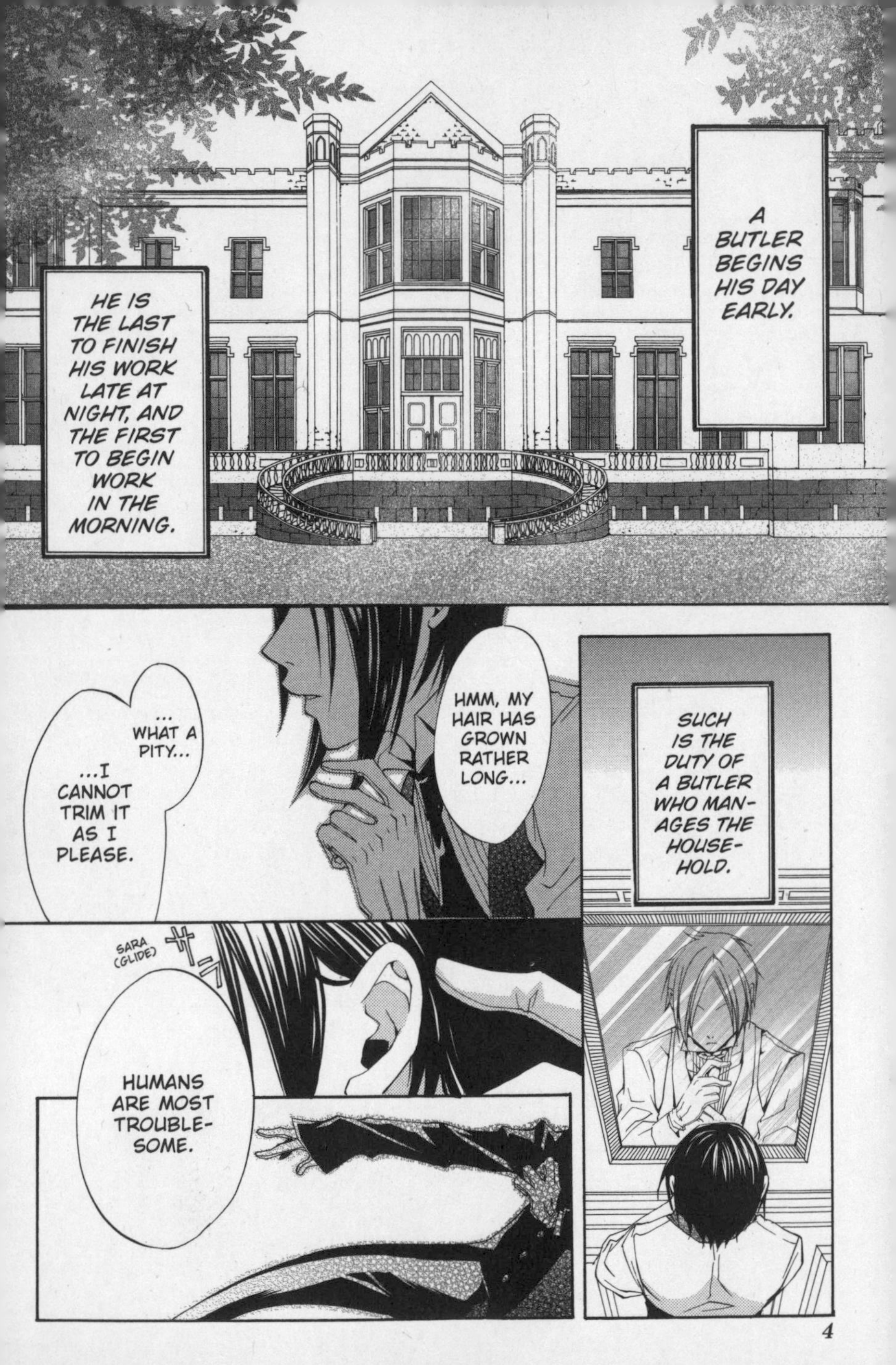
A BUTLER BEGINS HIS DAY EARLY.
HE IS THE LAST TO FINISH HIS WORK LATE AT NIGHT, AND THE FIRST TO BEGIN WORK IN THE MORNING.
SUCH IS THE DUTY OF A BUTLER WHO MAN-AGES THE HOUSE-HOLD.
HMM, MY HAIR HAS GROWN RATHER LONG...
...WHAT A PITY...
...I CANNOT TRIM IT AS I PLEASE.
SARA (GLIDE)
HUMANS ARE MOST TROUBLE-SOME.

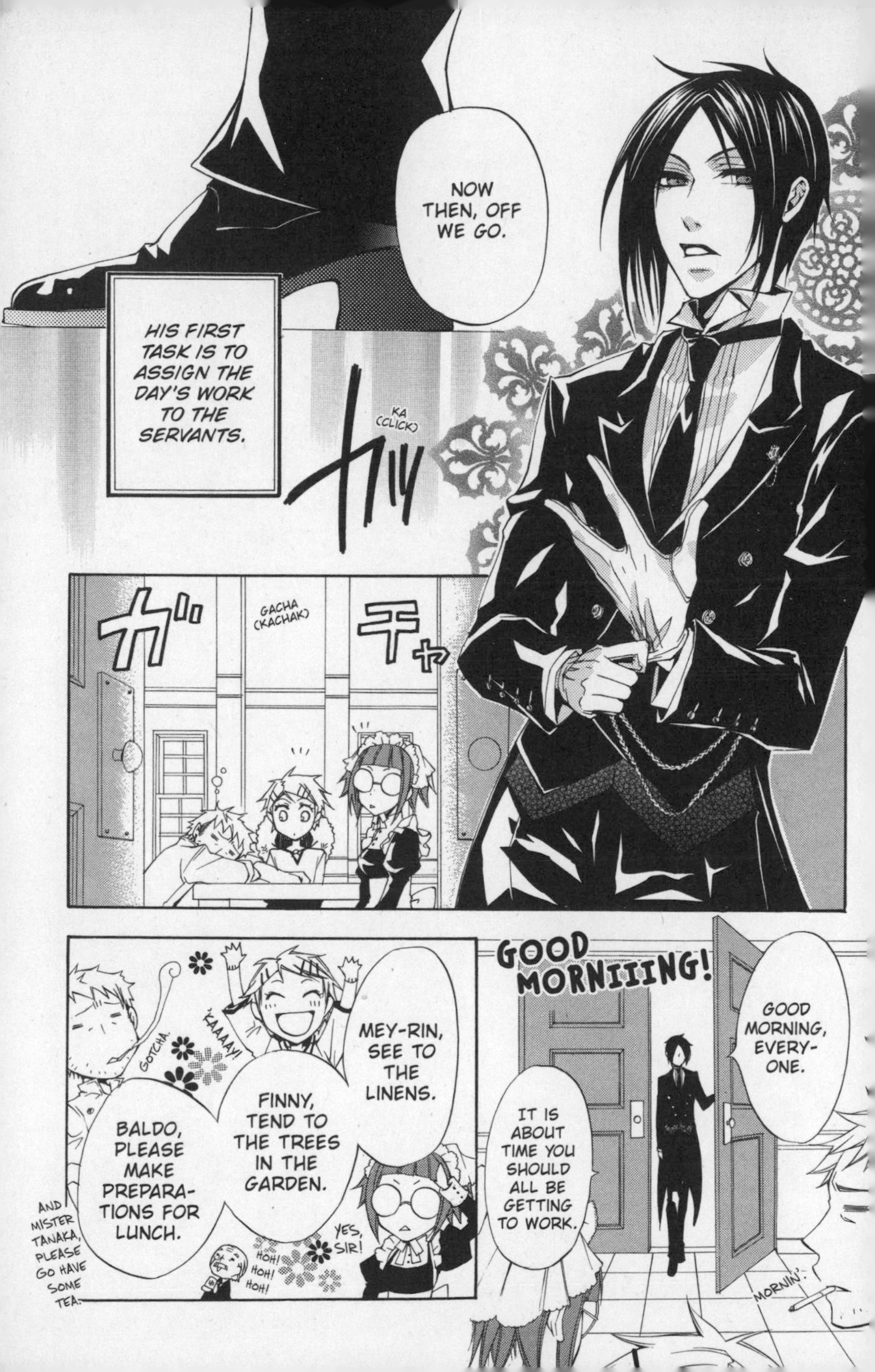
NOW THEN, OFF WE GO.
HIS FIRST TASK IS TO ASSIGN THE DAY'S WORK TO THE SERVANTS.
KA (CLICK)
GACHA (KACHAK)
GOOD MORNIIING!
GOOD MORNING, EVERY-ONE.
IT IS ABOUT TIME YOU SHOULD ALL BE GETTING TO WORK.
MORNIN'.
MEY-RIN, SEE TO THE LINENS.
KAAAAAY!
GOTCHA.
FINNY, TEND TO THE TREES IN THE GARDEN.
BALDO, PLEASE MAKE PREPARA-TIONS FOR LUNCH.
YES, SIR!
HOH! HOH! HOH!
AND MISTER TANAKA, PLEASE GO HAVE SOME TEA.

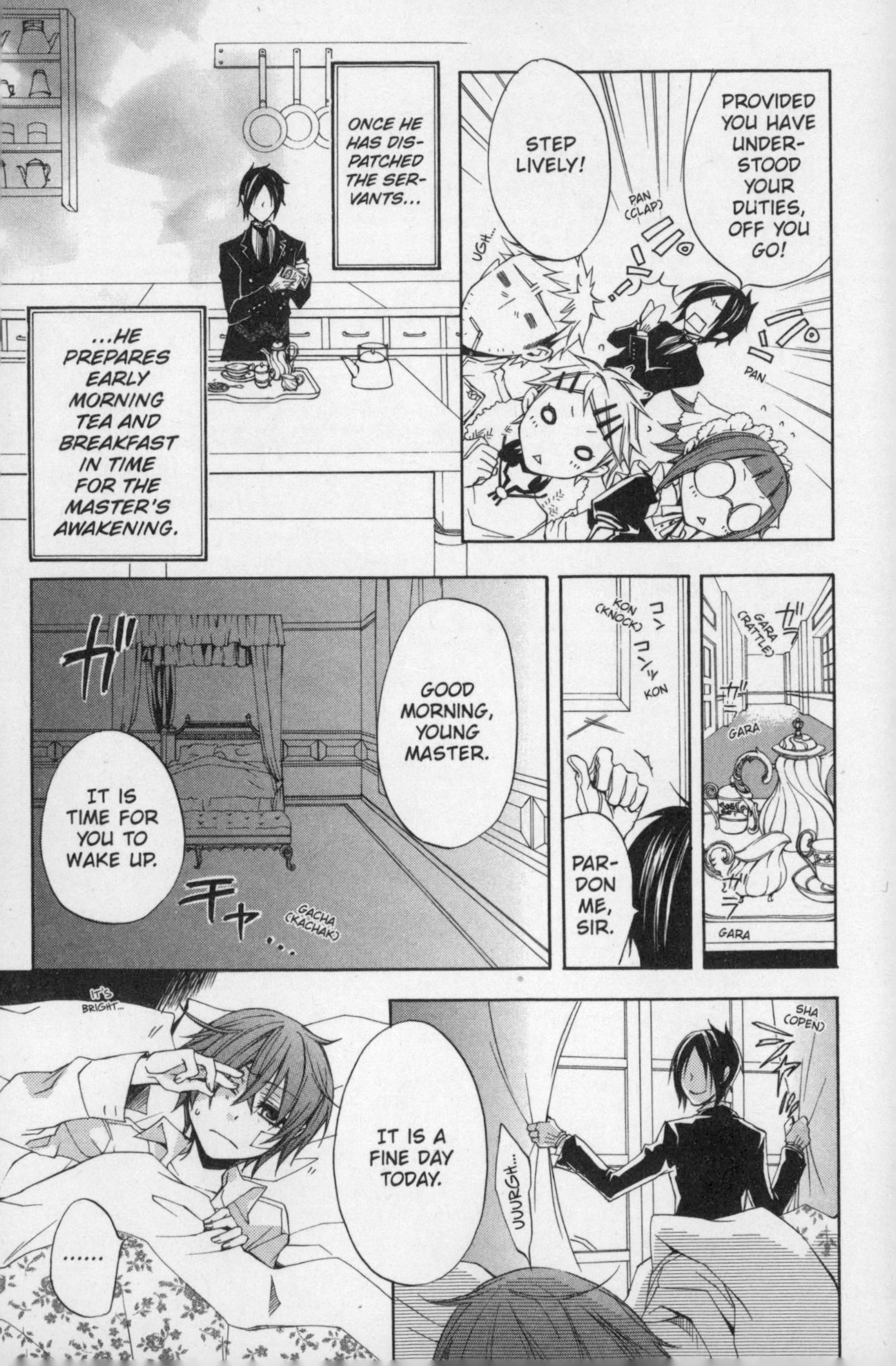
PROVIDED YOU HAVE UNDER-STOOD YOUR DUTIES, OFF YOU GO!
STEP LIVELY!
PAN (CLAP)
UGH...
PAN
ONCE HE HAS DIS-PATCHED THE SER-VANTS...
...HE PREPARES EARLY MORNING TEA AND BREAKFAST IN TIME FOR THE MASTER'S AWAKENING.
GARA (RATTLE)
GARA
GARA
KON (KNOCK)
KON
PAR-DON ME, SIR.
GOOD MORNING, YOUNG MASTER.
IT IS TIME FOR YOU TO WAKE UP.
GACHA (KACHAK)
...
SHA (OPEN)
IT IS A FINE DAY TODAY.
UUURGH...
IT'S BRIGHT...
......

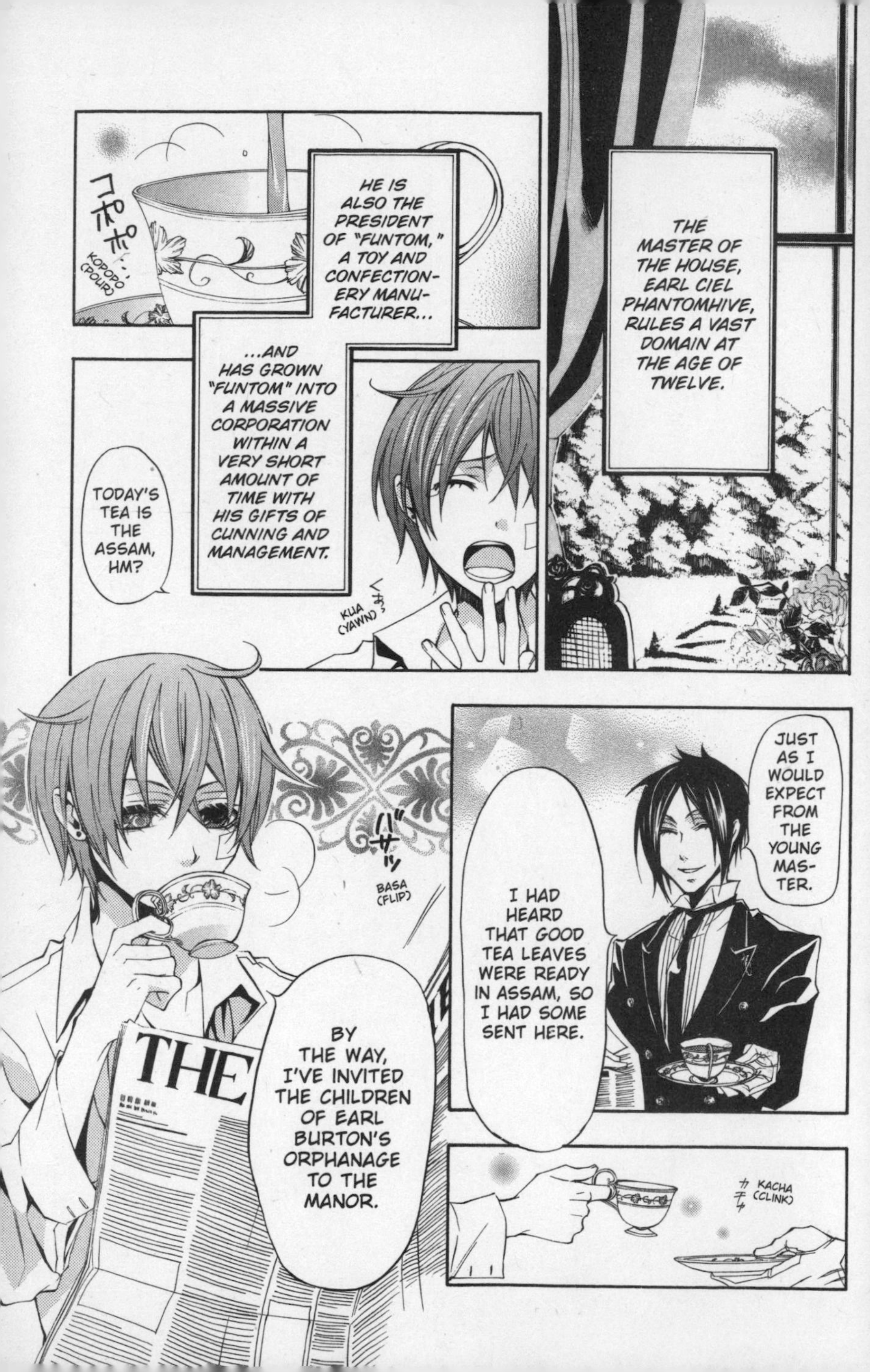
THE MASTER OF THE HOUSE, EARL CIEL PHANTOMHIVE, RULES A VAST DOMAIN AT THE AGE OF TWELVE.
HE IS ALSO THE PRESIDENT OF "FUNTOM," A TOY AND CONFECTION-ERY MANU-FACTURER...
コポポ
KOPOPO (POUR)
...AND HAS GROWN "FUNTOM" INTO A MASSIVE CORPORATION WITHIN A VERY SHORT AMOUNT OF TIME WITH HIS GIFTS OF CUNNING AND MANAGEMENT.
TODAY'S TEA IS THE ASSAM, HM?
KUA (YAWN)
JUST AS I WOULD EXPECT FROM THE YOUNG MAS-TER.
I HAD HEARD THAT GOOD TEA LEAVES WERE READY IN ASSAM, SO I HAD SOME SENT HERE.
カチャ
KACHA (CLINK)
バサッ
BASA (FLIP)
BY THE WAY, I'VE INVITED THE CHILDREN OF EARL BURTON'S ORPHANAGE TO THE MANOR.
THE

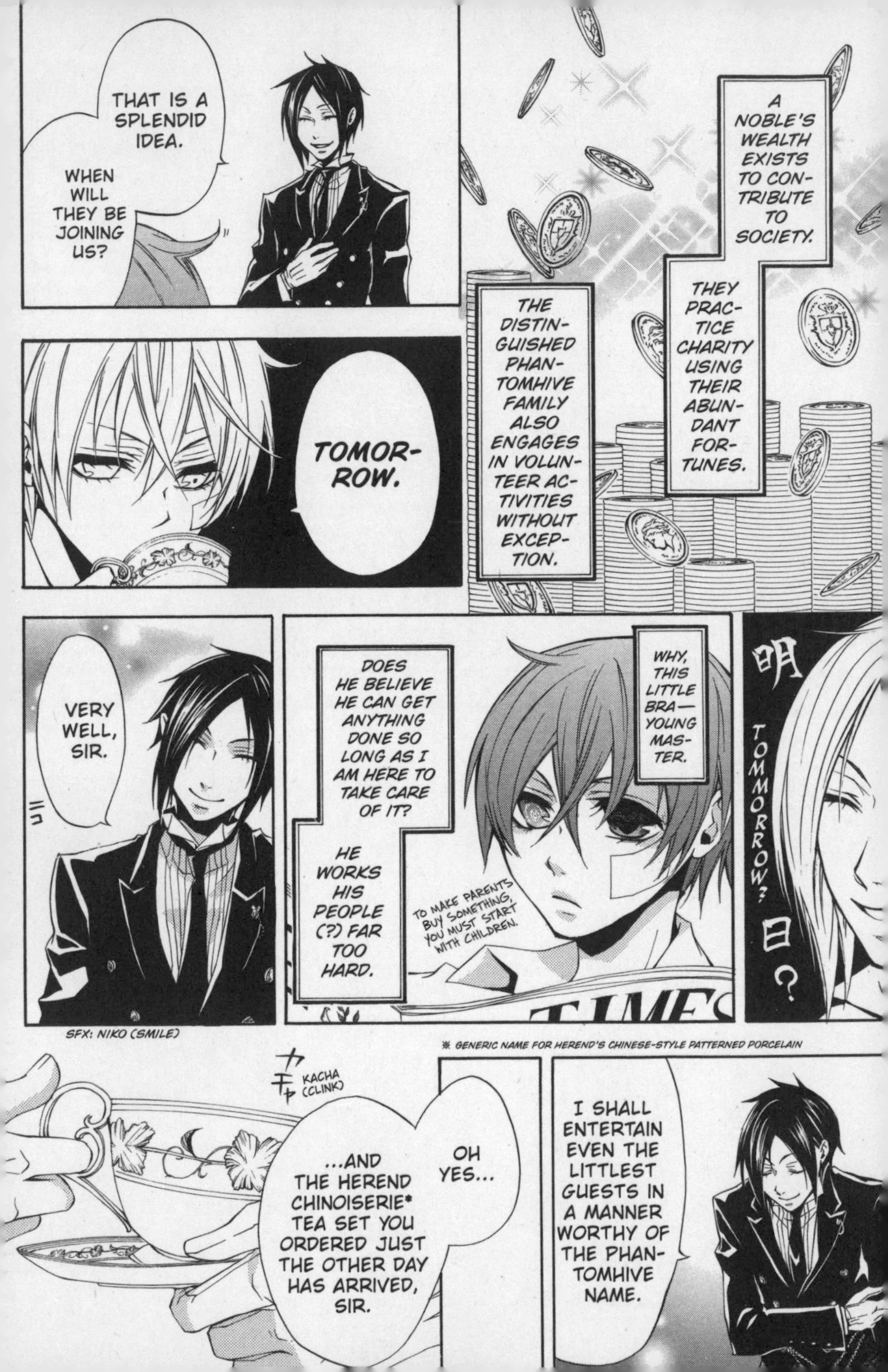
A NOBLE'S WEALTH EXISTS TO CONTRIBUTE TO SOCIETY.
THEY PRACTICE CHARITY USING THEIR ABUNDANT FORTUNES.
THE DISTINGUISHED PHANTOMHIVE FAMILY ALSO ENGAGES IN VOLUNTEER ACTIVITIES WITHOUT EXCEPTION.
THAT IS A SPLENDID IDEA.
WHEN WILL THEY BE JOINING US?
TOMORROW.
明日?
TOMMORROW?
WHY, THIS LITTLE BRA— YOUNG MASTER.
DOES HE BELIEVE HE CAN GET ANYTHING DONE SO LONG AS I AM HERE TO TAKE CARE OF IT?
HE WORKS HIS PEOPLE (?) FAR TOO HARD.
TO MAKE PARENTS BUY SOMETHING, YOU MUST START WITH CHILDREN.
TIMES
VERY WELL, SIR.
ニコ
SFX: NIKO (SMILE)
※ GENERIC NAME FOR HEREND'S CHINESE-STYLE PATTERNED PORCELAIN
I SHALL ENTERTAIN EVEN THE LITTLEST GUESTS IN A MANNER WORTHY OF THE PHANTOMHIVE NAME.
OH YES...
...AND THE HEREND CHINOISERIE* TEA SET YOU ORDERED JUST THE OTHER DAY HAS ARRIVED, SIR.
カチャ
KACHA (CLINK)

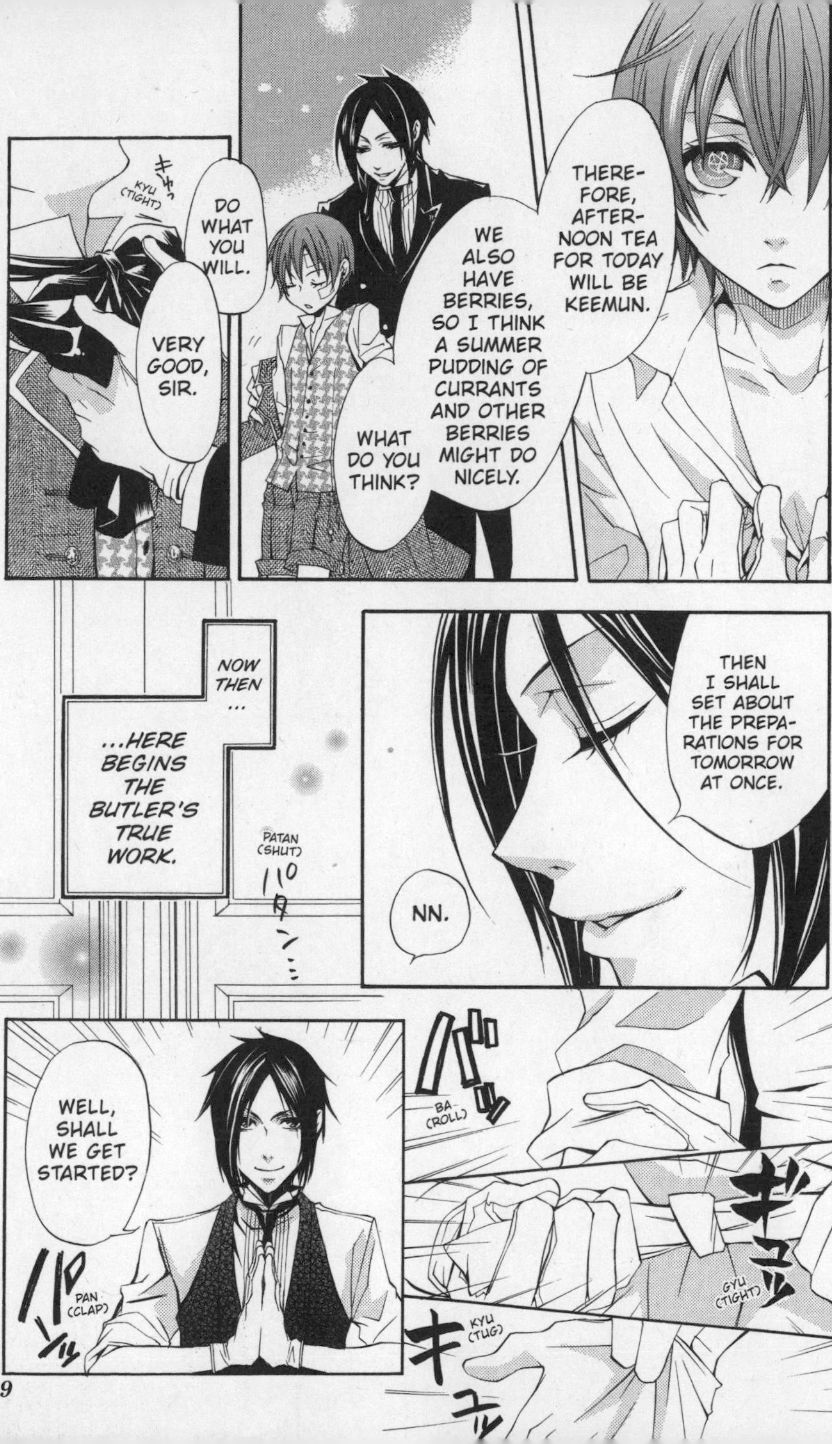
THEREFORE, AFTERNOON TEA FOR TODAY WILL BE KEEMUN.
WE ALSO HAVE BERRIES, SO I THINK A SUMMER PUDDING OF CURRANTS AND OTHER BERRIES MIGHT DO NICELY.
WHAT DO YOU THINK?
DO WHAT YOU WILL.
VERY GOOD, SIR.
KYU (TIGHT)
THEN I SHALL SET ABOUT THE PREPARATIONS FOR TOMORROW AT ONCE.
NN.
PATAN (SHUT)
NOW THEN ...
...HERE BEGINS THE BUTLER'S TRUE WORK.
BA (ROLL)
GYU (TIGHT)
KYU (TUG)
WELL, SHALL WE GET STARTED?
PAN (CLAP)

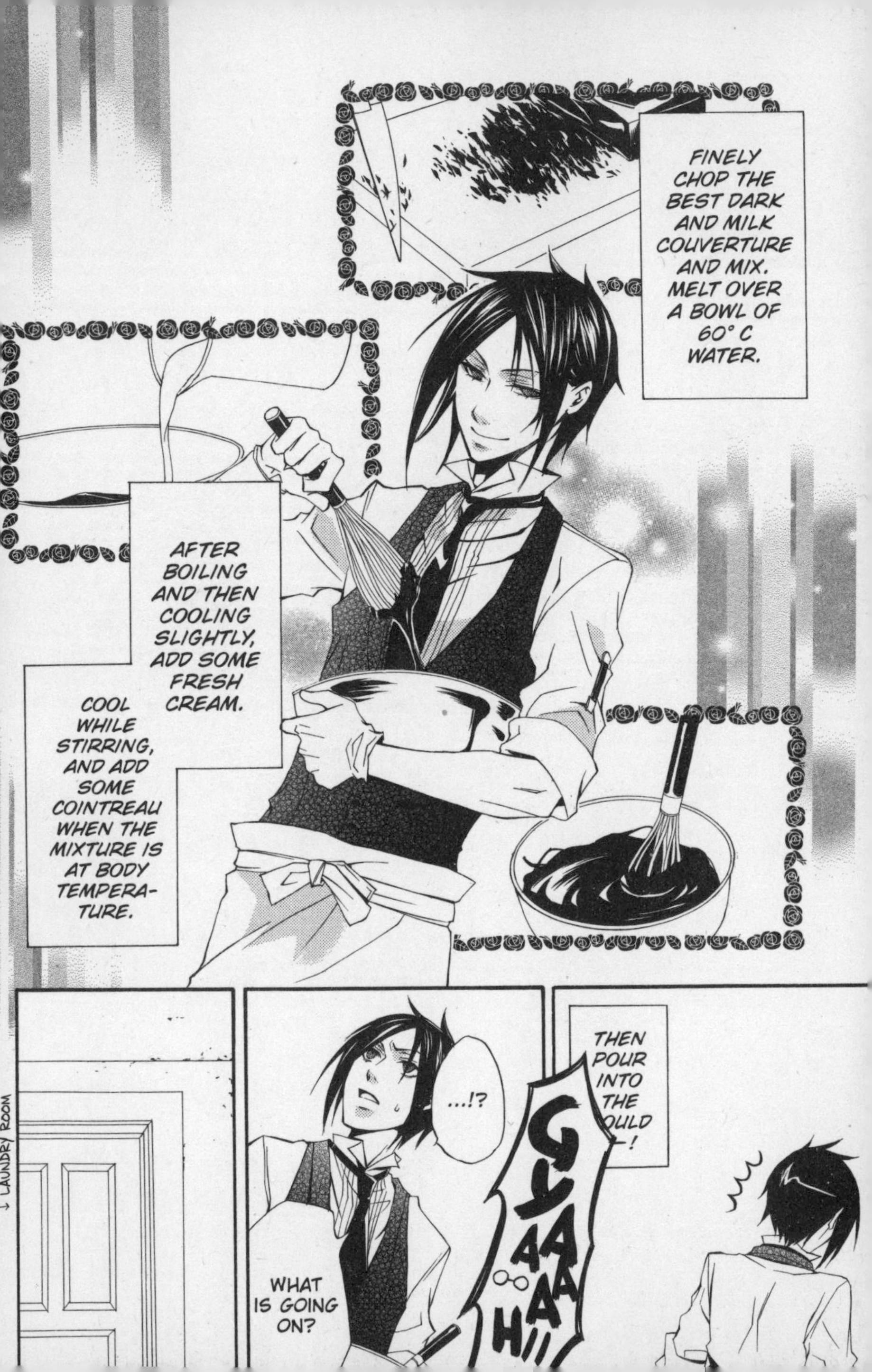

FINELY CHOP THE BEST DARK AND MILK COUVERTURE AND MIX. MELT OVER A BOWL OF 60° C WATER.
AFTER BOILING AND THEN COOLING SLIGHTLY, ADD SOME FRESH CREAM.
COOL WHILE STIRRING, AND ADD SOME COINTREAU WHEN THE MIXTURE IS AT BODY TEMPERA-TURE.
THEN POUR INTO THE OULD!
GYAAAAAH!!
...!?
WHAT IS GOING ON?
↓ LAUNDRY ROOM

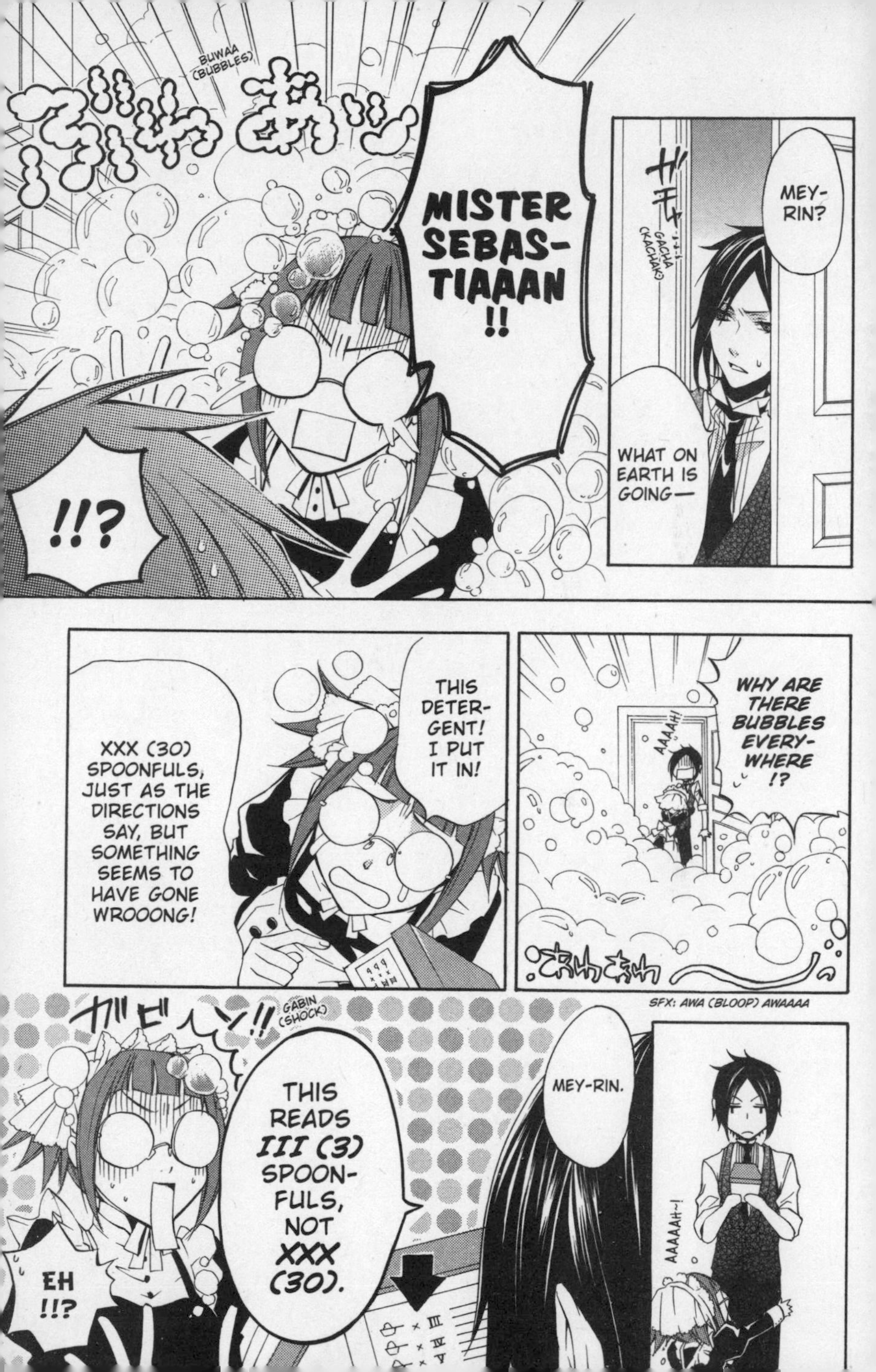
MEY-RIN?
GACHA (KACHAK)
WHAT ON EARTH IS GOING—
MISTER SEBASTIAAAN!!
BUWAA (BUBBLES)
!!?
WHY ARE THERE BUBBLES EVERYWHERE!?
AAAAH!
SFX: AWA (BLOOP) AWAAAA
THIS DETERGENT! I PUT IT IN!
XXX (30) SPOONFULS, JUST AS THE DIRECTIONS SAY, BUT SOMETHING SEEMS TO HAVE GONE WROOONG!
MEY-RIN.
AAAAAH~!
GABIN (SHOCK)
THIS READS III (3) SPOONFULS, NOT XXX (30).
EH!!?

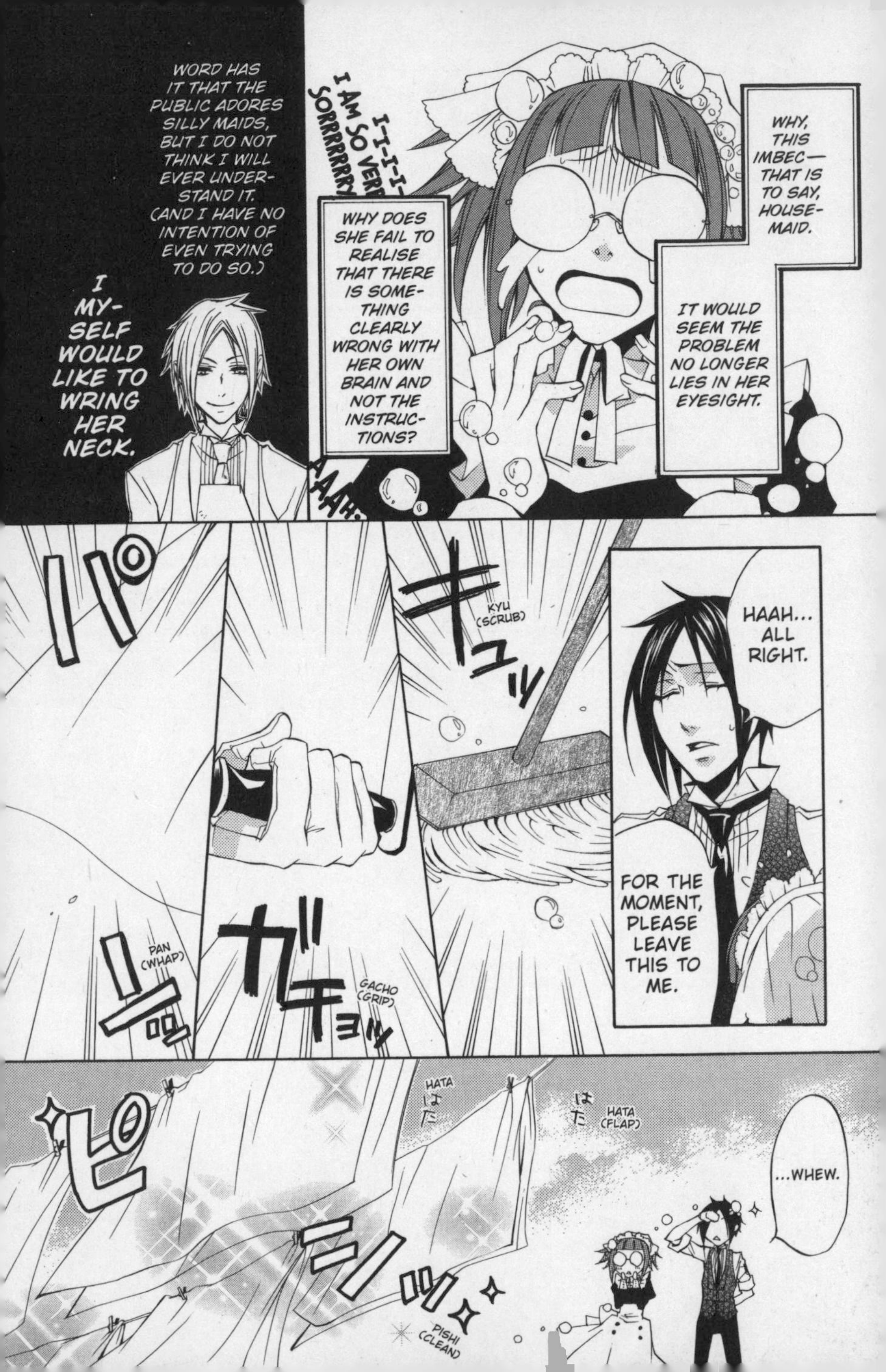
WHY, THIS IMBEC— THAT IS TO SAY, HOUSE-MAID.
IT WOULD SEEM THE PROBLEM NO LONGER LIES IN HER EYESIGHT.
I-I-I-I-
I AM SO VER
SORRRRRRRR
AAAH.
WHY DOES SHE FAIL TO REALISE THAT THERE IS SOME-THING CLEARLY WRONG WITH HER OWN BRAIN AND NOT THE INSTRUC-TIONS?
WORD HAS IT THAT THE PUBLIC ADORES SILLY MAIDS, BUT I DO NOT THINK I WILL EVER UNDER-STAND IT. (AND I HAVE NO INTENTION OF EVEN TRYING TO DO SO.)
I MY-SELF WOULD LIKE TO WRING HER NECK.
HAAH... ALL RIGHT.
FOR THE MOMENT, PLEASE LEAVE THIS TO ME.
KYU (SCRUB)
GACHO (GRIP)
PAN (WHAP)
...WHEW.
HATA (FLAP)
HATA
PISHI (CLEAN)

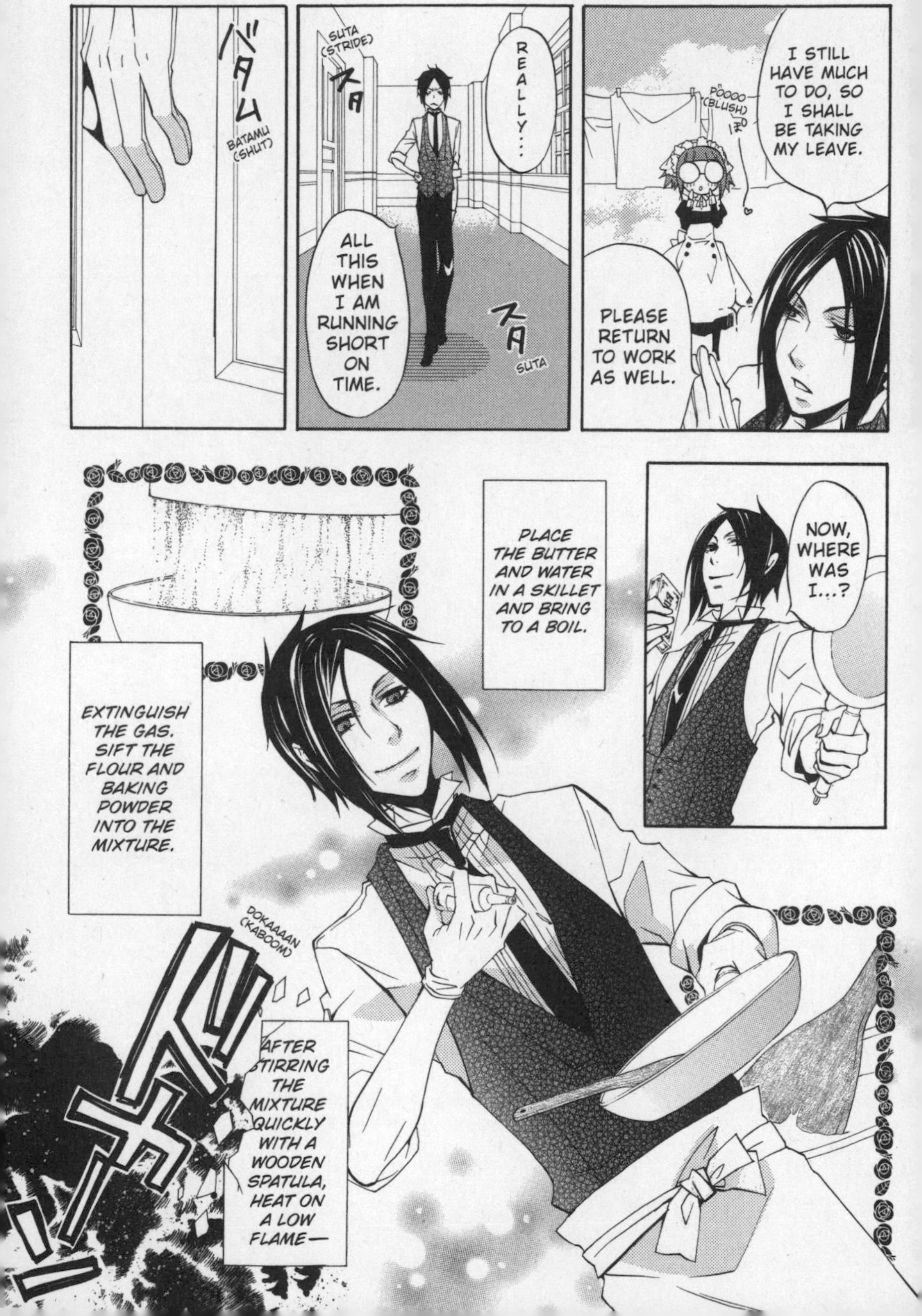
I STILL HAVE MUCH TO DO, SO I SHALL BE TAKING MY LEAVE.
POOOO (BLUSH)
PLEASE RETURN TO WORK AS WELL.
REALLY...
SUTA (STRIDE)
ALL THIS WHEN I AM RUNNING SHORT ON TIME.
SUTA
BATAMU (SHUT)
NOW, WHERE WAS I...?
PLACE THE BUTTER AND WATER IN A SKILLET AND BRING TO A BOIL.
EXTINGUISH THE GAS. SIFT THE FLOUR AND BAKING POWDER INTO THE MIXTURE.
DOKAAAAN (KABOOM)
AFTER STIRRING THE MIXTURE QUICKLY WITH A WOODEN SPATULA, HEAT ON A LOW FLAME—

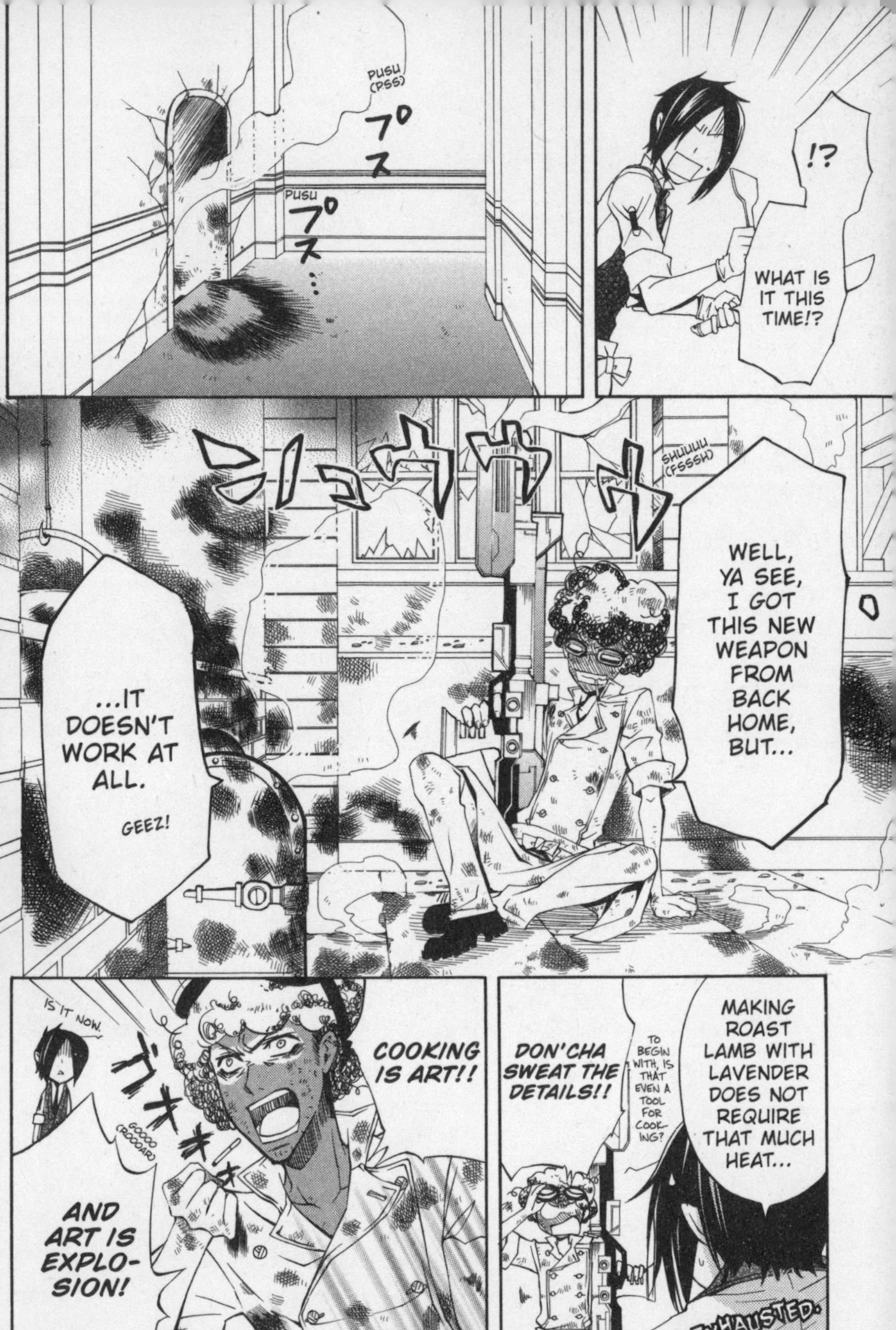
!?
WHAT IS IT THIS TIME!?
PUSU (PSS)
プス
PUSU
プス
SHUUUU (FSSSH)
WELL, YA SEE, I GOT THIS NEW WEAPON FROM BACK HOME, BUT...
...IT DOESN'T WORK AT ALL.
GEEZ!
MAKING ROAST LAMB WITH LAVENDER DOES NOT REQUIRE THAT MUCH HEAT...
TO BEGIN WITH, IS THAT EVEN A TOOL FOR COOKING?
DON'CHA SWEAT THE DETAILS!!
EXHAUSTED.
COOKING IS ART!!
GOOOO (ROOOAR)
IS IT NOW.
AND ART IS EXPLOSION!

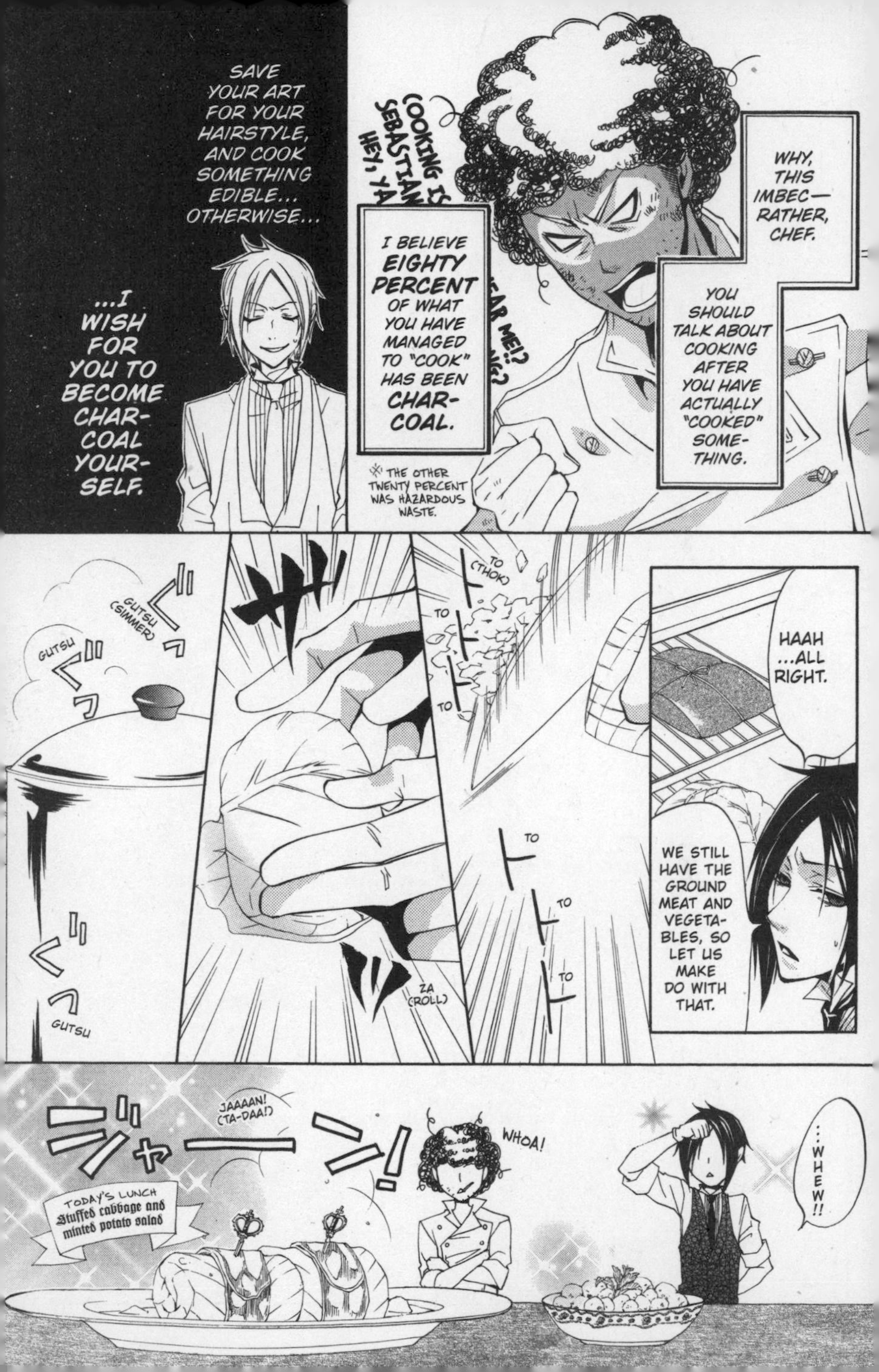
WHY, THIS IMBEC— RATHER, CHEF.
YOU SHOULD TALK ABOUT COOKING AFTER YOU HAVE ACTUALLY "COOKED" SOMETHING.
I BELIEVE EIGHTY PERCENT OF WHAT YOU HAVE MANAGED TO "COOK" HAS BEEN CHARCOAL.
※ THE OTHER TWENTY PERCENT WAS HAZARDOUS WASTE.
SAVE YOUR ART FOR YOUR HAIRSTYLE, AND COOK SOMETHING EDIBLE... OTHERWISE...
...I WISH FOR YOU TO BECOME CHARCOAL YOURSELF.
HAAH ...ALL RIGHT.
WE STILL HAVE THE GROUND MEAT AND VEGETABLES, SO LET US MAKE DO WITH THAT.
TO (THOK)
TO
TO
TO
TO
TO
ZA (ROLL)
GUTSU (SIMMER)
GUTSU
GUTSU
...WHEW!!
WHOA!
JAAAAN! (TA-DAA!)
TODAY'S LUNCH
Stuffed cabbage and minted potato salad

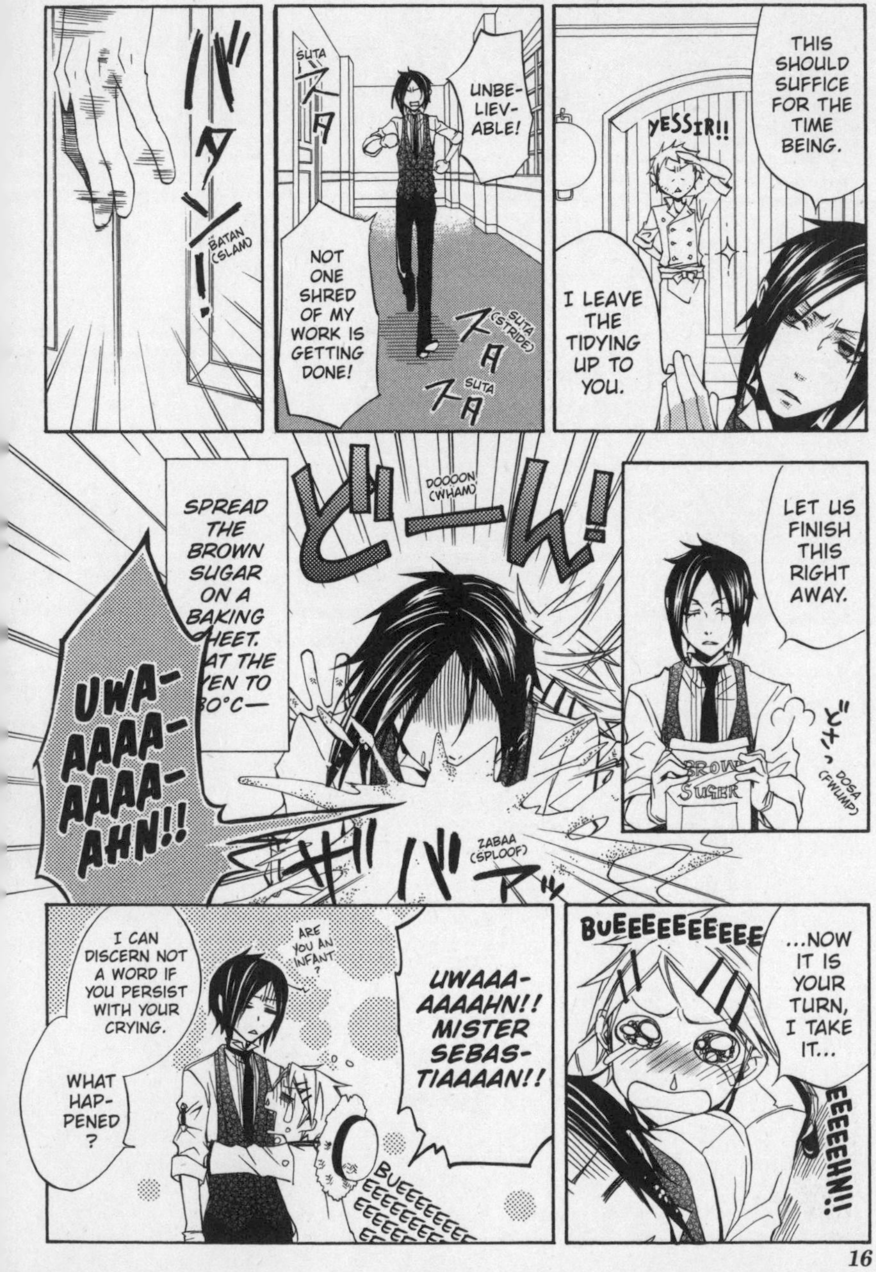
THIS SHOULD SUFFICE FOR THE TIME BEING.
YESSIR!!
I LEAVE THE TIDYING UP TO YOU.
SUTA
UNBE-LIEV-ABLE!
NOT ONE SHRED OF MY WORK IS GETTING DONE!
SUTA (STRIDE)
SUTA
BATAN (SLAM)
LET US FINISH THIS RIGHT AWAY.
BROWN SUGER
DOSA (FWUMP)
DOOOON (WHAM)
SPREAD THE BROWN SUGAR ON A BAKING HEET. AT THE VEN TO 0°C—
UWA-AAAA-AAAA-AHN!!
ZABAA (SPLOOF)
BUEEEEEEEEEE
...NOW IT IS YOUR TURN, I TAKE IT...
EEEEEHN!!
UWAAA-AAAAAHN!! MISTER SEBAS-TIAAAAN!!
ARE YOU AN INFANT?
I CAN DISCERN NOT A WORD IF YOU PERSIST WITH YOUR CRYING.
WHAT HAP-PENED?
BUEEEEEEEEEEEEEEEEEEEEEEEEEE

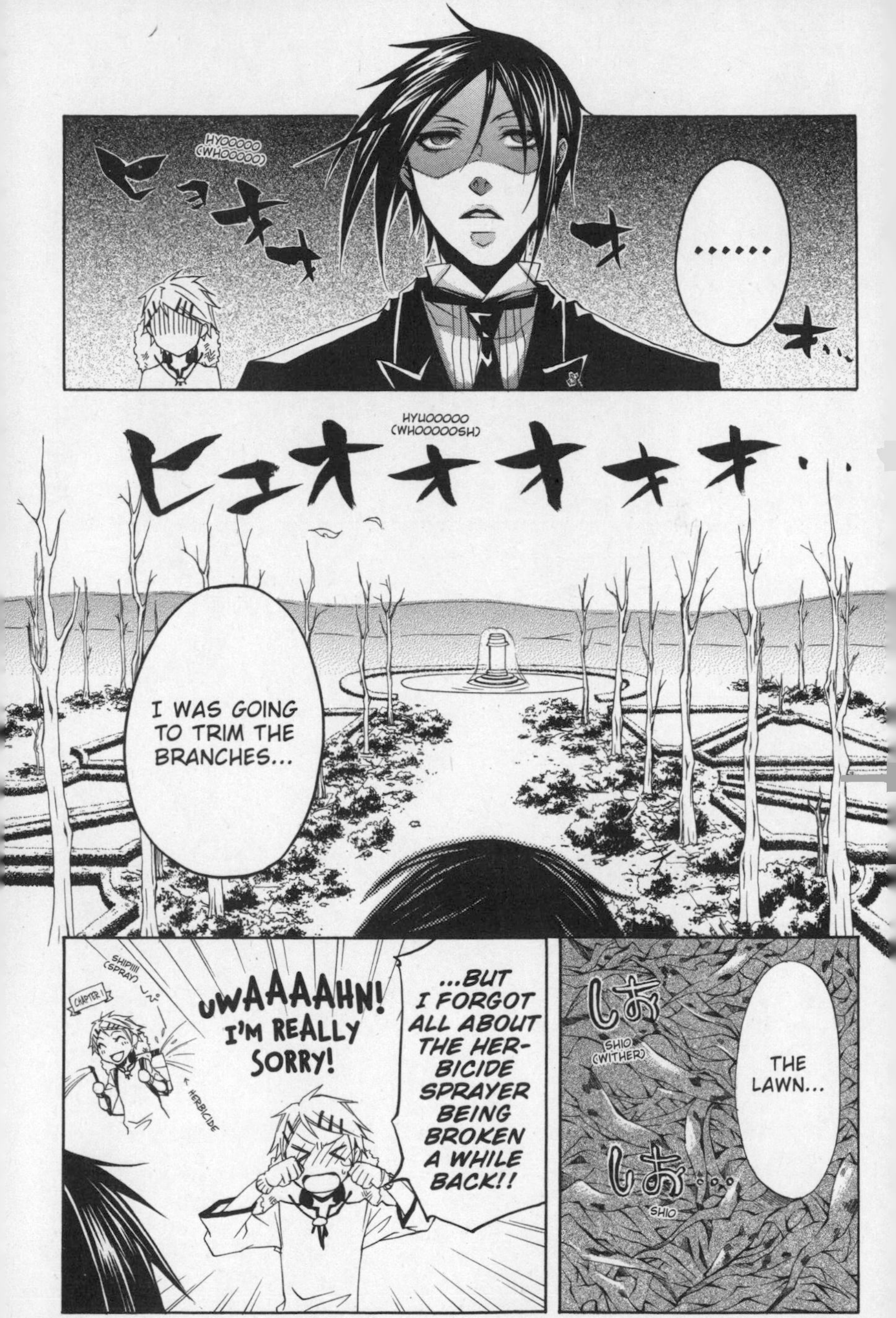
HYOOOOO (WHOOOOOO)
......
HYUOOOOO (WHOOOOOSH)
I WAS GOING TO TRIM THE BRANCHES...
SHIO (WITHER)
THE LAWN...
SHIO
...BUT I FORGOT ALL ABOUT THE HER-BICIDE SPRAYER BEING BROKEN A WHILE BACK!!
UWAAAAAHN! I'M REALLY SORRY!
SHIPIIII (SPRAY)
CHAPTER 1
HERBICIDE

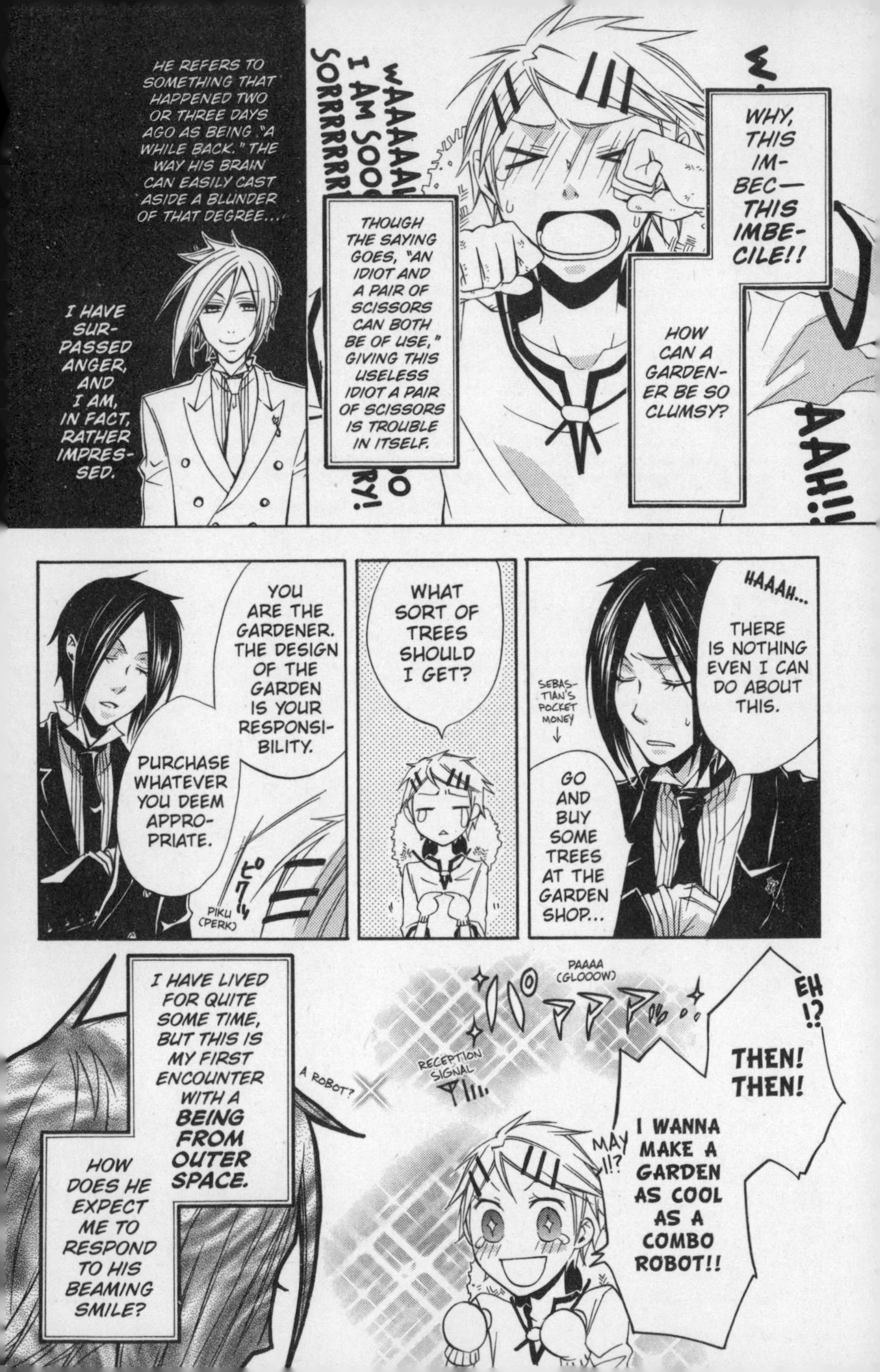
W
AAH!!!
WHY, THIS IM-BEC—THIS IMBECILE!!
HOW CAN A GARDENER BE SO CLUMSY?
WAAAAA
I AM SOOO
SORRRRRR
OO
RY!
THOUGH THE SAYING GOES, "AN IDIOT AND A PAIR OF SCISSORS CAN BOTH BE OF USE," GIVING THIS USELESS IDIOT A PAIR OF SCISSORS IS TROUBLE IN ITSELF.
HE REFERS TO SOMETHING THAT HAPPENED TWO OR THREE DAYS AGO AS BEING "A WHILE BACK." THE WAY HIS BRAIN CAN EASILY CAST ASIDE A BLUNDER OF THAT DEGREE...
I HAVE SURPASSED ANGER, AND I AM, IN FACT, RATHER IMPRESSED.
HAAAH...
THERE IS NOTHING EVEN I CAN DO ABOUT THIS.
SEBASTIAN'S POCKET MONEY
GO AND BUY SOME TREES AT THE GARDEN SHOP...
WHAT SORT OF TREES SHOULD I GET?
YOU ARE THE GARDENER. THE DESIGN OF THE GARDEN IS YOUR RESPONSIBILITY.
PURCHASE WHATEVER YOU DEEM APPROPRIATE.
PIKU (PERK)
EH!?
THEN! THEN!
I WANNA MAKE A GARDEN AS COOL AS A COMBO ROBOT!!
MAY!!?
PAAAA (GLOOOW)
RECEPTION SIGNAL
A ROBOT?
I HAVE LIVED FOR QUITE SOME TIME, BUT THIS IS MY FIRST ENCOUNTER WITH A BEING FROM OUTER SPACE.
HOW DOES HE EXPECT ME TO RESPOND TO HIS BEAMING SMILE?

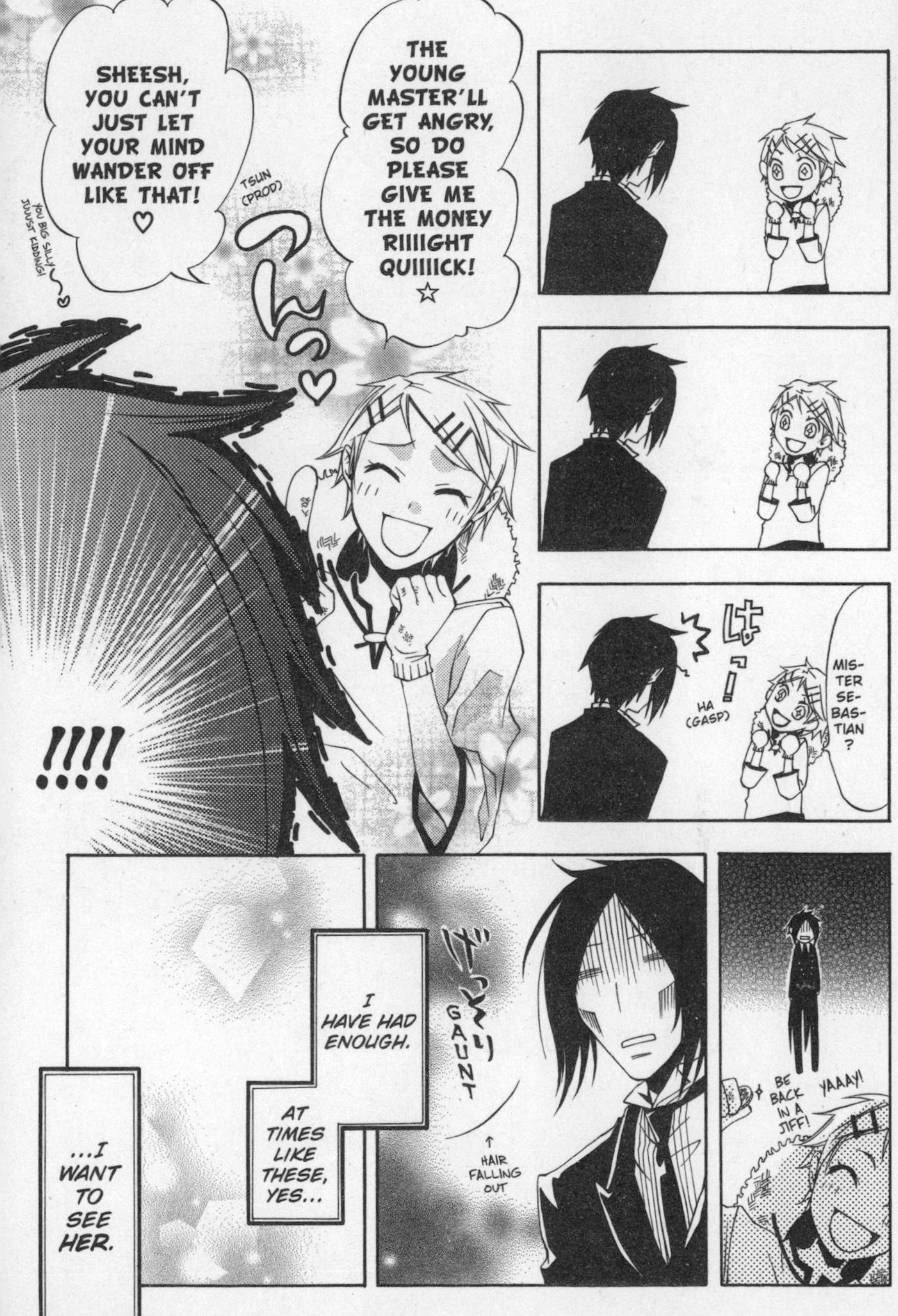
HA (GASP)
MISTER SEBASTIAN?
THE YOUNG MASTER'LL GET ANGRY, SO DO PLEASE GIVE ME THE MONEY RIIIIGHT QUIIIICK! ☆
TSUN (PROD)
SHEESH, YOU CAN'T JUST LET YOUR MIND WANDER OFF LIKE THAT! ♡
YOU BIG SILLY JUUUST KIDDING!
!!!!
YAAAY!
BE BACK IN A JIFF!
GAUNT
HAIR FALLING OUT
I HAVE HAD ENOUGH.
AT TIMES LIKE THESE, YES...
...I WANT TO SEE HER.

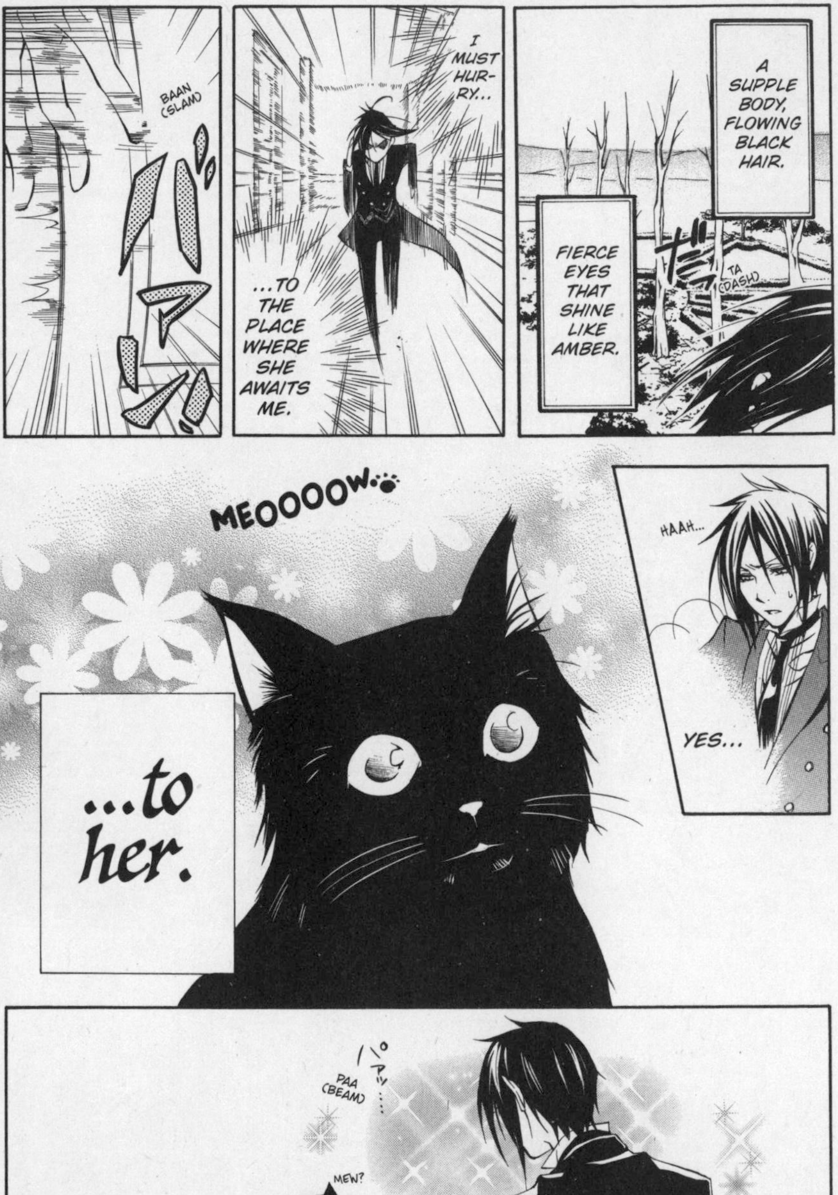
A SUPPLE BODY, FLOWING BLACK HAIR.
FIERCE EYES THAT SHINE LIKE AMBER.
TA (DASH)
I MUST HURRY...
...TO THE PLACE WHERE SHE AWAITS ME.
BAAN (SLAM)
HAAH...
YES...
MEOOOOW
...to her.
PAA (BEAM)
MEW?

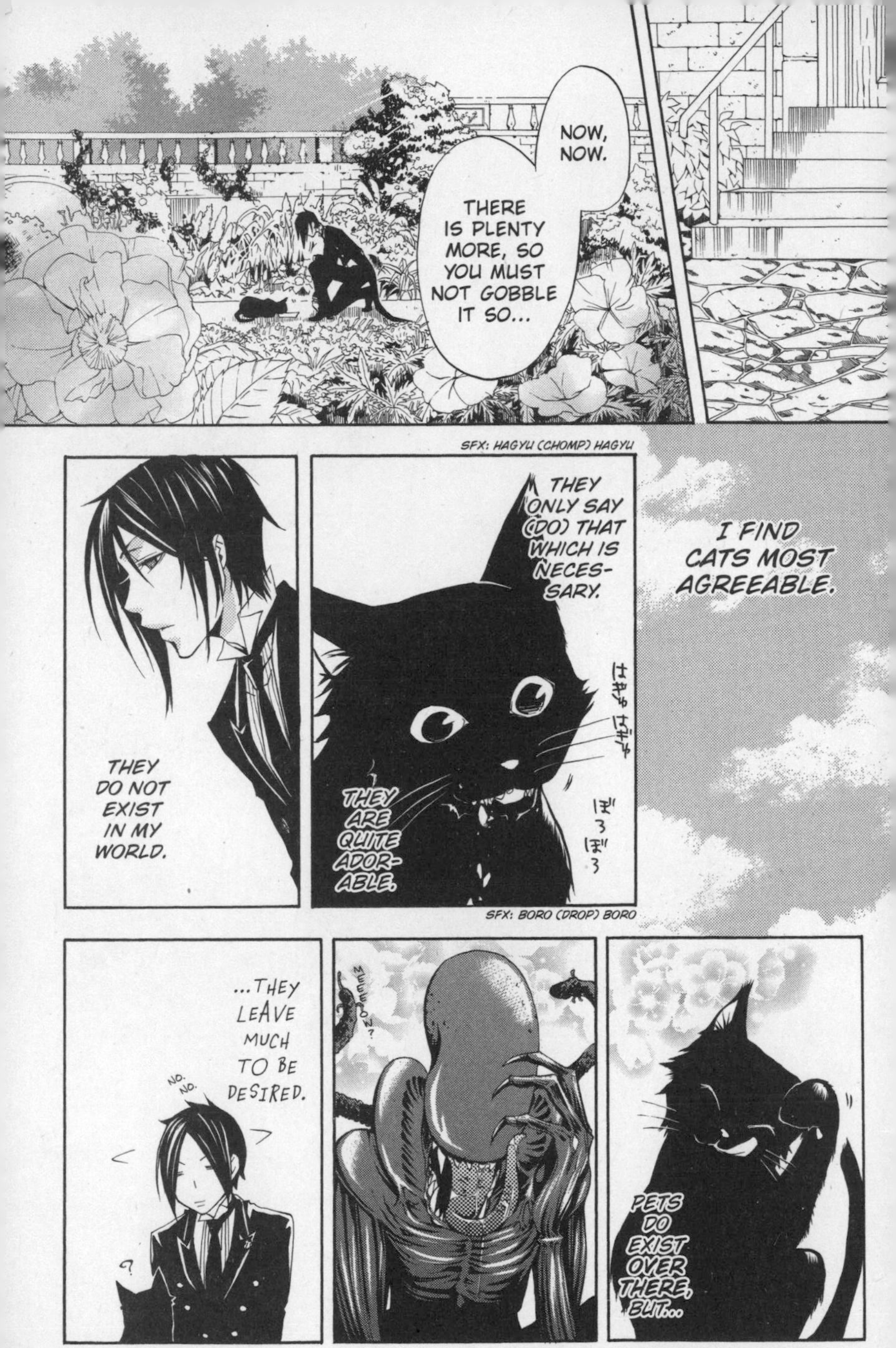
NOW, NOW.
THERE IS PLENTY MORE, SO YOU MUST NOT GOBBLE IT SO...
SFX: HAGYU (CHOMP) HAGYU
I FIND CATS MOST AGREEABLE.
THEY ONLY SAY (DO) THAT WHICH IS NECES-SARY.
はぎゅ はぎゅ
THEY ARE QUITE ADOR-ABLE.
ぼろ ぼろ
THEY DO NOT EXIST IN MY WORLD.
SFX: BORO (DROP) BORO
PETS DO EXIST OVER THERE, BUT...
MEEOW?
...THEY LEAVE MUCH TO BE DESIRED.
NO. NO.

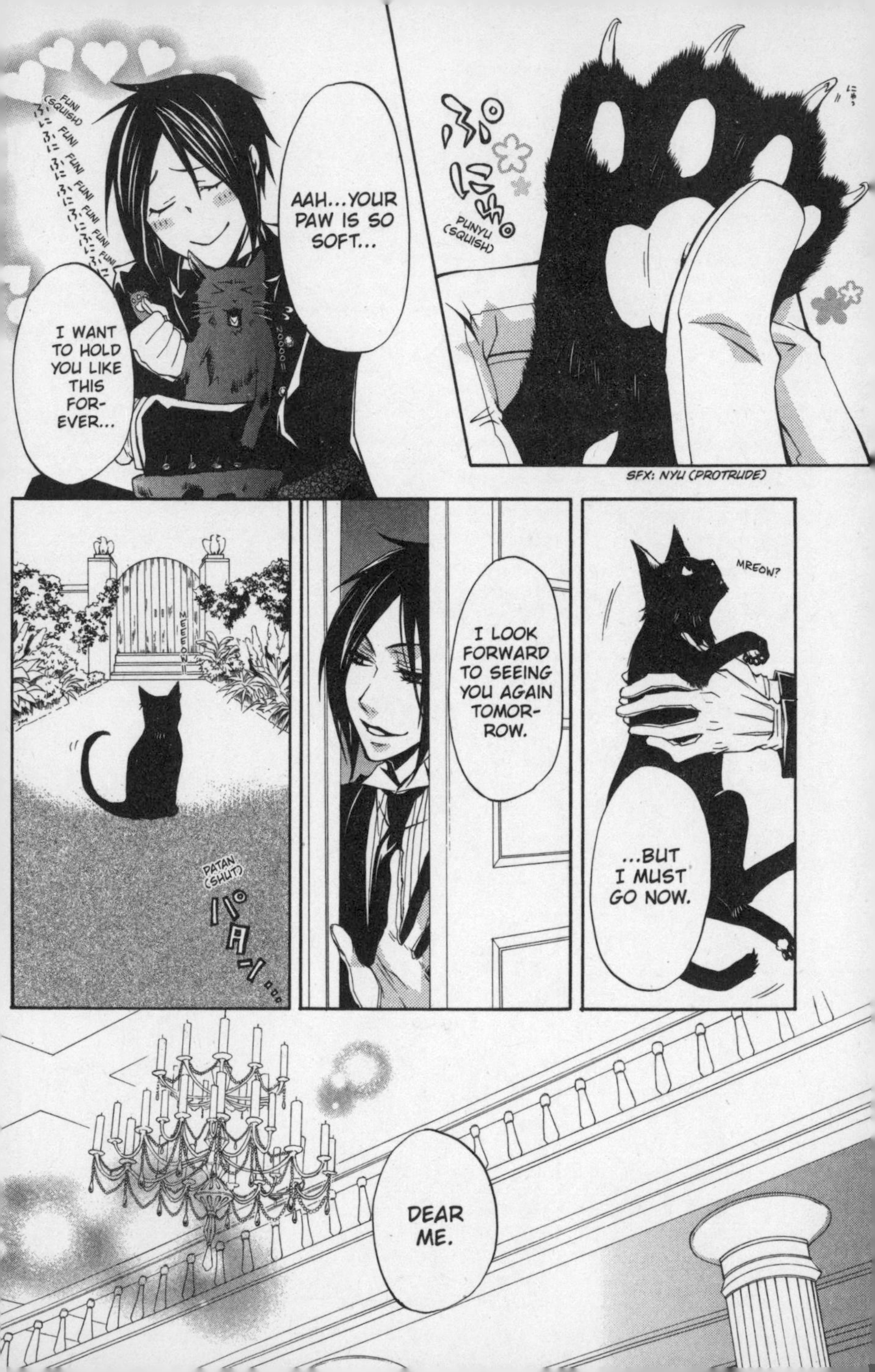

PUNYU (SQUISH)
SFX: NYU (PROTRUDE)
FUNI (SQUISH) FUNI FUNI FUNI FUNI FUNI
AAH...YOUR PAW IS SO SOFT...
I WANT TO HOLD YOU LIKE THIS FOR-EVER...
MREOW?
...BUT I MUST GO NOW.
I LOOK FORWARD TO SEEING YOU AGAIN TOMOR-ROW.
MEEEOW
PATAN (SHUT)
DEAR ME.

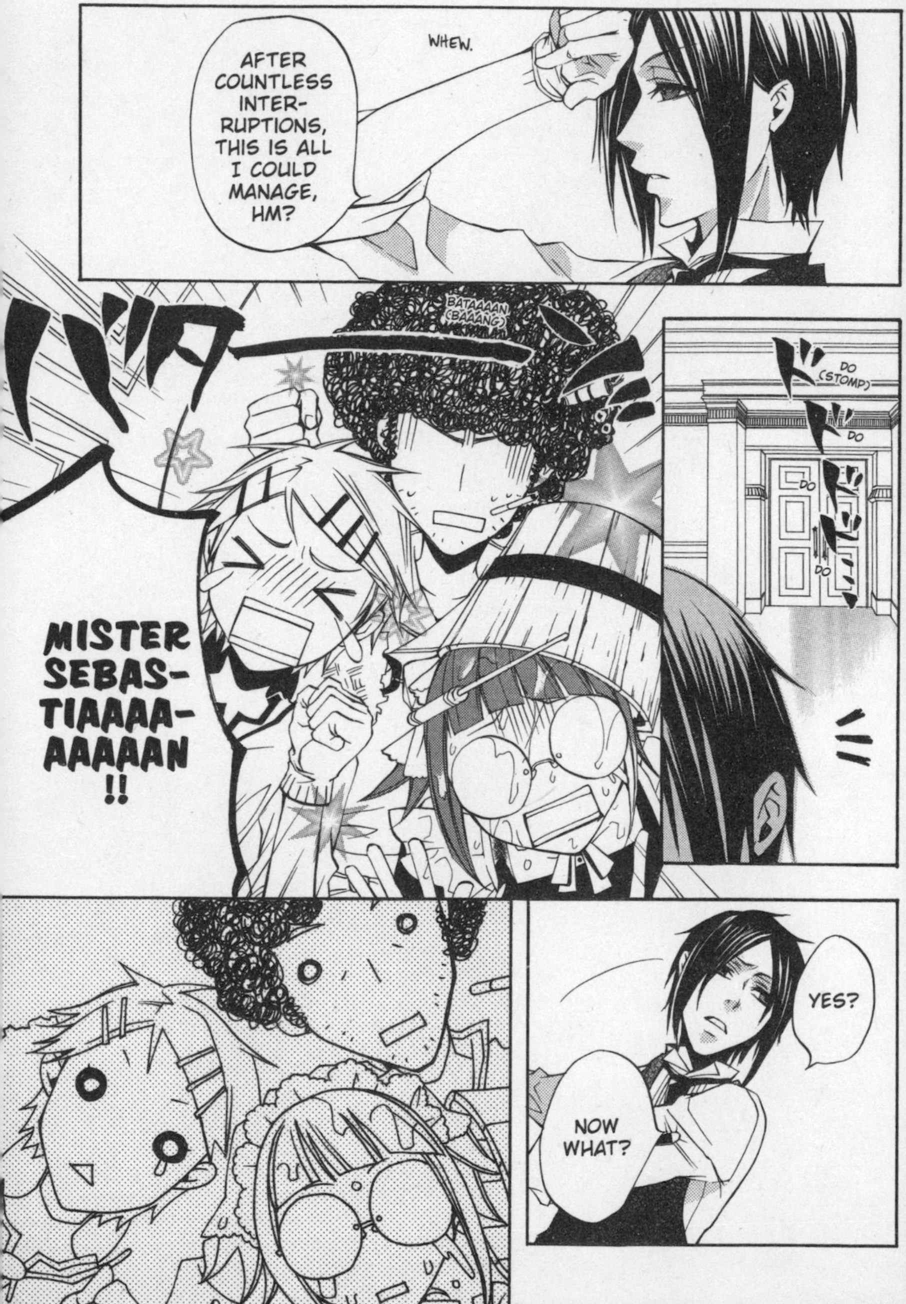
WHEW.
AFTER COUNTLESS INTER-RUPTIONS, THIS IS ALL I COULD MANAGE, HM?
DO (STOMP)
DO
DO
DO
BATAAAAN (BAAANG)
MISTER SEBAS-TIAAAA-AAAAAN!!
YES?
NOW WHAT?

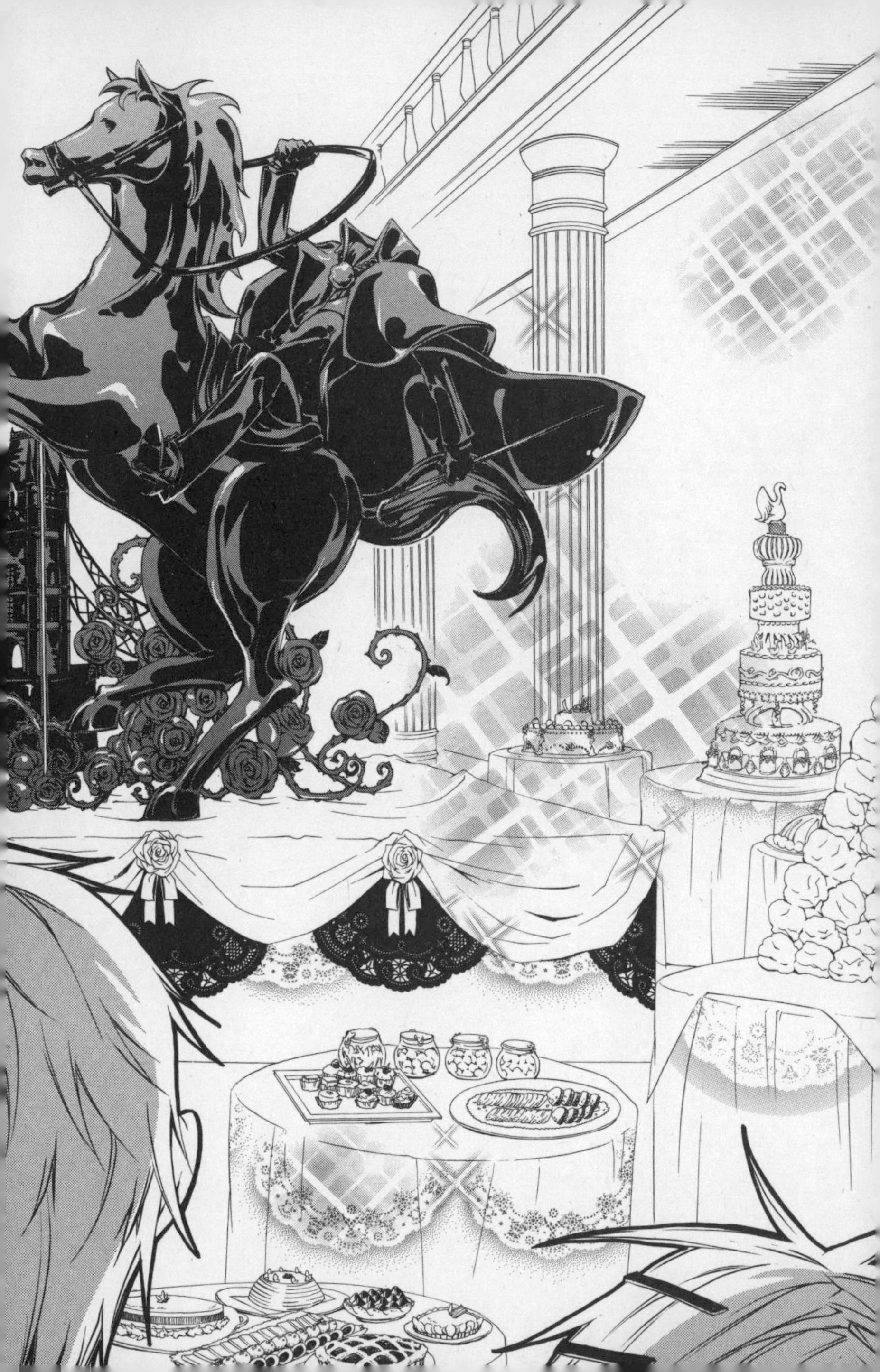

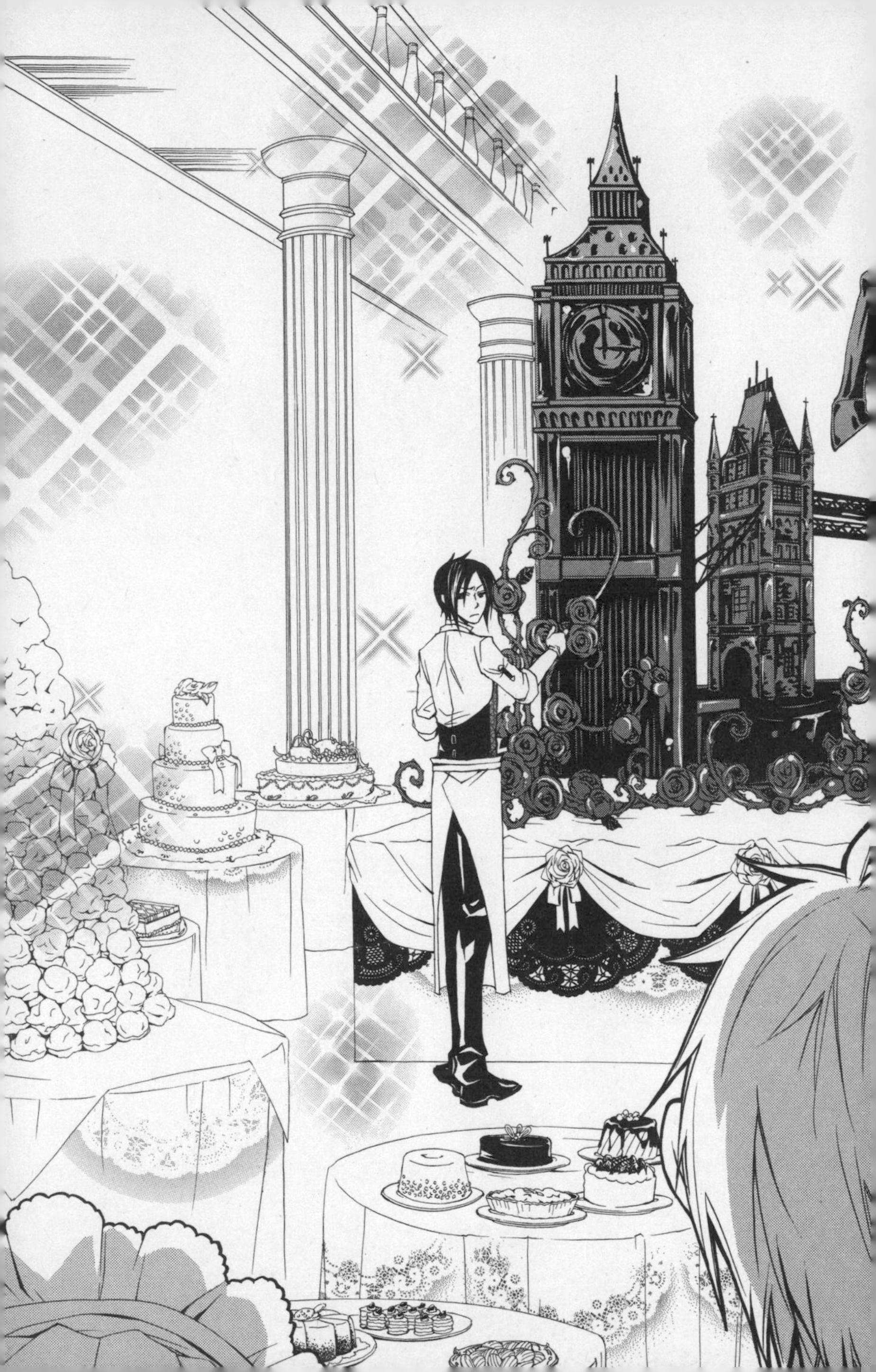

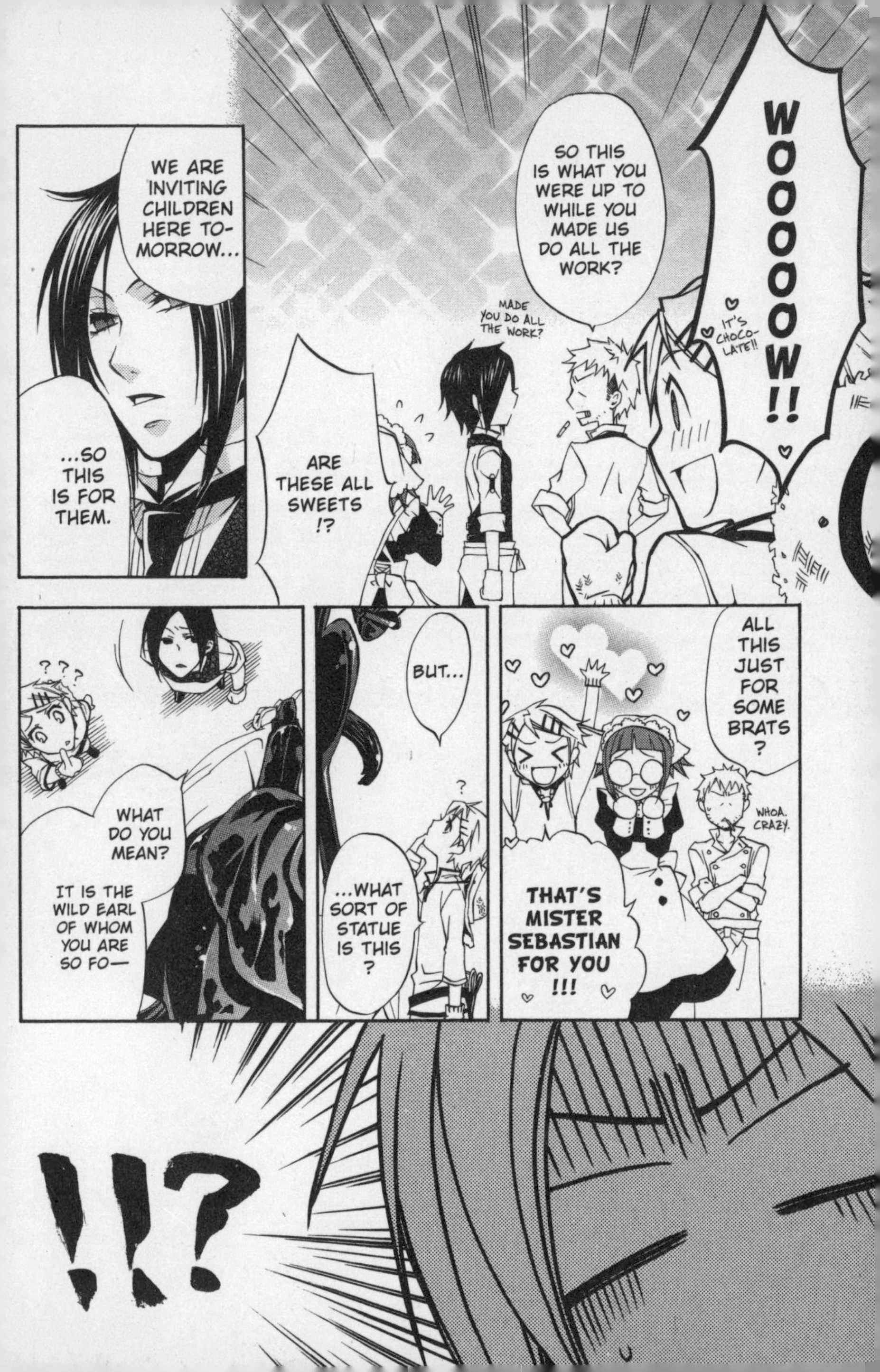
WOOOOOOW!!
IT'S CHOCO-LATE!!
SO THIS IS WHAT YOU WERE UP TO WHILE YOU MADE US DO ALL THE WORK?
MADE YOU DO ALL THE WORK?
ARE THESE ALL SWEETS!?
WE ARE INVITING CHILDREN HERE TO-MORROW...
...SO THIS IS FOR THEM.
ALL THIS JUST FOR SOME BRATS?
WHOA. CRAZY.
THAT'S MISTER SEBASTIAN FOR YOU!!!
BUT...
...WHAT SORT OF STATUE IS THIS?
???
WHAT DO YOU MEAN?
IT IS THE WILD EARL OF WHOM YOU ARE SO FO—
!!?

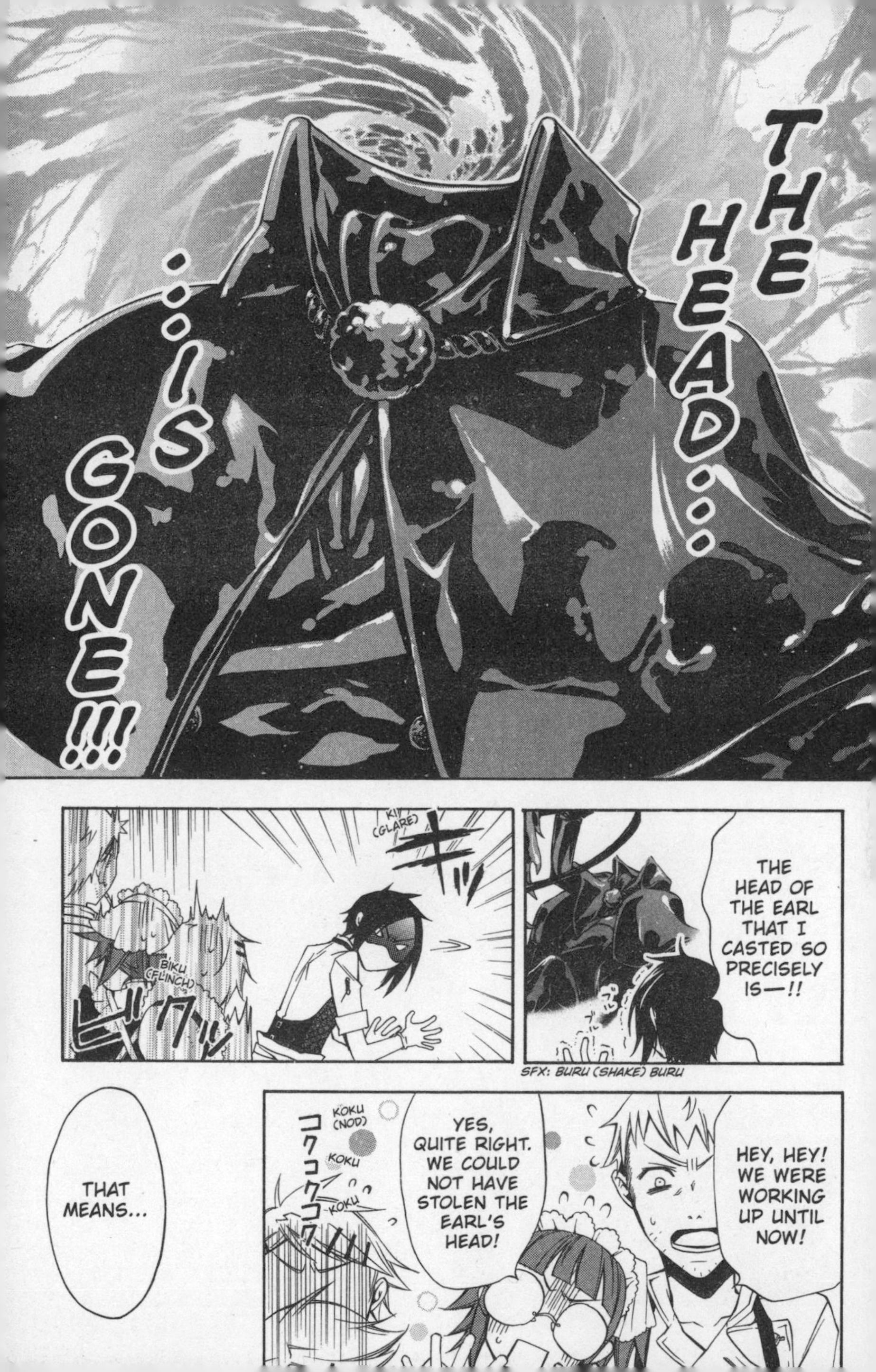
THE HEAD...
...IS GONE!!!
THE HEAD OF THE EARL THAT I CASTED SO PRECISELY IS—!!
SFX: BURU (SHAKE) BURU
KI (GLARE)
BIKU (FLINCH)
HEY, HEY! WE WERE WORKING UP UNTIL NOW!
YES, QUITE RIGHT. WE COULD NOT HAVE STOLEN THE EARL'S HEAD!
KOKU (NOD)
KOKU
KOKU
THAT MEANS...

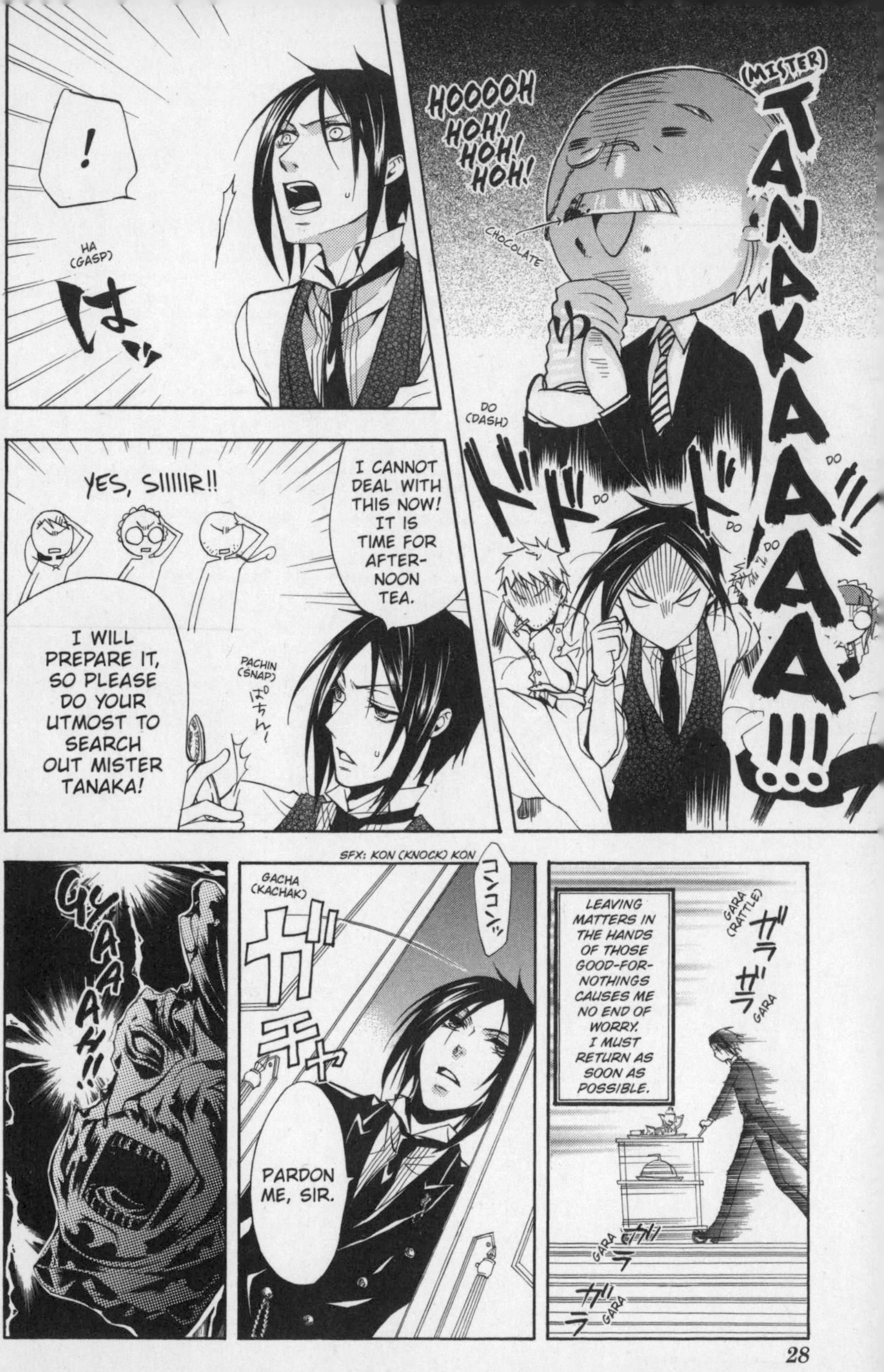
(MISTER) TANAKAAAA!!!...
HOOOOH HOH! HOH! HOH!
CHOCOLATE
DO (DASH)
DO
DO
DO
DO
!
HA (GASP)
I CANNOT DEAL WITH THIS NOW! IT IS TIME FOR AFTER-NOON TEA.
YES, SIIIIR!!
I WILL PREPARE IT, SO PLEASE DO YOUR UTMOST TO SEARCH OUT MISTER TANAKA!
PACHIN (SNAP)
LEAVING MATTERS IN THE HANDS OF THOSE GOOD-FOR-NOTHINGS CAUSES ME NO END OF WORRY. I MUST RETURN AS SOON AS POSSIBLE.
GARA (RATTLE)
GARA
GARA
GARA
SFX: KON (KNOCK) KON
GACHA (KACHAK)
PARDON ME, SIR.
GYAAAAH!!

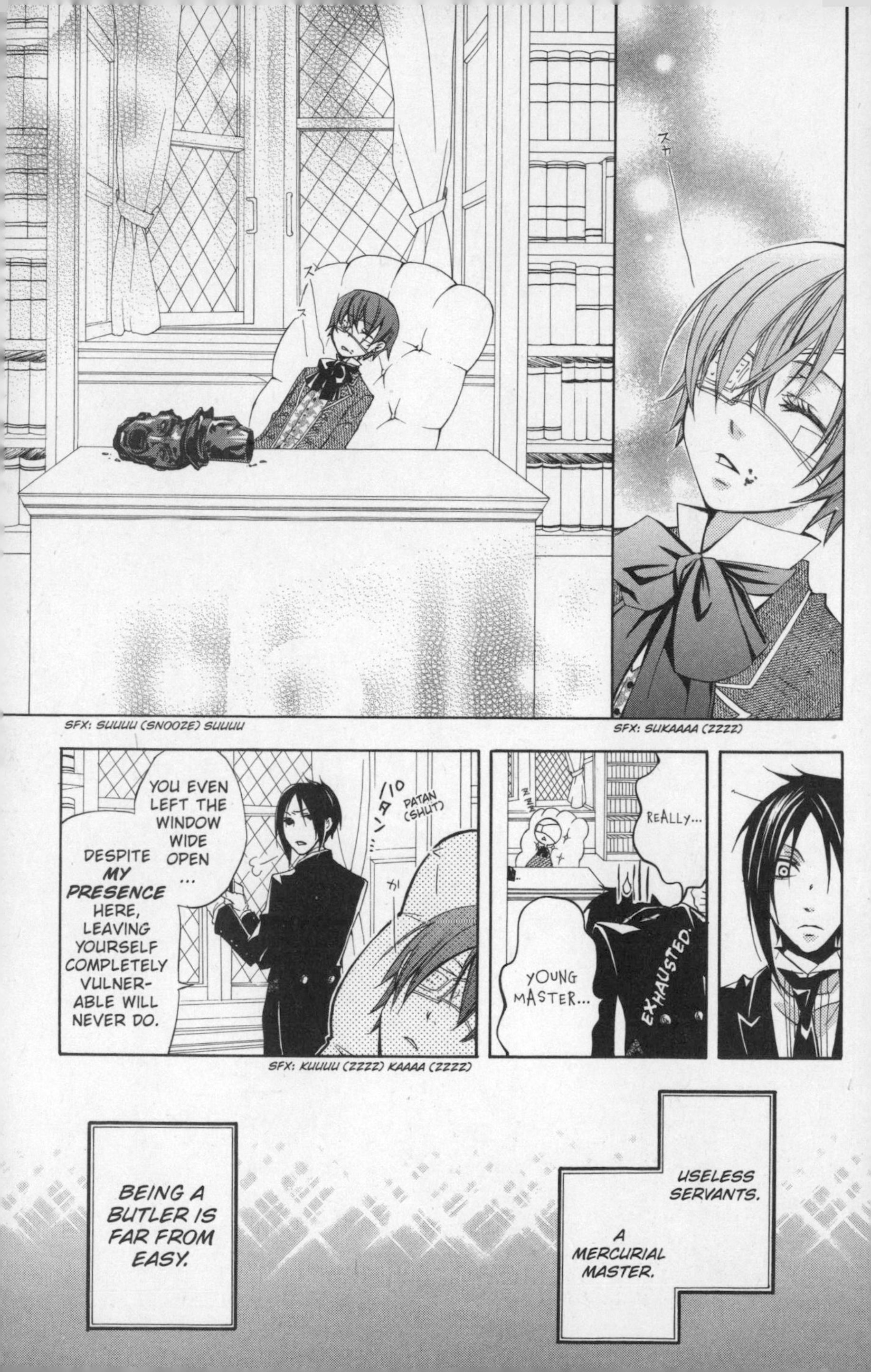
SFX: SUKAAAA (ZZZZ)
SFX: SUUUU (SNOOZE) SUUUU
REALLY...
EXHAUSTED.
YOUNG MASTER...
PATAN (SHUT)
YOU EVEN LEFT THE WINDOW WIDE OPEN...
DESPITE MY PRESENCE HERE, LEAVING YOURSELF COMPLETELY VULNERABLE WILL NEVER DO.
SFX: KUUUU (ZZZZ) KAAAA (ZZZZ)
USELESS SERVANTS.
A MERCURIAL MASTER.
BEING A BUTLER IS FAR FROM EASY.

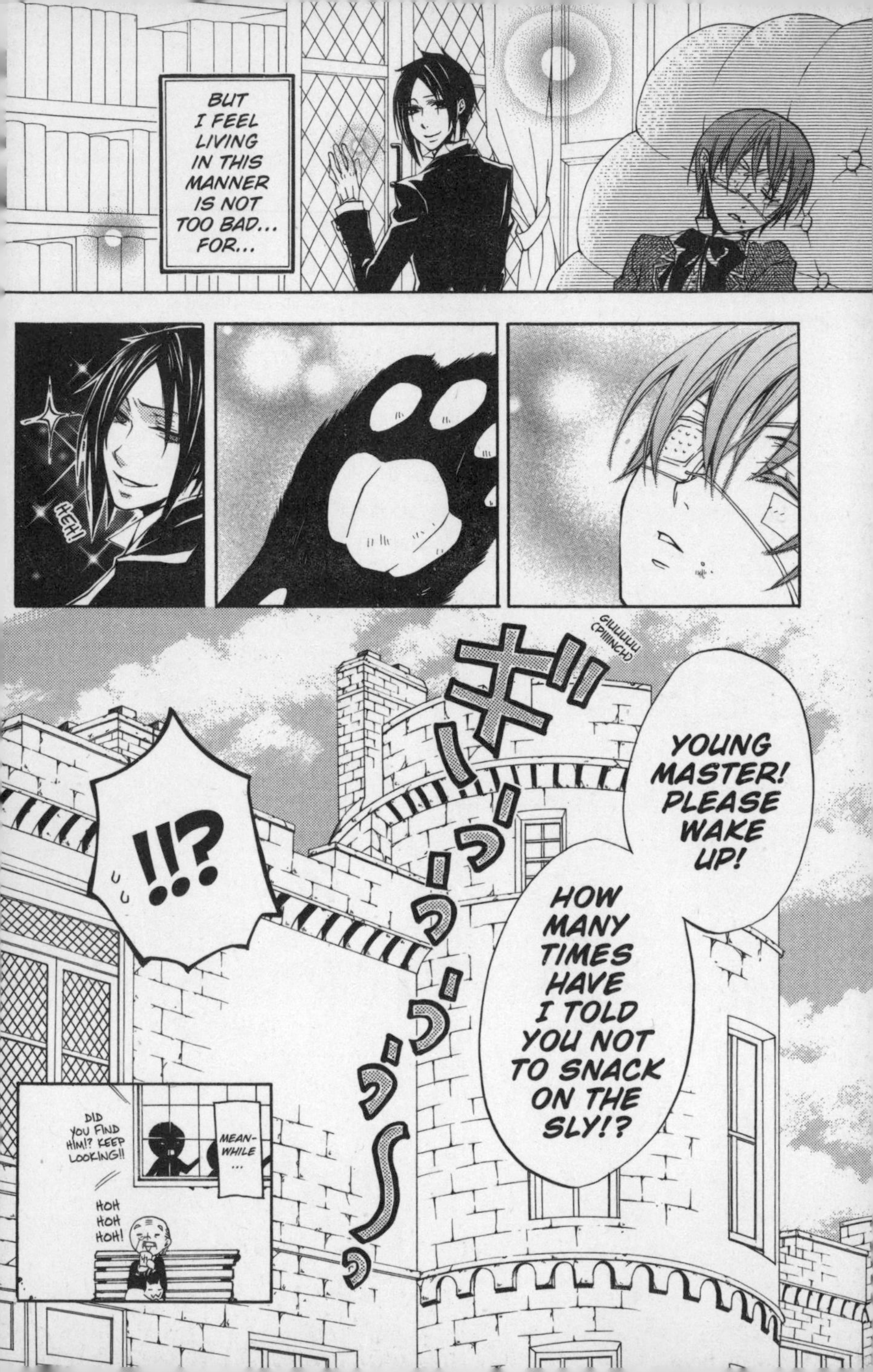
BUT I FEEL LIVING IN THIS MANNER IS NOT TOO BAD... FOR...
HEH!
GIUUUUU (PIIIINCH)
YOUNG MASTER! PLEASE WAKE UP!
HOW MANY TIMES HAVE I TOLD YOU NOT TO SNACK ON THE SLY!?
!!?
MEAN-WHILE...
DID YOU FIND HIM!? KEEP LOOKING!!
HOH HOH HOH!

Black Butler

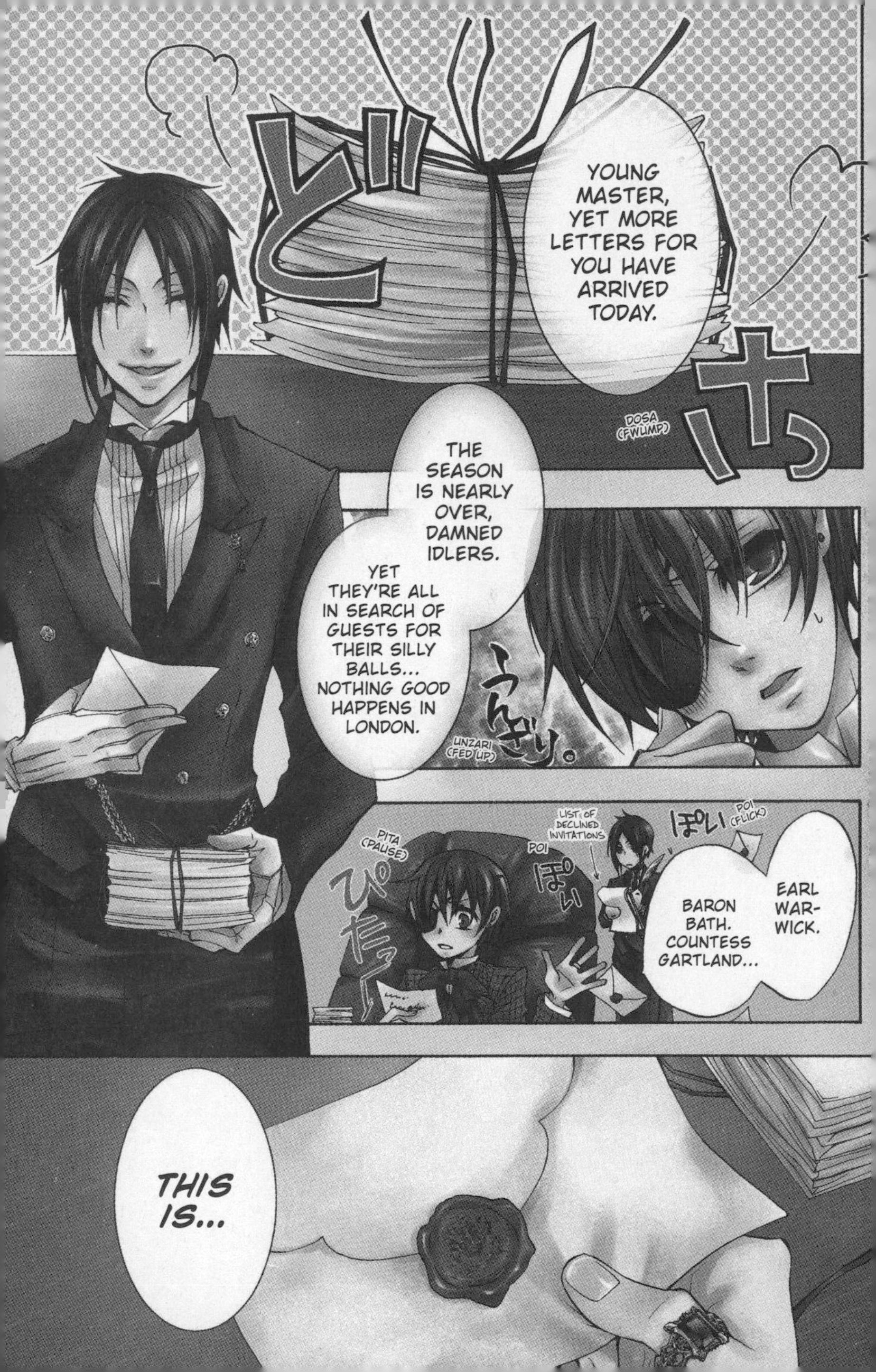
YOUNG MASTER, YET MORE LETTERS FOR YOU HAVE ARRIVED TODAY.
DOSA (FWUMP)
THE SEASON IS NEARLY OVER, DAMNED IDLERS.
YET THEY'RE ALL IN SEARCH OF GUESTS FOR THEIR SILLY BALLS... NOTHING GOOD HAPPENS IN LONDON.
UNZARI (FED UP)
EARL WAR-WICK.
BARON BATH. COUNTESS GARTLAND...
POI (FLICK)
LIST OF DECLINED INVITATIONS
POI
PITA (PAUSE)
THIS IS...

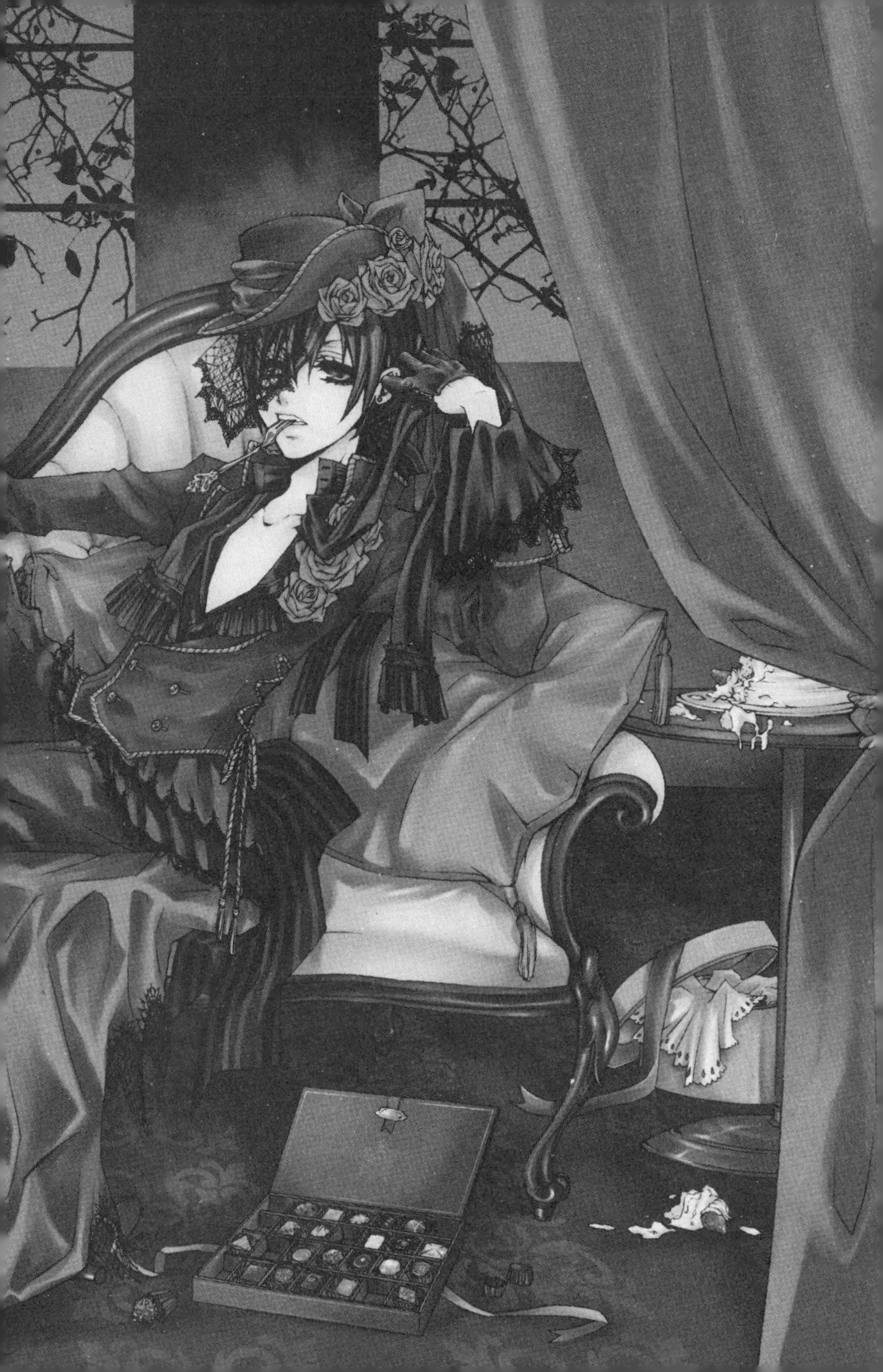

Chapter 6

At noon : The Butler, Activated

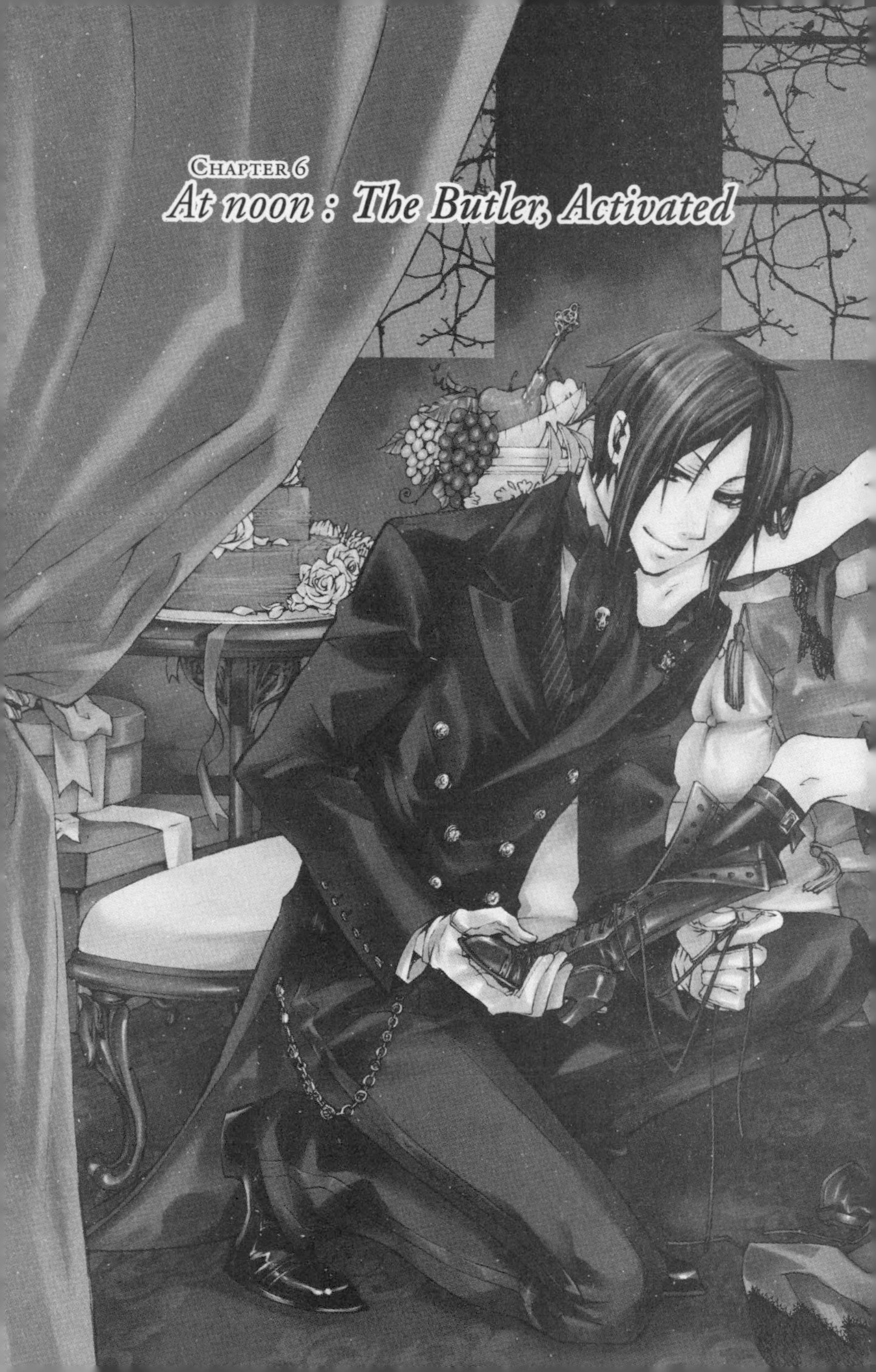

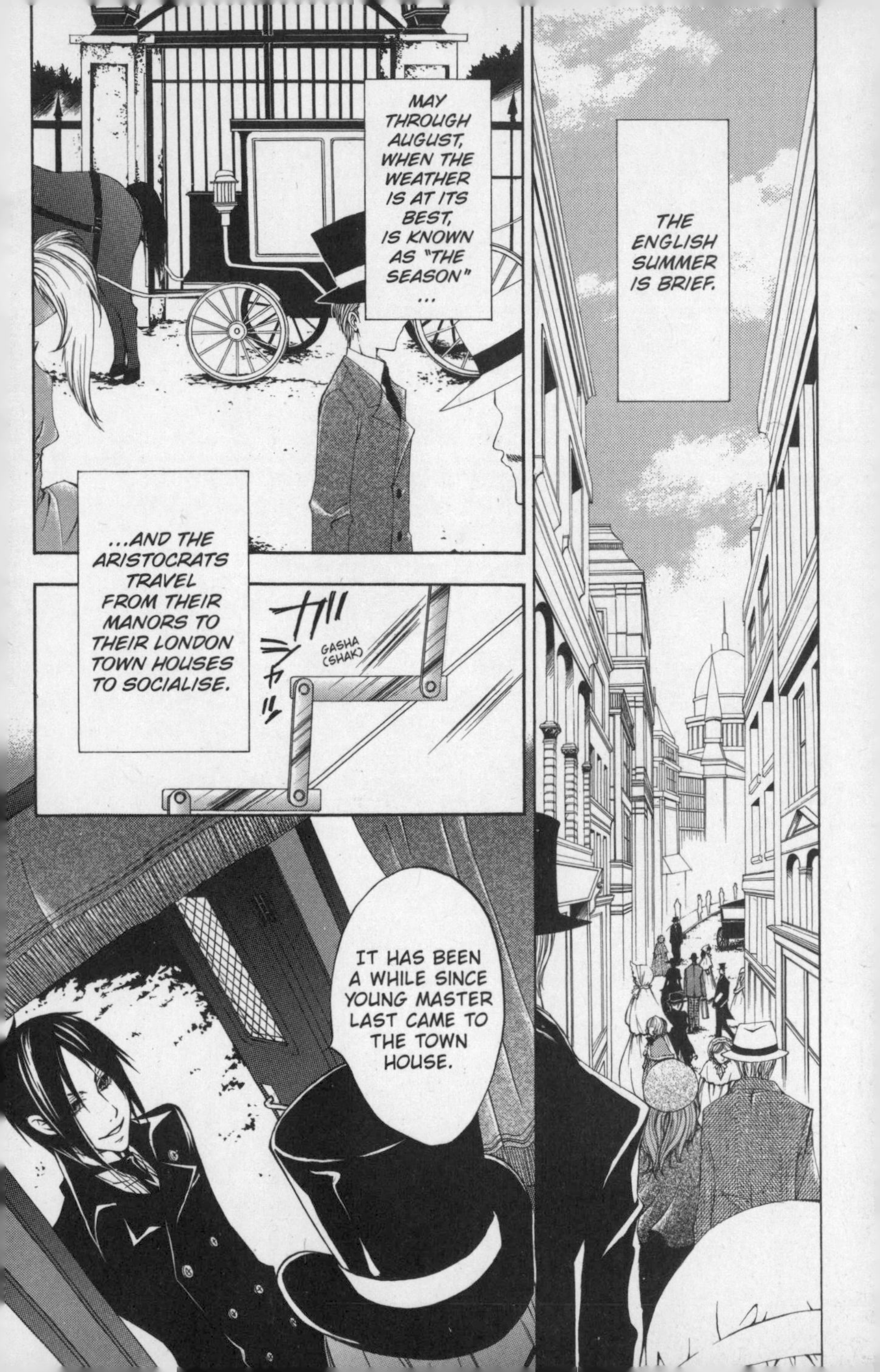
THE ENGLISH SUMMER IS BRIEF.
MAY THROUGH AUGUST, WHEN THE WEATHER IS AT ITS BEST, IS KNOWN AS "THE SEASON" ...
...AND THE ARISTOCRATS TRAVEL FROM THEIR MANORS TO THEIR LONDON TOWN HOUSES TO SOCIALISE.
GASHA (SHAK)
IT HAS BEEN A WHILE SINCE YOUNG MASTER LAST CAME TO THE TOWN HOUSE.

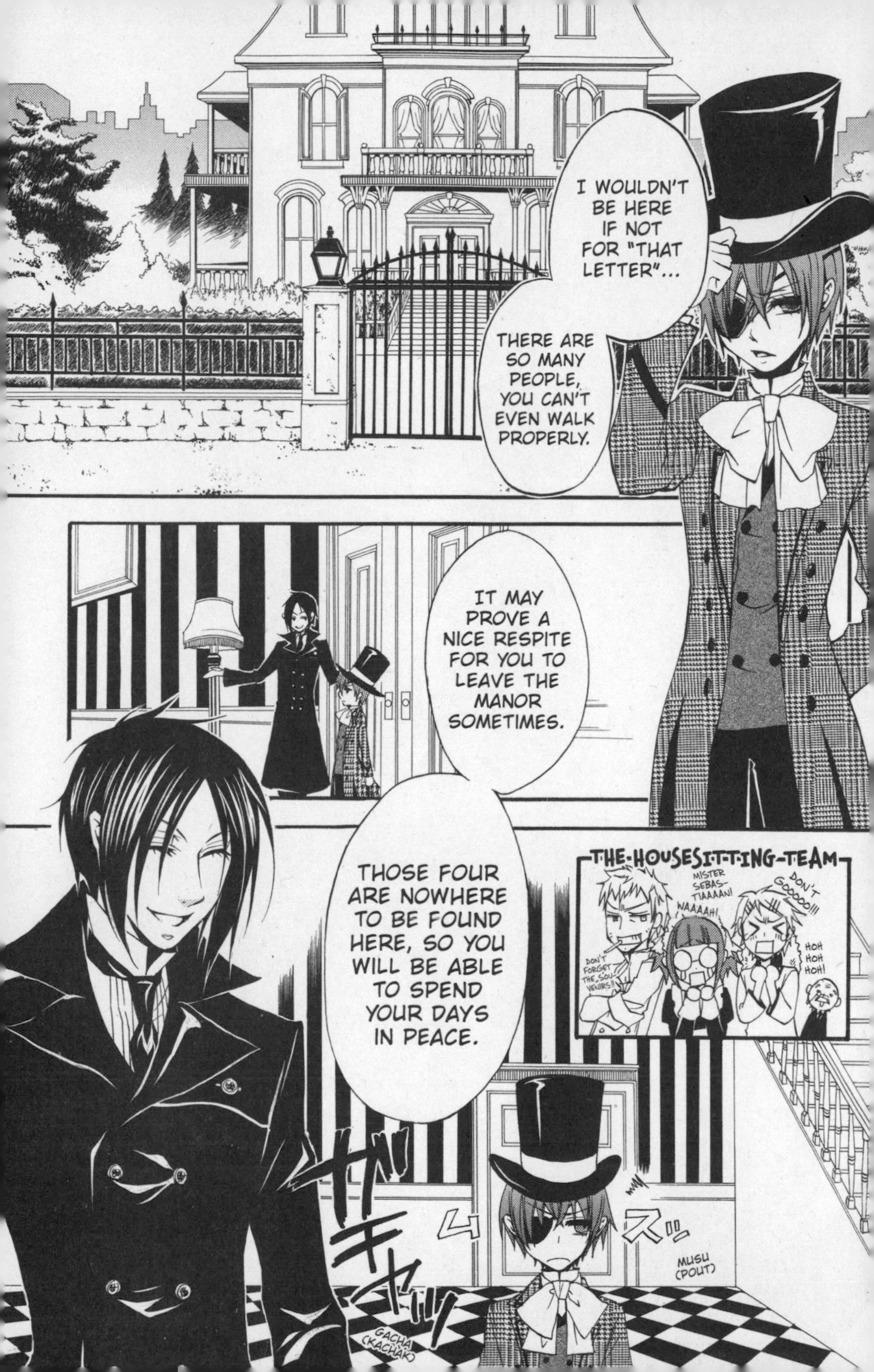
I WOULDN'T BE HERE IF NOT FOR "THAT LETTER"...
THERE ARE SO MANY PEOPLE, YOU CAN'T EVEN WALK PROPERLY.
IT MAY PROVE A NICE RESPITE FOR YOU TO LEAVE THE MANOR SOMETIMES.
THOSE FOUR ARE NOWHERE TO BE FOUND HERE, SO YOU WILL BE ABLE TO SPEND YOUR DAYS IN PEACE.
THE-HOUSESITTING-TEAM
DON'T GOOOOOO!!!
HOH HOH HOH!
MISTER SEBAS-TIAAAAN!
WAAAAH!
DON'T FORGET THE SOU-VENIRS!!
MUSU (POUT)
GACHA (KACHAK)

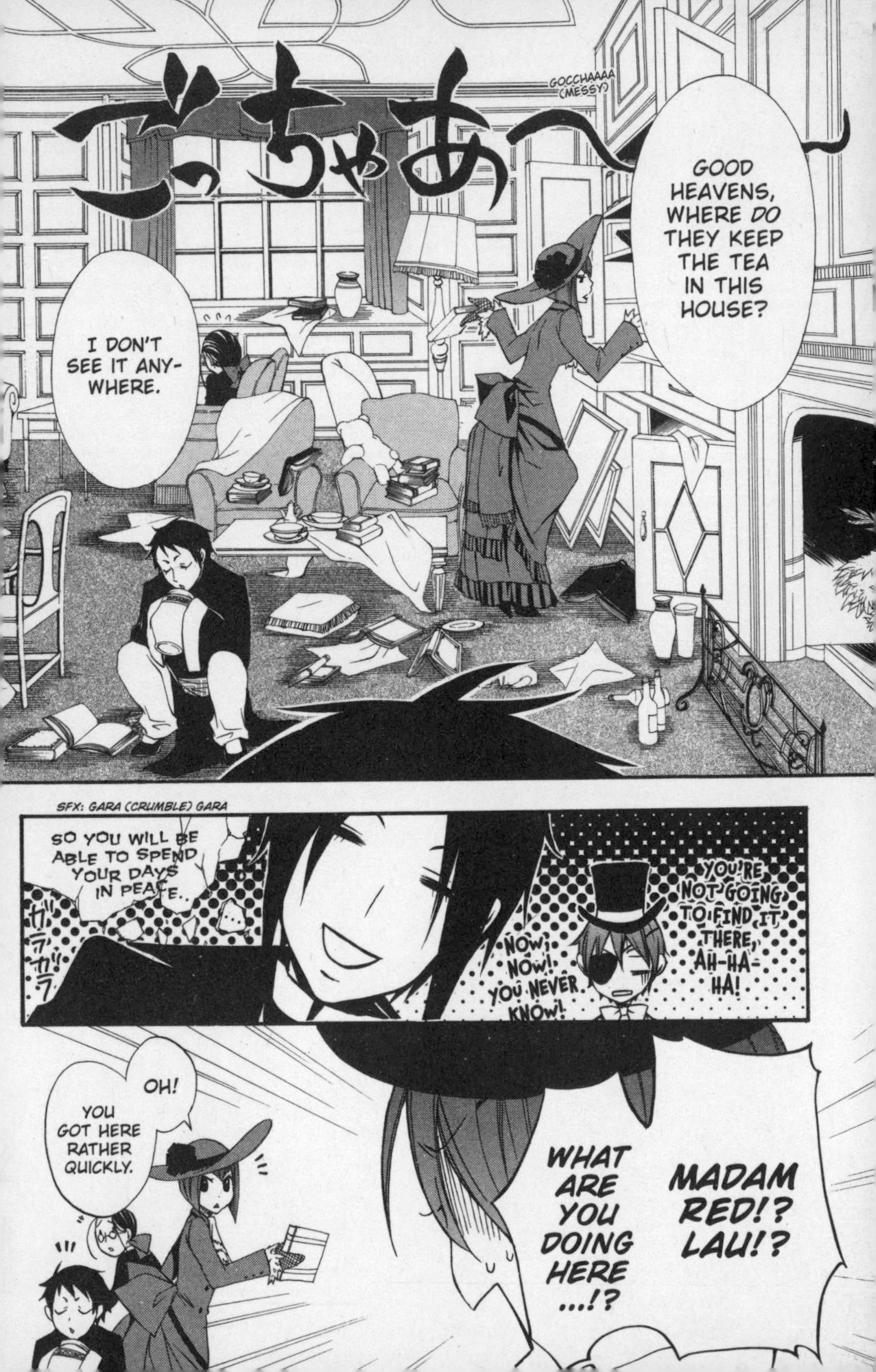
GOCCHAAAA (MESSY)
GOOD HEAVENS, WHERE *DO* THEY KEEP THE TEA IN THIS HOUSE?
I DON'T SEE IT ANY-WHERE.
SFX: GARA (CRUMBLE) GARA
YOU'RE NOT GOING TO FIND IT THERE, AH-HA-HA!
NOW, NOW! YOU NEVER KNOW!
SO YOU WILL BE ABLE TO SPEND YOUR DAYS IN PEACE...
MADAM RED!? LAU!?
WHAT ARE YOU DOING HERE ...!?
OH!
YOU GOT HERE RATHER QUICKLY.

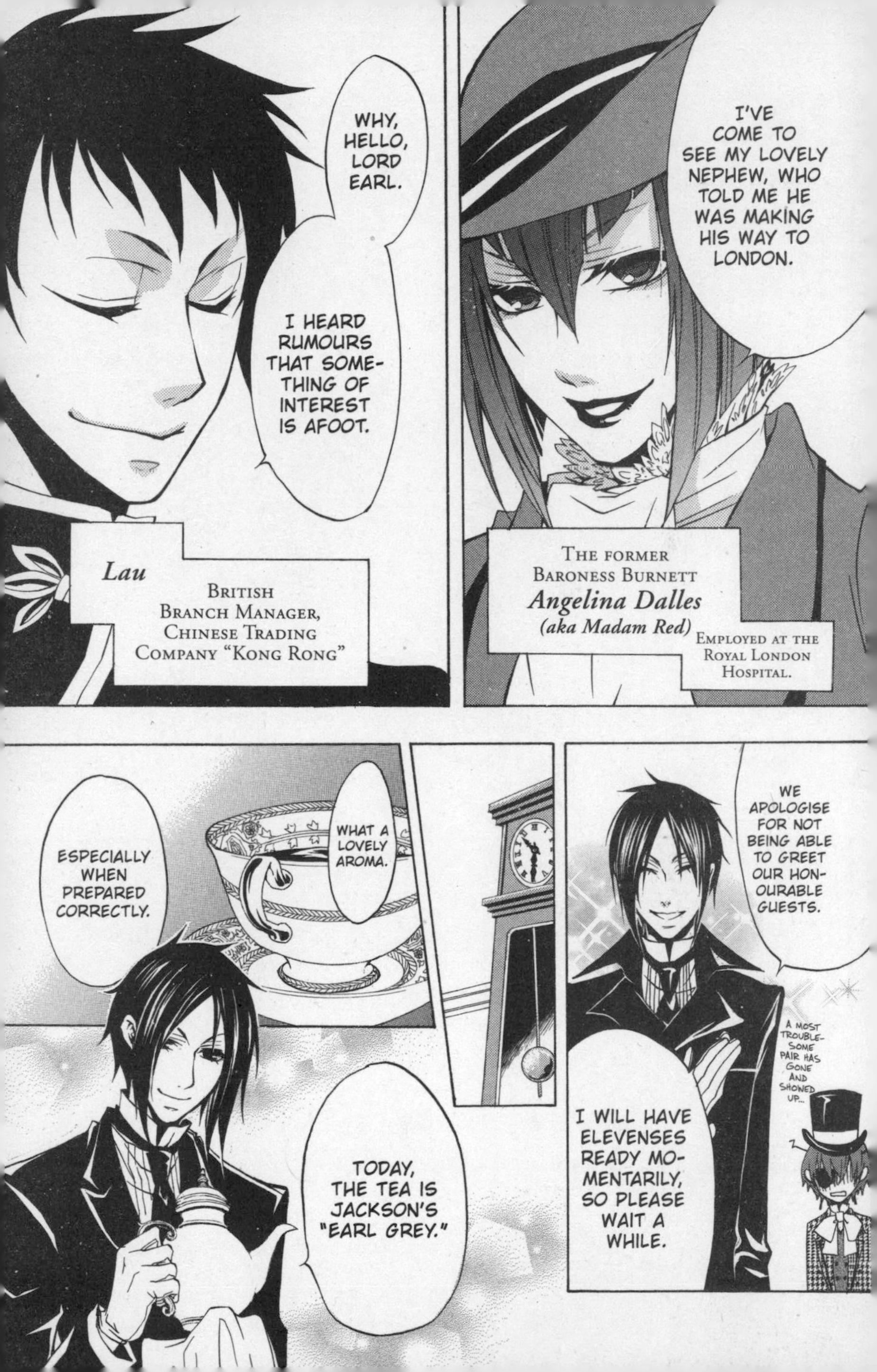
I'VE COME TO SEE MY LOVELY NEPHEW, WHO TOLD ME HE WAS MAKING HIS WAY TO LONDON.
The former Baroness Burnett *Angelina Dalles* *(aka Madam Red)*
Employed at the Royal London Hospital.
WHY, HELLO, LORD EARL.
I HEARD RUMOURS THAT SOME-THING OF INTEREST IS AFOOT.
Lau
British Branch Manager, Chinese Trading Company "Kong Rong"
WE APOLOGISE FOR NOT BEING ABLE TO GREET OUR HON-OURABLE GUESTS.
A MOST TROUBLE-SOME PAIR HAS GONE AND SHOWED UP...
I WILL HAVE ELEVENSES READY MO-MENTARILY, SO PLEASE WAIT A WHILE.
WHAT A LOVELY AROMA.
ESPECIALLY WHEN PREPARED CORRECTLY.
TODAY, THE TEA IS JACKSON'S "EARL GREY."

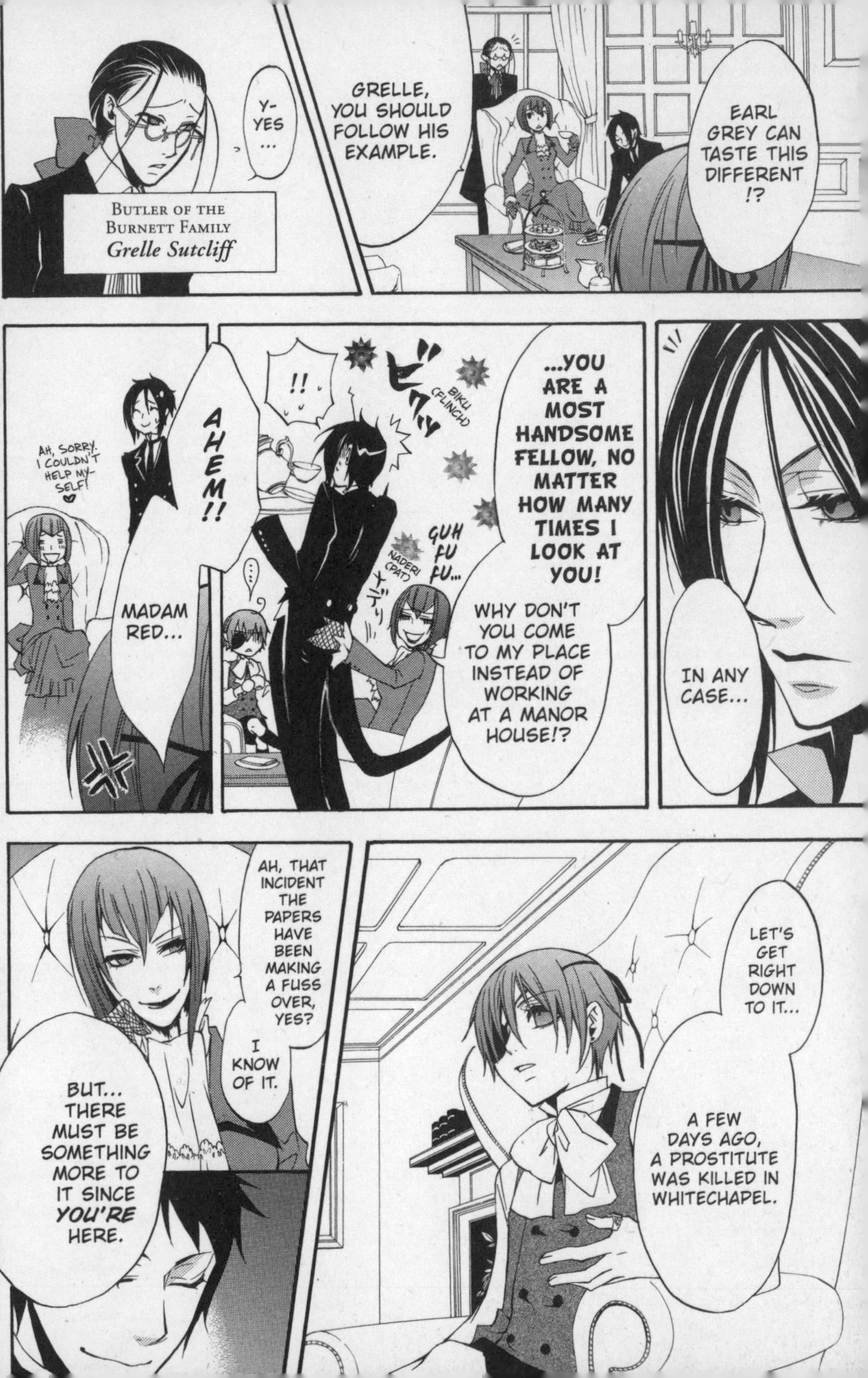
EARL GREY CAN TASTE THIS DIFFERENT!?
GRELLE, YOU SHOULD FOLLOW HIS EXAMPLE.
Y-YES...
Butler of the Burnett Family *Grelle Sutcliff*
IN ANY CASE...
...YOU ARE A MOST HANDSOME FELLOW, NO MATTER HOW MANY TIMES I LOOK AT YOU!
WHY DON'T YOU COME TO MY PLACE INSTEAD OF WORKING AT A MANOR HOUSE!?
BIKU (FLINCH)
!!
GUH FU FU...
NADERI (PAT)
...
AHEM!!
MADAM RED...
AH, SORRY. I COULDN'T HELP MYSELF!
LET'S GET RIGHT DOWN TO IT...
A FEW DAYS AGO, A PROSTITUTE WAS KILLED IN WHITECHAPEL.
AH, THAT INCIDENT THE PAPERS HAVE BEEN MAKING A FUSS OVER, YES?
I KNOW OF IT.
BUT... THERE MUST BE SOMETHING MORE TO IT SINCE *YOU'RE* HERE.

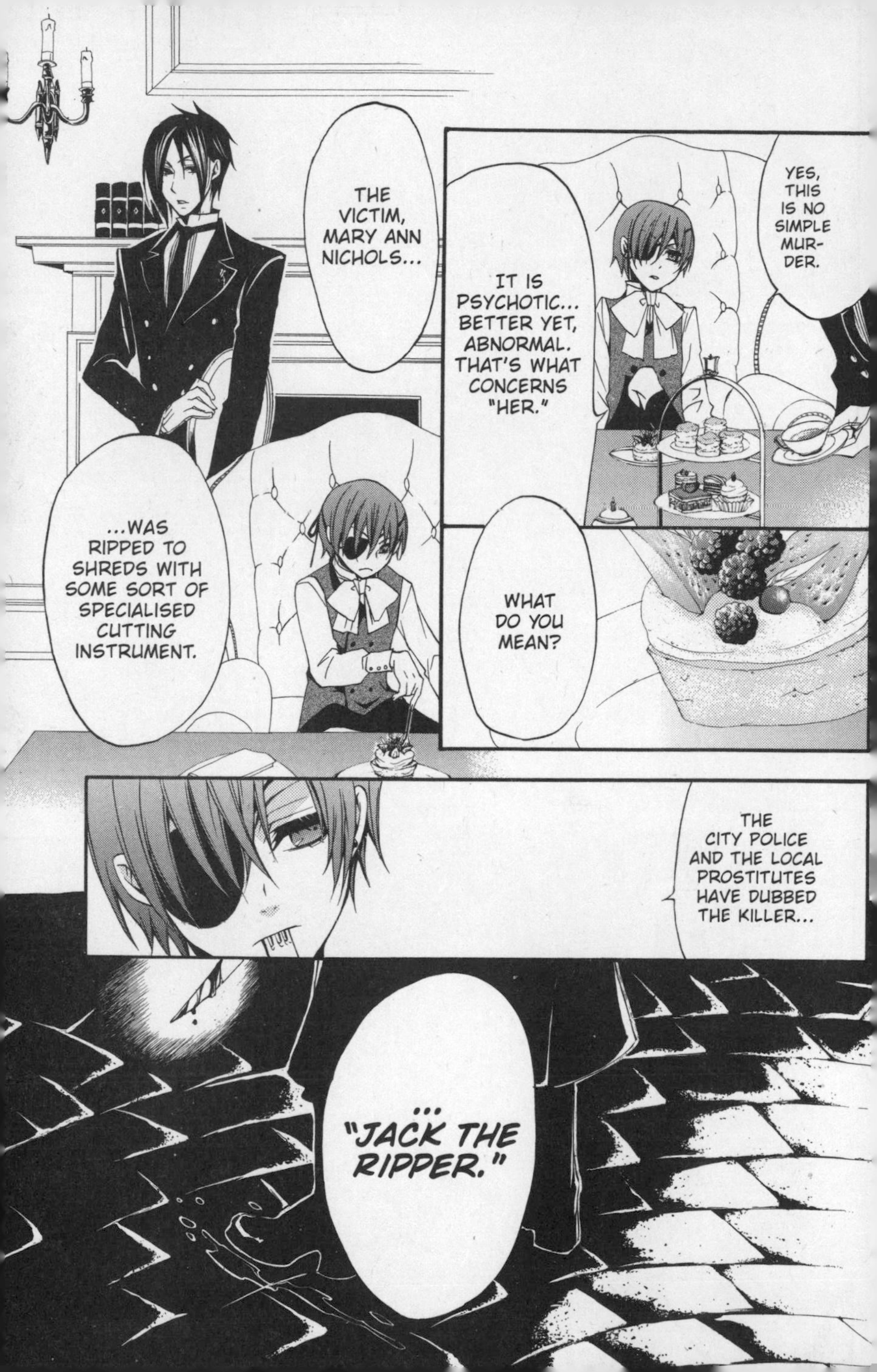
YES, THIS IS NO SIMPLE MUR-DER.
IT IS PSYCHOTIC... BETTER YET, ABNORMAL. THAT'S WHAT CONCERNS "HER."
WHAT DO YOU MEAN?
THE VICTIM, MARY ANN NICHOLS...
...WAS RIPPED TO SHREDS WITH SOME SORT OF SPECIALISED CUTTING INSTRUMENT.
THE CITY POLICE AND THE LOCAL PROSTITUTES HAVE DUBBED THE KILLER...
... "JACK THE RIPPER."

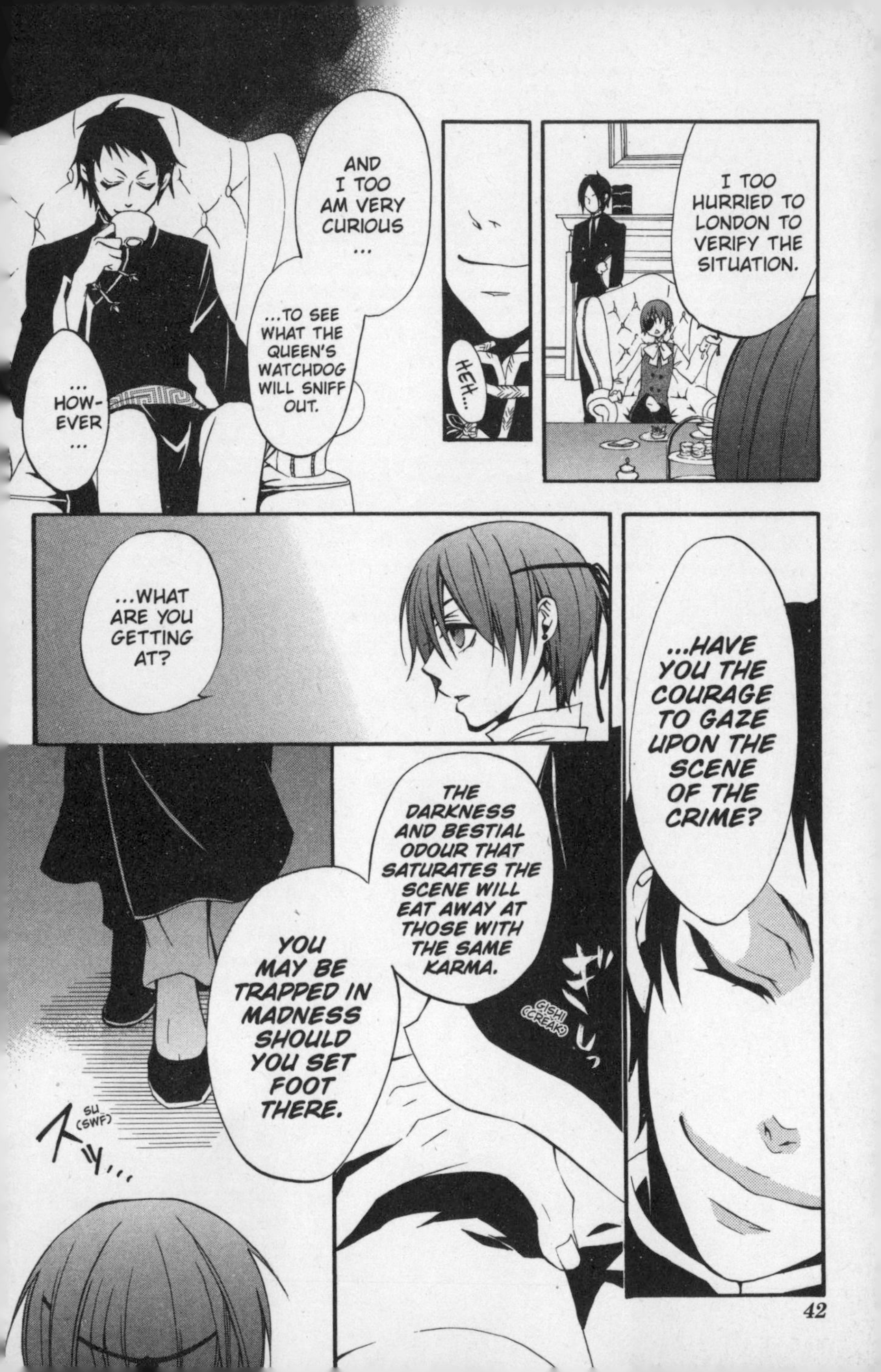
I TOO HURRIED TO LONDON TO VERIFY THE SITUATION.
HEH...
AND I TOO AM VERY CURIOUS ...
...TO SEE WHAT THE QUEEN'S WATCHDOG WILL SNIFF OUT.
... HOW-EVER ...
...HAVE YOU THE COURAGE TO GAZE UPON THE SCENE OF THE CRIME?
...WHAT ARE YOU GETTING AT?
THE DARKNESS AND BESTIAL ODOUR THAT SATURATES THE SCENE WILL EAT AWAY AT THOSE WITH THE SAME KARMA.
GISHI (CREAK)
YOU MAY BE TRAPPED IN MADNESS SHOULD YOU SET FOOT THERE.
SU (SWF)

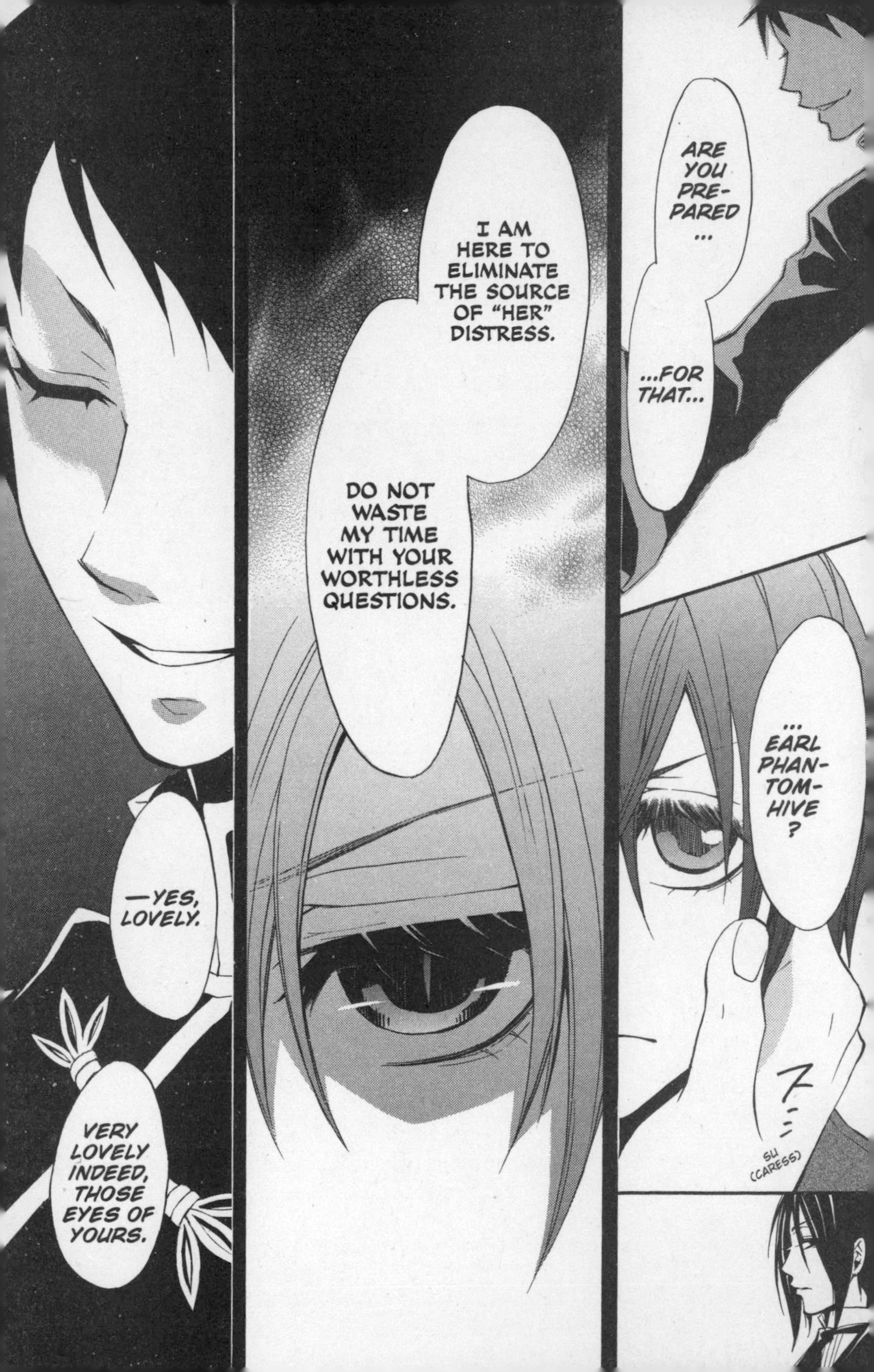
ARE YOU PRE-PARED...
...FOR THAT...
...EARL PHAN-TOM-HIVE?
SU (CARESS)
I AM HERE TO ELIMINATE THE SOURCE OF "HER" DISTRESS.
DO NOT WASTE MY TIME WITH YOUR WORTHLESS QUESTIONS.
—YES, LOVELY.
VERY LOVELY INDEED, THOSE EYES OF YOURS.

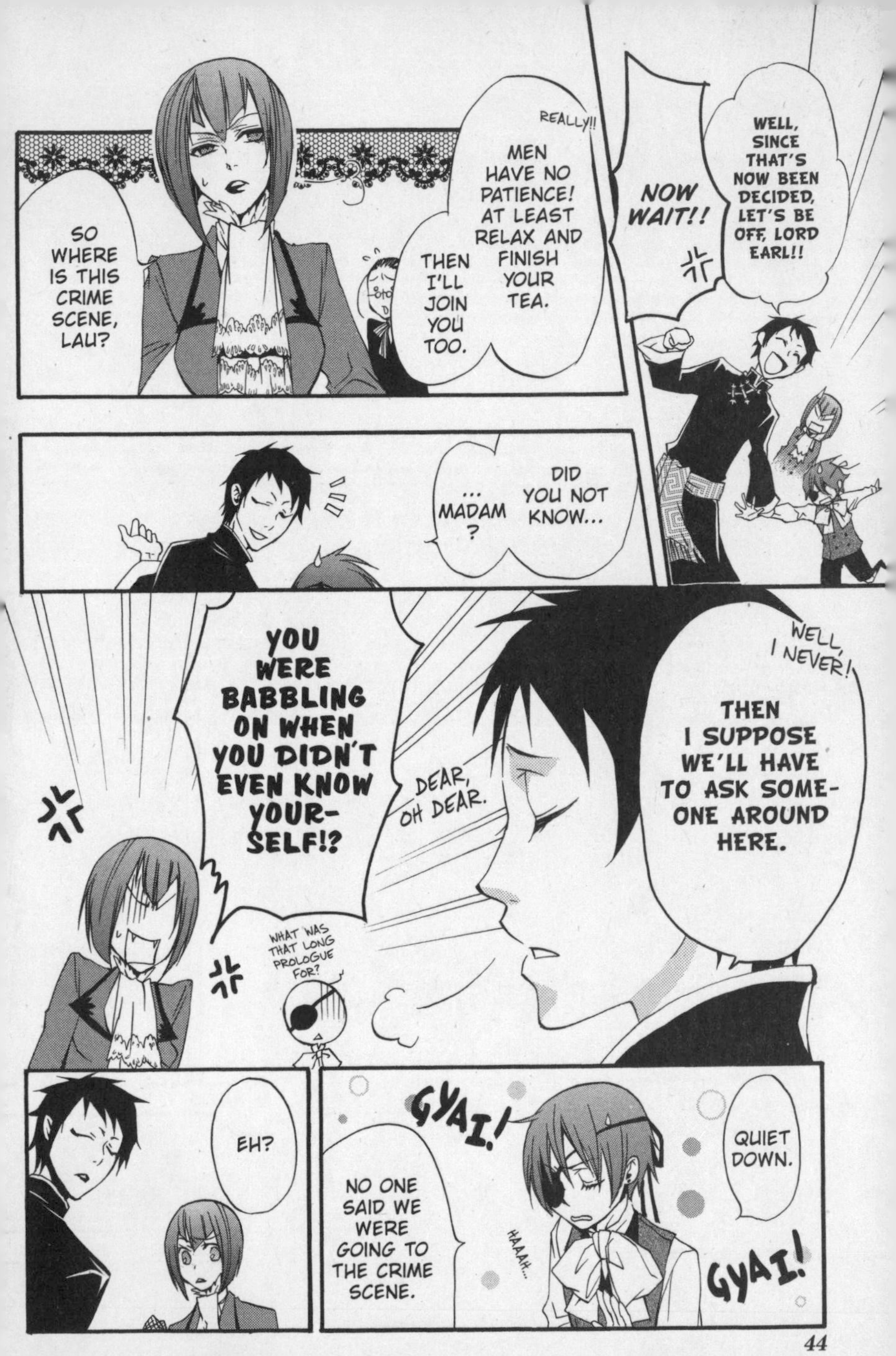
WELL, SINCE THAT'S NOW BEEN DECIDED, LET'S BE OFF, LORD EARL!!
NOW WAIT!!
MEN HAVE NO PATIENCE! AT LEAST RELAX AND FINISH YOUR TEA. THEN I'LL JOIN YOU TOO.
REALLY!!
SO WHERE IS THIS CRIME SCENE, LAU?
DID YOU NOT KNOW... ...MADAM?
WELL, I NEVER!
THEN I SUPPOSE WE'LL HAVE TO ASK SOMEONE AROUND HERE.
DEAR, OH DEAR.
YOU WERE BABBLING ON WHEN YOU DIDN'T EVEN KNOW YOURSELF!?
WHAT WAS THAT LONG PROLOGUE FOR?
QUIET DOWN.
GYAI!
NO ONE SAID WE WERE GOING TO THE CRIME SCENE.
HAAAH...
GYAI!
EH?

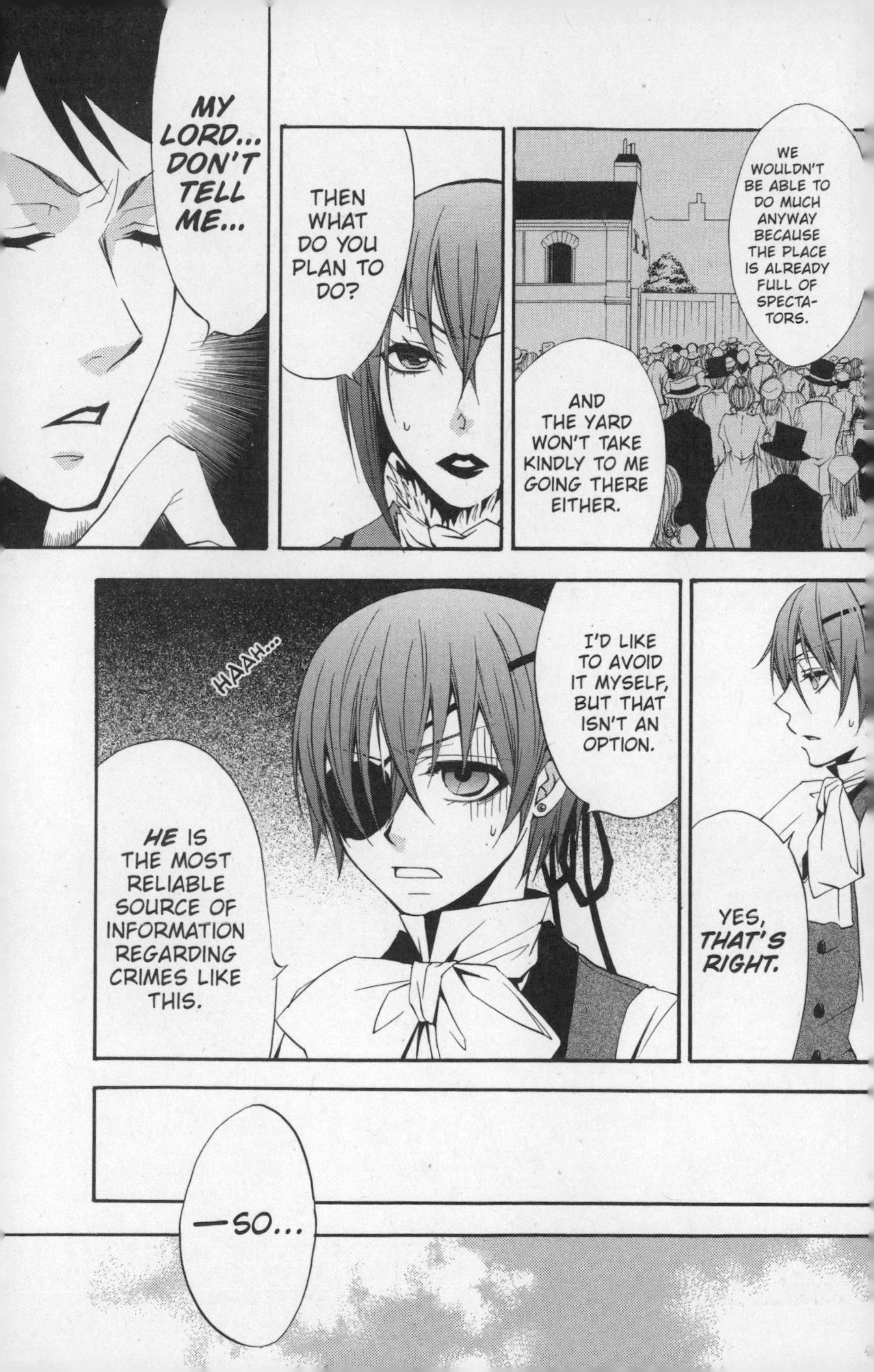
WE WOULDN'T BE ABLE TO DO MUCH ANYWAY BECAUSE THE PLACE IS ALREADY FULL OF SPECTATORS.
AND THE YARD WON'T TAKE KINDLY TO ME GOING THERE EITHER.
THEN WHAT DO YOU PLAN TO DO?
MY LORD... DON'T TELL ME...
YES, THAT'S RIGHT.
I'D LIKE TO AVOID IT MYSELF, BUT THAT ISN'T AN OPTION.
HAAAH...
HE IS THE MOST RELIABLE SOURCE OF INFORMATION REGARDING CRIMES LIKE THIS.
—SO...

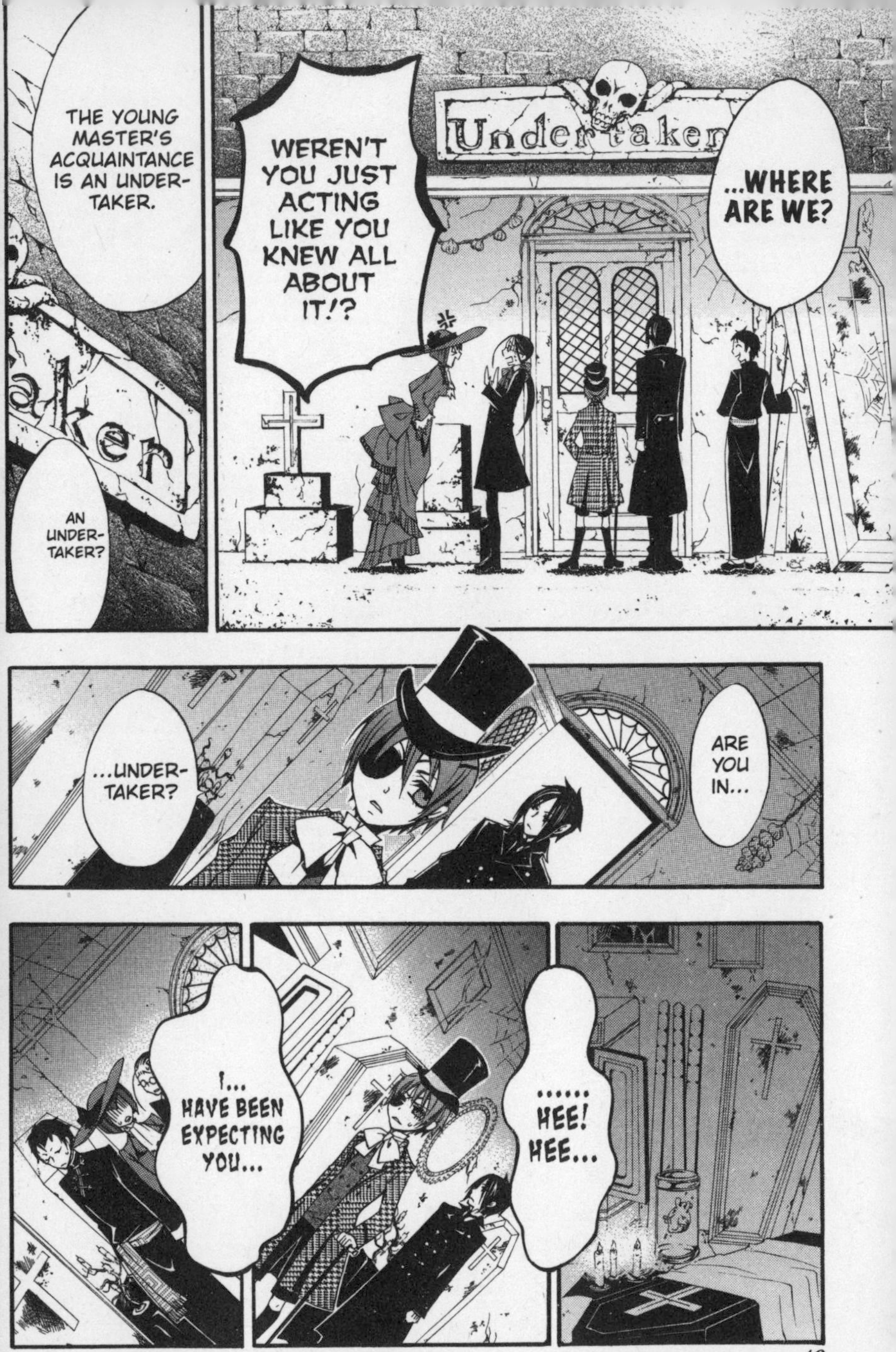
Undertaker
...WHERE ARE WE?
WEREN'T YOU JUST ACTING LIKE YOU KNEW ALL ABOUT IT!?
THE YOUNG MASTER'S ACQUAINTANCE IS AN UNDER-TAKER.
AN UNDER-TAKER?
ARE YOU IN...
...UNDER-TAKER?
...... HEE! HEE...
I... HAVE BEEN EXPECTING YOU...

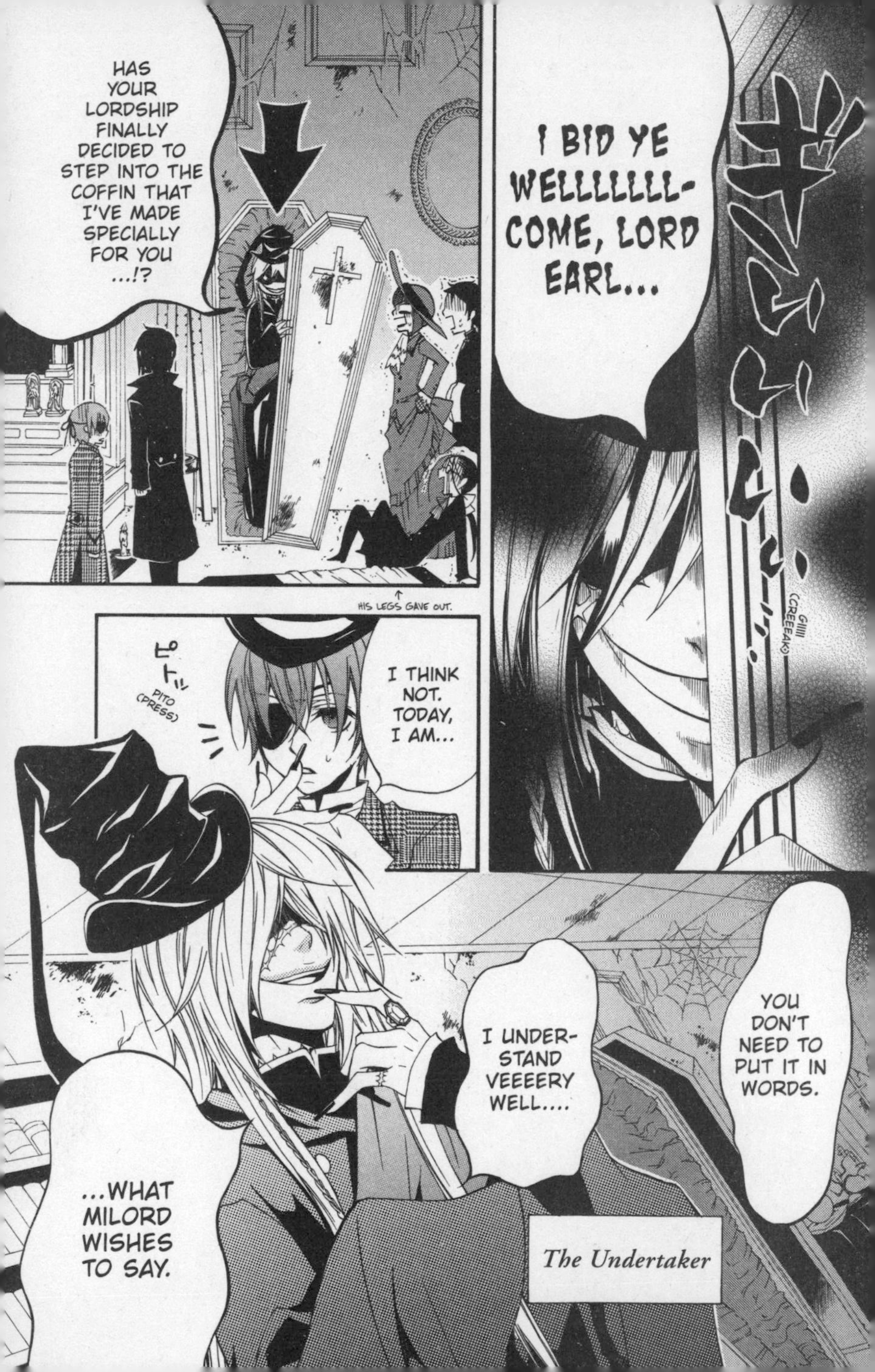
I BID YE WELLLLLLL-COME, LORD EARL...
GIIIII (CREEEAK)
HAS YOUR LORDSHIP FINALLY DECIDED TO STEP INTO THE COFFIN THAT I'VE MADE SPECIALLY FOR YOU ...!?
HIS LEGS GAVE OUT.
ピトッ
PITO (PRESS)
I THINK NOT. TODAY, I AM...
YOU DON'T NEED TO PUT IT IN WORDS.
I UNDER-STAND VEEEERY WELL....
...WHAT MILORD WISHES TO SAY.
The Undertaker

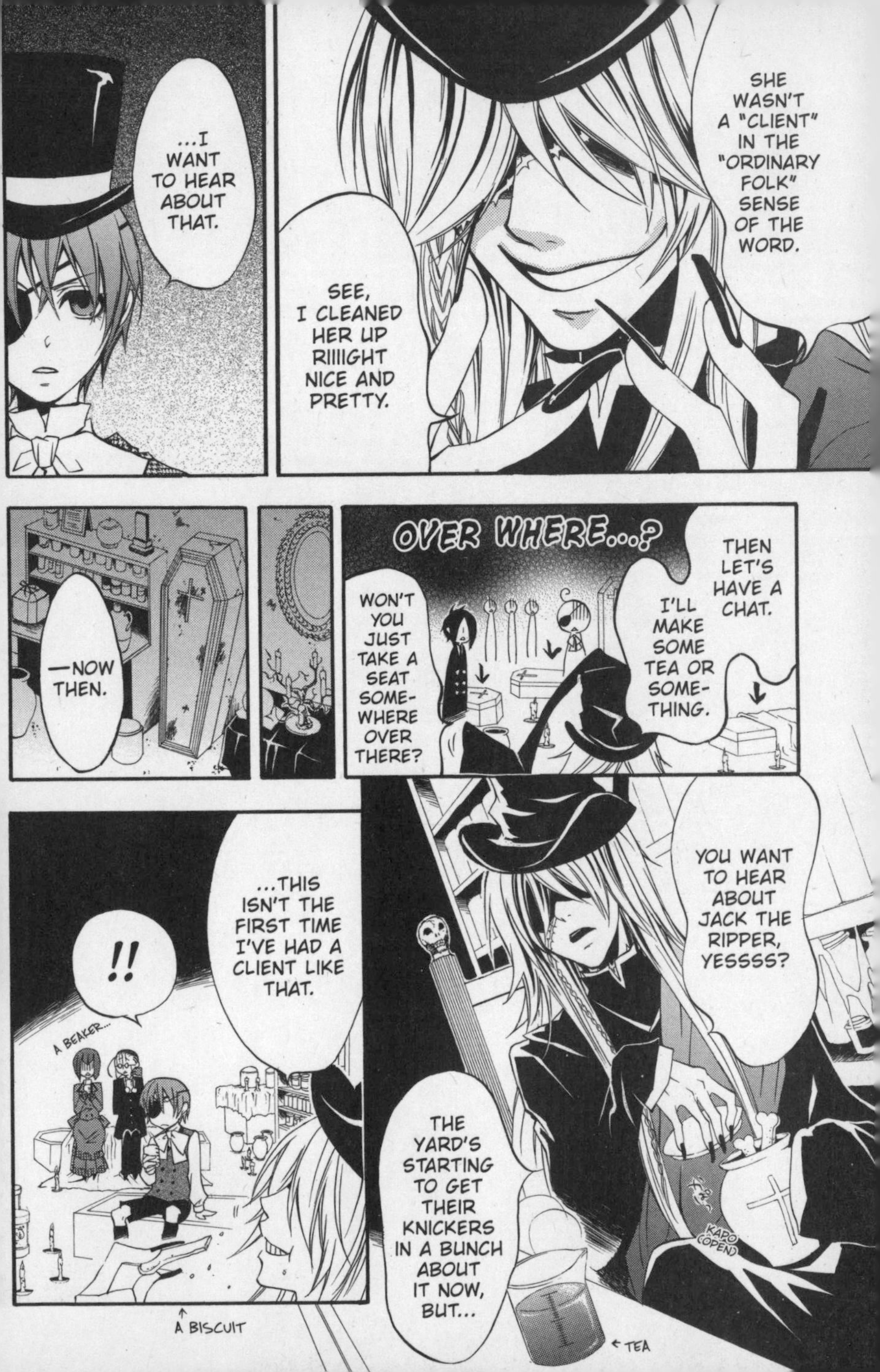
SHE WASN'T A "CLIENT" IN THE "ORDINARY FOLK" SENSE OF THE WORD.
SEE, I CLEANED HER UP RIIIIGHT NICE AND PRETTY.
...I WANT TO HEAR ABOUT THAT.
THEN LET'S HAVE A CHAT.
I'LL MAKE SOME TEA OR SOME-THING.
OVER WHERE...?
WON'T YOU JUST TAKE A SEAT SOME-WHERE OVER THERE?
—NOW THEN.
YOU WANT TO HEAR ABOUT JACK THE RIPPER, YESSSS?
KAPO (OPEN)
THE YARD'S STARTING TO GET THEIR KNICKERS IN A BUNCH ABOUT IT NOW, BUT...
← TEA
...THIS ISN'T THE FIRST TIME I'VE HAD A CLIENT LIKE THAT.
!!
A BEAKER...
↑ A BISCUIT

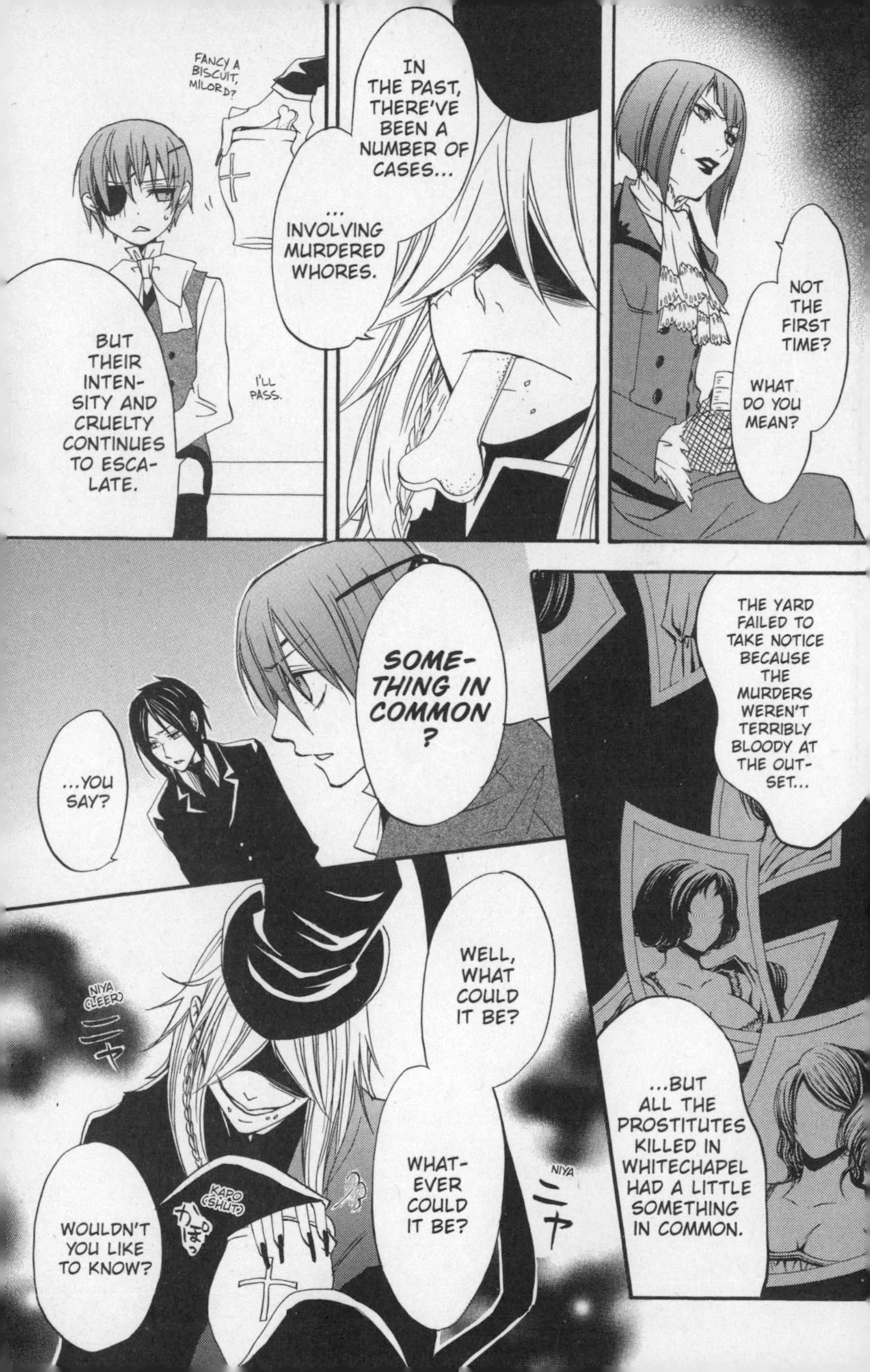
NOT THE FIRST TIME?
WHAT DO YOU MEAN?
IN THE PAST, THERE'VE BEEN A NUMBER OF CASES...
...INVOLVING MURDERED WHORES.
FANCY A BISCUIT, MILORD?
I'LL PASS.
BUT THEIR INTEN-SITY AND CRUELTY CONTINUES TO ESCA-LATE.
THE YARD FAILED TO TAKE NOTICE BECAUSE THE MURDERS WEREN'T TERRIBLY BLOODY AT THE OUT-SET...
...BUT ALL THE PROSTITUTES KILLED IN WHITECHAPEL HAD A LITTLE SOMETHING IN COMMON.
SOME-THING IN COMMON?
...YOU SAY?
WELL, WHAT COULD IT BE?
NIYA
ニヤ
WHAT-EVER COULD IT BE?
NIYA (LEER)
ニヤ
KAPO (SHUT)
WOULDN'T YOU LIKE TO KNOW?

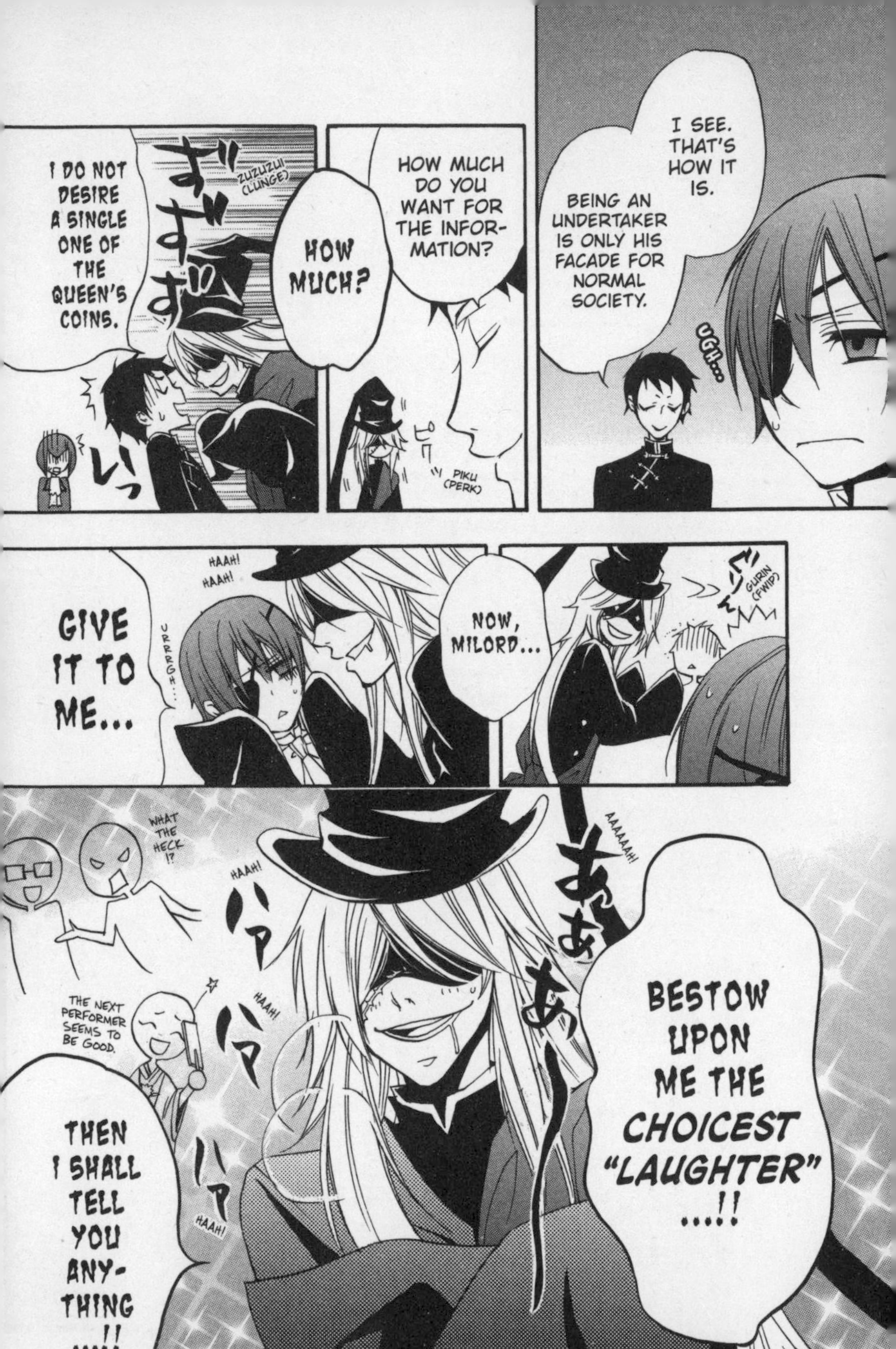
I SEE. THAT'S HOW IT IS.
BEING AN UNDERTAKER IS ONLY HIS FACADE FOR NORMAL SOCIETY.
UGH...
HOW MUCH DO YOU WANT FOR THE INFORMATION?
HOW MUCH?
PIKU (PERK)
ZUZUZUI (LUNGE)
I DO NOT DESIRE A SINGLE ONE OF THE QUEEN'S COINS.
GURIN (FWIP)
NOW, MILORD...
HAAH! HAAH!
URRRGH...
GIVE IT TO ME...
AAAAAAH!
BESTOW UPON ME THE CHOICEST "LAUGHTER" ...!!
WHAT THE HECK!?
HAAH!
HAAH!
THE NEXT PERFORMER SEEMS TO BE GOOD.
HAAH!
THEN I SHALL TELL YOU ANYTHING ...!!

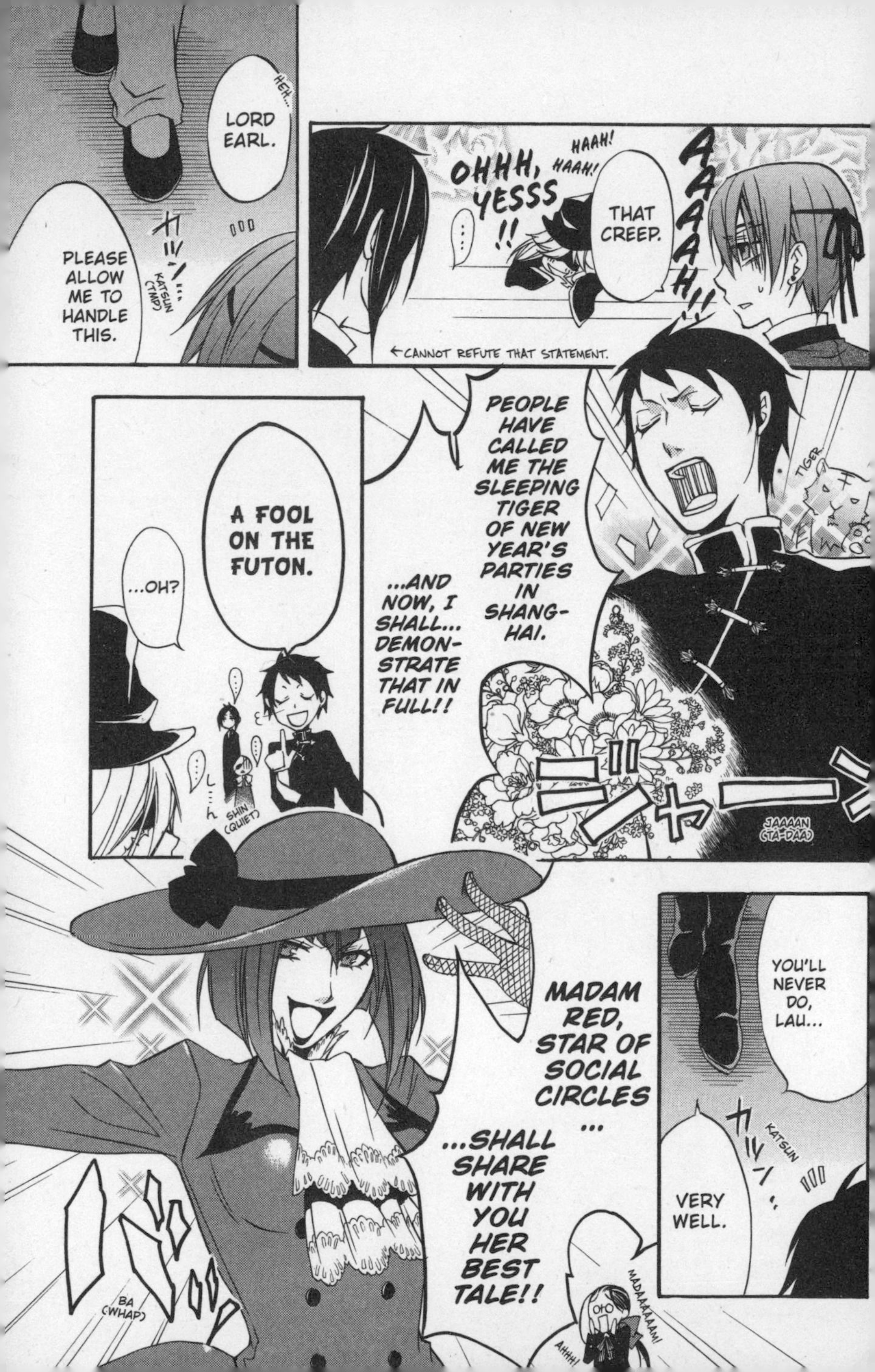
AAAAAH!!
THAT CREEP.
HAAH! HAAH!
OHHH, YESSS!!
...
←CANNOT REFUTE THAT STATEMENT.
HEH...
LORD EARL.
KATSUN (TMP)
PLEASE ALLOW ME TO HANDLE THIS.
PEOPLE HAVE CALLED ME THE SLEEPING TIGER OF NEW YEAR'S PARTIES IN SHANG-HAI.
...AND NOW, I SHALL... DEMON-STRATE THAT IN FULL!!
TIGER
JAAAAN (TA-DAA)
A FOOL ON THE FUTON.
...OH?
...
...
...
SHIN (QUIET)
YOU'LL NEVER DO, LAU...
KATSUN
VERY WELL.
MADAM RED, STAR OF SOCIAL CIRCLES...
...SHALL SHARE WITH YOU HER BEST TALE!!
MADAAAAAM!
AHHH!
BA (WHAP)

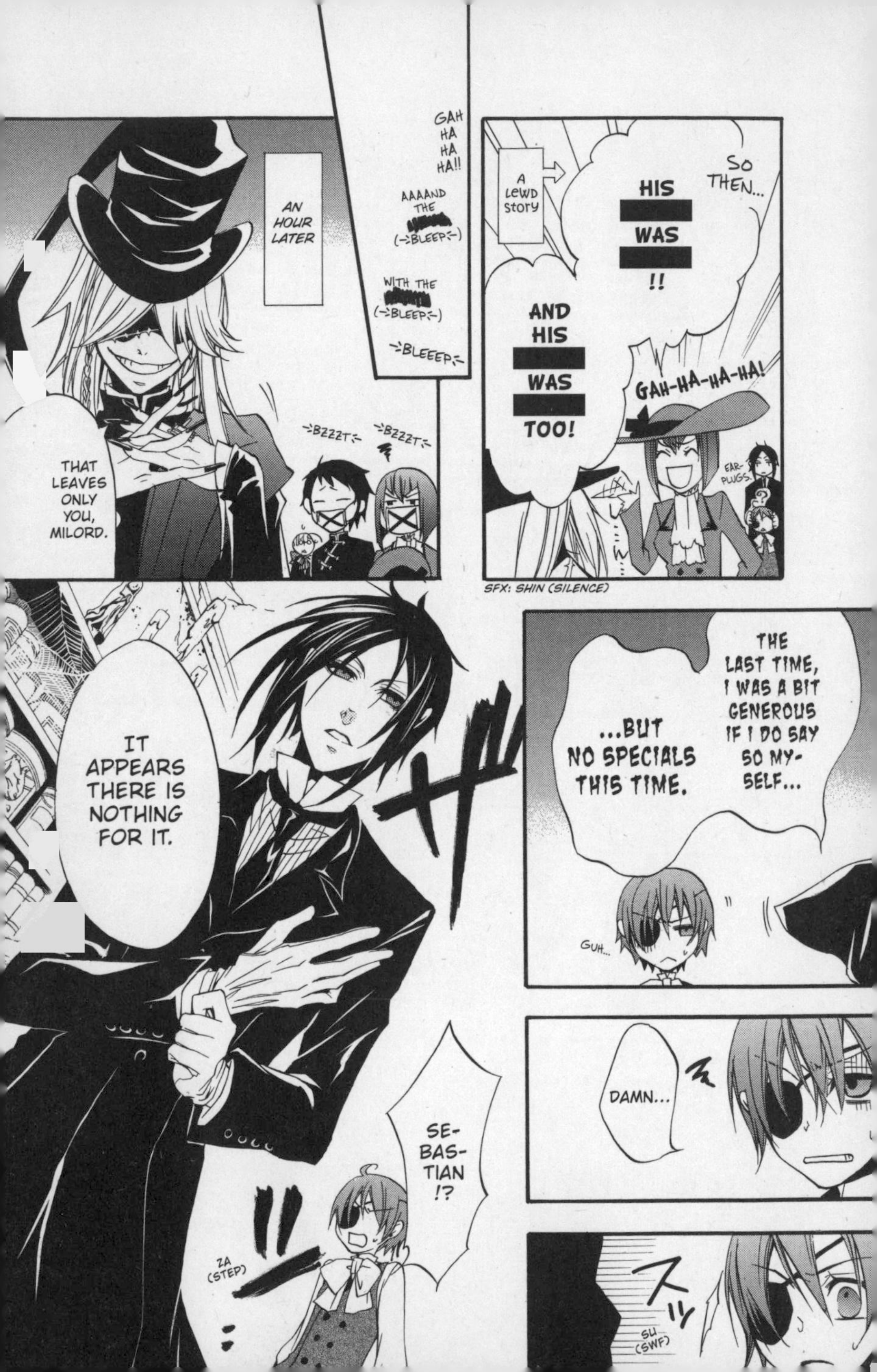

SO THEN...
HIS [redacted] WAS [redacted] !!
A LEWD STORY
AND HIS [redacted] WAS [redacted] TOO!
GAH-HA-HA-HA!
EAR-PLUGS
SFX: SHIN (SILENCE)
GAH HA HA HA!!
AAAAND THE [redacted] (-BLEEP-)
WITH THE [redacted] (-BLEEP-)
-BLEEEP-
AN HOUR LATER
-BZZZT-
-BZZZT-
THAT LEAVES ONLY YOU, MILORD.
THE LAST TIME, I WAS A BIT GENEROUS IF I DO SAY SO MY-SELF...
...BUT NO SPECIALS THIS TIME.
GUH...
DAMN...
SU (SWF)
IT APPEARS THERE IS NOTHING FOR IT.
SE-BAS-TIAN !?
ZA (STEP)

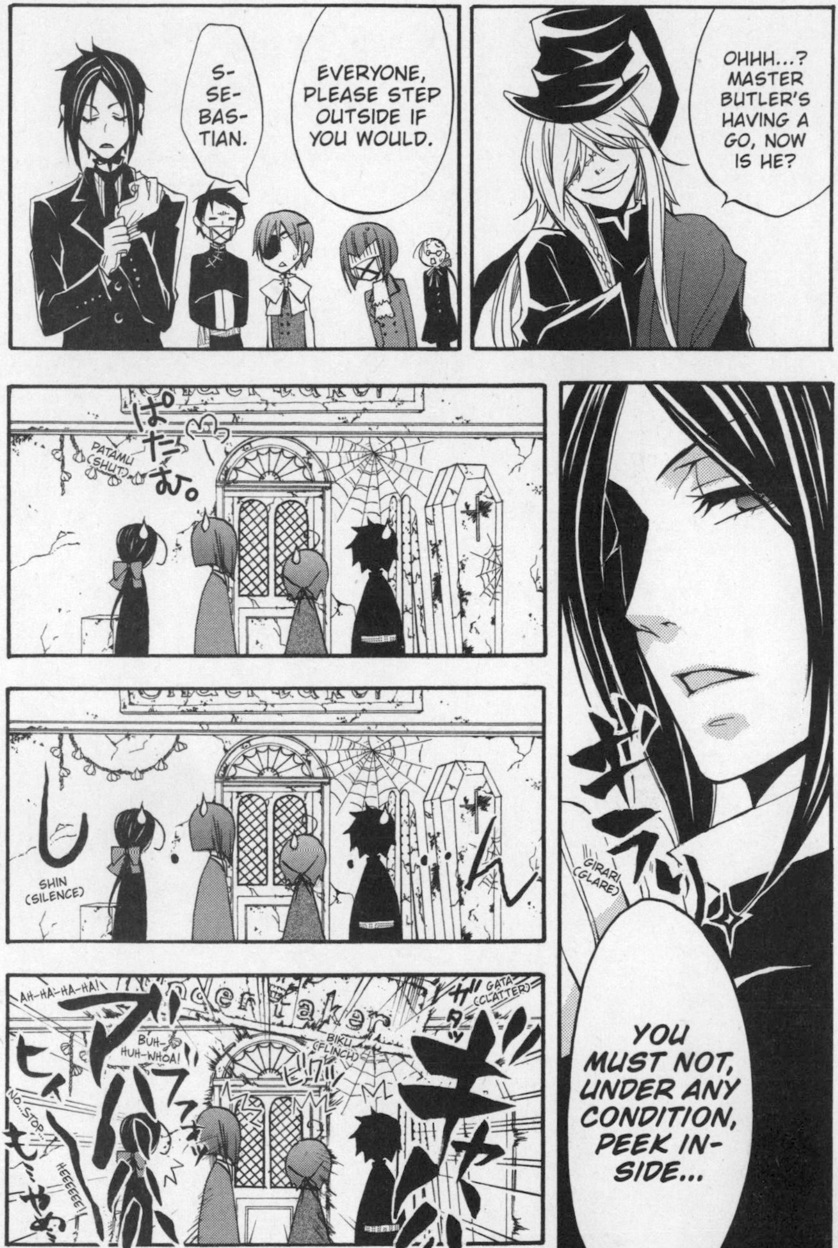

OHHH...? MASTER BUTLER'S HAVING A GO, NOW IS HE?
EVERYONE, PLEASE STEP OUTSIDE IF YOU WOULD.
S-SE-BAS-TIAN.
GIRARI (GLARE)
YOU MUST NOT, UNDER ANY CONDITION, PEEK IN-SIDE...
PATAMU (SHUT)
SHIN (SILENCE)
GATA (CLATTER)
AH-HA-HA-HA!
BIKU (FLINCH)
BUH-HUH-WHOA!
NO...STOP...
HEEEEEEE
GYAH-HA-HA-HA!

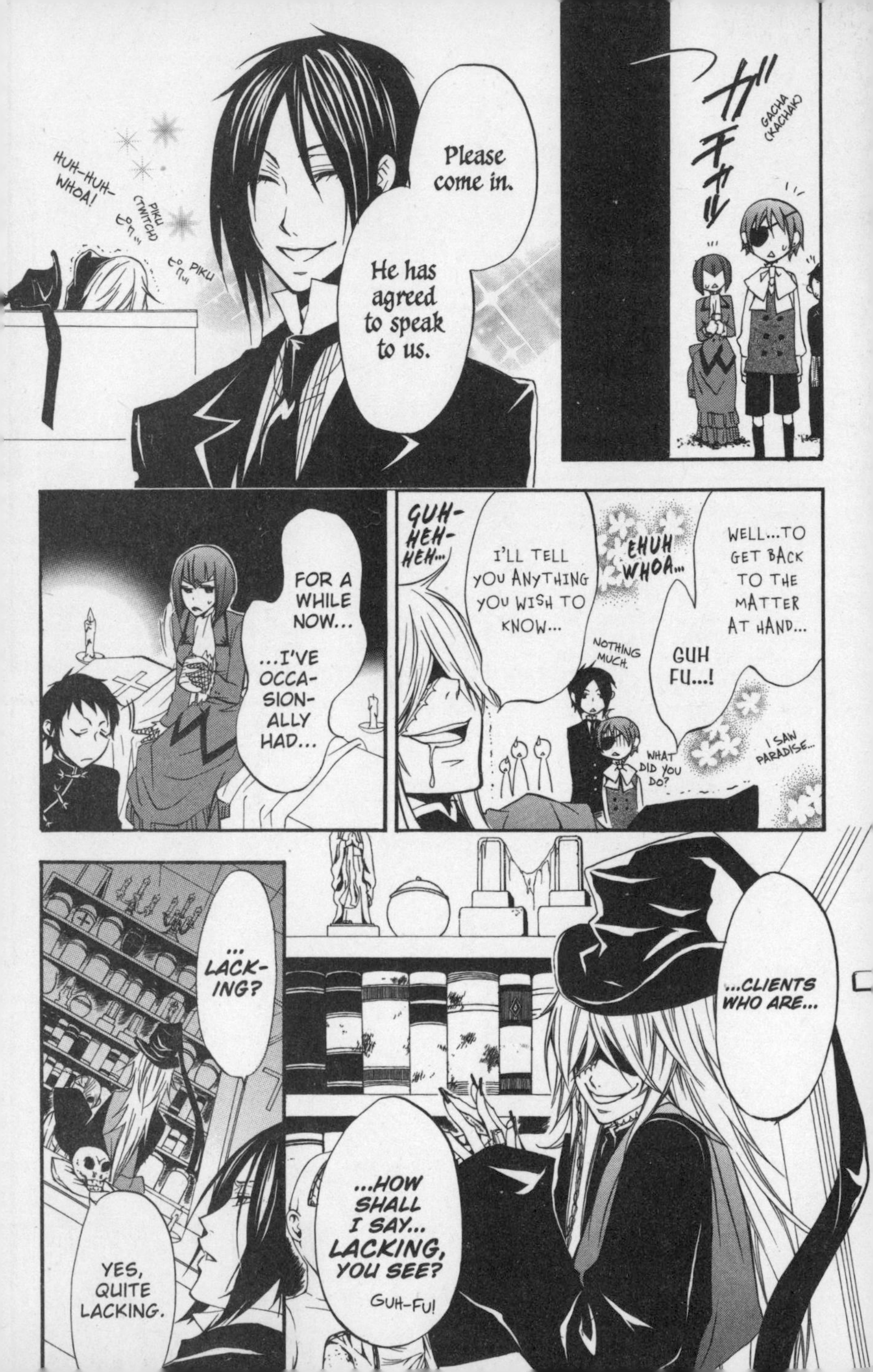
GACHA (KACHAK)
Please come in.
He has agreed to speak to us.
HUH-HUH-WHOA!
PIKU (TWITCH)
PIKU
WELL...TO GET BACK TO THE MATTER AT HAND...
EHUH WHOA...
GUH FU...!
I SAW PARADISE...
I'LL TELL YOU ANYTHING YOU WISH TO KNOW...
GUH-HEH-HEH...
WHAT DID YOU DO?
NOTHING MUCH.
FOR A WHILE NOW...
...I'VE OCCASIONALLY HAD...
...CLIENTS WHO ARE...
...HOW SHALL I SAY... LACKING, YOU SEE?
GUH-FU!
...LACKING?
YES, QUITE LACKING.

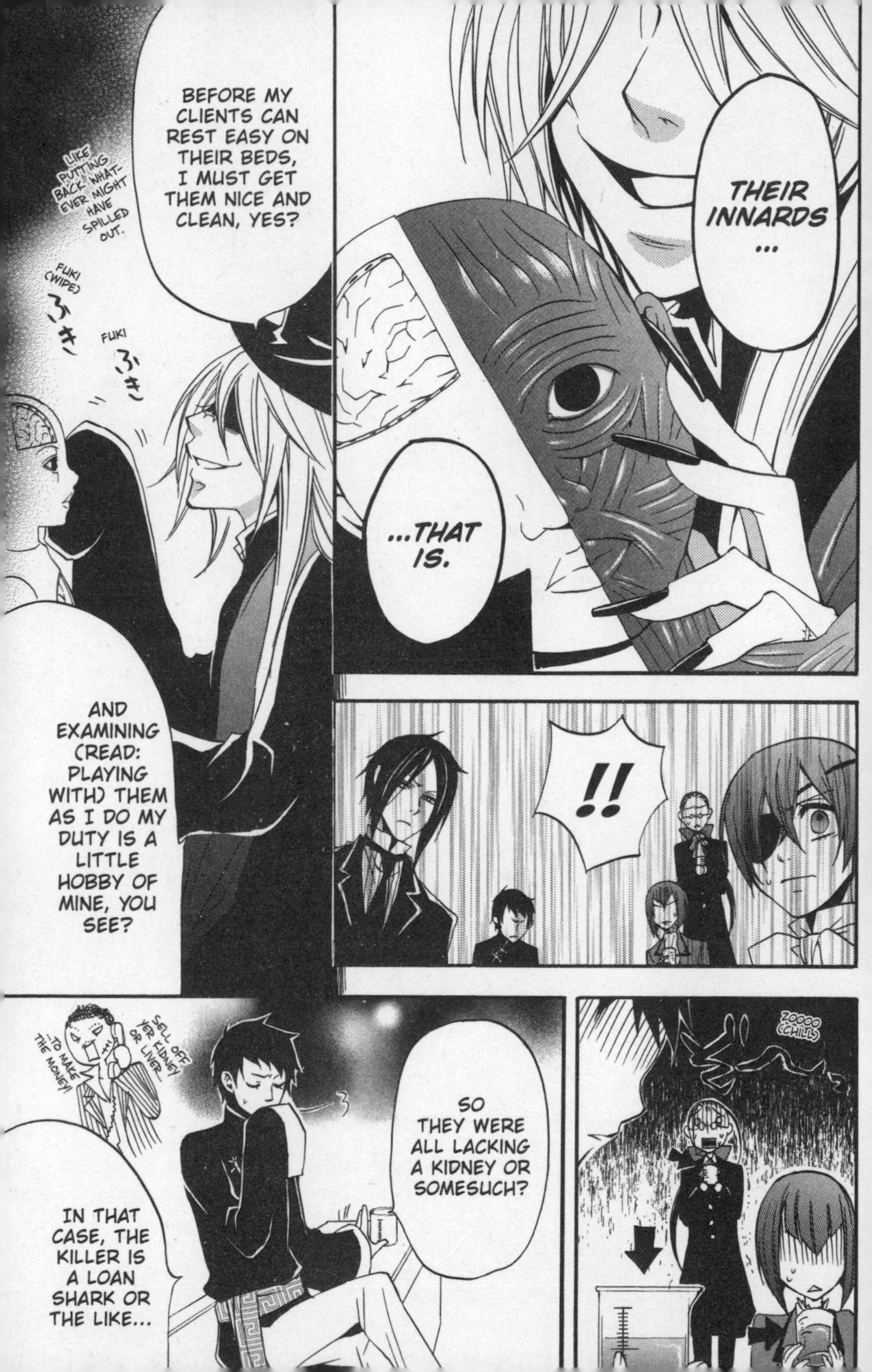

THEIR INNARDS ...
...THAT IS.
!!
BEFORE MY CLIENTS CAN REST EASY ON THEIR BEDS, I MUST GET THEM NICE AND CLEAN, YES?
LIKE PUTTING BACK WHATEVER MIGHT HAVE SPILLED OUT.
FUKI (WIPE) ふき
FUKI ふき
AND EXAMINING (READ: PLAYING WITH) THEM AS I DO MY DUTY IS A LITTLE HOBBY OF MINE, YOU SEE?
ZOOOO (CHILL)
SO THEY WERE ALL LACKING A KIDNEY OR SOMESUCH?
SELL OFF YER KIDNEY OR LIVER...
...TO MAKE THE MONEY!
IN THAT CASE, THE KILLER IS A LOAN SHARK OR THE LIKE...

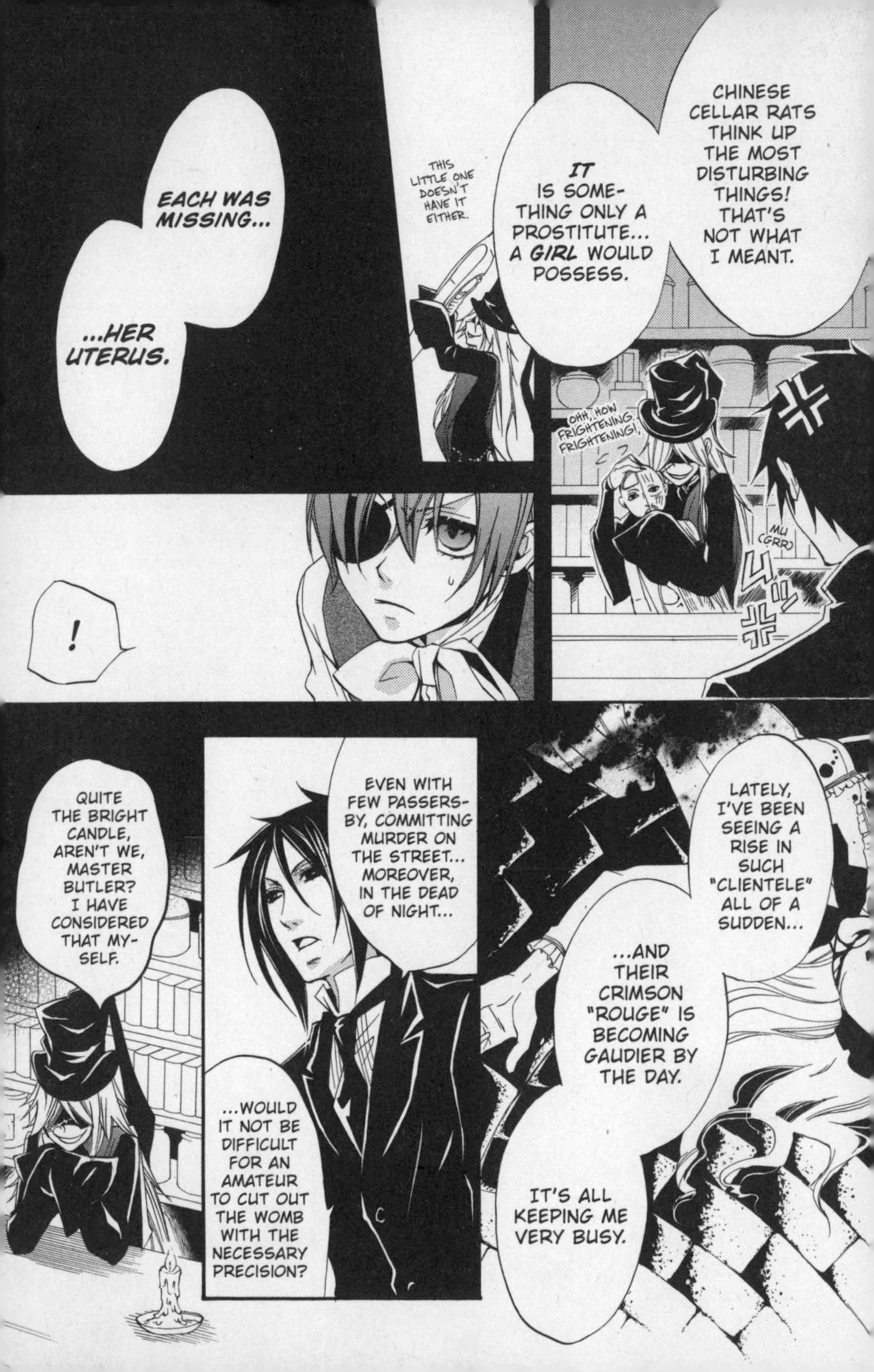
CHINESE CELLAR RATS THINK UP THE MOST DISTURBING THINGS! THAT'S NOT WHAT I MEANT.
IT IS SOME-THING ONLY A PROSTITUTE... A *GIRL* WOULD POSSESS.
THIS LITTLE ONE DOESN'T HAVE IT EITHER.
EACH WAS MISSING...
...HER UTERUS.
OHH, HOW FRIGHTENING, FRIGHTENING!
MU (GRR)
!
LATELY, I'VE BEEN SEEING A RISE IN SUCH "CLIENTELE" ALL OF A SUDDEN...
...AND THEIR CRIMSON "ROUGE" IS BECOMING GAUDIER BY THE DAY.
IT'S ALL KEEPING ME VERY BUSY.
EVEN WITH FEW PASSERS-BY, COMMITTING MURDER ON THE STREET... MOREOVER, IN THE DEAD OF NIGHT...
...WOULD IT NOT BE DIFFICULT FOR AN AMATEUR TO CUT OUT THE WOMB WITH THE NECESSARY PRECISION?
QUITE THE BRIGHT CANDLE, AREN'T WE, MASTER BUTLER? I HAVE CONSIDERED THAT MY-SELF.

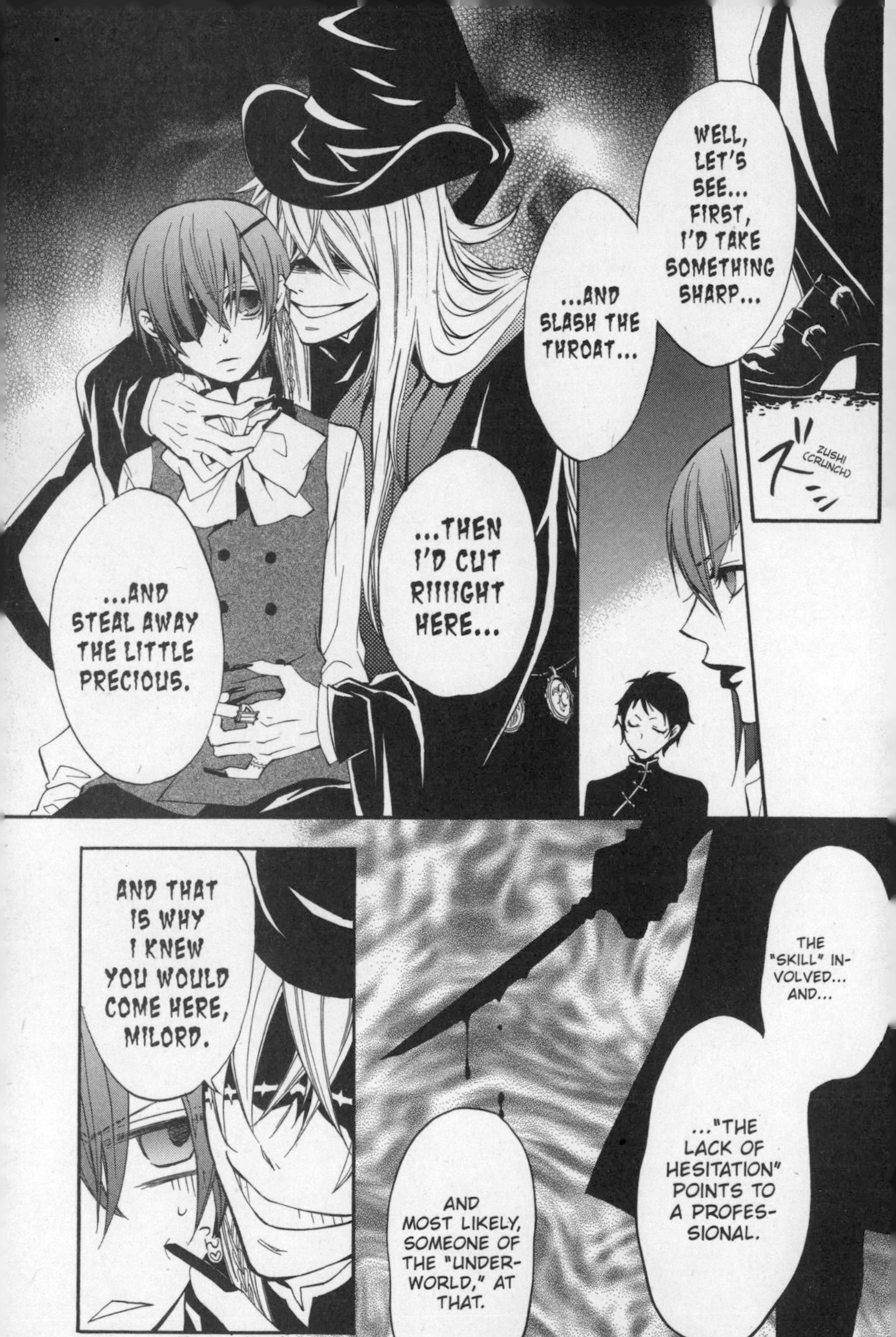
ZUSHI (CRUNCH)
WELL, LET'S SEE... FIRST, I'D TAKE SOMETHING SHARP...
...AND SLASH THE THROAT...
...THEN I'D CUT RIIIIGHT HERE...
...AND STEAL AWAY THE LITTLE PRECIOUS.
THE "SKILL" IN-VOLVED... AND...
..."THE LACK OF HESITATION" POINTS TO A PROFES-SIONAL.
AND MOST LIKELY, SOMEONE OF THE "UNDER-WORLD," AT THAT.
AND THAT IS WHY I KNEW YOU WOULD COME HERE, MILORD.
SFX: TSUN (POKE)

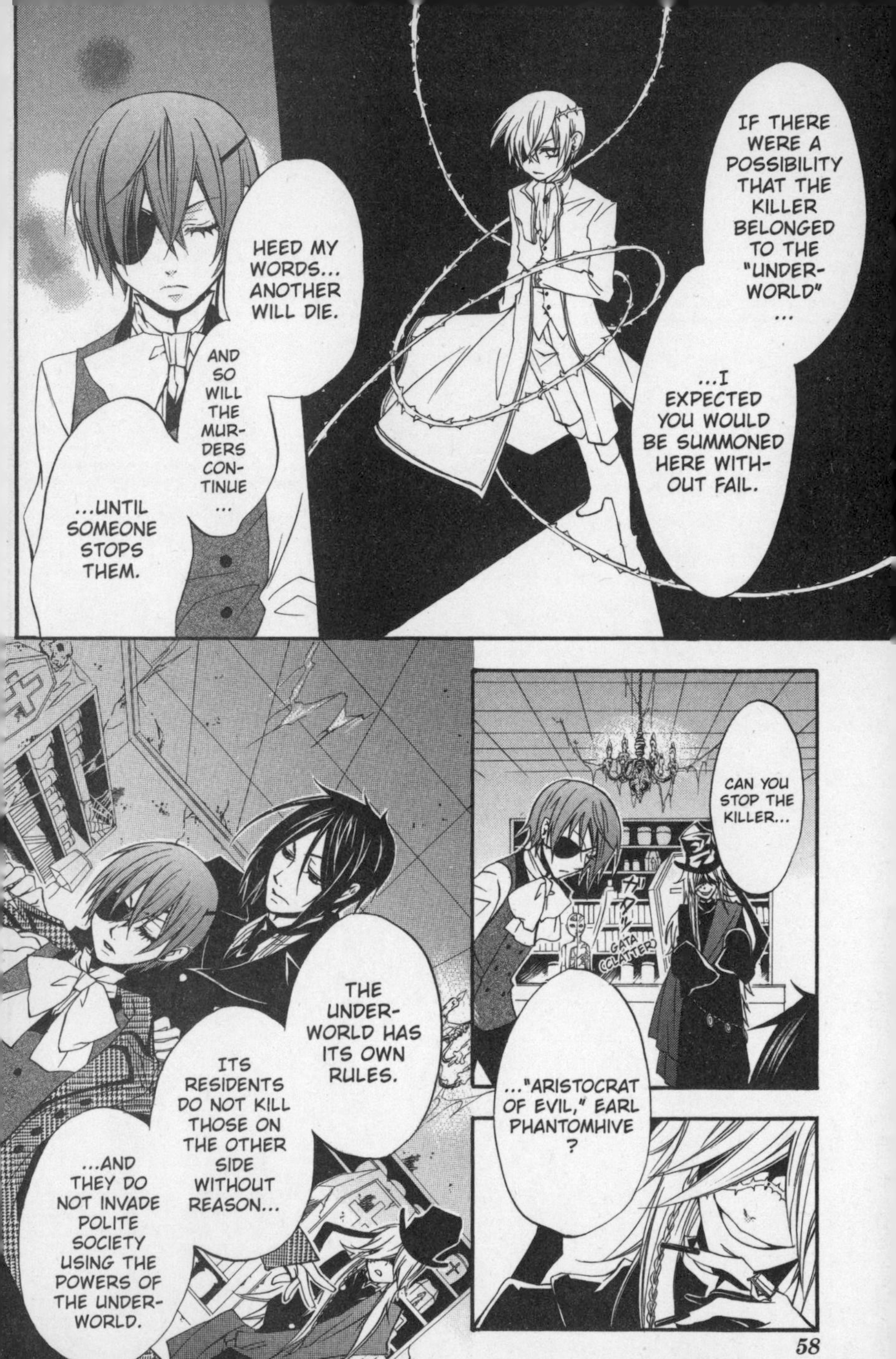
IF THERE WERE A POSSIBILITY THAT THE KILLER BELONGED TO THE "UNDER-WORLD"...
...I EXPECTED YOU WOULD BE SUMMONED HERE WITH-OUT FAIL.
HEED MY WORDS... ANOTHER WILL DIE.
AND SO WILL THE MUR-DERS CON-TINUE...
...UNTIL SOMEONE STOPS THEM.
CAN YOU STOP THE KILLER...
GATA
CLATTER
..."ARISTOCRAT OF EVIL," EARL PHANTOMHIVE?
THE UNDER-WORLD HAS ITS OWN RULES.
ITS RESIDENTS DO NOT KILL THOSE ON THE OTHER SIDE WITHOUT REASON...
...AND THEY DO NOT INVADE POLITE SOCIETY USING THE POWERS OF THE UNDER-WORLD.

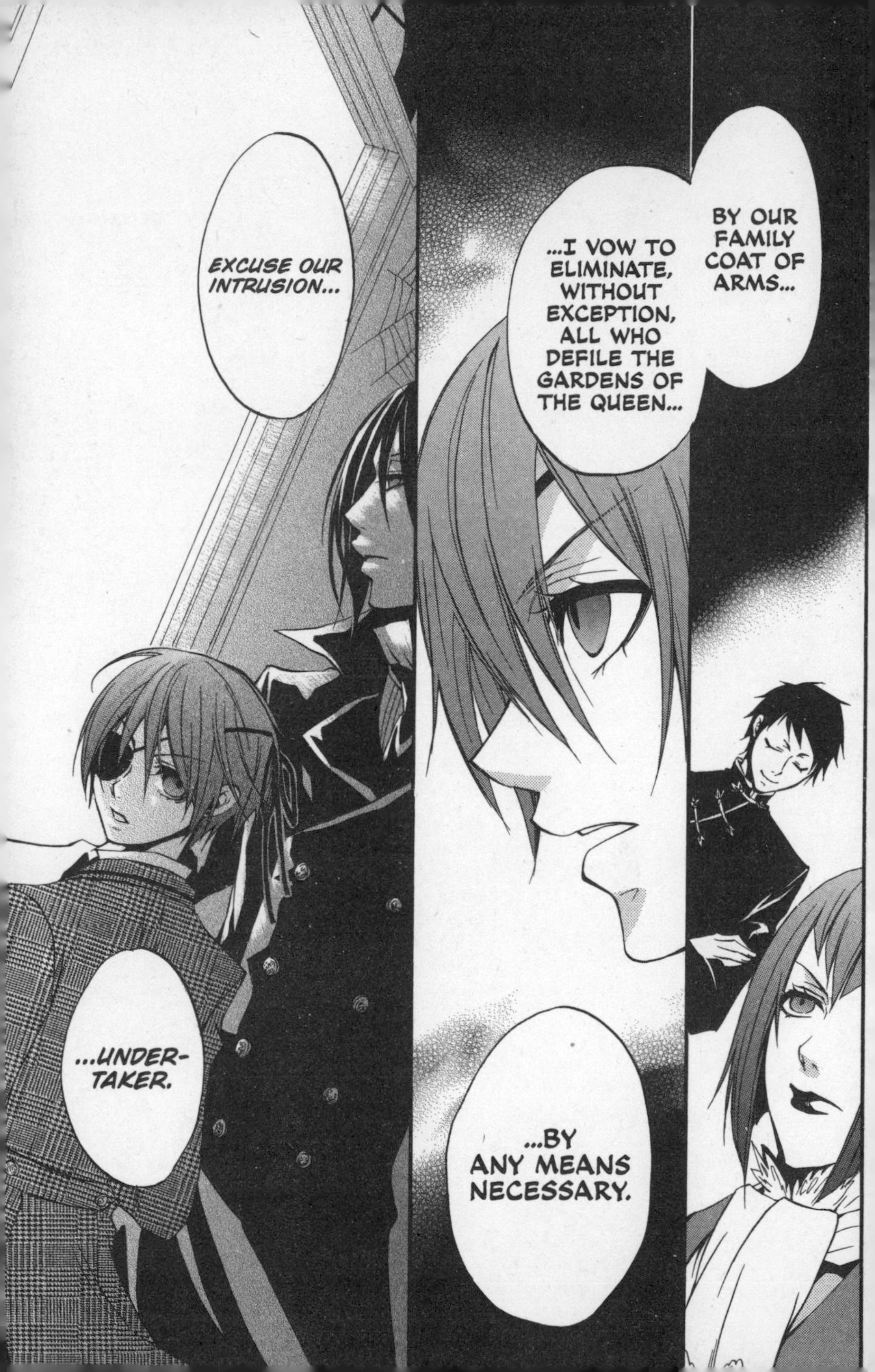
BY OUR FAMILY COAT OF ARMS...
...I VOW TO ELIMINATE, WITHOUT EXCEPTION, ALL WHO DEFILE THE GARDENS OF THE QUEEN...
...BY ANY MEANS NECESSARY.
EXCUSE OUR INTRUSION...
...UNDER-TAKER.

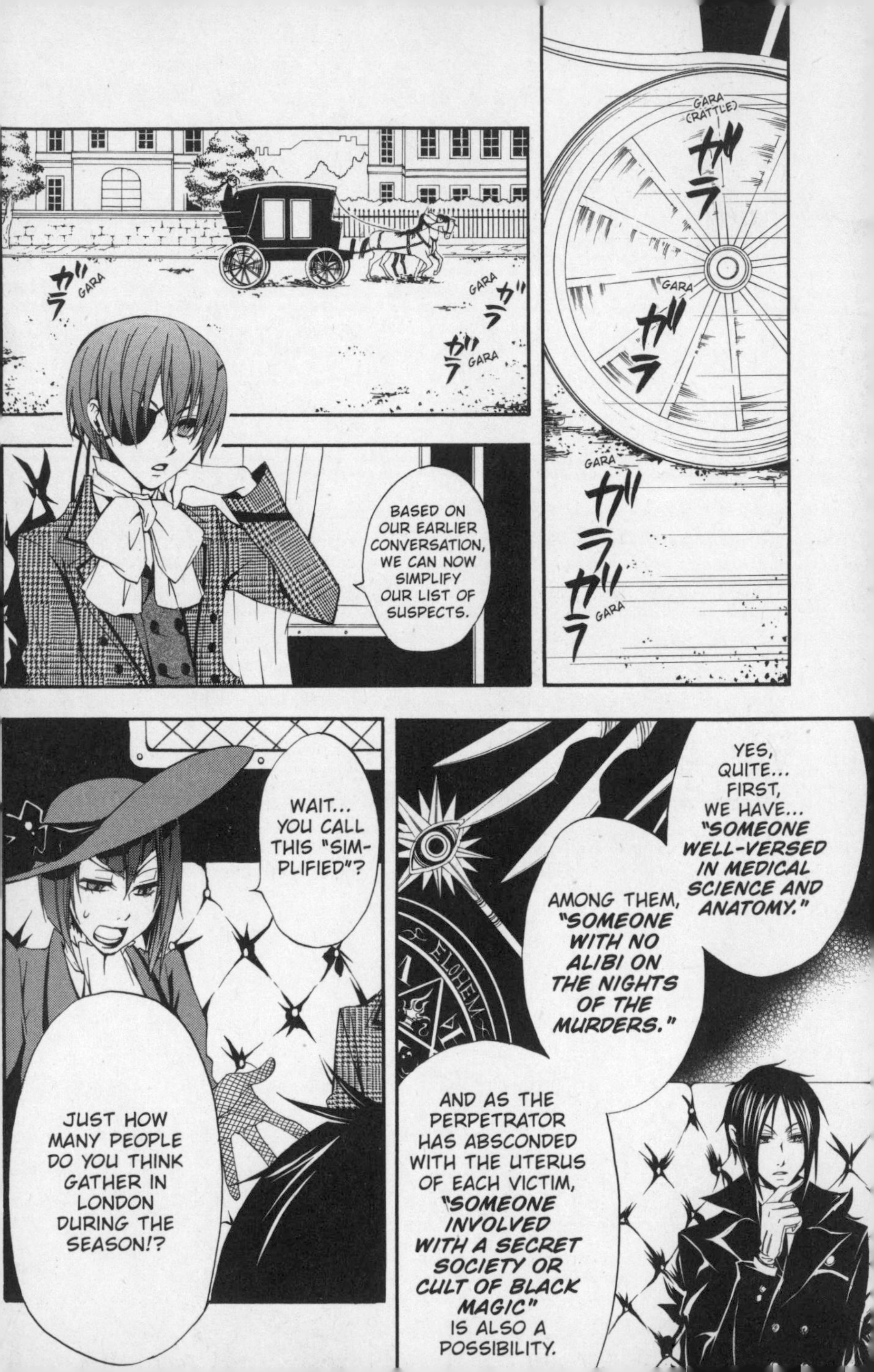

GARA (RATTLE)
ガラ
GARA
ガラ
GARA
ガラ
GARA
ガラ
ガラ
GARA
ガラ
GARA
ガラ
GARA
BASED ON OUR EARLIER CONVERSATION, WE CAN NOW SIMPLIFY OUR LIST OF SUSPECTS.
YES, QUITE... FIRST, WE HAVE... "SOMEONE WELL-VERSED IN MEDICAL SCIENCE AND ANATOMY."
AMONG THEM, "SOMEONE WITH NO ALIBI ON THE NIGHTS OF THE MURDERS."
AND AS THE PERPETRATOR HAS ABSCONDED WITH THE UTERUS OF EACH VICTIM, "SOMEONE INVOLVED WITH A SECRET SOCIETY OR CULT OF BLACK MAGIC" IS ALSO A POSSIBILITY.
WAIT... YOU CALL THIS "SIMPLIFIED"?
JUST HOW MANY PEOPLE DO YOU THINK GATHER IN LONDON DURING THE SEASON!?

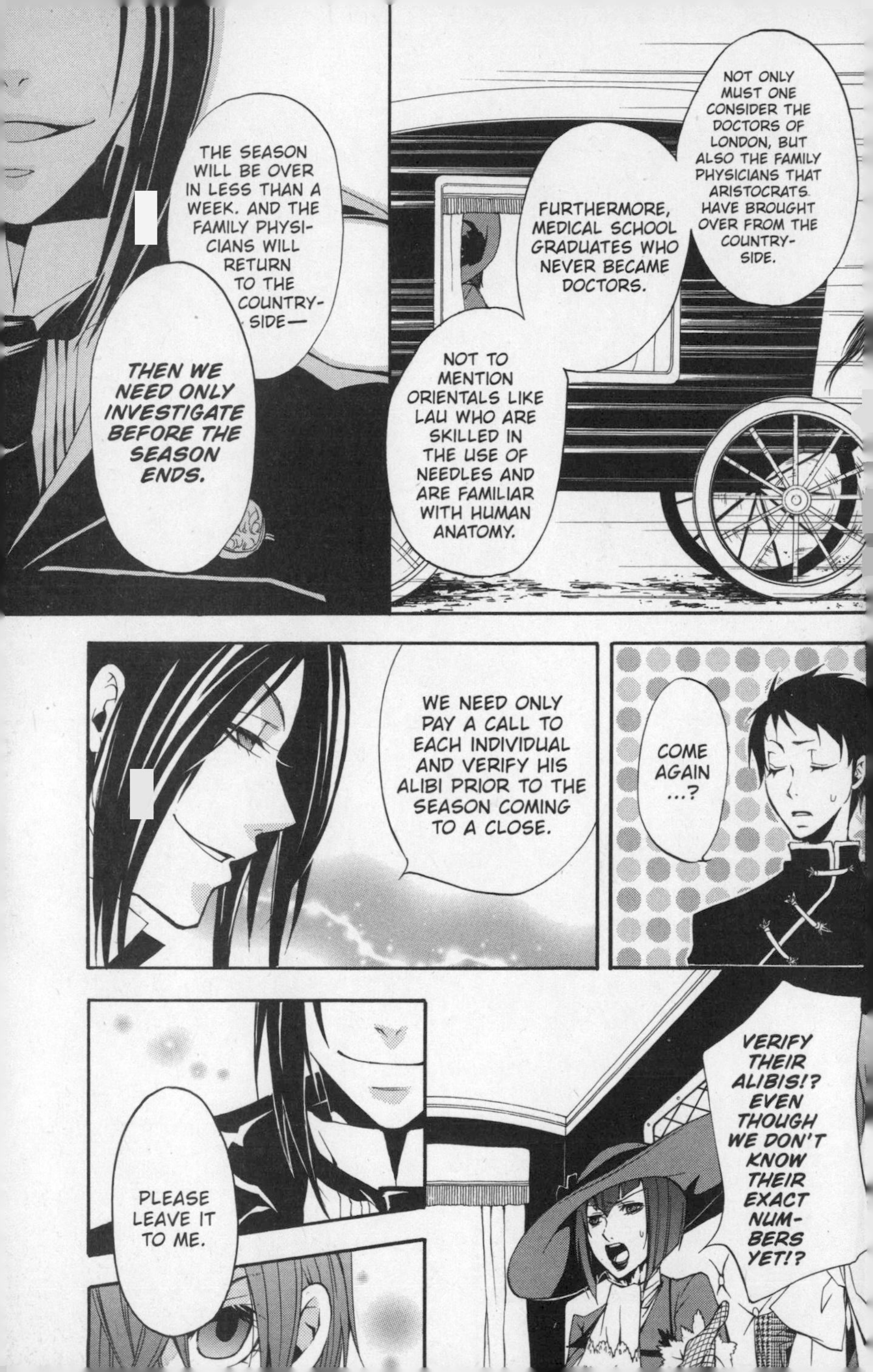
NOT ONLY MUST ONE CONSIDER THE DOCTORS OF LONDON, BUT ALSO THE FAMILY PHYSICIANS THAT ARISTOCRATS HAVE BROUGHT OVER FROM THE COUNTRY-SIDE.
FURTHERMORE, MEDICAL SCHOOL GRADUATES WHO NEVER BECAME DOCTORS.
NOT TO MENTION ORIENTALS LIKE LAU WHO ARE SKILLED IN THE USE OF NEEDLES AND ARE FAMILIAR WITH HUMAN ANATOMY.
THE SEASON WILL BE OVER IN LESS THAN A WEEK. AND THE FAMILY PHYSI-CIANS WILL RETURN TO THE COUNTRY-SIDE—
THEN WE NEED ONLY INVESTIGATE BEFORE THE SEASON ENDS.
COME AGAIN ...?
WE NEED ONLY PAY A CALL TO EACH INDIVIDUAL AND VERIFY HIS ALIBI PRIOR TO THE SEASON COMING TO A CLOSE.
VERIFY THEIR ALIBIS!? EVEN THOUGH WE DON'T KNOW THEIR EXACT NUM-BERS YET!?
PLEASE LEAVE IT TO ME.

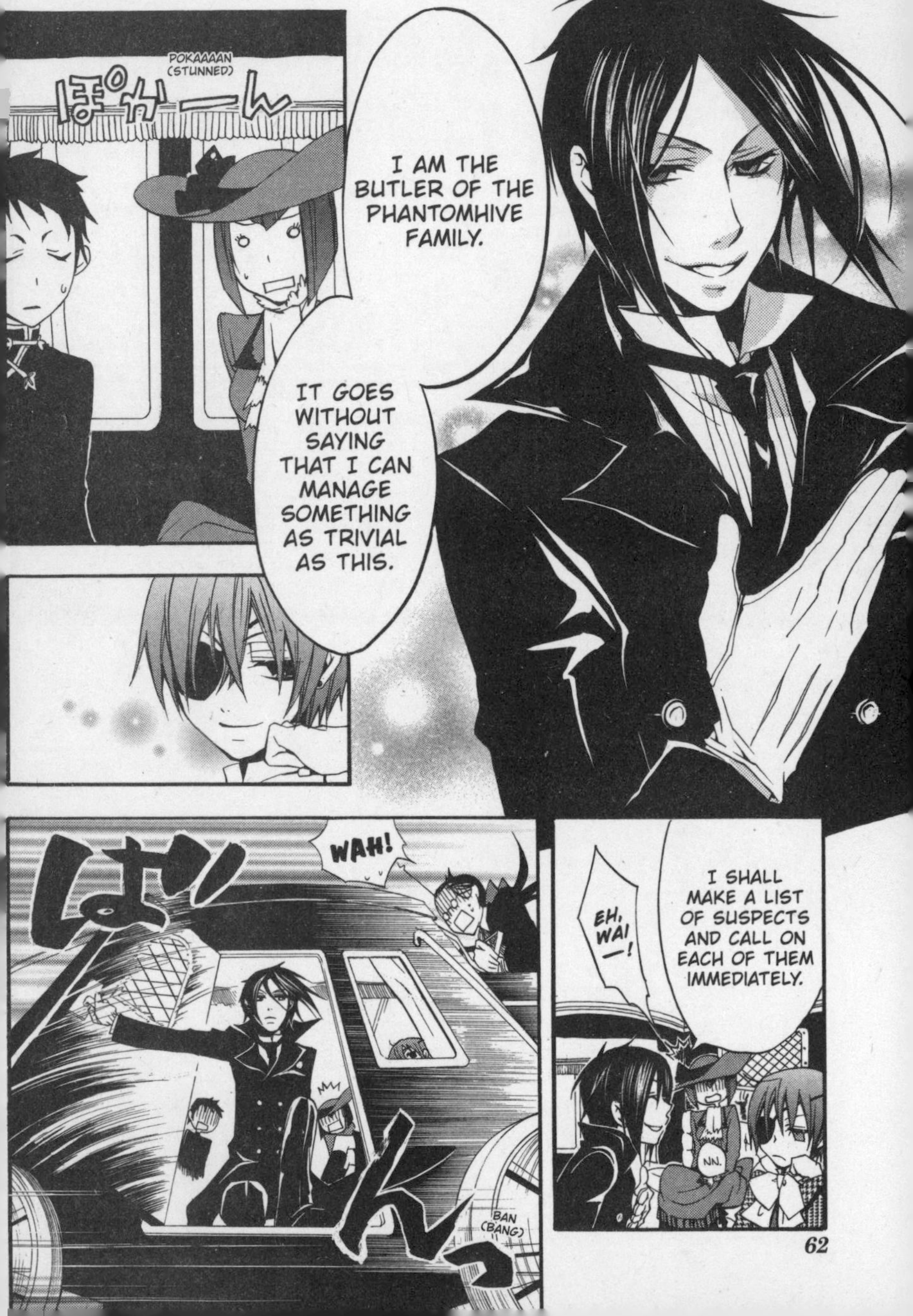
I AM THE BUTLER OF THE PHANTOMHIVE FAMILY.
IT GOES WITHOUT SAYING THAT I CAN MANAGE SOMETHING AS TRIVIAL AS THIS.
POKAAAAN (STUNNED)
I SHALL MAKE A LIST OF SUSPECTS AND CALL ON EACH OF THEM IMMEDIATELY.
EH, WAI—!
NN.
WAH!
BAN (BANG)

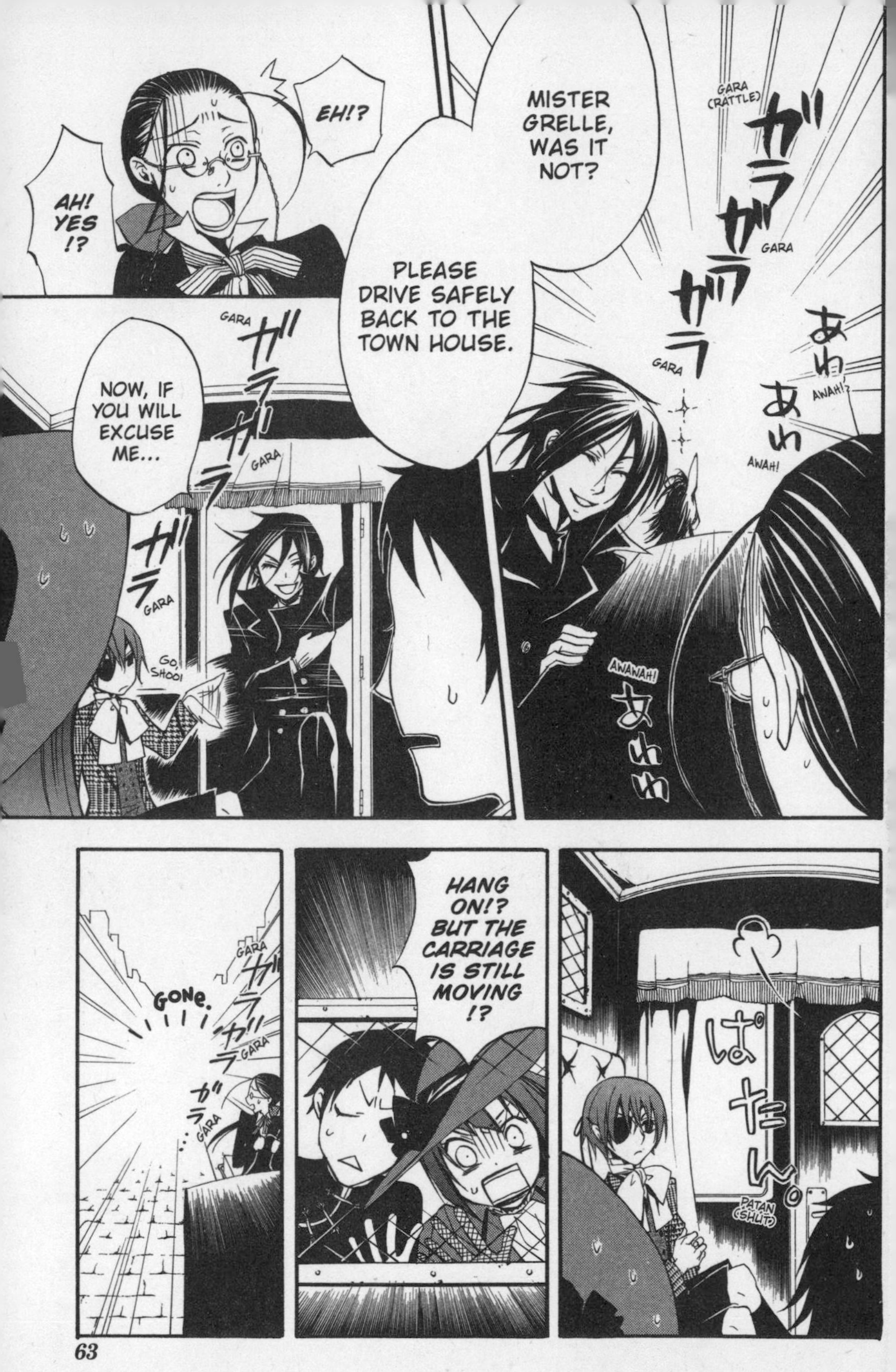

ガラ
GARA (RATTLE)
ガラ
GARA
ガラ
GARA
MISTER GRELLE, WAS IT NOT?
PLEASE DRIVE SAFELY BACK TO THE TOWN HOUSE.
あわ
AWAH!?
あわ
AWAH!
AWAWAH!
あわわわ
EH!?
AH! YES!?
ガラ
GARA
ガラ
GARA
ガラ
GARA
NOW, IF YOU WILL EXCUSE ME...
GO, SHOO!
ぱたん。
PATAN (SHUT)
HANG ON!? BUT THE CARRIAGE IS STILL MOVING!?
ガラ
GARA
ガラ
GARA
ガラ
GARA
GONE.

SFX: PO (BLUSH)

SFX: GARA (RATTLE) GARA GARA

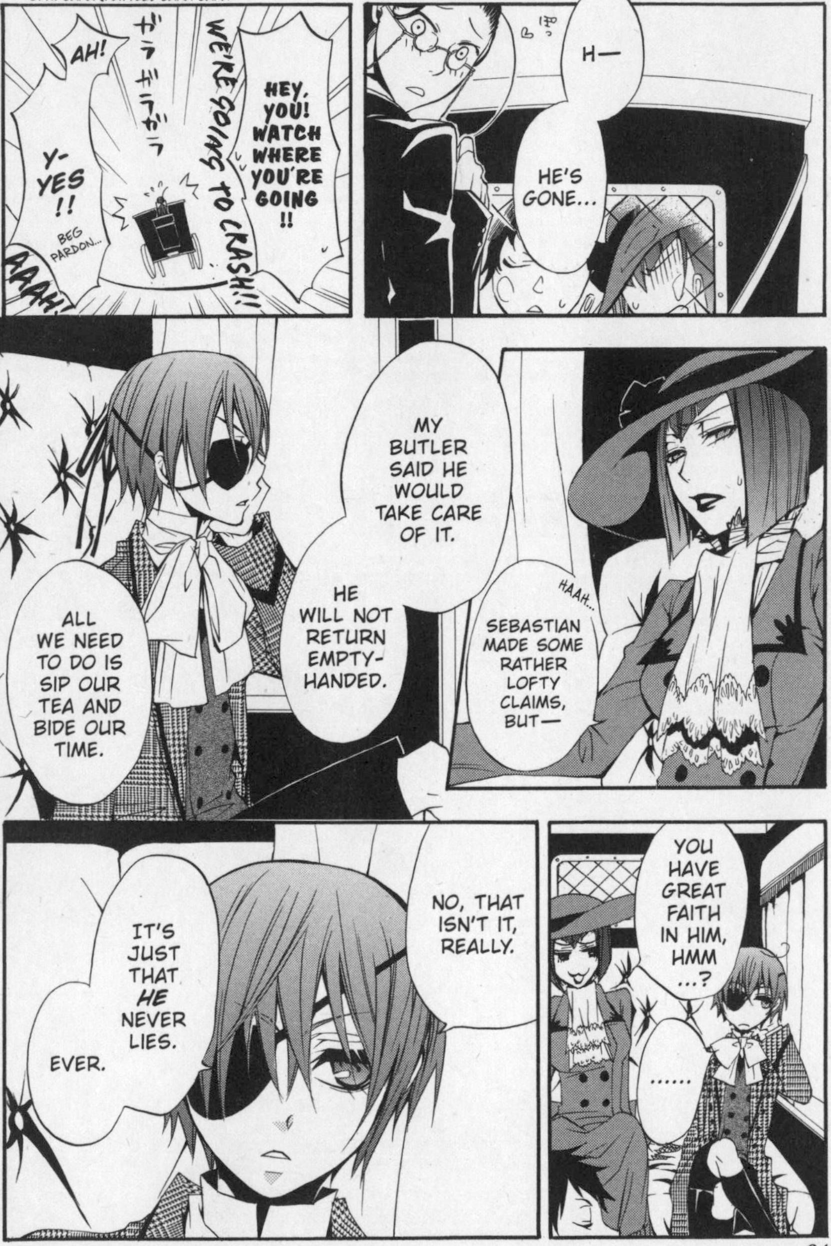

ぽっ
H—
HE'S GONE...
HEY, YOU! WATCH WHERE YOU'RE GOING!!
WE'RE GOING TO CRASH!!
ガラガラガラ
AH!
Y-YES!!
BEG PARDON...
AAAAH!
HAAAH...
SEBASTIAN MADE SOME RATHER LOFTY CLAIMS, BUT—
MY BUTLER SAID HE WOULD TAKE CARE OF IT.
HE WILL NOT RETURN EMPTY-HANDED.
ALL WE NEED TO DO IS SIP OUR TEA AND BIDE OUR TIME.
YOU HAVE GREAT FAITH IN HIM, HMM...?
......
NO, THAT ISN'T IT, REALLY.
IT'S JUST THAT *HE* NEVER LIES.
EVER.

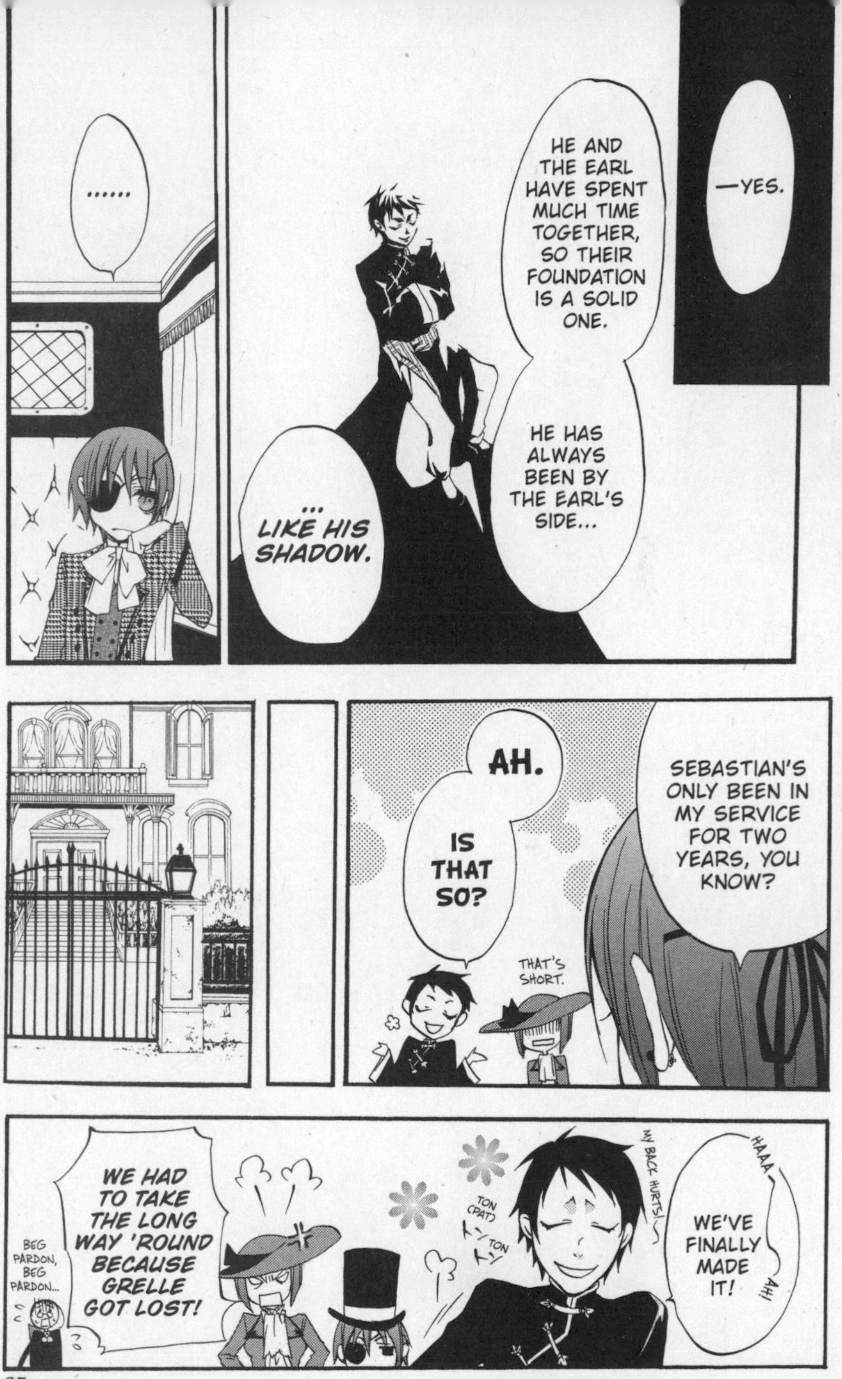
—YES.
HE AND THE EARL HAVE SPENT MUCH TIME TOGETHER, SO THEIR FOUNDATION IS A SOLID ONE.
HE HAS ALWAYS BEEN BY THE EARL'S SIDE...
...LIKE HIS SHADOW.
......
SEBASTIAN'S ONLY BEEN IN MY SERVICE FOR TWO YEARS, YOU KNOW?
AH.
IS THAT SO?
THAT'S SHORT.
HAAA—AH!
WE'VE FINALLY MADE IT!
MY BACK HURTS!
TON (PAT)
TON
WE HAD TO TAKE THE LONG WAY 'ROUND BECAUSE GRELLE GOT LOST!
BEG PARDON, BEG PARDON...

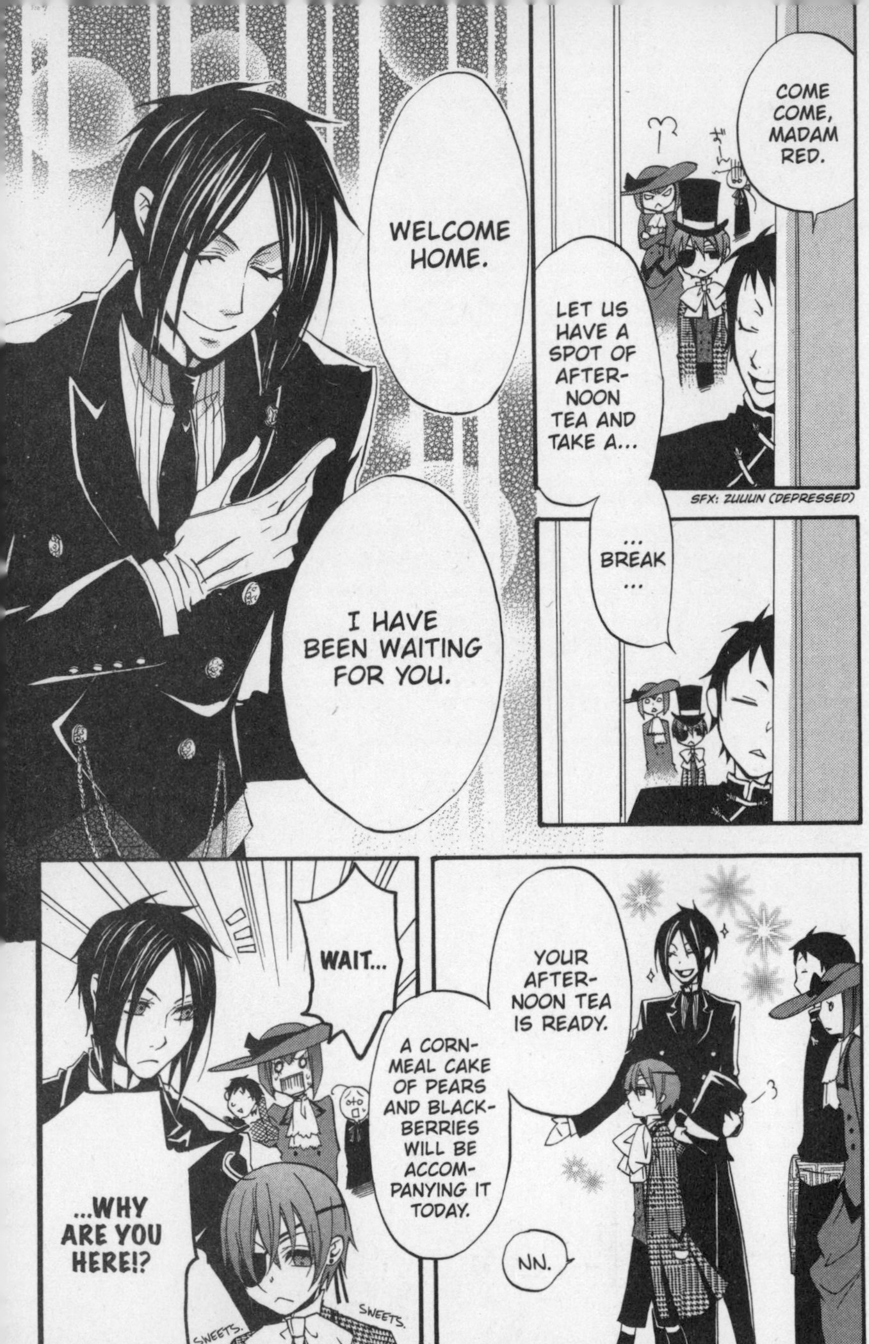
COME COME, MADAM RED.
LET US HAVE A SPOT OF AFTER-NOON TEA AND TAKE A...
SFX: ZUUUN (DEPRESSED)
... BREAK ...
WELCOME HOME.
I HAVE BEEN WAITING FOR YOU.
YOUR AFTER-NOON TEA IS READY.
A CORN-MEAL CAKE OF PEARS AND BLACK-BERRIES WILL BE ACCOM-PANYING IT TODAY.
NN.
WAIT...
...WHY ARE YOU HERE!?
SWEETS.
SWEETS.

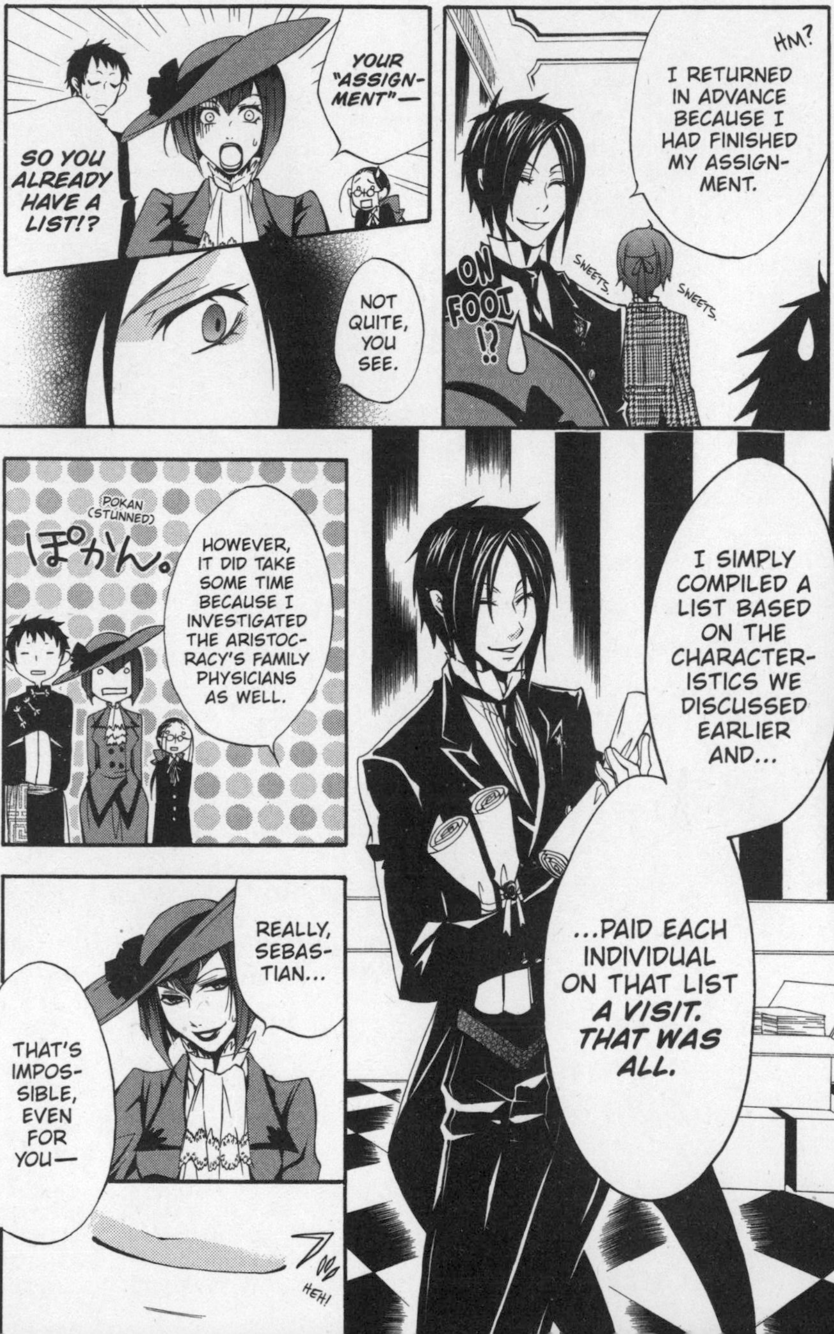
HM?
I RETURNED IN ADVANCE BECAUSE I HAD FINISHED MY ASSIGNMENT.
SWEETS. SWEETS.
ON FOOT!?
YOUR "ASSIGNMENT"—
SO YOU ALREADY HAVE A LIST!?
NOT QUITE, YOU SEE.
I SIMPLY COMPILED A LIST BASED ON THE CHARACTERISTICS WE DISCUSSED EARLIER AND...
...PAID EACH INDIVIDUAL ON THAT LIST A VISIT. THAT WAS ALL.
POKAN (STUNNED)
ぽかん。
HOWEVER, IT DID TAKE SOME TIME BECAUSE I INVESTIGATED THE ARISTOCRACY'S FAMILY PHYSICIANS AS WELL.
REALLY, SEBASTIAN...
THAT'S IMPOSSIBLE, EVEN FOR YOU—
HEH!

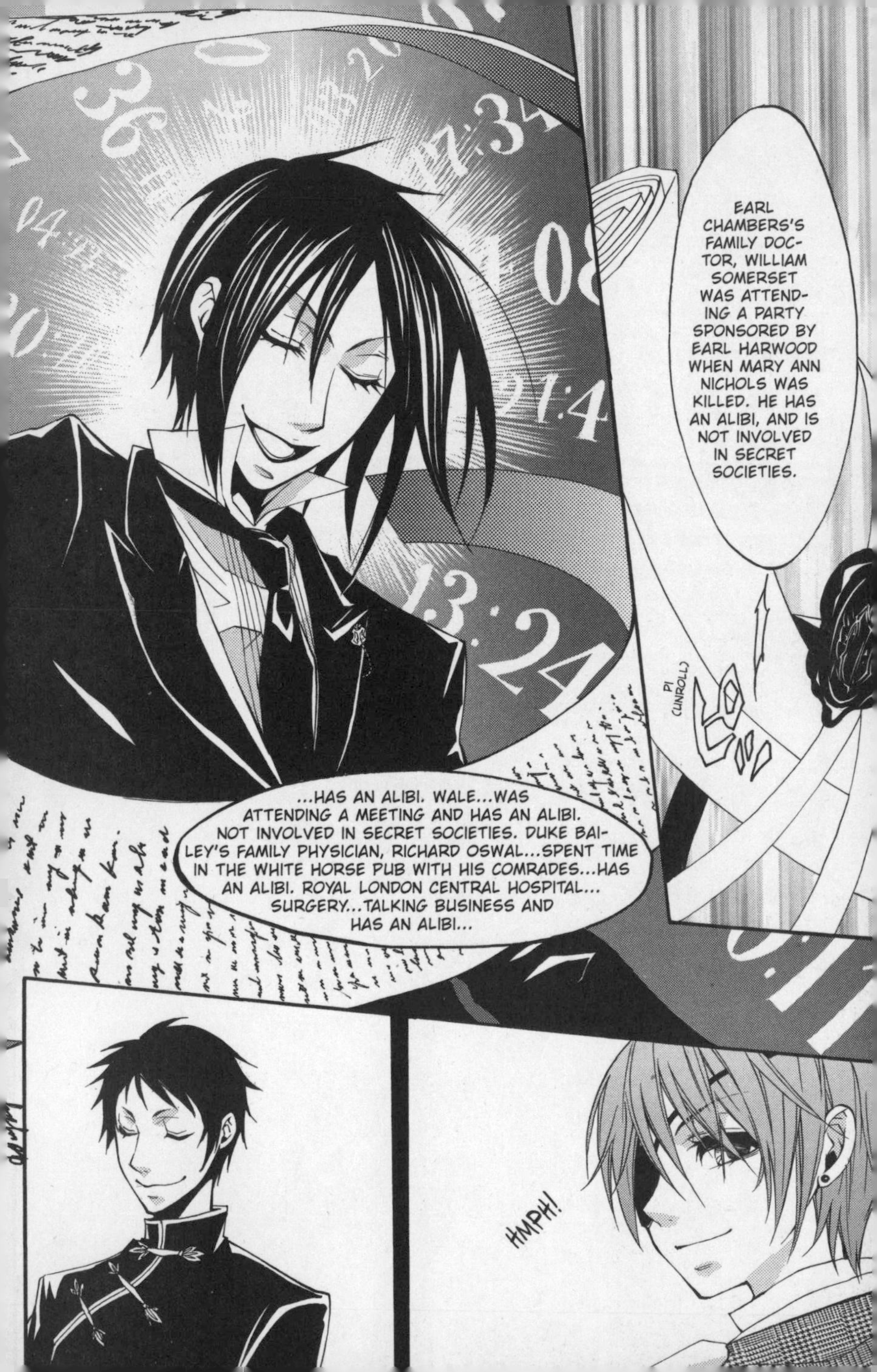
EARL CHAMBERS'S FAMILY DOCTOR, WILLIAM SOMERSET WAS ATTENDING A PARTY SPONSORED BY EARL HARWOOD WHEN MARY ANN NICHOLS WAS KILLED. HE HAS AN ALIBI, AND IS NOT INVOLVED IN SECRET SOCIETIES.
PI (UNROLL)
...HAS AN ALIBI. WALE...WAS ATTENDING A MEETING AND HAS AN ALIBI. NOT INVOLVED IN SECRET SOCIETIES. DUKE BAILEY'S FAMILY PHYSICIAN, RICHARD OSWAL...SPENT TIME IN THE WHITE HORSE PUB WITH HIS COMRADES...HAS AN ALIBI. ROYAL LONDON CENTRAL HOSPITAL... SURGERY...TALKING BUSINESS AND HAS AN ALIBI...
HMPH!

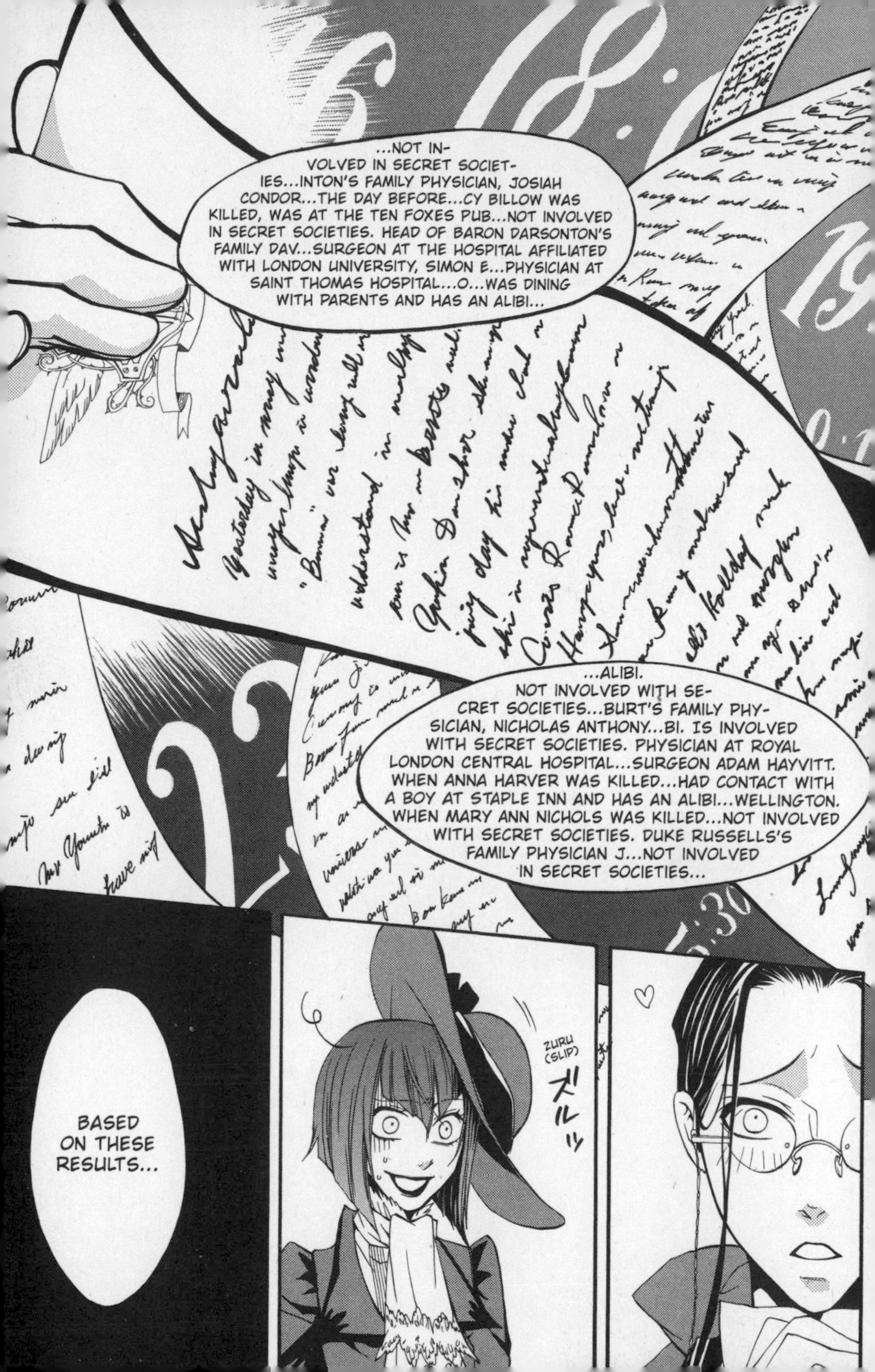
...NOT INVOLVED IN SECRET SOCIETIES...INTON'S FAMILY PHYSICIAN, JOSIAH CONDOR...THE DAY BEFORE...CY BILLOW WAS KILLED, WAS AT THE TEN FOXES PUB...NOT INVOLVED IN SECRET SOCIETIES. HEAD OF BARON DARSONTON'S FAMILY DAV...SURGEON AT THE HOSPITAL AFFILIATED WITH LONDON UNIVERSITY, SIMON E...PHYSICIAN AT SAINT THOMAS HOSPITAL...O...WAS DINING WITH PARENTS AND HAS AN ALIBI...
...ALIBI. NOT INVOLVED WITH SECRET SOCIETIES...BURT'S FAMILY PHYSICIAN, NICHOLAS ANTHONY...BI. IS INVOLVED WITH SECRET SOCIETIES. PHYSICIAN AT ROYAL LONDON CENTRAL HOSPITAL...SURGEON ADAM HAYVITT. WHEN ANNA HARVER WAS KILLED...HAD CONTACT WITH A BOY AT STAPLE INN AND HAS AN ALIBI...WELLINGTON. WHEN MARY ANN NICHOLS WAS KILLED...NOT INVOLVED WITH SECRET SOCIETIES. DUKE RUSSELLS'S FAMILY PHYSICIAN J...NOT INVOLVED IN SECRET SOCIETIES...
ZURU (SLIP)
ズルッ
BASED ON THESE RESULTS...

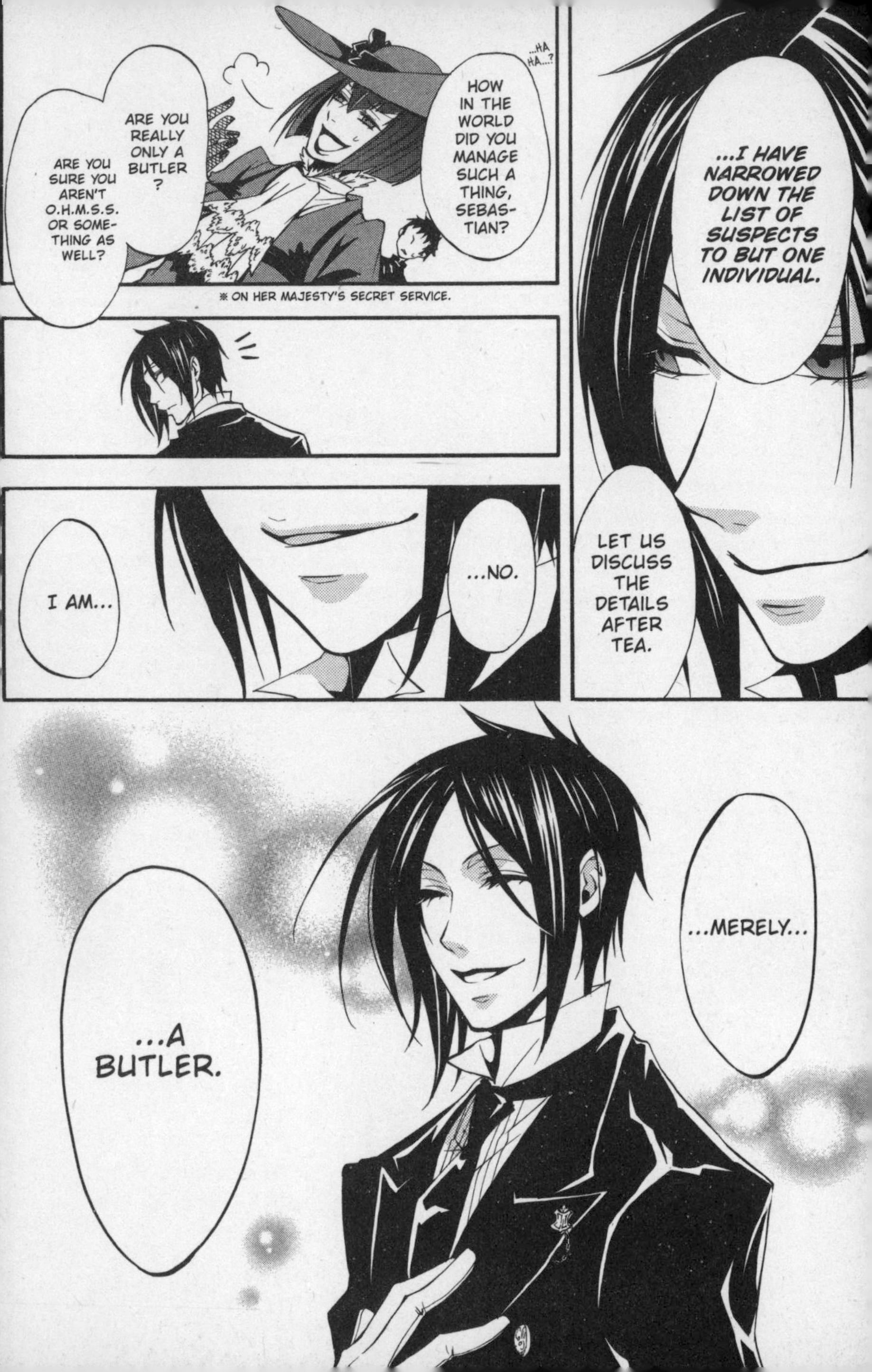
...I HAVE NARROWED DOWN THE LIST OF SUSPECTS TO BUT ONE INDIVIDUAL.
LET US DISCUSS THE DETAILS AFTER TEA.
...HA HA...?
HOW IN THE WORLD DID YOU MANAGE SUCH A THING, SEBASTIAN?
ARE YOU REALLY ONLY A BUTLER?
ARE YOU SURE YOU AREN'T O.H.M.S.S. OR SOMETHING AS WELL?
※ ON HER MAJESTY'S SECRET SERVICE.
...NO.
I AM...
...MERELY...
...A BUTLER.

Black Butler

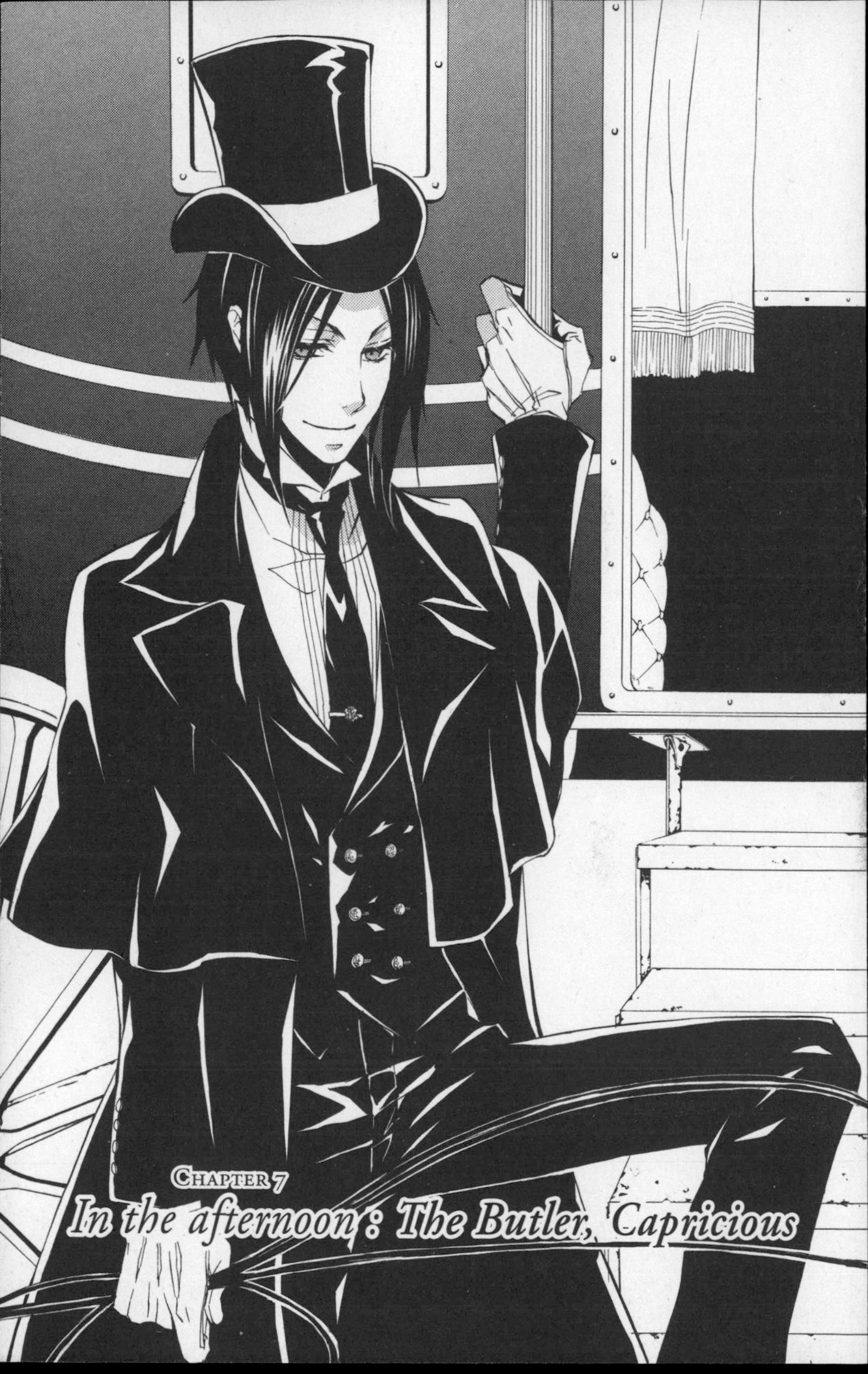
Chapter 7
In the afternoon : The Butler, Capricious

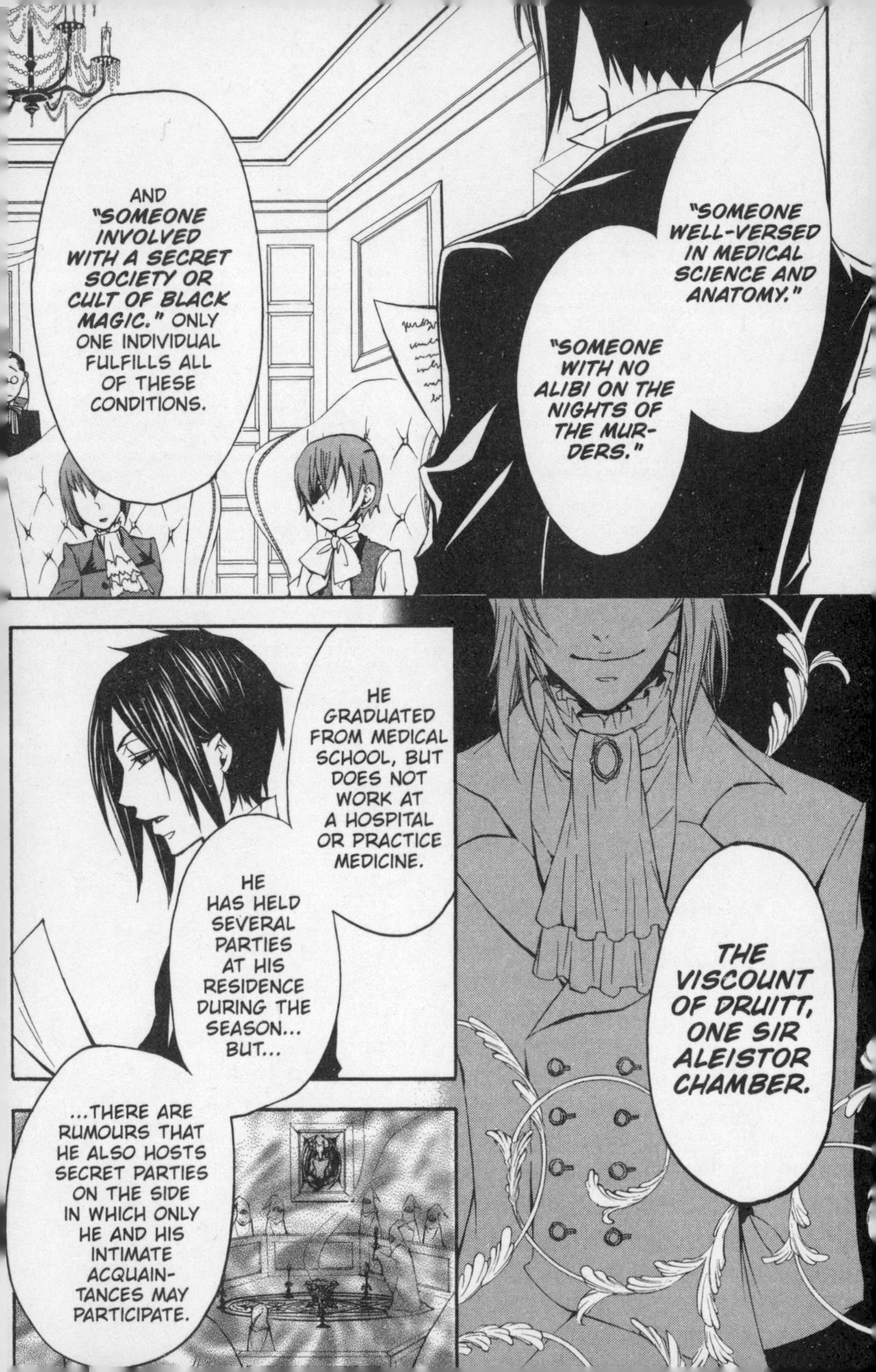
"SOMEONE WELL-VERSED IN MEDICAL SCIENCE AND ANATOMY."
"SOMEONE WITH NO ALIBI ON THE NIGHTS OF THE MUR-DERS."
AND "SOMEONE INVOLVED WITH A SECRET SOCIETY OR CULT OF BLACK MAGIC." ONLY ONE INDIVIDUAL FULFILLS ALL OF THESE CONDITIONS.
THE VISCOUNT OF DRUITT, ONE SIR ALEISTOR CHAMBER.
HE GRADUATED FROM MEDICAL SCHOOL, BUT DOES NOT WORK AT A HOSPITAL OR PRACTICE MEDICINE.
HE HAS HELD SEVERAL PARTIES AT HIS RESIDENCE DURING THE SEASON... BUT...
...THERE ARE RUMOURS THAT HE ALSO HOSTS SECRET PARTIES ON THE SIDE IN WHICH ONLY HE AND HIS INTIMATE ACQUAIN-TANCES MAY PARTICIPATE.

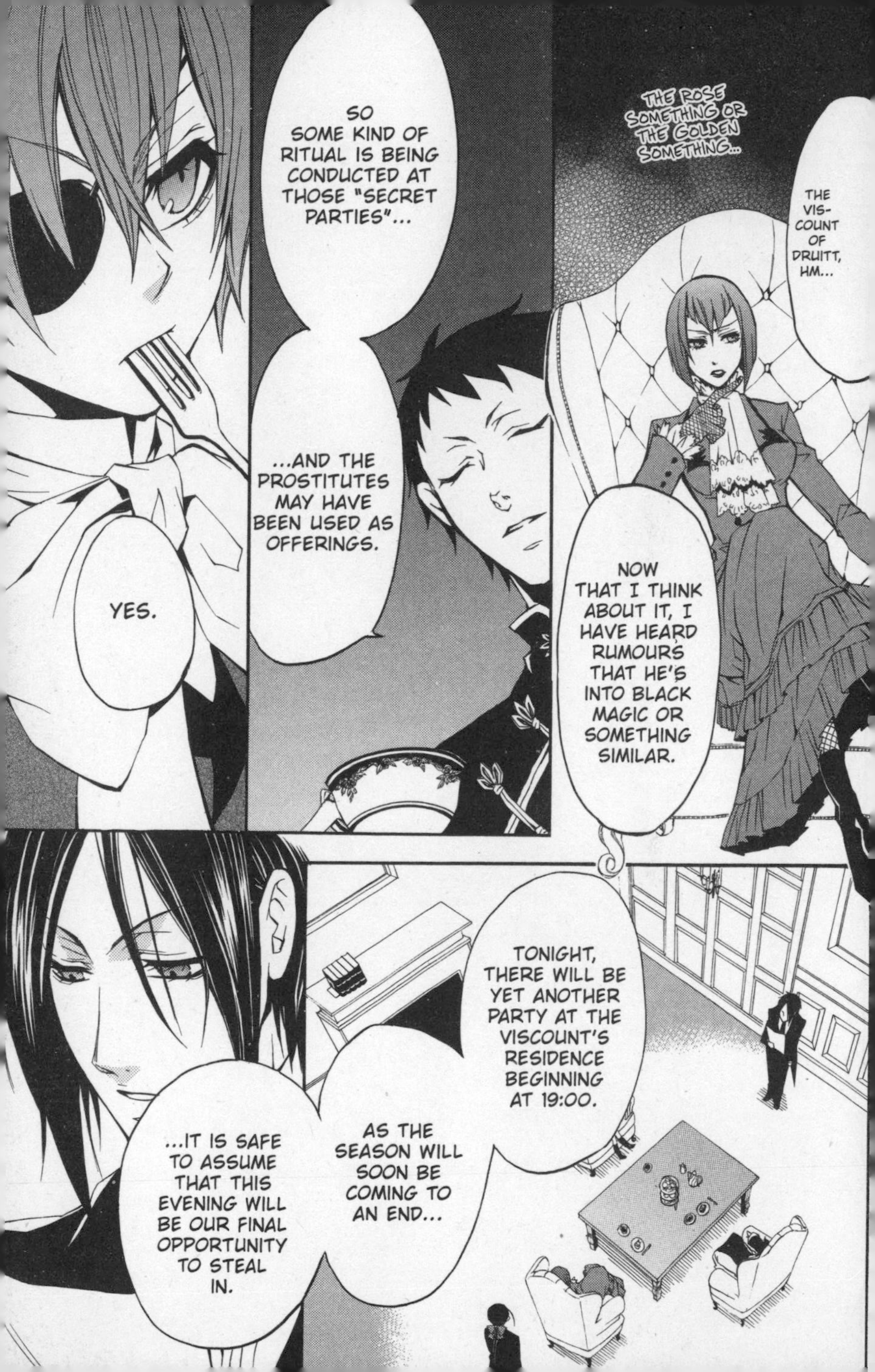
THE VIS-COUNT OF DRUITT, HM...
THE ROSE SOMETHING OR THE GOLDEN SOMETHING...
NOW THAT I THINK ABOUT IT, I HAVE HEARD RUMOURS THAT HE'S INTO BLACK MAGIC OR SOMETHING SIMILAR.
SO SOME KIND OF RITUAL IS BEING CONDUCTED AT THOSE "SECRET PARTIES"...
...AND THE PROSTITUTES MAY HAVE BEEN USED AS OFFERINGS.
YES.
TONIGHT, THERE WILL BE YET ANOTHER PARTY AT THE VISCOUNT'S RESIDENCE BEGINNING AT 19:00.
AS THE SEASON WILL SOON BE COMING TO AN END...
...IT IS SAFE TO ASSUME THAT THIS EVENING WILL BE OUR FINAL OPPORTUNITY TO STEAL IN.

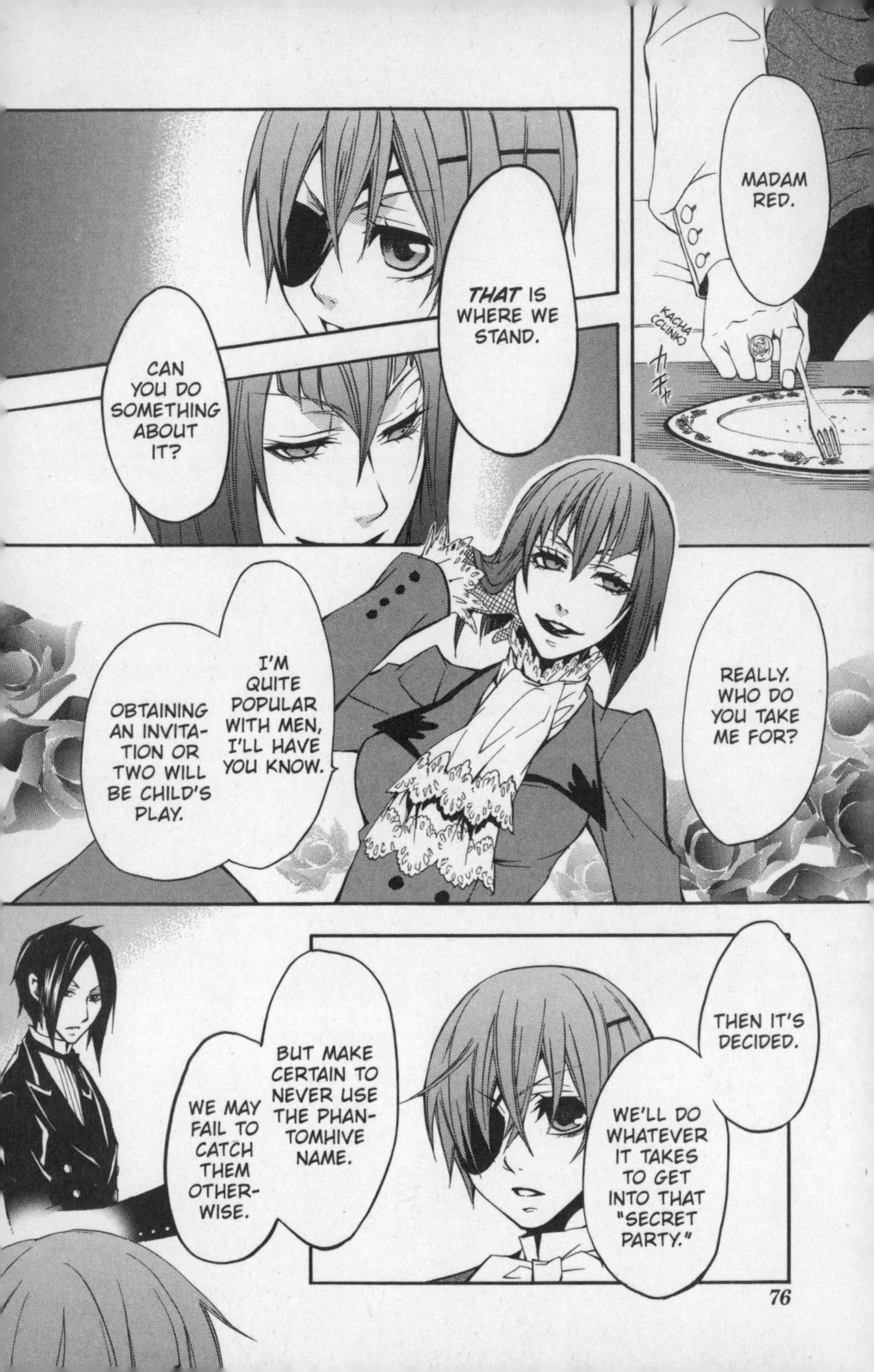
MADAM RED.
KACHA (CLINK)
THAT IS WHERE WE STAND.
CAN YOU DO SOMETHING ABOUT IT?
REALLY. WHO DO YOU TAKE ME FOR?
I'M QUITE POPULAR WITH MEN, I'LL HAVE YOU KNOW.
OBTAINING AN INVITATION OR TWO WILL BE CHILD'S PLAY.
THEN IT'S DECIDED.
WE'LL DO WHATEVER IT TAKES TO GET INTO THAT "SECRET PARTY."
BUT MAKE CERTAIN TO NEVER USE THE PHANTOMHIVE NAME.
WE MAY FAIL TO CATCH THEM OTHERWISE.

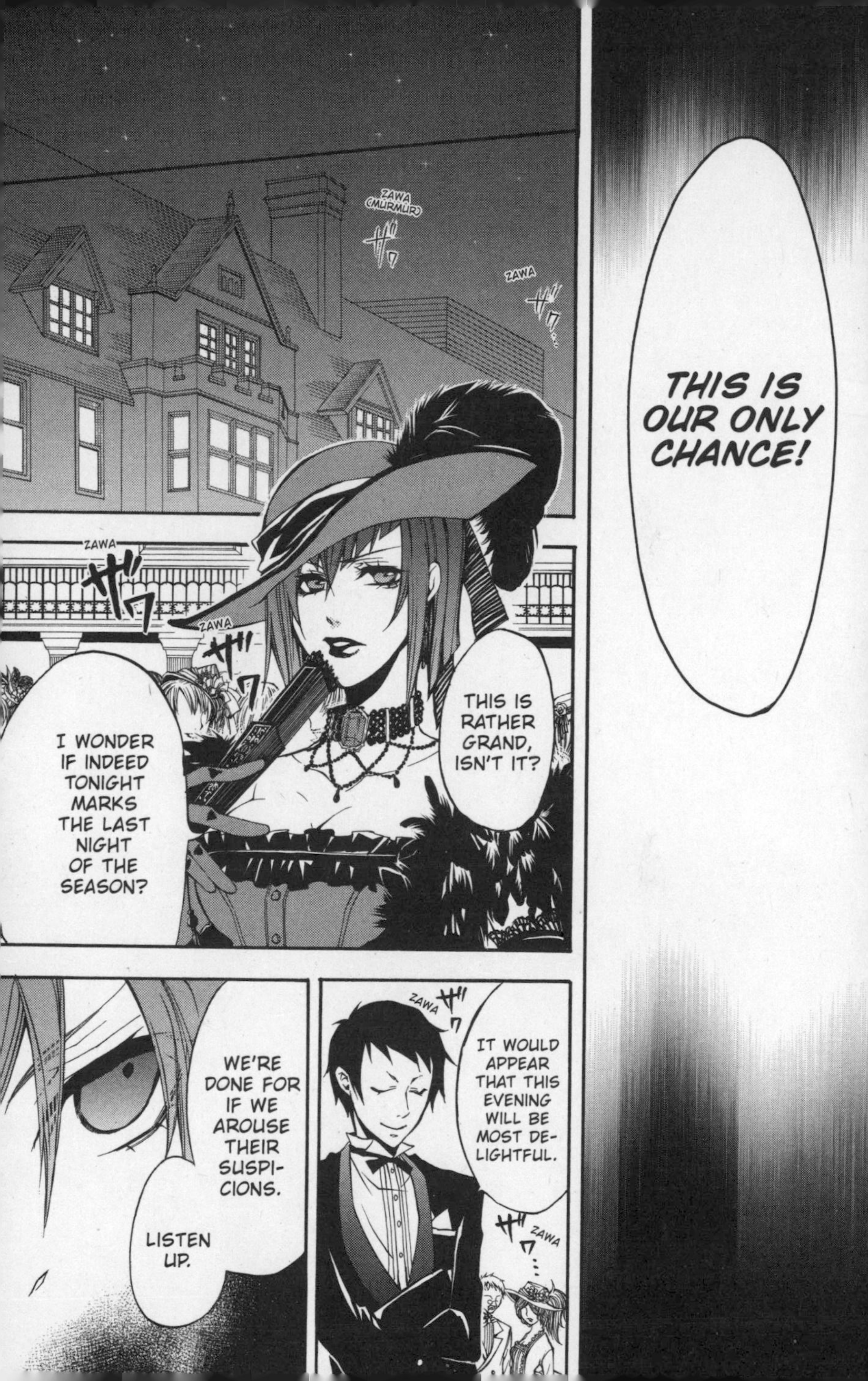
THIS IS OUR ONLY CHANCE!
ZAWA (MURMUR)
ZAWA
ZAWA
ZAWA
THIS IS RATHER GRAND, ISN'T IT?
I WONDER IF INDEED TONIGHT MARKS THE LAST NIGHT OF THE SEASON?
ZAWA
IT WOULD APPEAR THAT THIS EVENING WILL BE MOST DE-LIGHTFUL.
ZAWA
WE'RE DONE FOR IF WE AROUSE THEIR SUSPI-CIONS.
LISTEN UP.

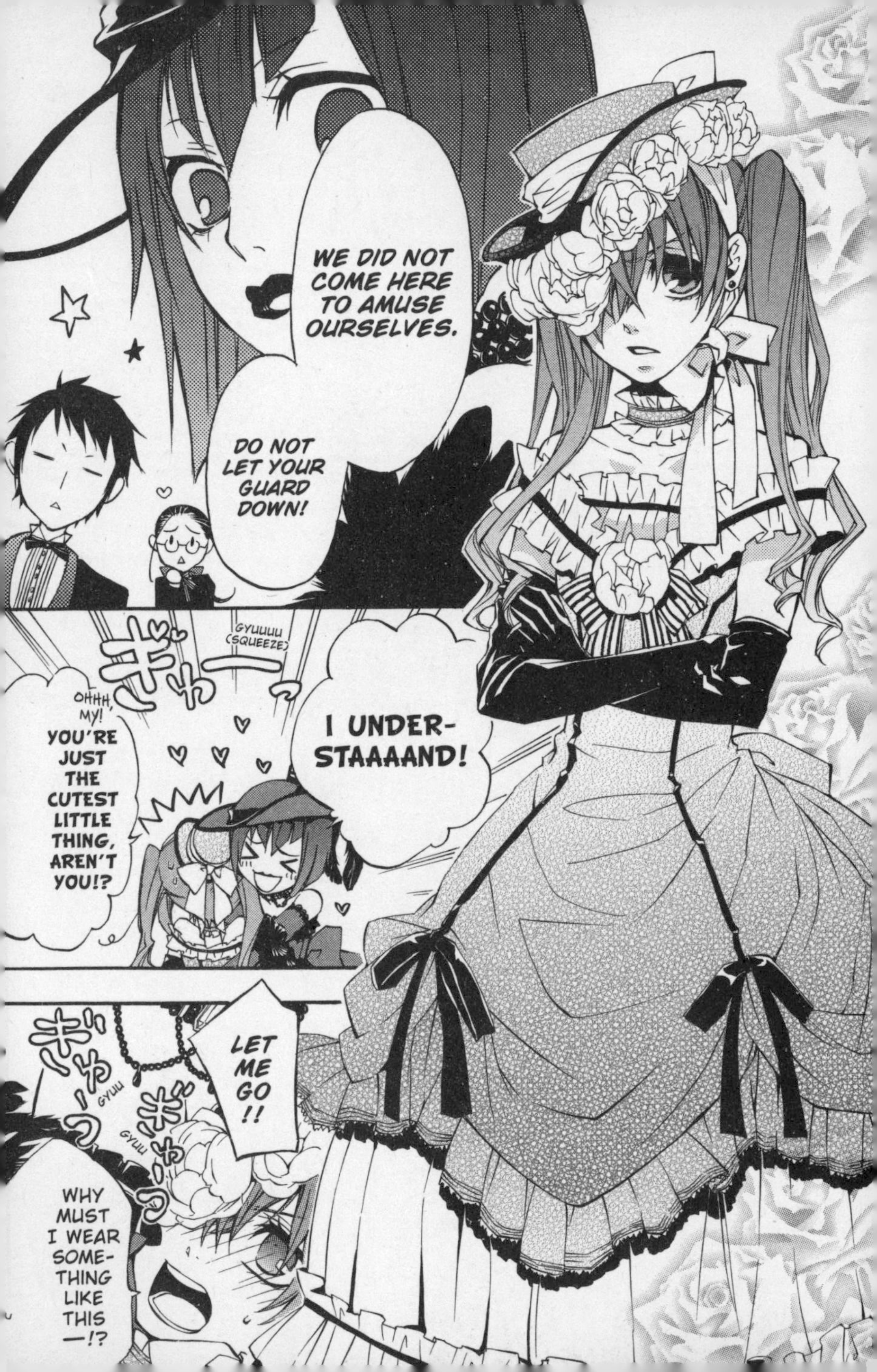
WE DID NOT COME HERE TO AMUSE OURSELVES.
DO NOT LET YOUR GUARD DOWN!
I UNDER-STAAAAND!
GYUUUU (SQUEEZE)
OHHH, MY! YOU'RE JUST THE CUTEST LITTLE THING, AREN'T YOU!?
LET ME GO!!
GYUU
GYUU
WHY MUST I WEAR SOME-THING LIKE THIS—!?

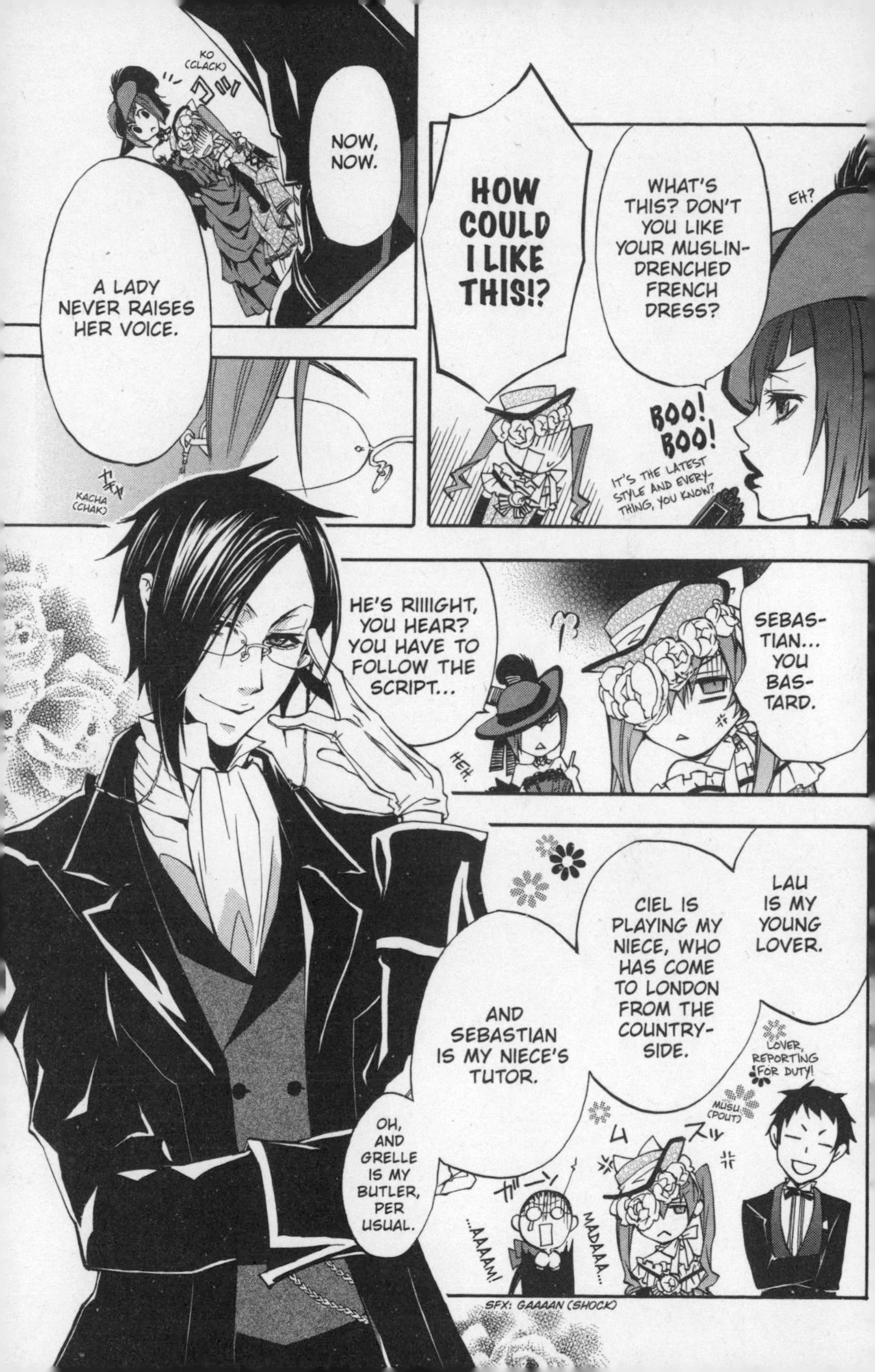
EH?
WHAT'S THIS? DON'T YOU LIKE YOUR MUSLIN-DRENCHED FRENCH DRESS?
HOW COULD I LIKE THIS!?
BOO! BOO!
IT'S THE LATEST STYLE AND EVERYTHING, YOU KNOW?
KO (CLACK)
NOW, NOW.
A LADY NEVER RAISES HER VOICE.
KACHA (CHAK)
SEBASTIAN... YOU BASTARD.
HE'S RIIIIGHT, YOU HEAR? YOU HAVE TO FOLLOW THE SCRIPT...
HEH.
LAU IS MY YOUNG LOVER.
CIEL IS PLAYING MY NIECE, WHO HAS COME TO LONDON FROM THE COUNTRYSIDE.
AND SEBASTIAN IS MY NIECE'S TUTOR.
LOVER, REPORTING FOR DUTY!
MUSU (POUT)
MADAAA...
...AAAAM!
OH, AND GRELLE IS MY BUTLER, PER USUAL.
SFX: GAAAAN (SHOCK)

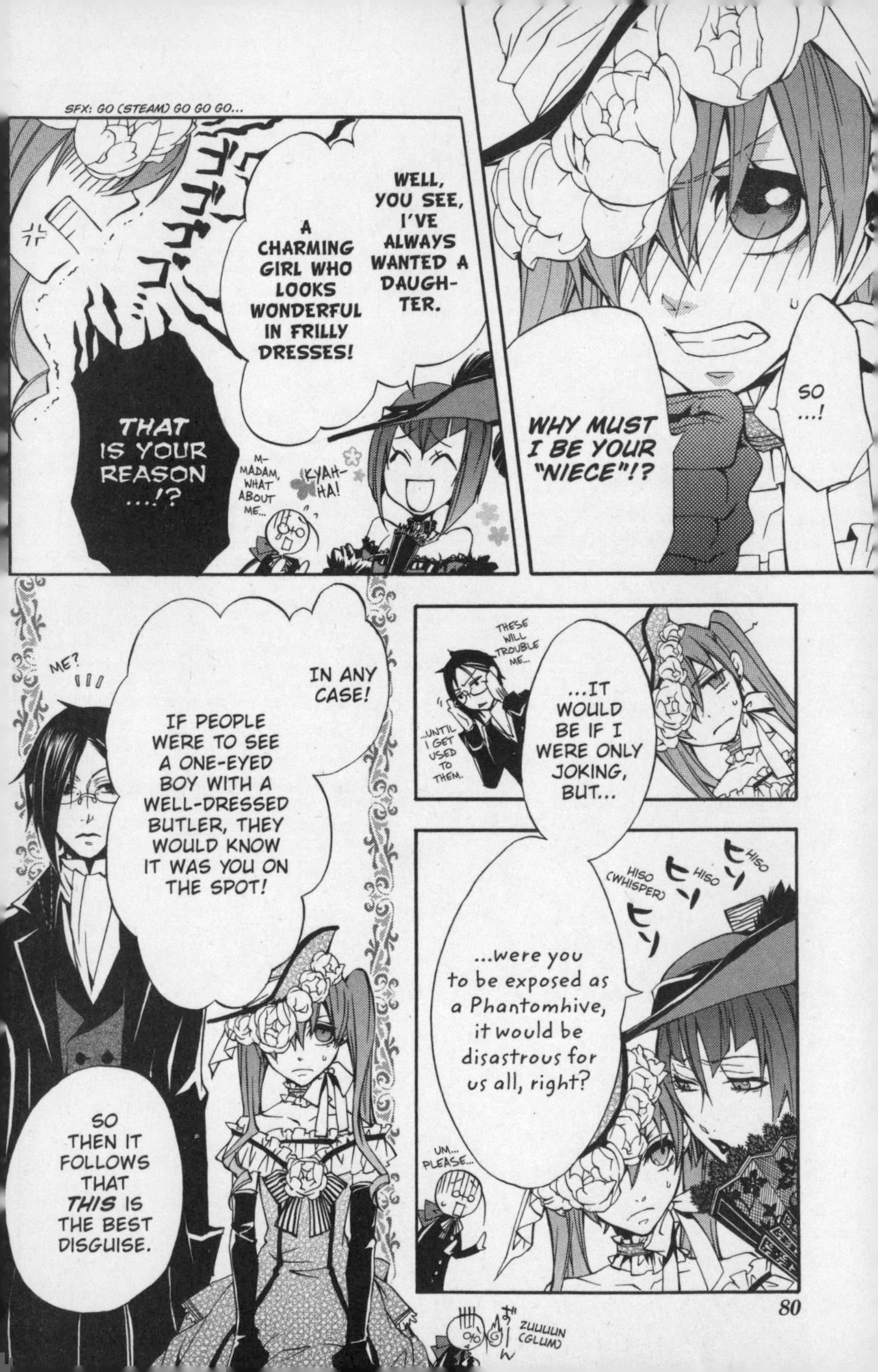
SFX: GO (STEAM) GO GO GO...
SO ...!
WHY MUST I BE YOUR "NIECE"!?
WELL, YOU SEE, I'VE ALWAYS WANTED A DAUGHTER.
A CHARMING GIRL WHO LOOKS WONDERFUL IN FRILLY DRESSES!
THAT IS YOUR REASON ...!?
KYAH-HA!
M-MADAM, WHAT ABOUT ME...
...IT WOULD BE IF I WERE ONLY JOKING, BUT...
THESE WILL TROUBLE ME...
...UNTIL I GET USED TO THEM.
HISO HISO HISO (WHISPER)
...were you to be exposed as a Phantomhive, it would be disastrous for us all, right?
UM... PLEASE...
IN ANY CASE!
IF PEOPLE WERE TO SEE A ONE-EYED BOY WITH A WELL-DRESSED BUTLER, THEY WOULD KNOW IT WAS YOU ON THE SPOT!
ME?
SO THEN IT FOLLOWS THAT THIS IS THE BEST DISGUISE.
ZUUUUN (GLUM)

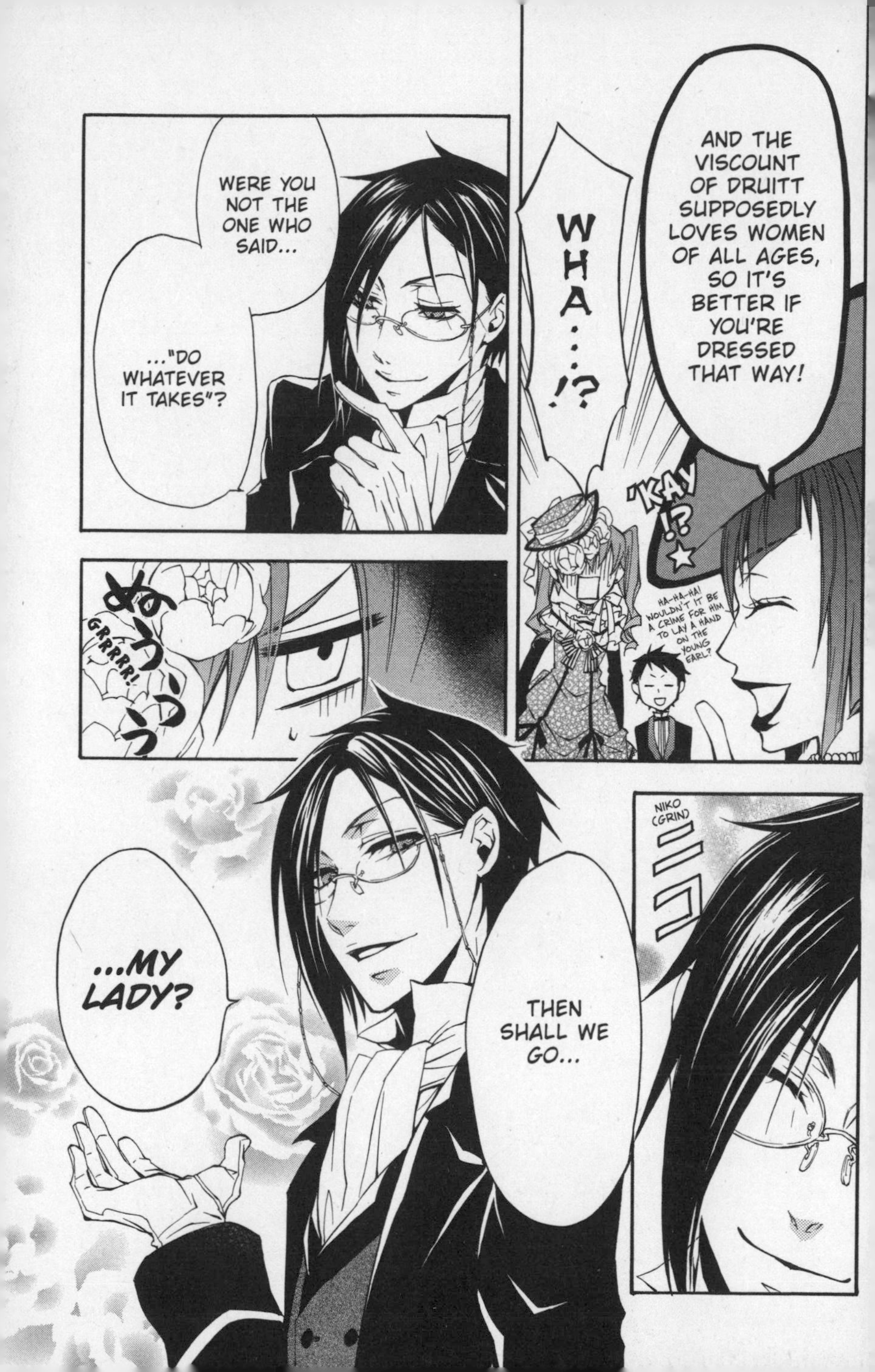
AND THE VISCOUNT OF DRUITT SUPPOSEDLY LOVES WOMEN OF ALL AGES, SO IT'S BETTER IF YOU'RE DRESSED THAT WAY!
WHA...!?
'KAY!?☆
HA-HA-HA! WOULDN'T IT BE A CRIME FOR HIM TO LAY A HAND ON THE YOUNG EARL?
WERE YOU NOT THE ONE WHO SAID...
..."DO WHATEVER IT TAKES"?
GRRRRR!
ニコ
NIKO (GRIN)
THEN SHALL WE GO...
...MY LADY?

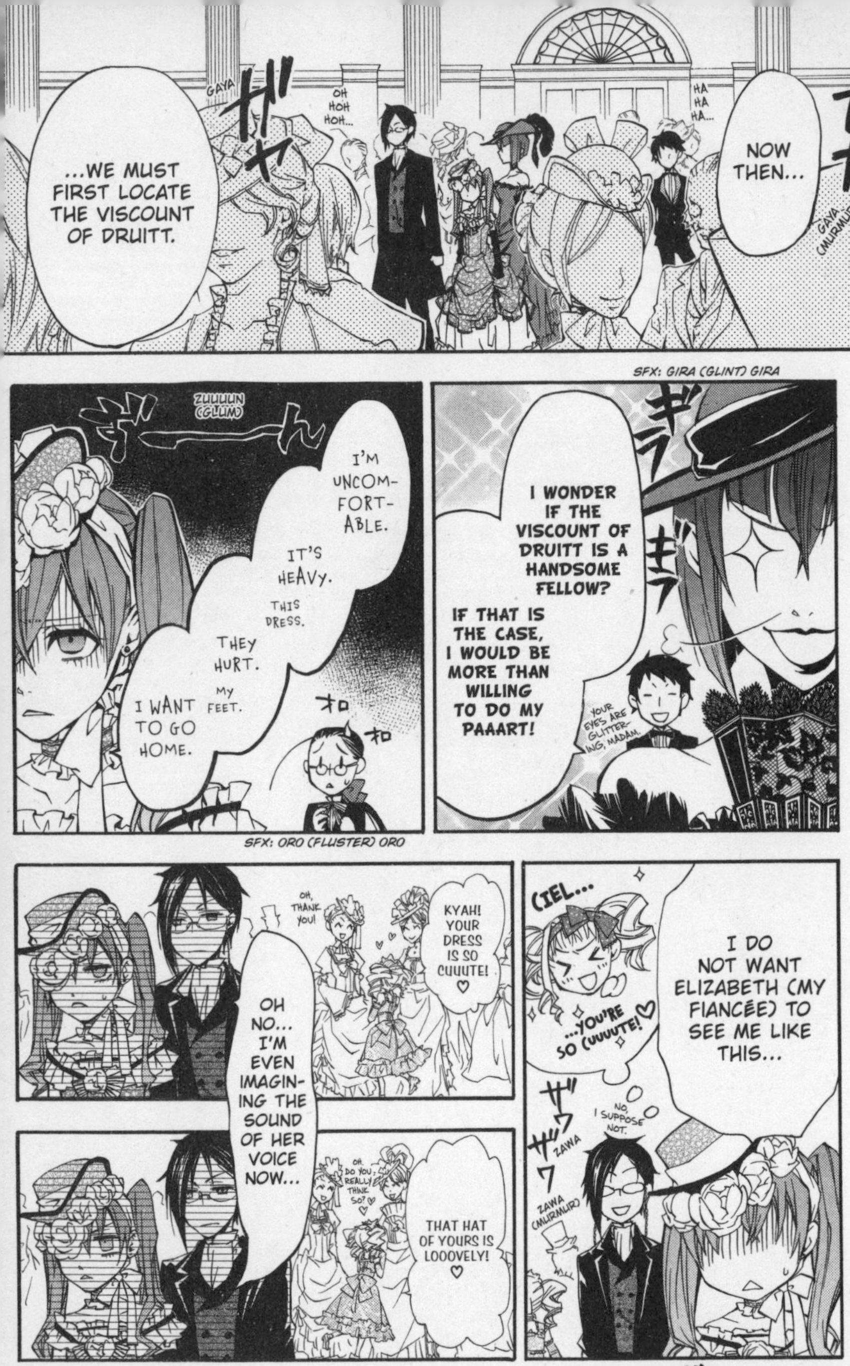

GAYA (MURMUR)
NOW THEN...
HA HA HA...
OH HOH HOH...
GAYA
...WE MUST FIRST LOCATE THE VISCOUNT OF DRUITT.
SFX: GIRA (GLINT) GIRA
I WONDER IF THE VISCOUNT OF DRUITT IS A HANDSOME FELLOW?
IF THAT IS THE CASE, I WOULD BE MORE THAN WILLING TO DO MY PAAART!
YOUR EYES ARE GLITTERING, MADAM.
ZUUUUN (GLUM)
I'M UNCOMFORTABLE.
IT'S HEAVY.
THIS DRESS.
THEY HURT.
MY FEET.
I WANT TO GO HOME.
SFX: ORO (FLUSTER) ORO
CIEL...
...YOU'RE SO CUUUUTE! ♥
I DO NOT WANT ELIZABETH (MY FIANCÉE) TO SEE ME LIKE THIS...
NO, I SUPPOSE NOT.
ZAWA
ZAWA (MURMUR)
KYAH! YOUR DRESS IS SO CUUUTE! ♥
OH, THANK YOU!
OH NO... I'M EVEN IMAGINING THE SOUND OF HER VOICE NOW...
THAT HAT OF YOURS IS LOOOVELY! ♥
OH, DO YOU REALLY THINK SO? ♥
ZUUUUUN

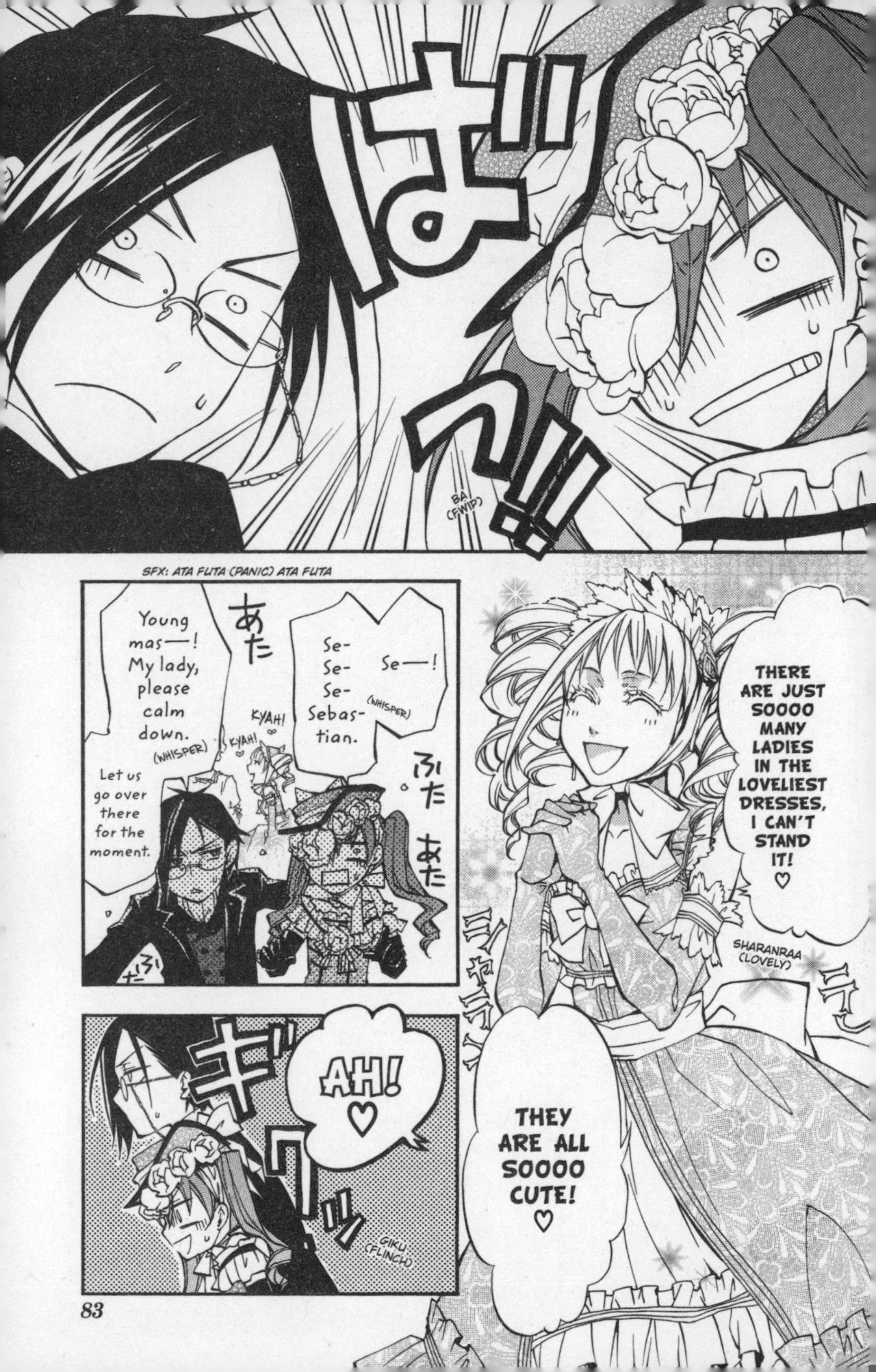
ばっ!!
BA (FWIP)
SFX: ATA FUTA (PANIC) ATA FUTA
THERE ARE JUST SOOOO MANY LADIES IN THE LOVELIEST DRESSES, I CAN'T STAND IT! ♡
SHARANRAA (LOVELY)
THEY ARE ALL SOOOO CUTE! ♡
Se—! (WHISPER)
Se-Se-Se-Sebastian.
あた
Young mas—! My lady, please calm down. (WHISPER)
KYAH! KYAH! ♡
Let us go over there for the moment.
ふた あた
AH! ♡
GIKU (FLINCH)

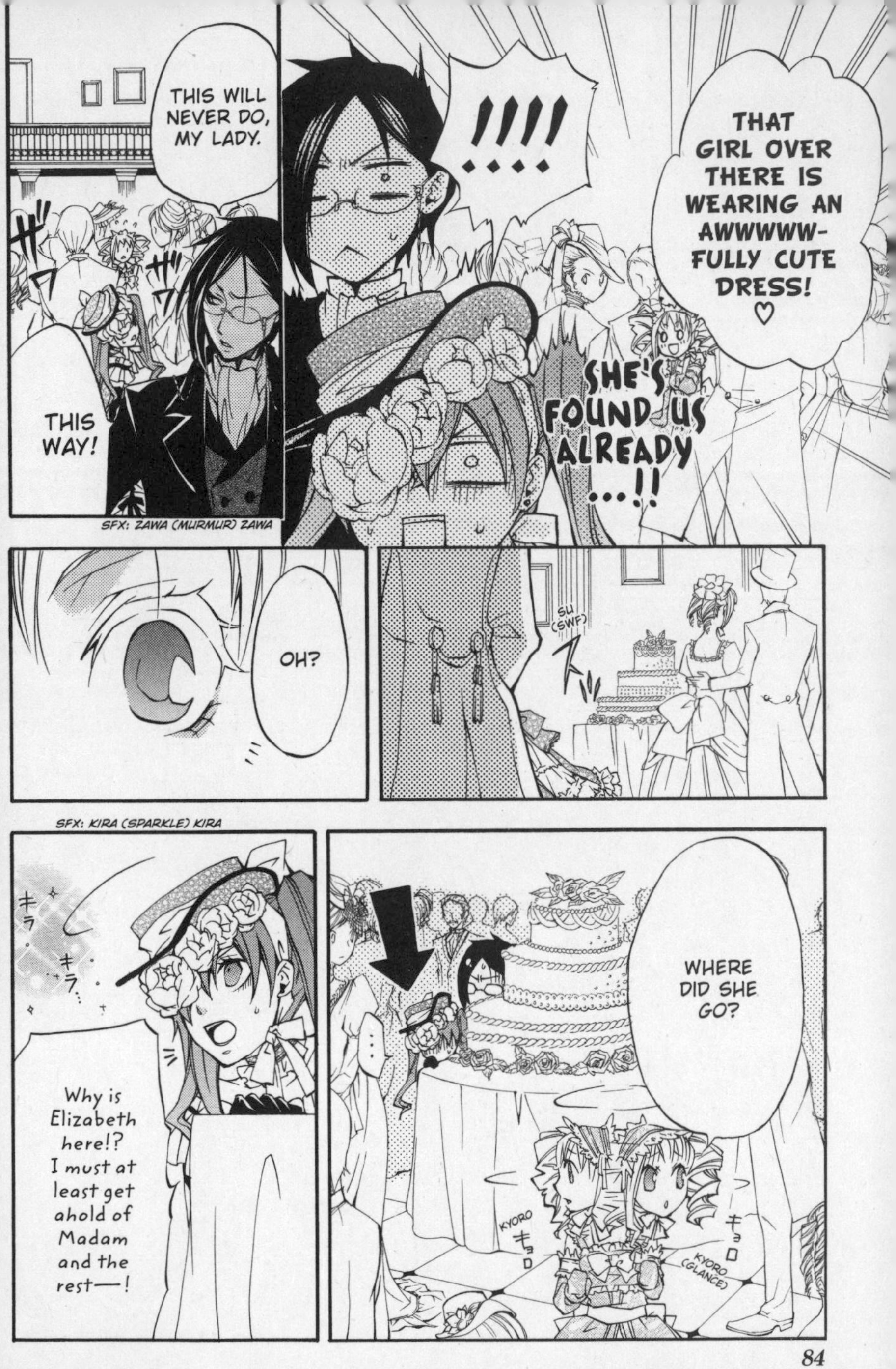
THAT GIRL OVER THERE IS WEARING AN AWWWWW-FULLY CUTE DRESS! ♡
!!!!
....
SHE'S FOUND US ALREADY ...!!
THIS WILL NEVER DO, MY LADY.
THIS WAY!
SFX: ZAWA (MURMUR) ZAWA
SU (SWF)
OH?
SFX: KIRA (SPARKLE) KIRA
WHERE DID SHE GO?
KYORO (GLANCE)
KYORO
...
Why is Elizabeth here!? I must at least get ahold of Madam and the rest—!

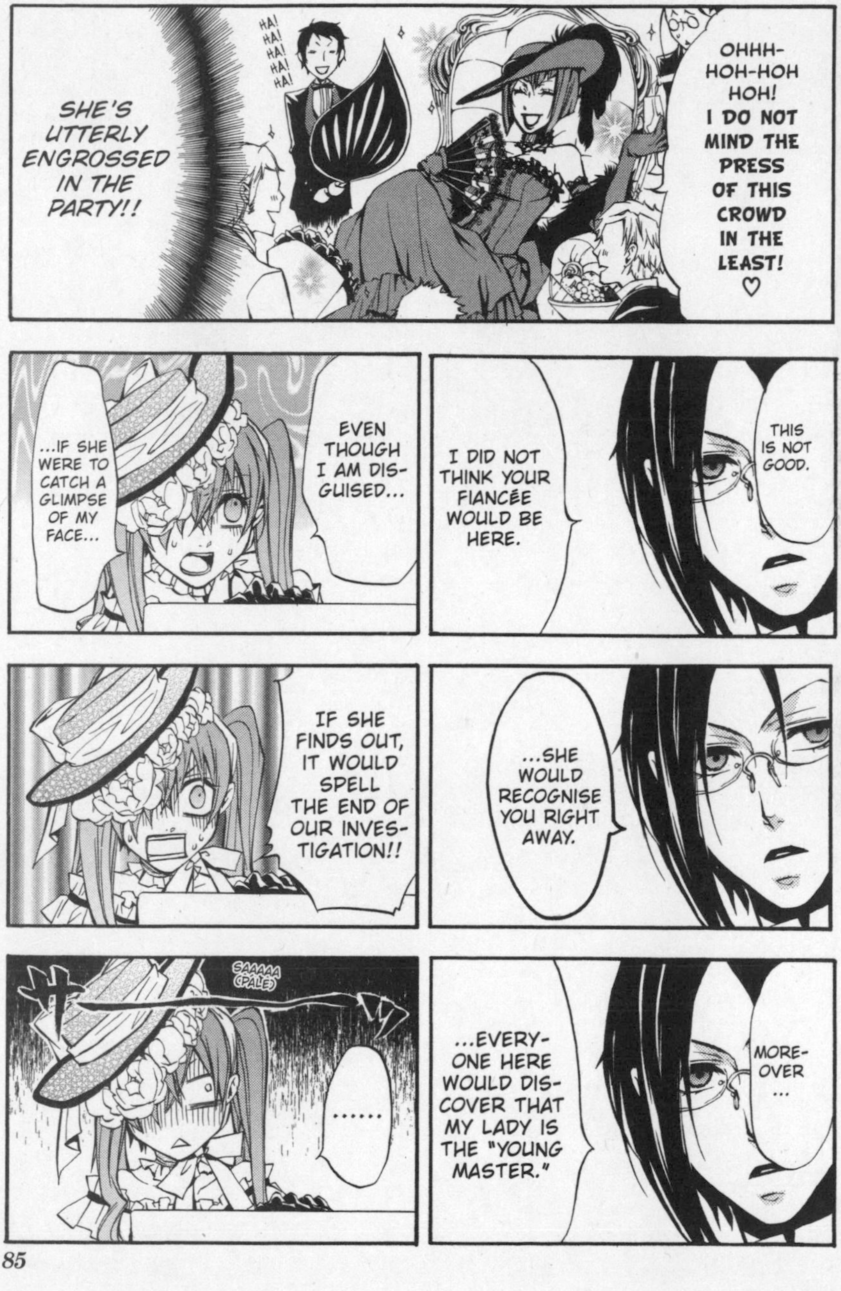

OHHH-HOH-HOH HOH! I DO NOT MIND THE PRESS OF THIS CROWD IN THE LEAST! ♡
HA! HA! HA! HA! HA!
SHE'S UTTERLY ENGROSSED IN THE PARTY!!
THIS IS NOT GOOD.
I DID NOT THINK YOUR FIANCÉE WOULD BE HERE.
EVEN THOUGH I AM DISGUISED...
...IF SHE WERE TO CATCH A GLIMPSE OF MY FACE...
...SHE WOULD RECOGNISE YOU RIGHT AWAY.
IF SHE FINDS OUT, IT WOULD SPELL THE END OF OUR INVESTIGATION!!
MOREOVER...
...EVERYONE HERE WOULD DISCOVER THAT MY LADY IS THE "YOUNG MASTER."
SAAAAA (PALE)
......

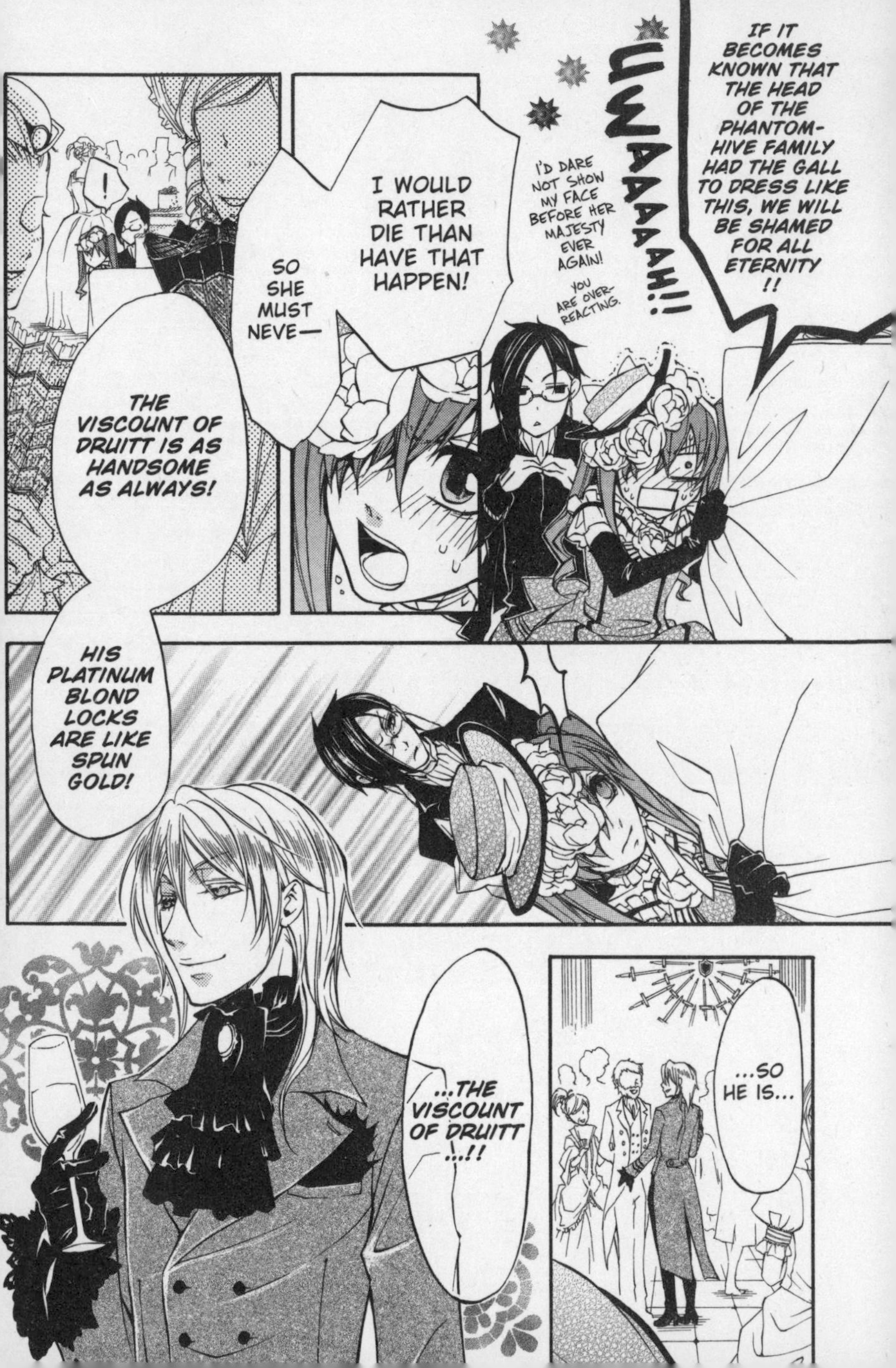
IF IT BECOMES KNOWN THAT THE HEAD OF THE PHANTOM-HIVE FAMILY HAD THE GALL TO DRESS LIKE THIS, WE WILL BE SHAMED FOR ALL ETERNITY !!
UWAAAAAH!!!
I'D DARE NOT SHOW MY FACE BEFORE HER MAJESTY EVER AGAIN!
YOU ARE OVER-REACTING.
I WOULD RATHER DIE THAN HAVE THAT HAPPEN!
SO SHE MUST NEVE—
!
THE VISCOUNT OF DRUITT IS AS HANDSOME AS ALWAYS!
HIS PLATINUM BLOND LOCKS ARE LIKE SPUN GOLD!
...SO HE IS...
...THE VISCOUNT OF DRUITT ...!!

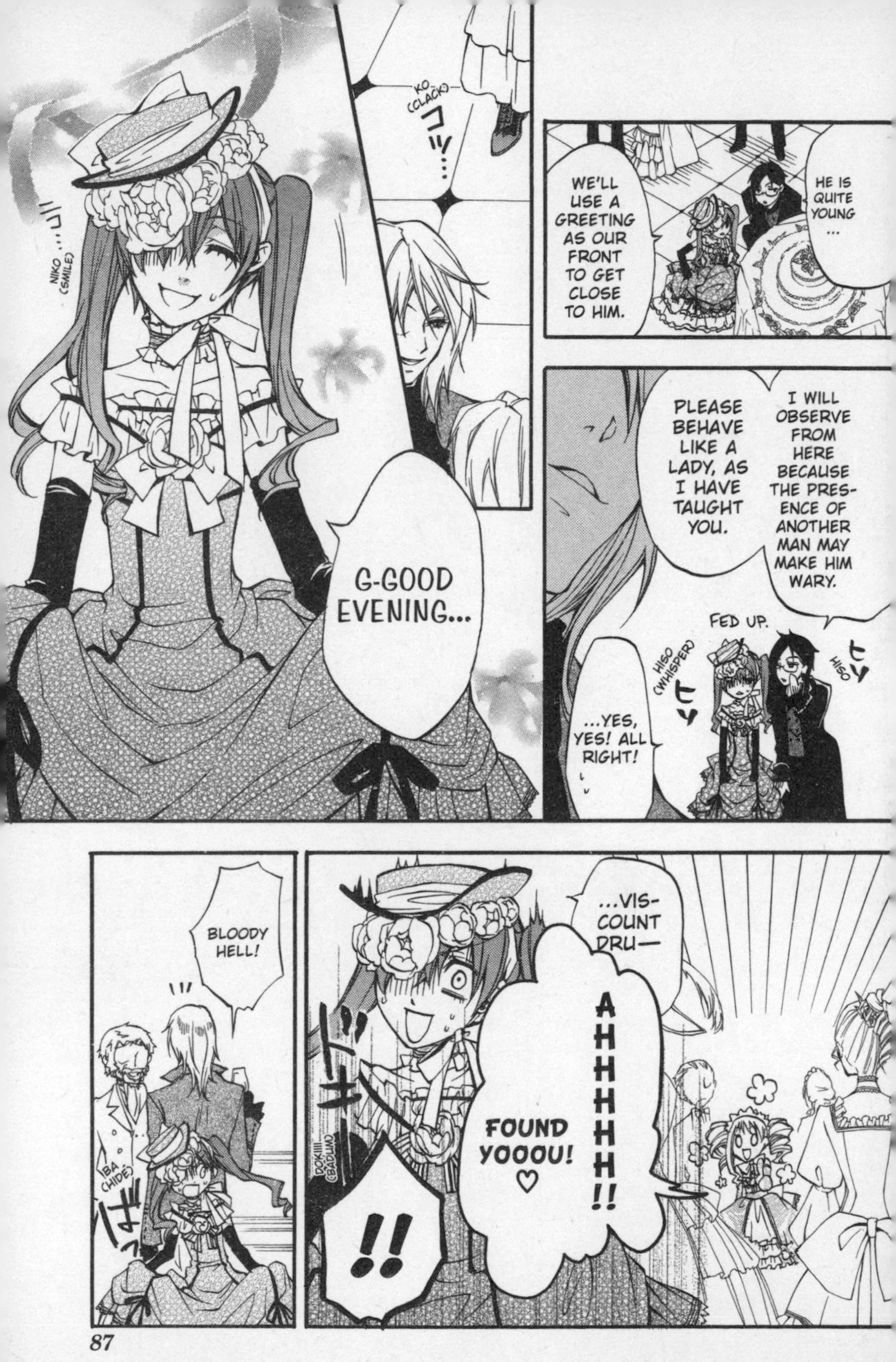
HE IS QUITE YOUNG...
WE'LL USE A GREETING AS OUR FRONT TO GET CLOSE TO HIM.
I WILL OBSERVE FROM HERE BECAUSE THE PRES-ENCE OF ANOTHER MAN MAY MAKE HIM WARY.
PLEASE BEHAVE LIKE A LADY, AS I HAVE TAUGHT YOU.
FED UP.
HISO
HISO (WHISPER)
...YES, YES! ALL RIGHT!
KO (CLACK)
NIKO (SMILE)
G-GOOD EVENING...
...VIS-COUNT DRU—
AHHHHHH!!
FOUND YOOOU! ♡
DOKIIII (BADUMP)
!!
BLOODY HELL!
!!!
BA (HIDE)

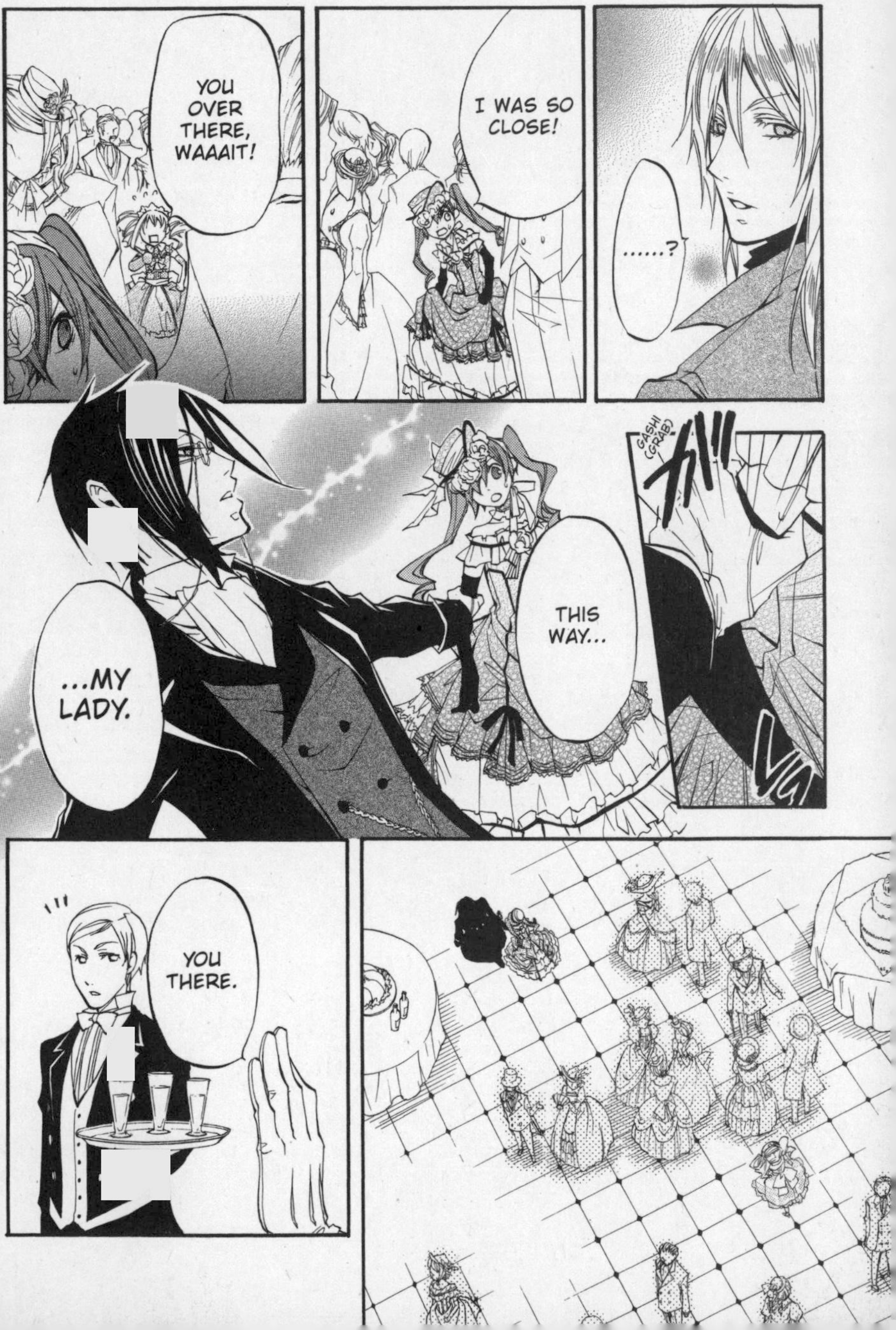
......?
I WAS SO CLOSE!
YOU OVER THERE, WAAAIT!
GASHI (GRAB)
THIS WAY...
...MY LADY.
YOU THERE.

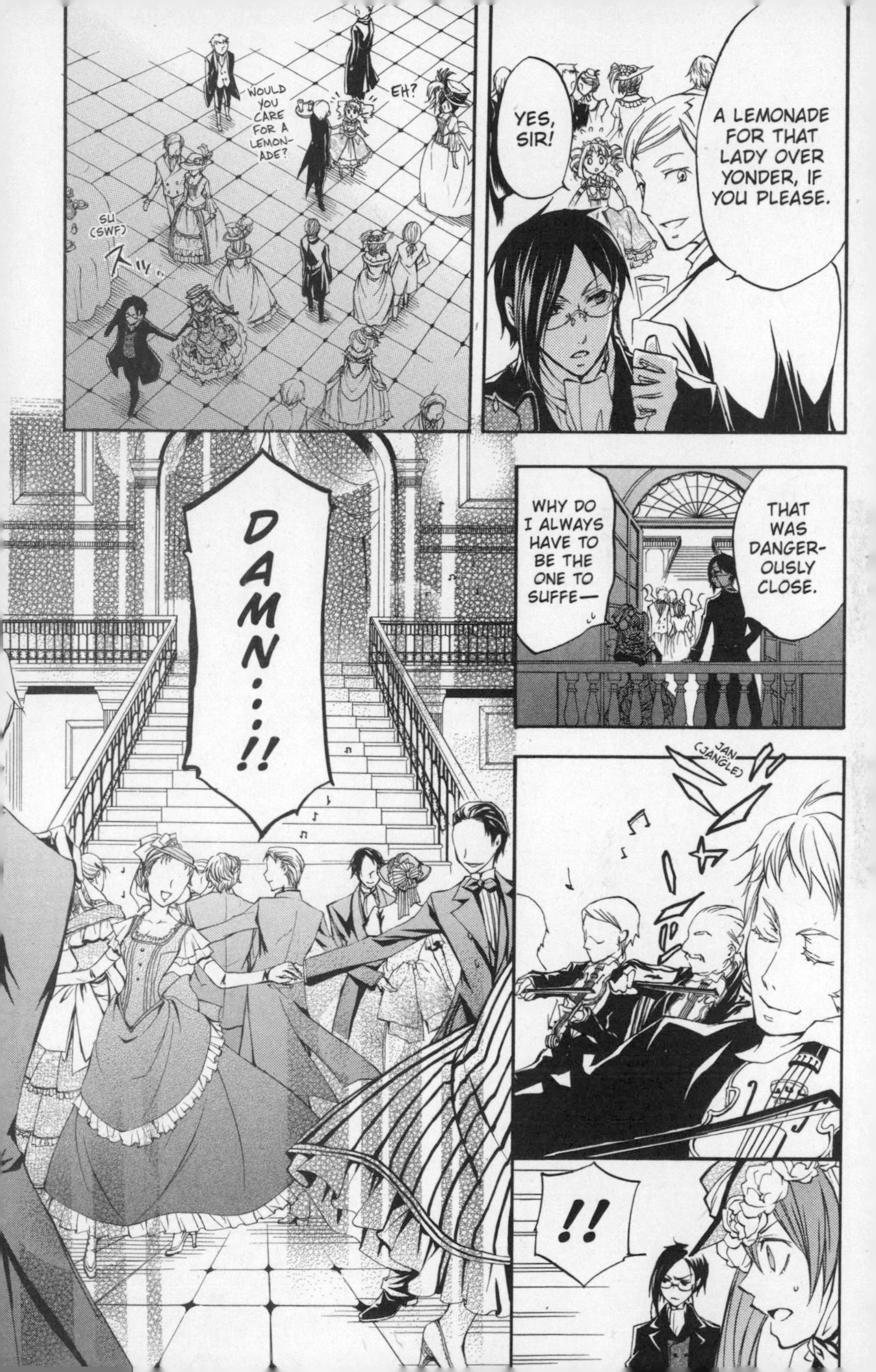
A LEMONADE FOR THAT LADY OVER YONDER, IF YOU PLEASE.
YES, SIR!
WOULD YOU CARE FOR A LEMON-ADE?
EH?
SU (SWF)
THAT WAS DANGER-OUSLY CLOSE.
WHY DO I ALWAYS HAVE TO BE THE ONE TO SUFFE—
JAN (JANGLE)
!!
DAMN...!!

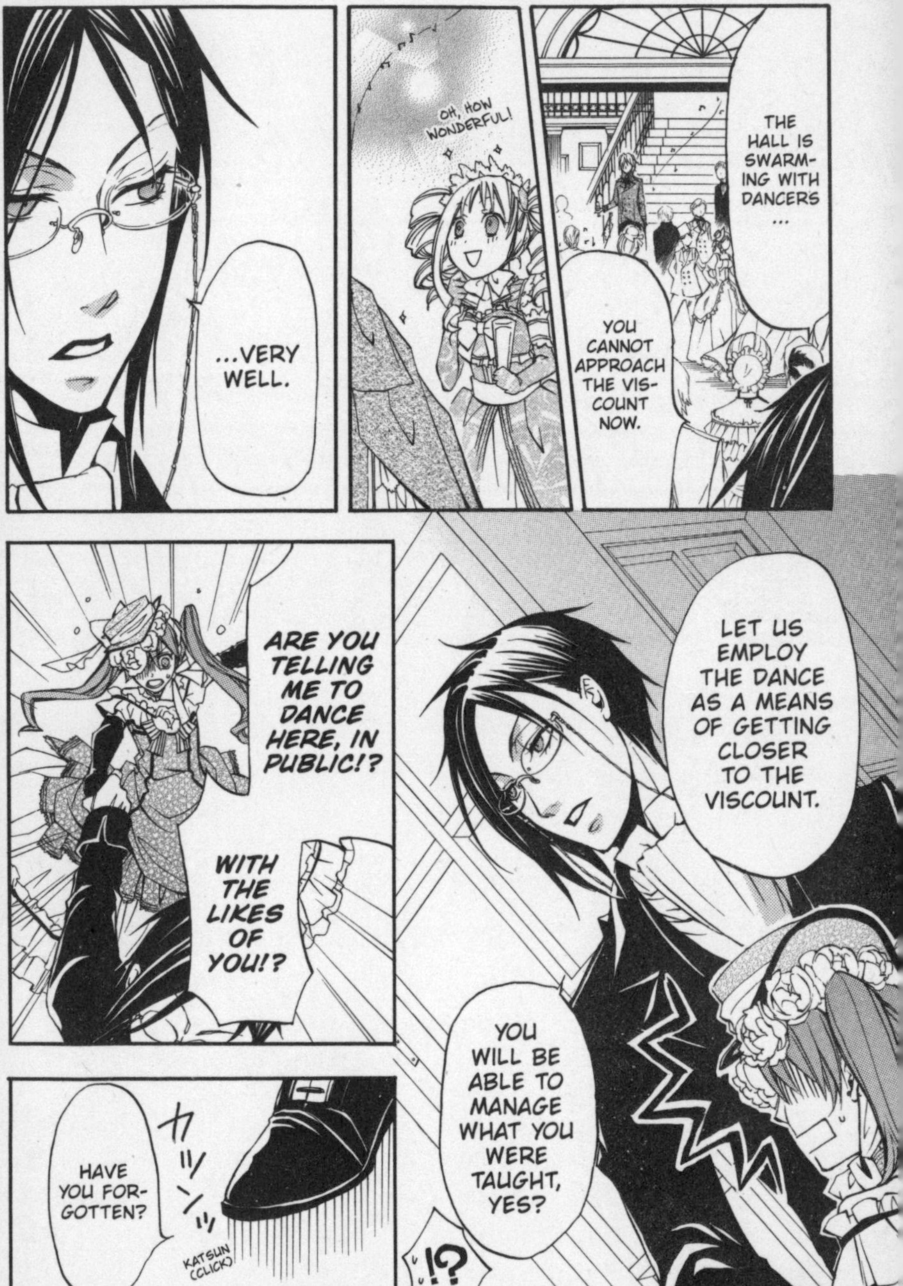
THE HALL IS SWARMING WITH DANCERS ...
YOU CANNOT APPROACH THE VISCOUNT NOW.
OH, HOW WONDERFUL!
...VERY WELL.
LET US EMPLOY THE DANCE AS A MEANS OF GETTING CLOSER TO THE VISCOUNT.
YOU WILL BE ABLE TO MANAGE WHAT YOU WERE TAUGHT, YES?
!?
ARE YOU TELLING ME TO DANCE HERE, IN PUBLIC!?
WITH THE LIKES OF YOU!?
KATSUN (CLICK)
HAVE YOU FORGOTTEN?

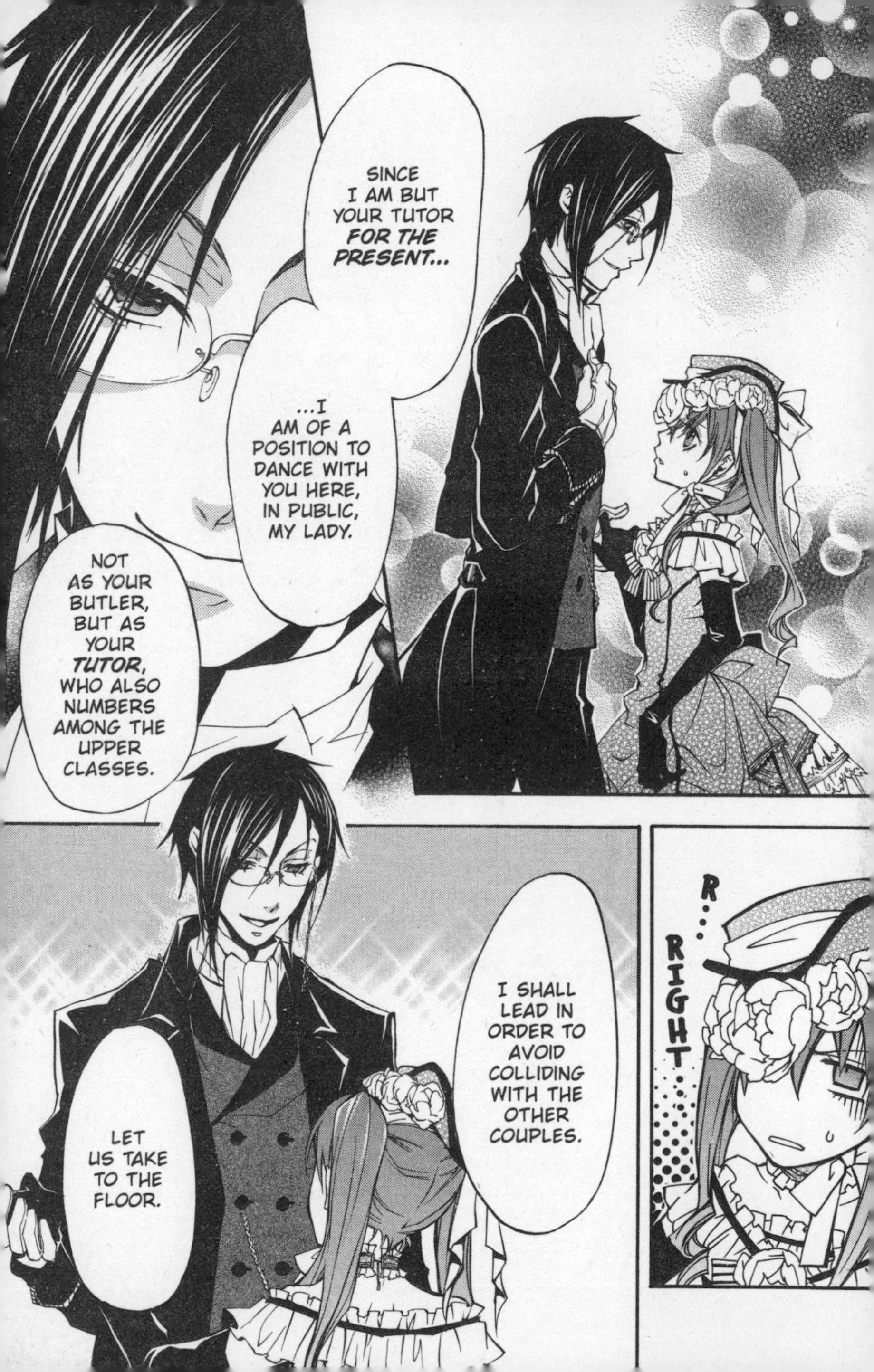
SINCE I AM BUT YOUR TUTOR *FOR THE PRESENT...*
...I AM OF A POSITION TO DANCE WITH YOU HERE, IN PUBLIC, MY LADY.
NOT AS YOUR BUTLER, BUT AS YOUR *TUTOR*, WHO ALSO NUMBERS AMONG THE UPPER CLASSES.
R... RIGHT...
I SHALL LEAD IN ORDER TO AVOID COLLIDING WITH THE OTHER COUPLES.
LET US TAKE TO THE FLOOR.

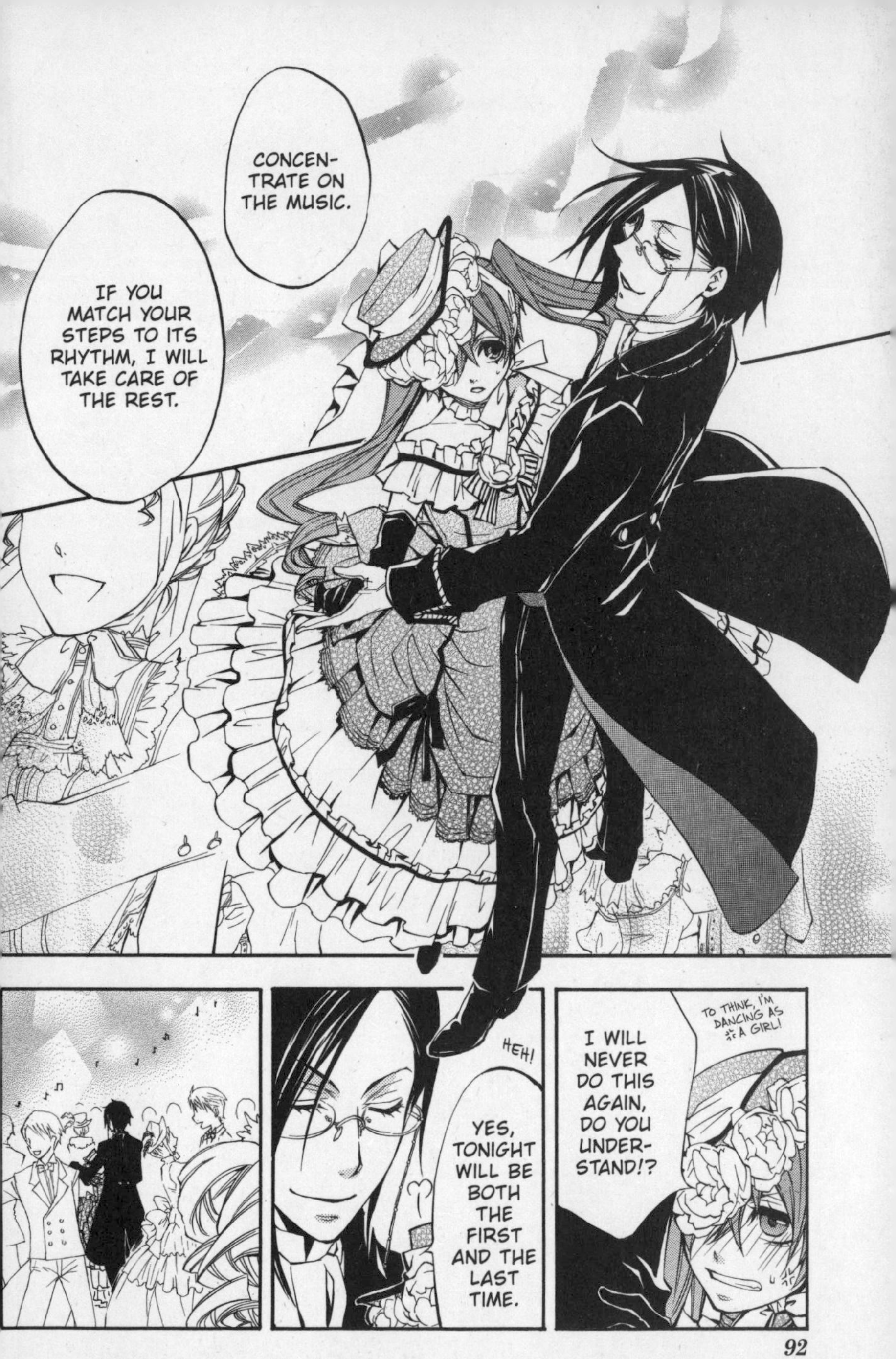
CONCENTRATE ON THE MUSIC.
IF YOU MATCH YOUR STEPS TO ITS RHYTHM, I WILL TAKE CARE OF THE REST.
TO THINK, I'M DANCING AS A GIRL!
I WILL NEVER DO THIS AGAIN, DO YOU UNDERSTAND!?
HEH!
YES, TONIGHT WILL BE BOTH THE FIRST AND THE LAST TIME.

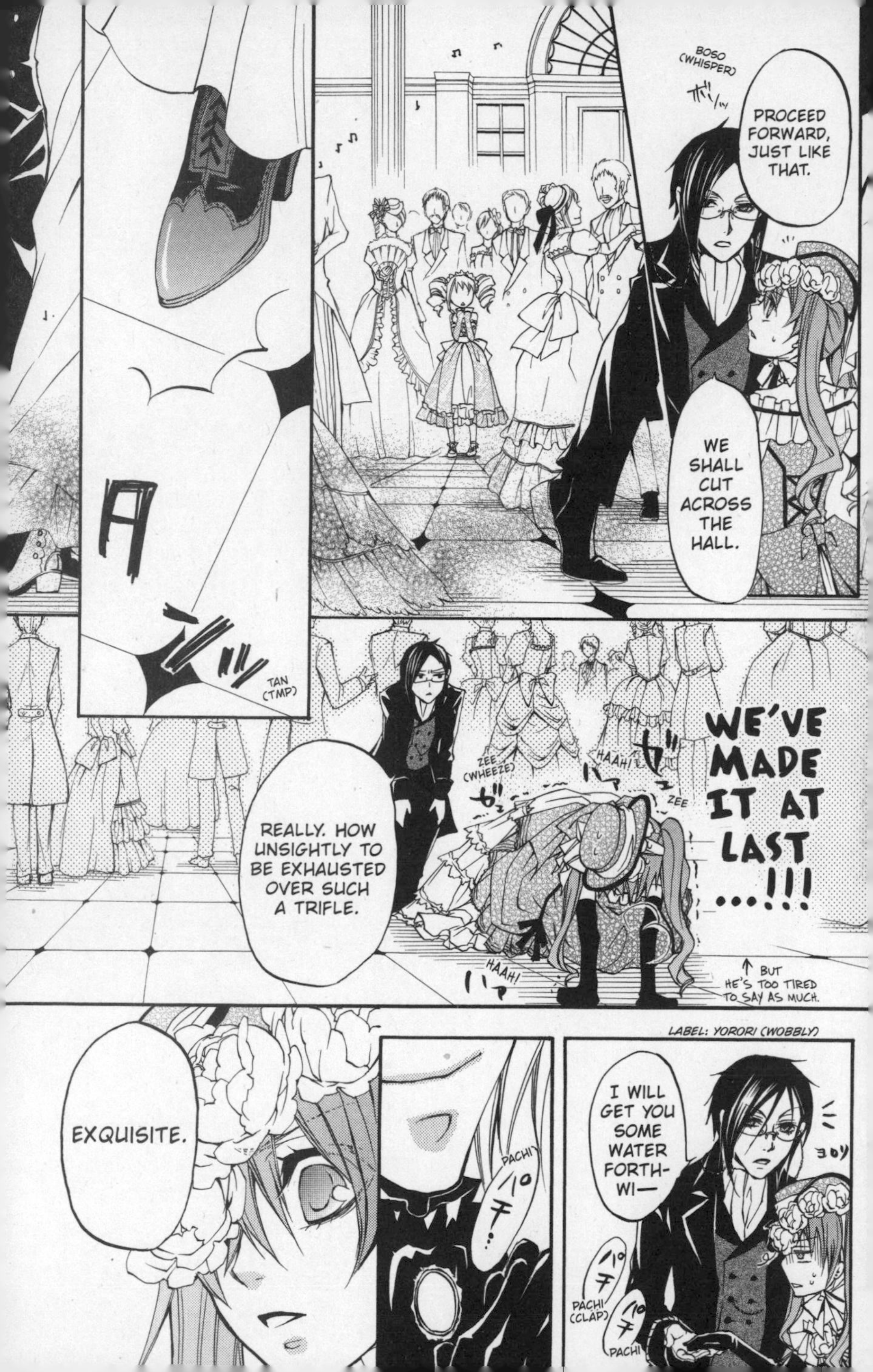
BOSO (WHISPER)
PROCEED FORWARD, JUST LIKE THAT.
WE SHALL CUT ACROSS THE HALL.
TAN (TMP)
WE'VE MADE IT AT LAST...!!!
↑ BUT HE'S TOO TIRED TO SAY AS MUCH.
HAAH!
ZEE (WHEEZE)
ZEE
REALLY. HOW UNSIGHTLY TO BE EXHAUSTED OVER SUCH A TRIFLE.
HAAH!
LABEL: YORORI (WOBBLY)
I WILL GET YOU SOME WATER FORTH-WI—
PACHI (CLAP)
PACHI
PACHI
EXQUISITE.

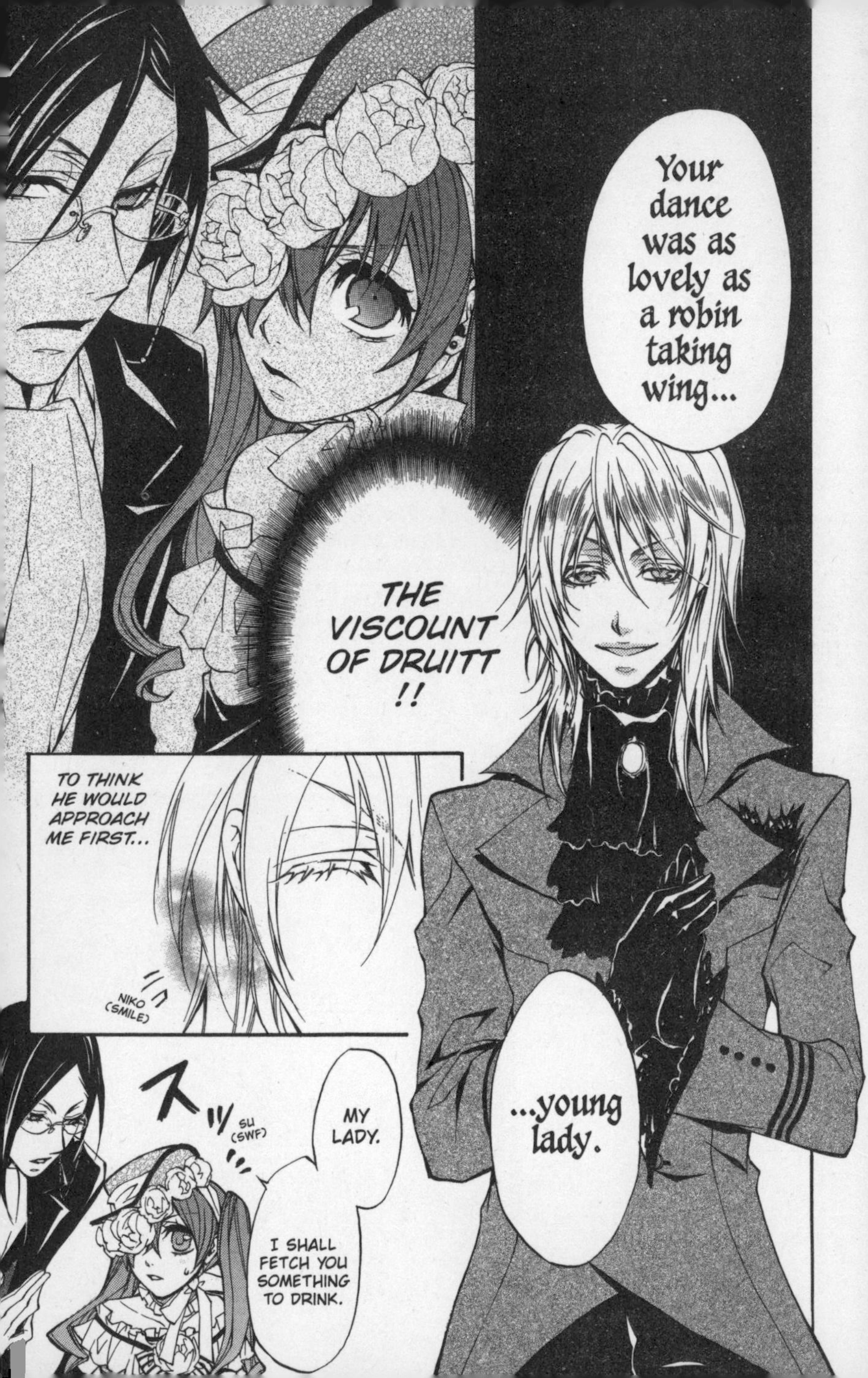
Your dance was as lovely as a robin taking wing...
...young lady.
THE VISCOUNT OF DRUITT !!
TO THINK HE WOULD APPROACH ME FIRST...
NIKO (SMILE)
SU (SWF)
MY LADY.
I SHALL FETCH YOU SOMETHING TO DRINK.

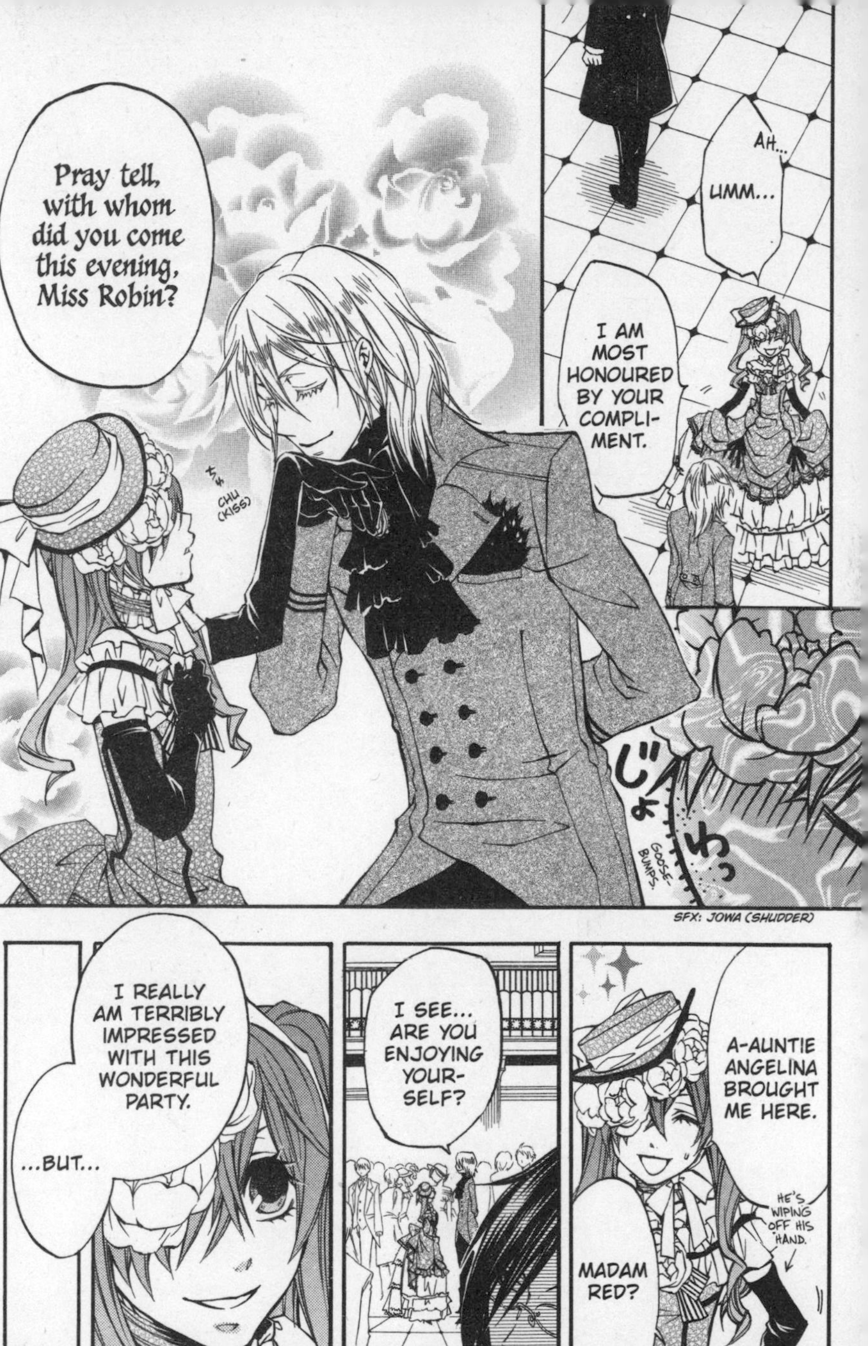
AH...
UMM...
I AM MOST HONOURED BY YOUR COMPLIMENT.
GOOSE-BUMPS.
SFX: JOWA (SHUDDER)
Pray tell, with whom did you come this evening, Miss Robin?
CHU (KISS)
A-AUNTIE ANGELINA BROUGHT ME HERE.
HE'S WIPING OFF HIS HAND.
MADAM RED?
I SEE... ARE YOU ENJOYING YOUR-SELF?
I REALLY AM TERRIBLY IMPRESSED WITH THIS WONDERFUL PARTY.
...BUT...

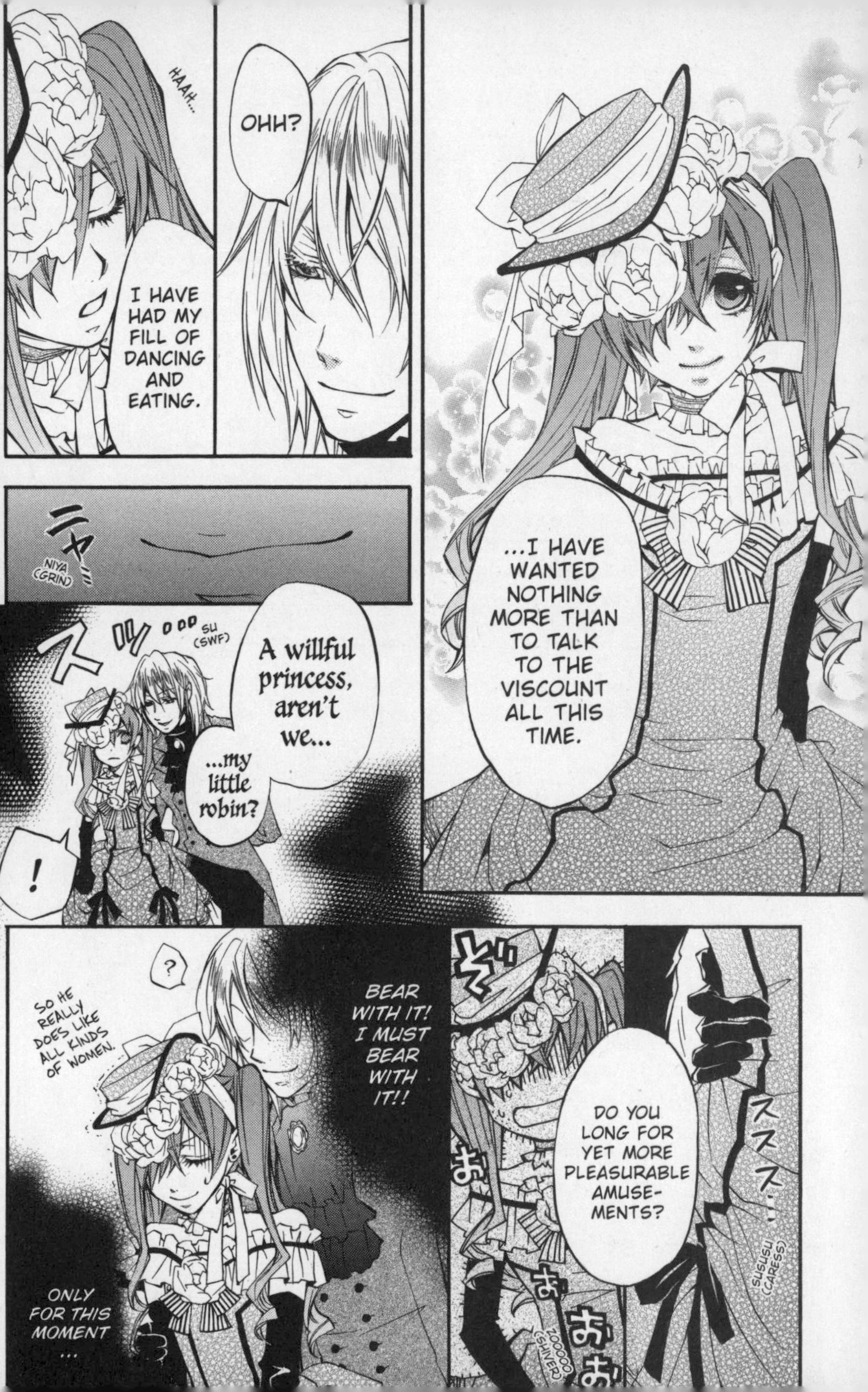
...I HAVE WANTED NOTHING MORE THAN TO TALK TO THE VISCOUNT ALL THIS TIME.
OHH?
HAAH...
I HAVE HAD MY FILL OF DANCING AND EATING.
ニヤ
NIYA (GRIN)
スッ
SU (SWF)
A willful princess, aren't we...
...my little robin?
!
ススス
SUSUSU (CARESS)
DO YOU LONG FOR YET MORE PLEASURABLE AMUSE-MENTS?
ぞぉぉぉぉ
ZOOOOO (SHIVER)
BEAR WITH IT! I MUST BEAR WITH IT!!
?
SO HE REALLY DOES LIKE ALL KINDS OF WOMEN.
ONLY FOR THIS MOMENT ...

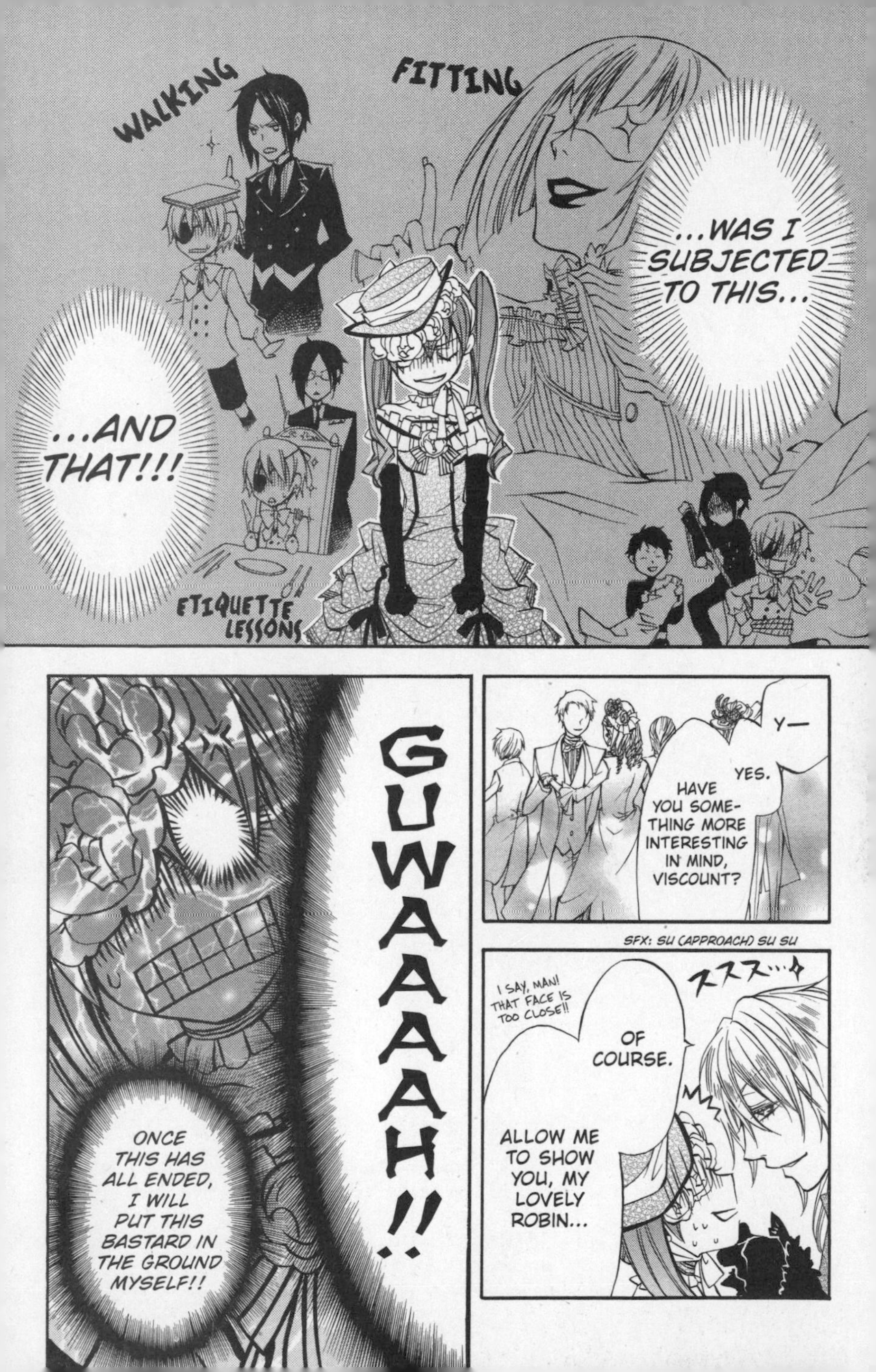
...WAS I SUBJECTED TO THIS...
FITTING
WALKING
...AND THAT!!!
ETIQUETTE LESSONS
Y—
YES. HAVE YOU SOMETHING MORE INTERESTING IN MIND, VISCOUNT?
SFX: SU (APPROACH) SU SU
ススス…♪
OF COURSE.
ALLOW ME TO SHOW YOU, MY LOVELY ROBIN...
I SAY, MAN! THAT FACE IS TOO CLOSE!!
GUWAAAAH!!
ONCE THIS HAS ALL ENDED, I WILL PUT THIS BASTARD IN THE GROUND MYSELF!!

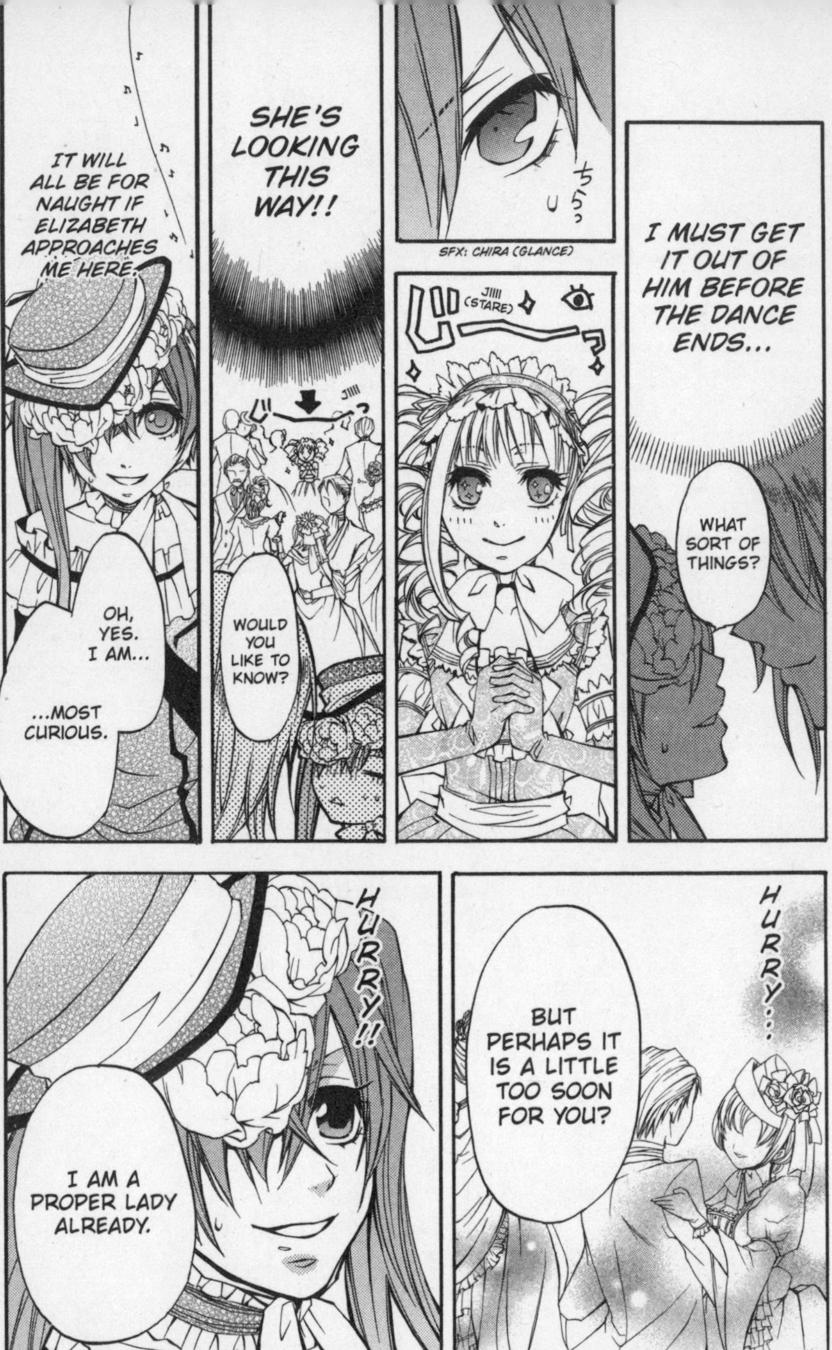
I MUST GET IT OUT OF HIM BEFORE THE DANCE ENDS...
WHAT SORT OF THINGS?
ちらっ
SFX: CHIRA (GLANCE)
JIIII (STARE)
SHE'S LOOKING THIS WAY!!
JIIII
WOULD YOU LIKE TO KNOW?
IT WILL ALL BE FOR NAUGHT IF ELIZABETH APPROACHES ME HERE.
OH, YES. I AM...
...MOST CURIOUS.
HURRY...
BUT PERHAPS IT IS A LITTLE TOO SOON FOR YOU?
HURRY!!
I AM A PROPER LADY ALREADY.

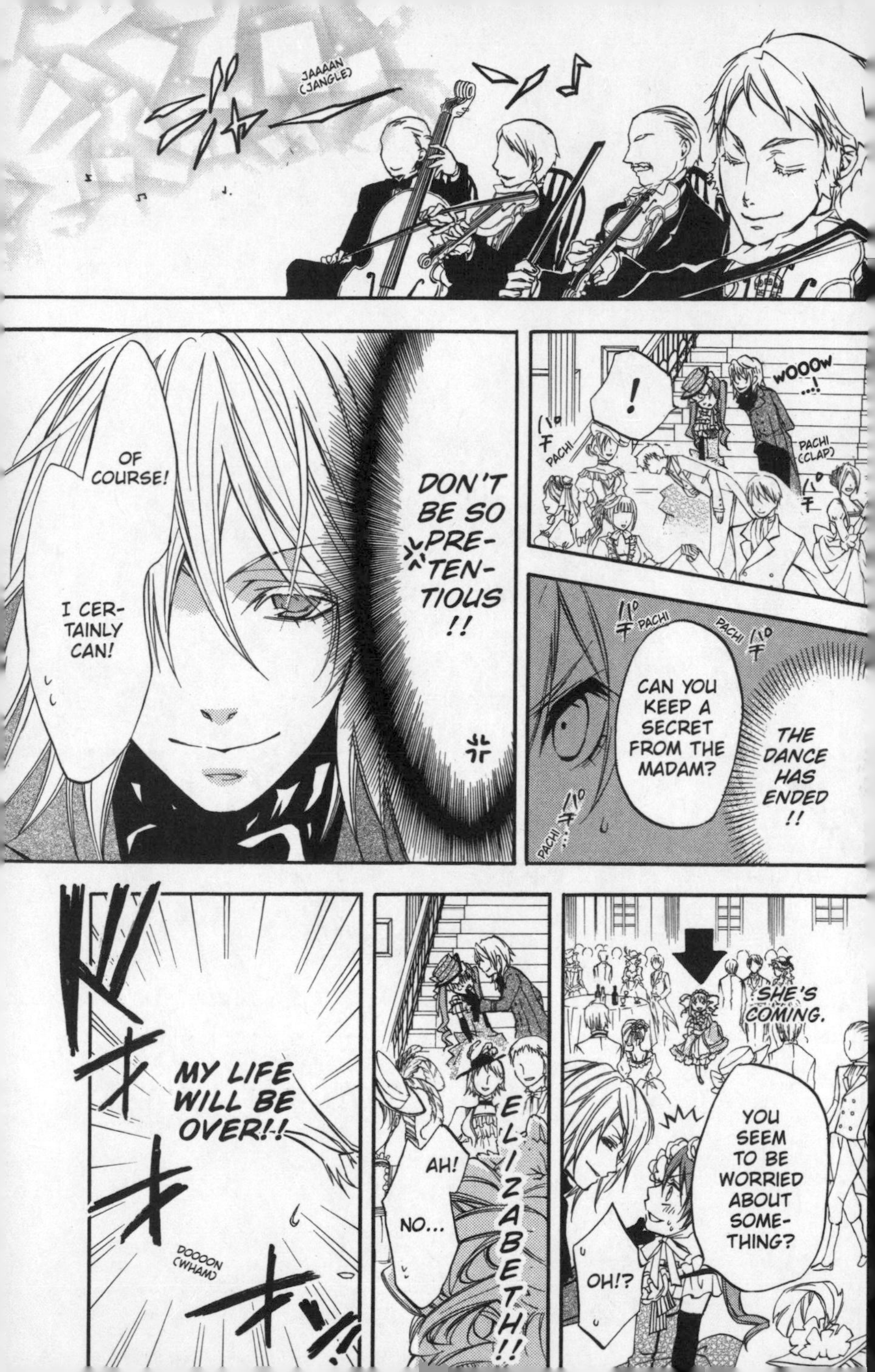
JAAAAN (JANGLE)
!
WOOOW ...!
PACHI
PACHI (CLAP)
PACHI
PACHI
CAN YOU KEEP A SECRET FROM THE MADAM?
THE DANCE HAS ENDED!!
PACHI...
DON'T BE SO PRETENTIOUS!!
OF COURSE!
I CERTAINLY CAN!
SHE'S COMING.
YOU SEEM TO BE WORRIED ABOUT SOMETHING?
OH!?
ELIZABETH!!
AH!
NO...
MY LIFE WILL BE OVER!-!
DOOOON (WHAM)

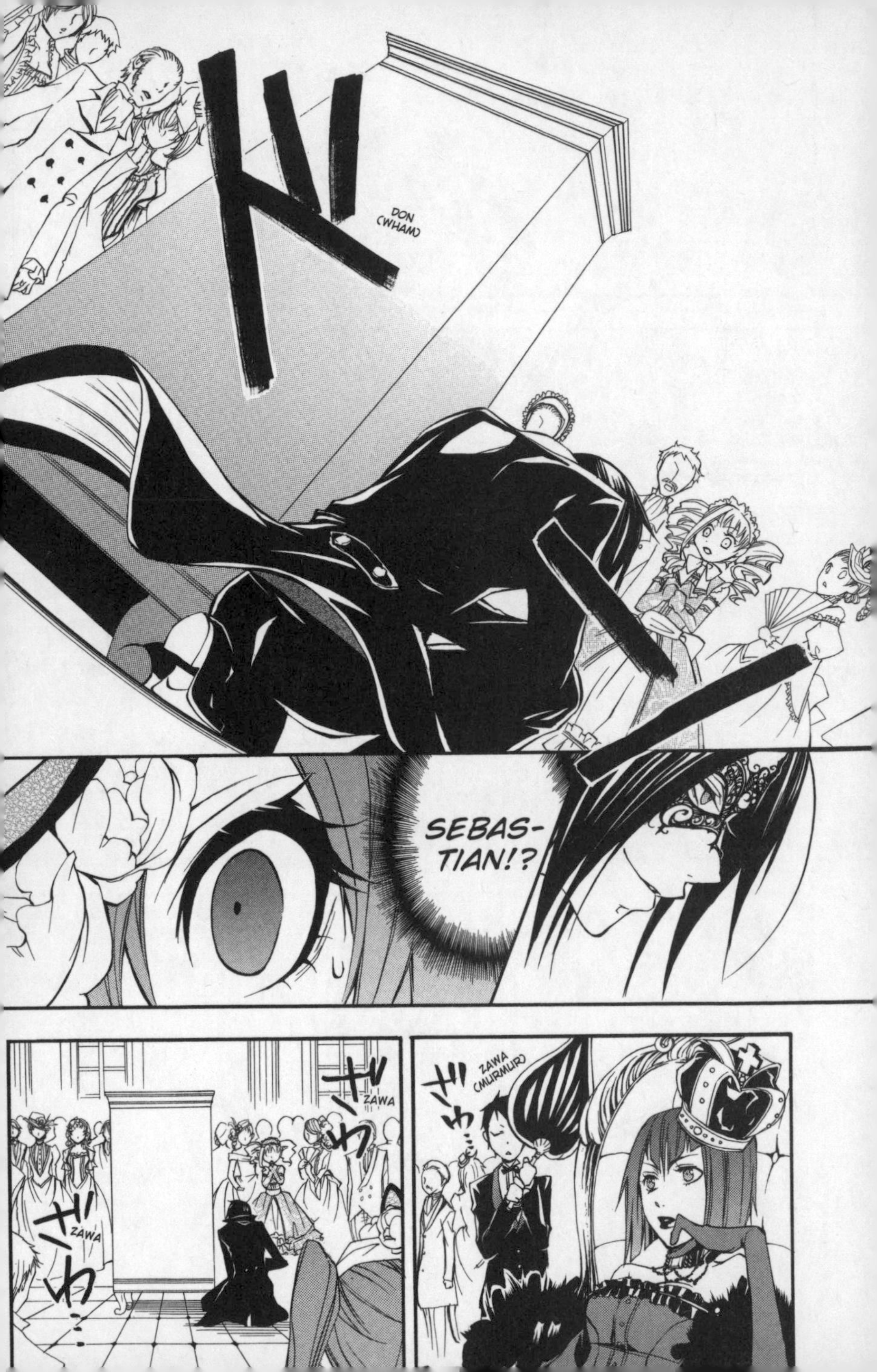
ドン
DON (WHAM)
SEBAS-TIAN!?
ざわ…
ZAWA (MURMUR)
ざわ
ZAWA
ざわ…
ZAWA

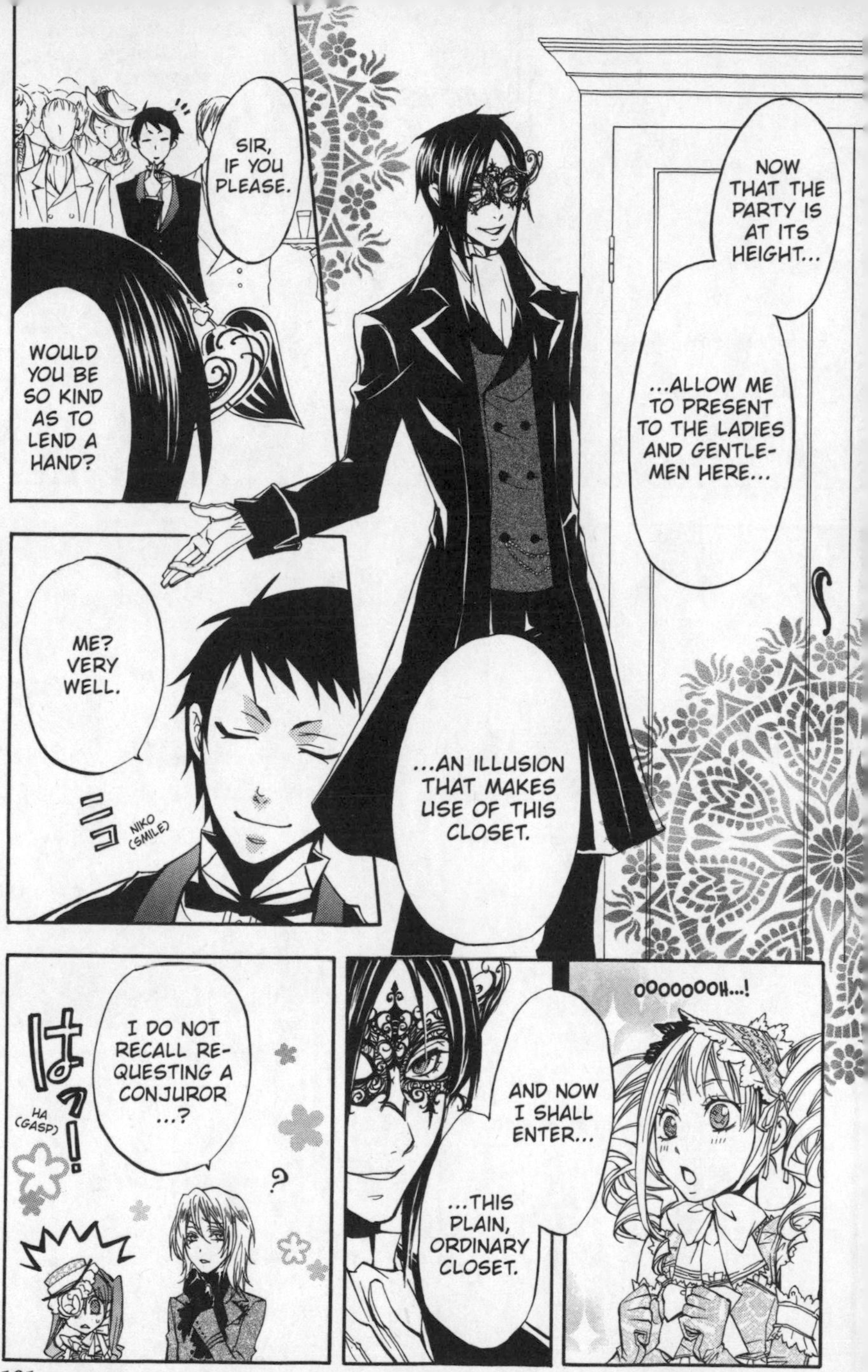
NOW THAT THE PARTY IS AT ITS HEIGHT...
...ALLOW ME TO PRESENT TO THE LADIES AND GENTLE-MEN HERE...
...AN ILLUSION THAT MAKES USE OF THIS CLOSET.
SIR, IF YOU PLEASE.
WOULD YOU BE SO KIND AS TO LEND A HAND?
ME? VERY WELL.
NIKO (SMILE)
OOOOOOOH...!
AND NOW I SHALL ENTER...
...THIS PLAIN, ORDINARY CLOSET.
I DO NOT RECALL RE-QUESTING A CONJUROR ...?
HA (GASP)

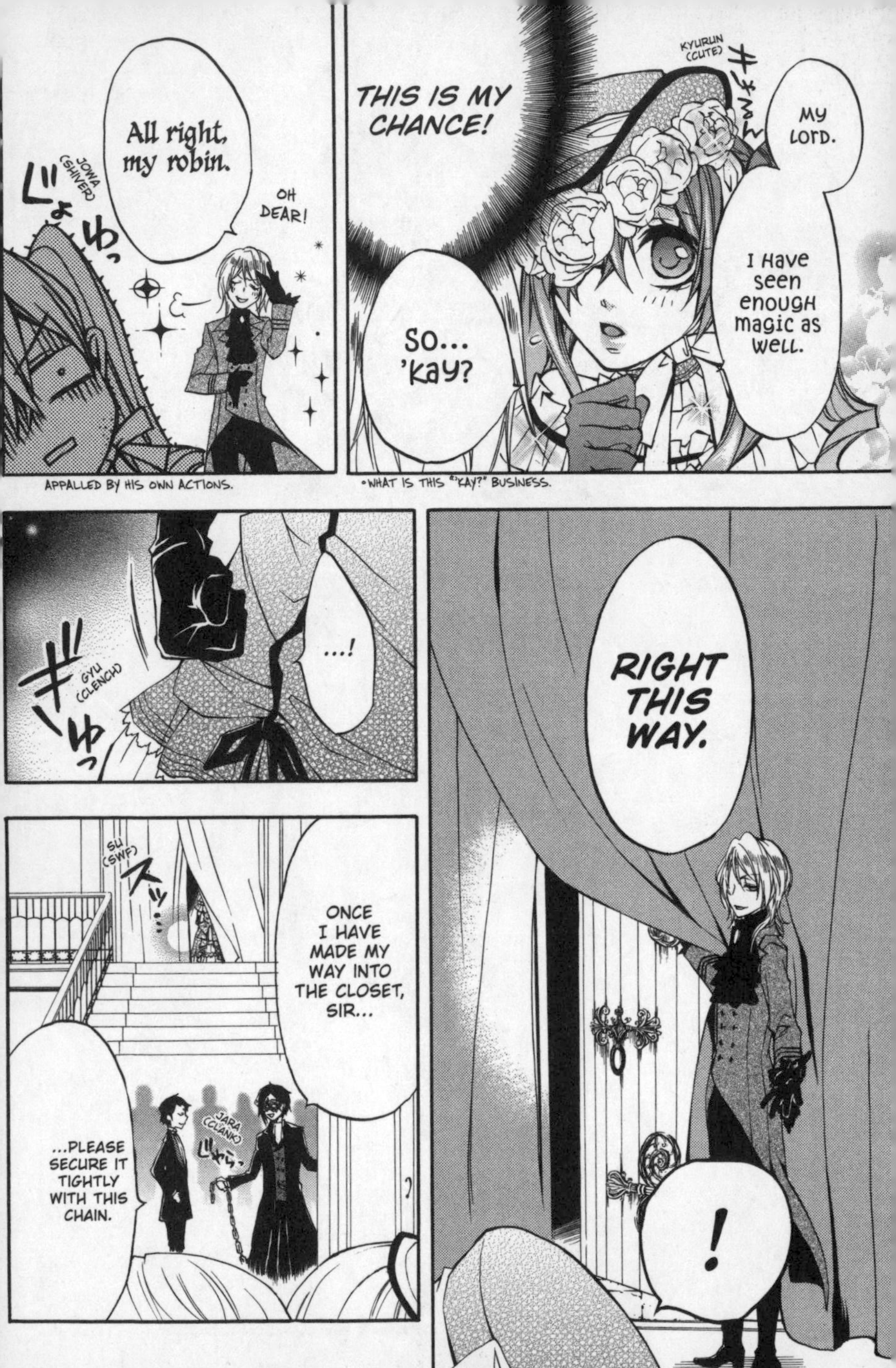
KYURUN (CUTE)
My Lord.
I have seen enough magic as well.
So... 'kay?
THIS IS MY CHANCE!
•WHAT IS THIS "'KAY?" BUSINESS.
All right, my robin.
OH DEAR!
JOWA (SHIVER)
APPALLED BY HIS OWN ACTIONS.
RIGHT THIS WAY.
!
...!
GYU (CLENCH)
ONCE I HAVE MADE MY WAY INTO THE CLOSET, SIR...
SU (SWF)
JARA (CLANK)
...PLEASE SECURE IT TIGHTLY WITH THIS CHAIN.

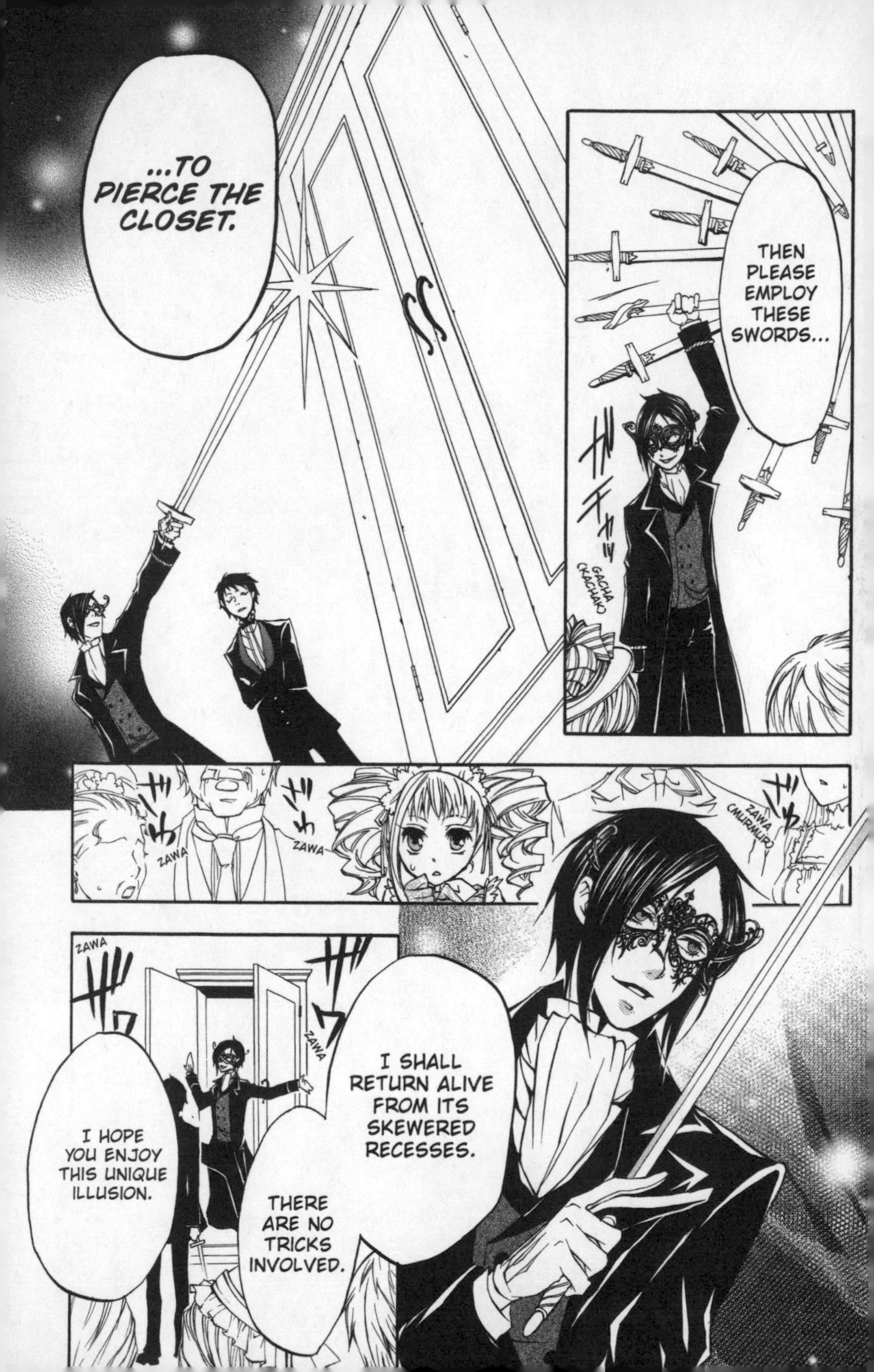
THEN PLEASE EMPLOY THESE SWORDS...
GACHA (KACHAK)
...TO PIERCE THE CLOSET.
ZAWA (MURMUR)
ZAWA
ZAWA
I SHALL RETURN ALIVE FROM ITS SKEWERED RECESSES.
THERE ARE NO TRICKS INVOLVED.
ZAWA
ZAWA
I HOPE YOU ENJOY THIS UNIQUE ILLUSION.

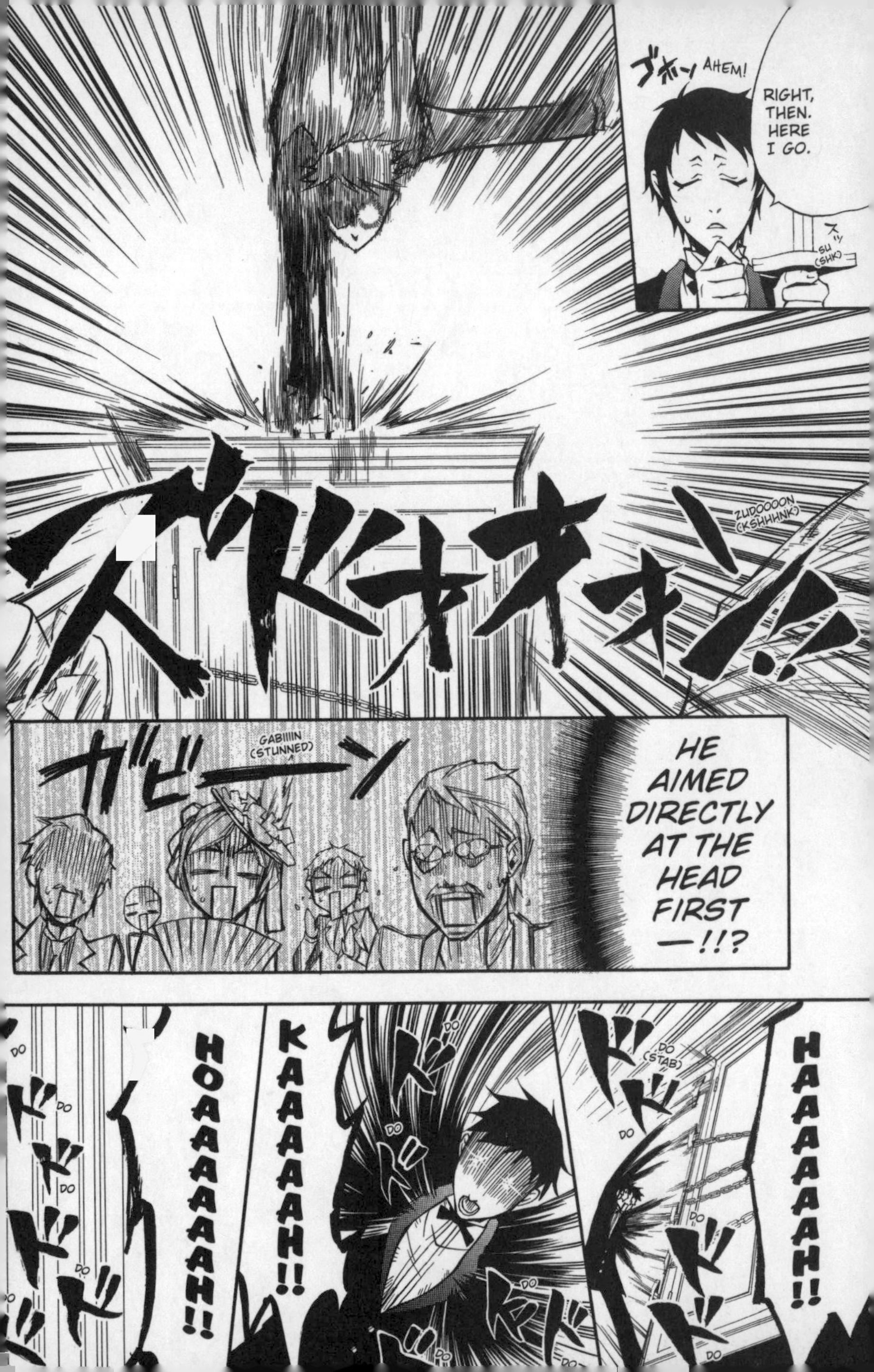
AHEM!
RIGHT, THEN. HERE I GO.
SU (SHK)
ZUDOOOOON (KSHHHHNK)
GABIIIIN (STUNNED)
HE AIMED DIRECTLY AT THE HEAD FIRST—!!?
DO (STAB)
HAAAAAAAAH!!
KAAAAAAAAH!!
HOAAAAAAAAH!!

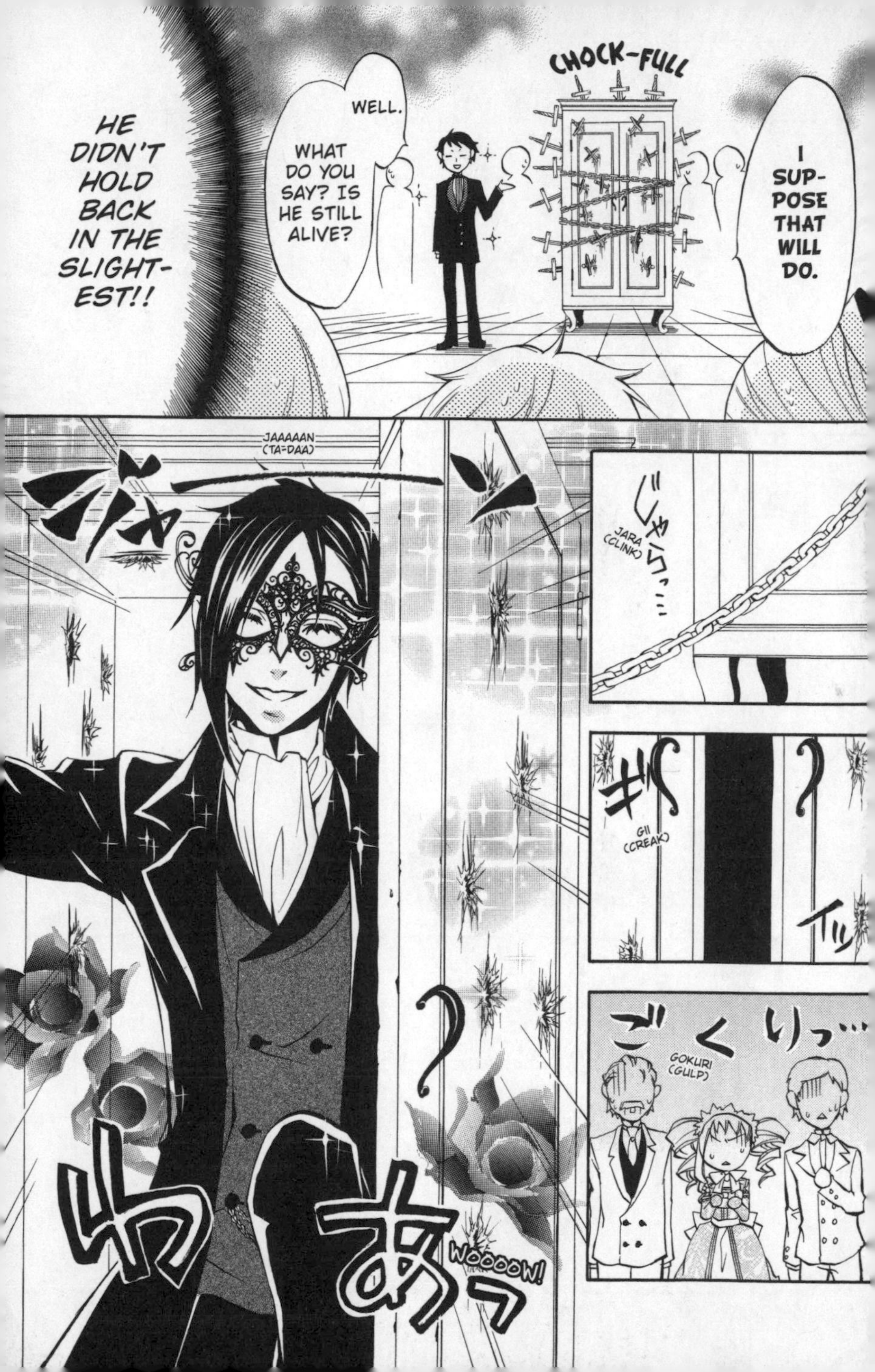
CHOCK-FULL
I SUPPOSE THAT WILL DO.
WELL.
WHAT DO YOU SAY? IS HE STILL ALIVE?
HE DIDN'T HOLD BACK IN THE SLIGHTEST!!
じゃらっ…
JARA (CLINK)
ギィ
GII (CREAK)
ごくりっ…
GOKURI (GULP)
ジャーン
JAAAAAN (TA-DAA)
わあっ
WOOOOW!

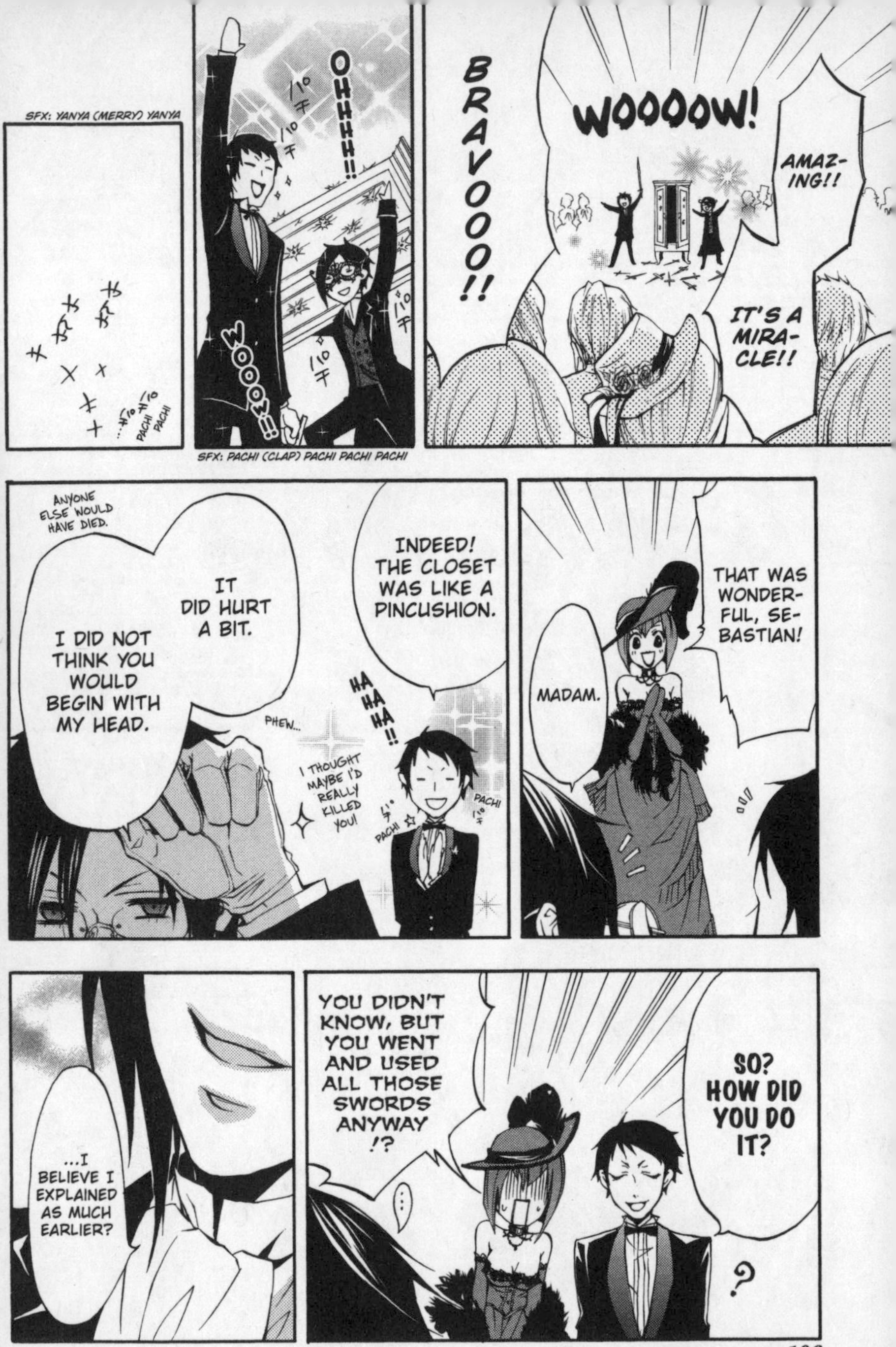
WOOOOW!
AMAZ-ING!!
IT'S A MIRA-CLE!!
BRAVOOOO!!
OHHHH!!
WOOOW!!
PACHI PACHI
SFX: PACHI (CLAP) PACHI PACHI PACHI
SFX: YANYA (MERRY) YANYA
THAT WAS WONDER-FUL, SE-BASTIAN!
MADAM.
INDEED! THE CLOSET WAS LIKE A PINCUSHION.
HA HA HA!!
PHEW...
I THOUGHT MAYBE I'D REALLY KILLED YOU!
PACHI PACHI
IT DID HURT A BIT.
I DID NOT THINK YOU WOULD BEGIN WITH MY HEAD.
ANYONE ELSE WOULD HAVE DIED.
SO? HOW DID YOU DO IT?
YOU DIDN'T KNOW, BUT YOU WENT AND USED ALL THOSE SWORDS ANYWAY!?
...
?
...I BELIEVE I EXPLAINED AS MUCH EARLIER?

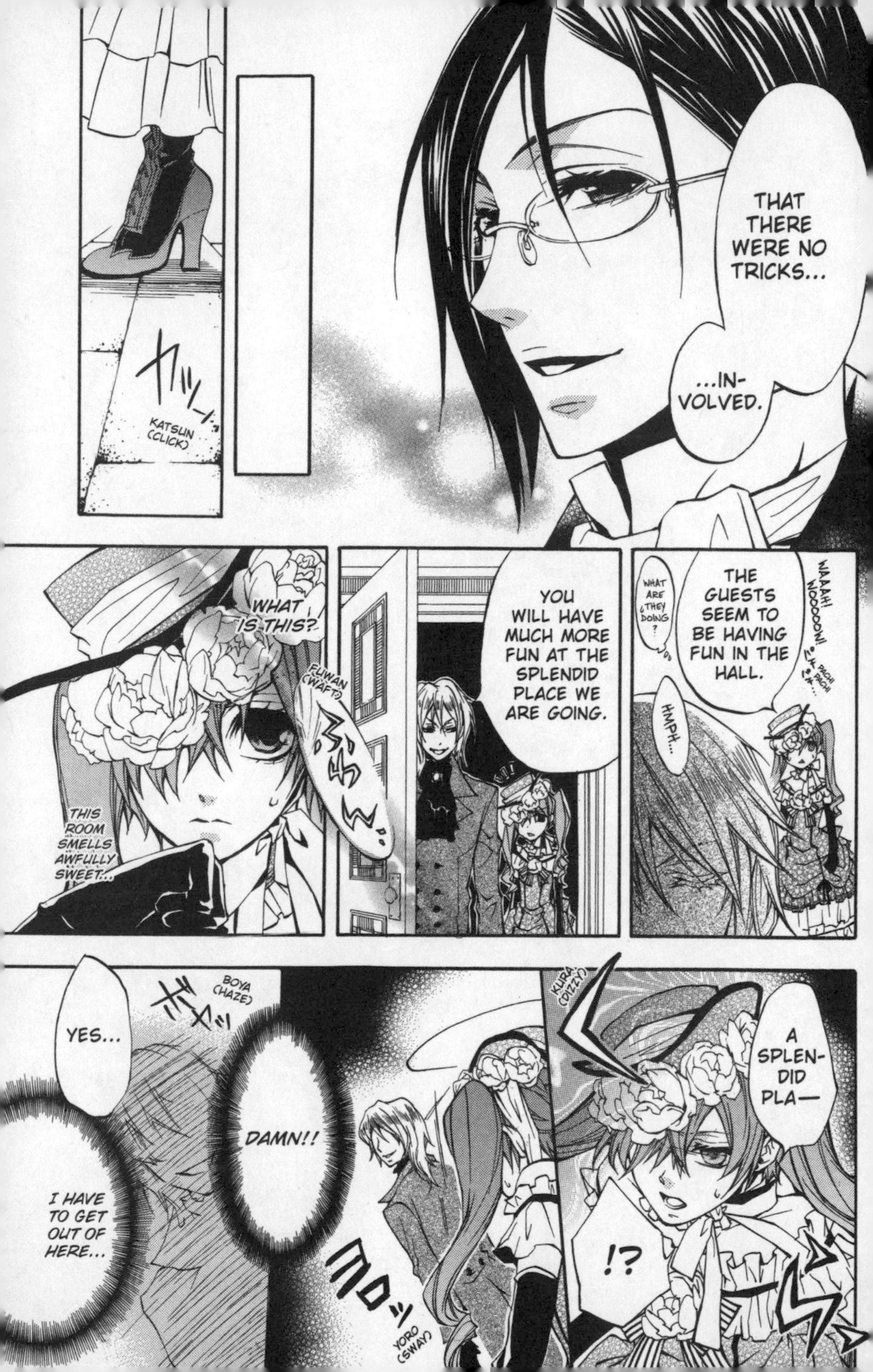
THAT THERE WERE NO TRICKS...
...IN-VOLVED.
KATSUN (CLICK)
THE GUESTS SEEM TO BE HAVING FUN IN THE HALL.
WHAT ARE THEY DOING?
WAAAH! WOOOOON!
PACHI PACHI...
HMPH...
YOU WILL HAVE MUCH MORE FUN AT THE SPLENDID PLACE WE ARE GOING.
WHAT IS THIS?
FUWAN (WAFT)
THIS ROOM SMELLS AWFULLY SWEET...
A SPLEN-DID PLA—
KURA (DIZZY)
!?
YORO (SWAY)
YES...
BOYA (HAZE)
DAMN!!
I HAVE TO GET OUT OF HERE...

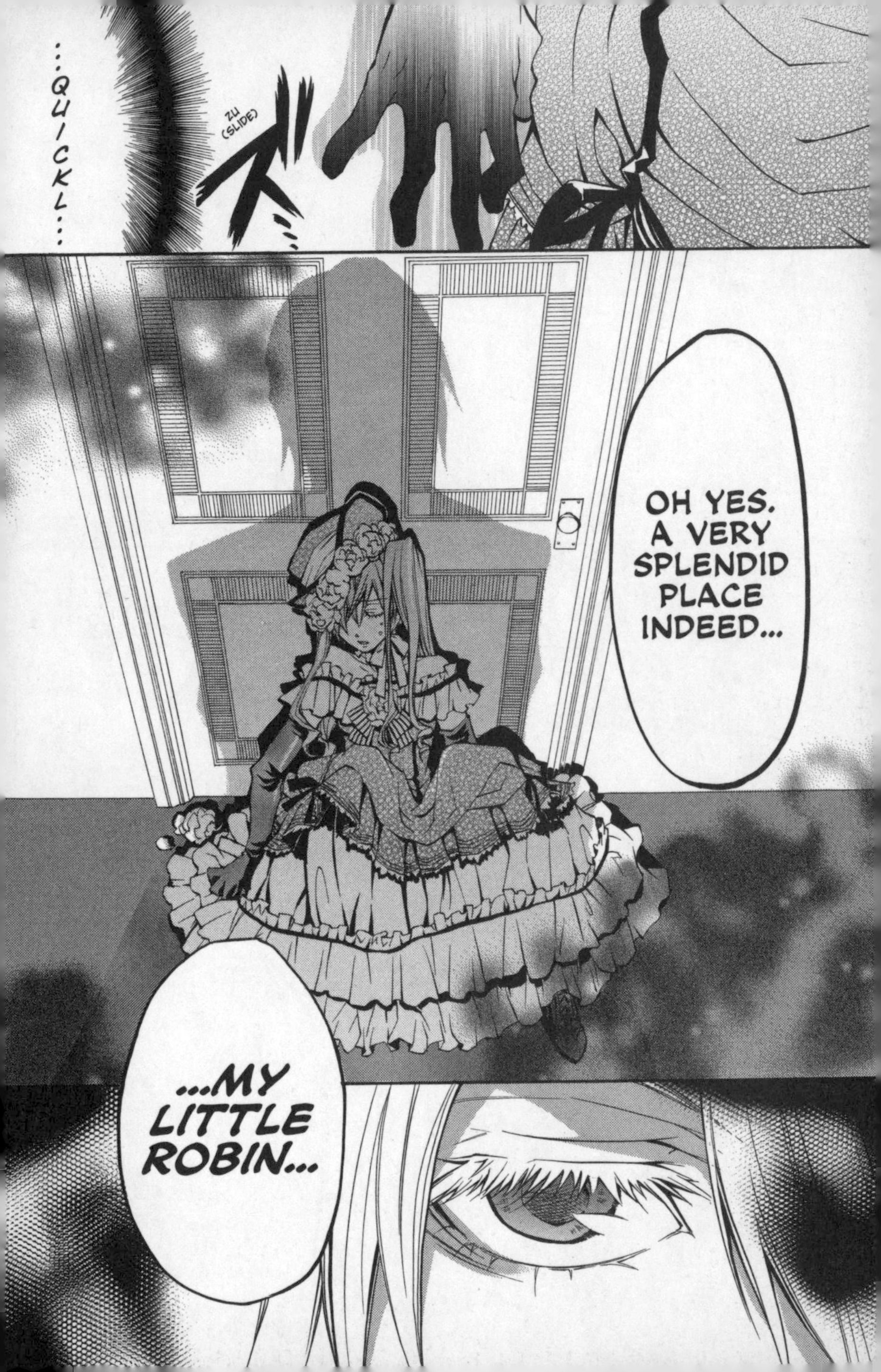
ZU (SLIDE)
...QUICKL...
OH YES. A VERY SPLENDID PLACE INDEED...
...MY LITTLE ROBIN...

Black Butler

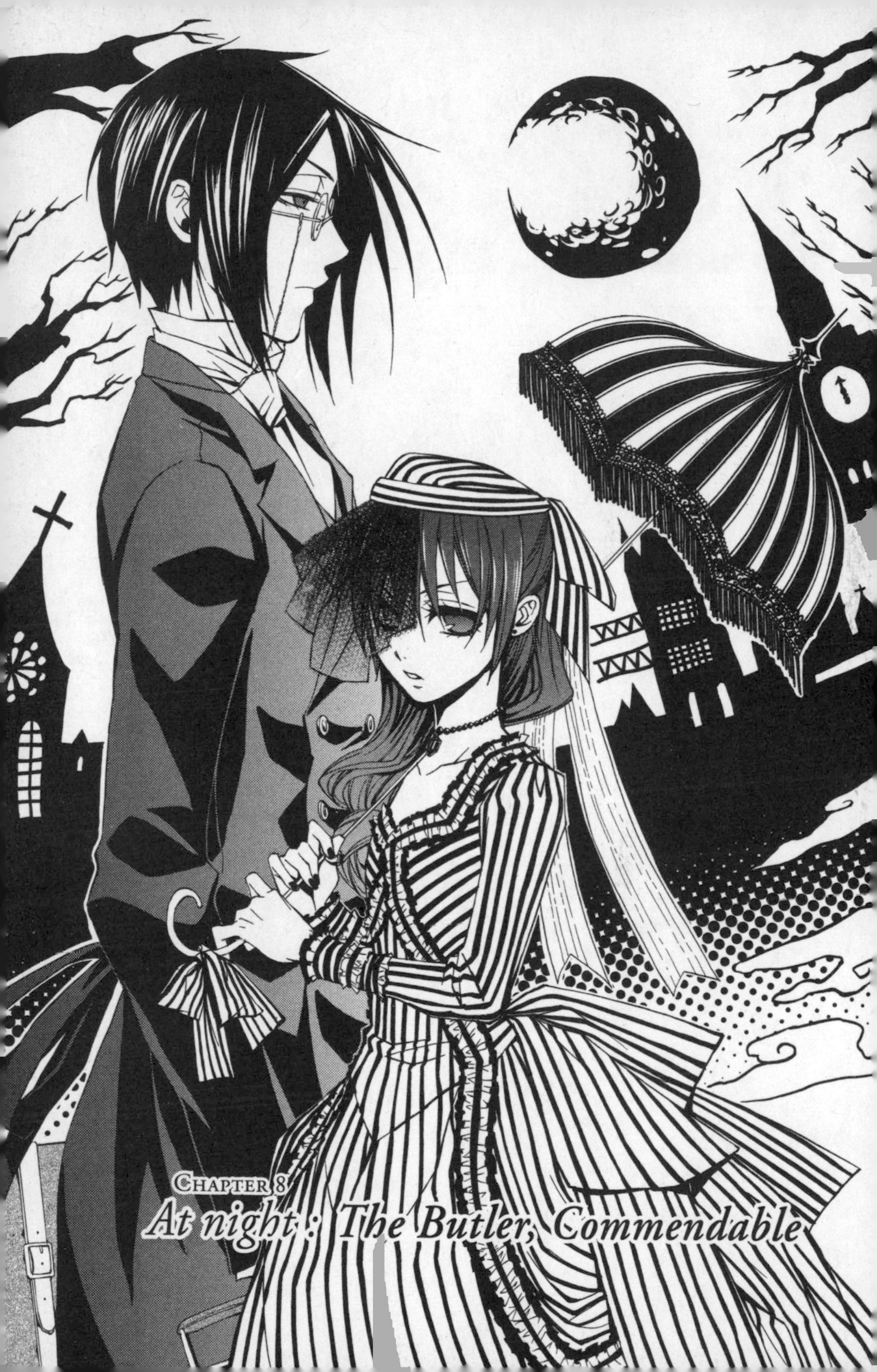
CHAPTER 8
At night : The Butler, Commendable

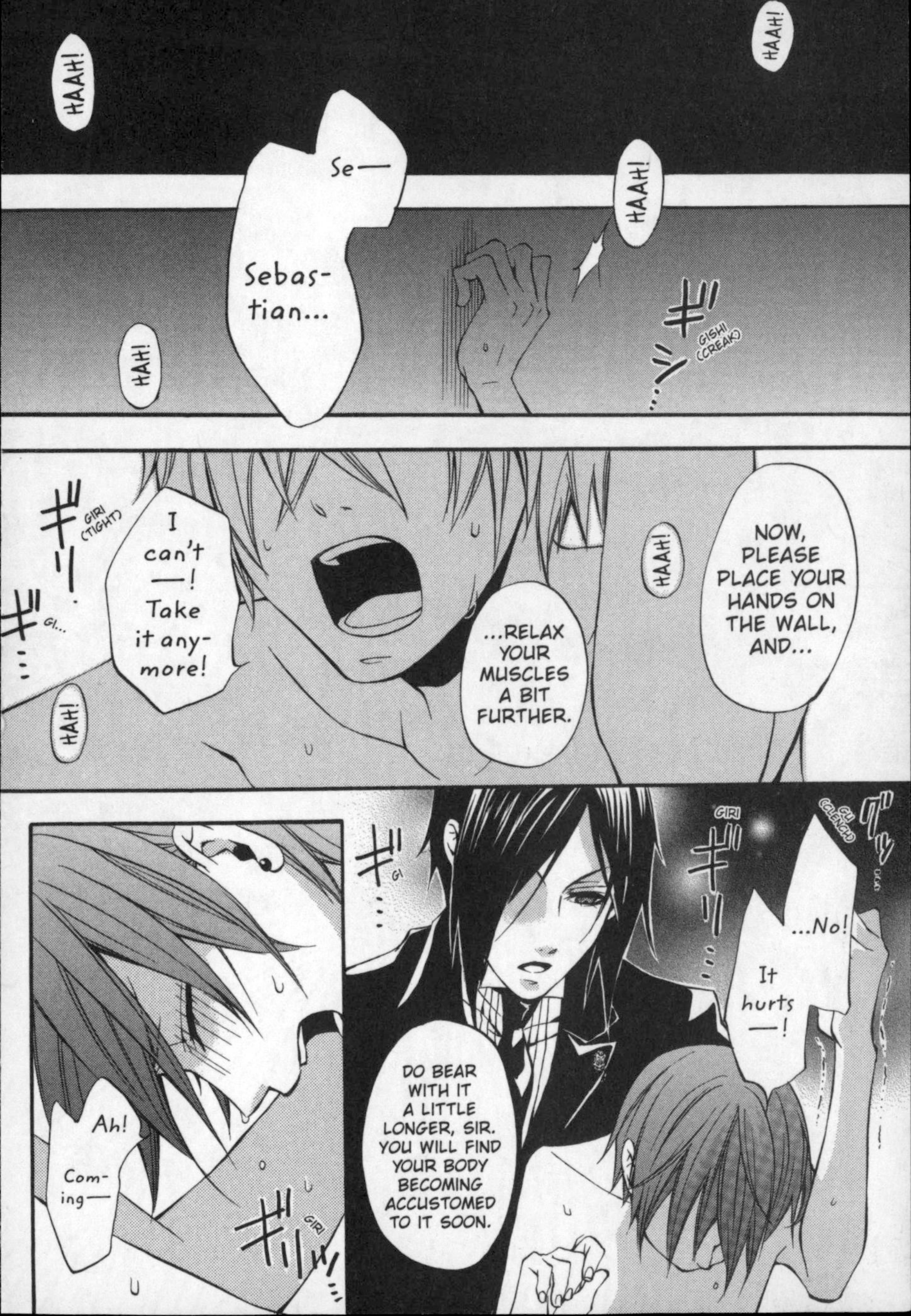
HAAAH!
HAAAH!
HAAAH!
GISHI (CREAK)
Se— Sebas-tian...
HAH!
NOW, PLEASE PLACE YOUR HANDS ON THE WALL, AND...
HAAAH!
...RELAX YOUR MUSCLES A BIT FURTHER.
I can't—! Take it any-more!
GIRI (TIGHT)
GI...
HAH!
GU (CLENCH)
GIRI
...No! It hurts—!
DO BEAR WITH IT A LITTLE LONGER, SIR. YOU WILL FIND YOUR BODY BECOMING ACCUSTOMED TO IT SOON.
GI
Ah! Com-ing—
GIRI

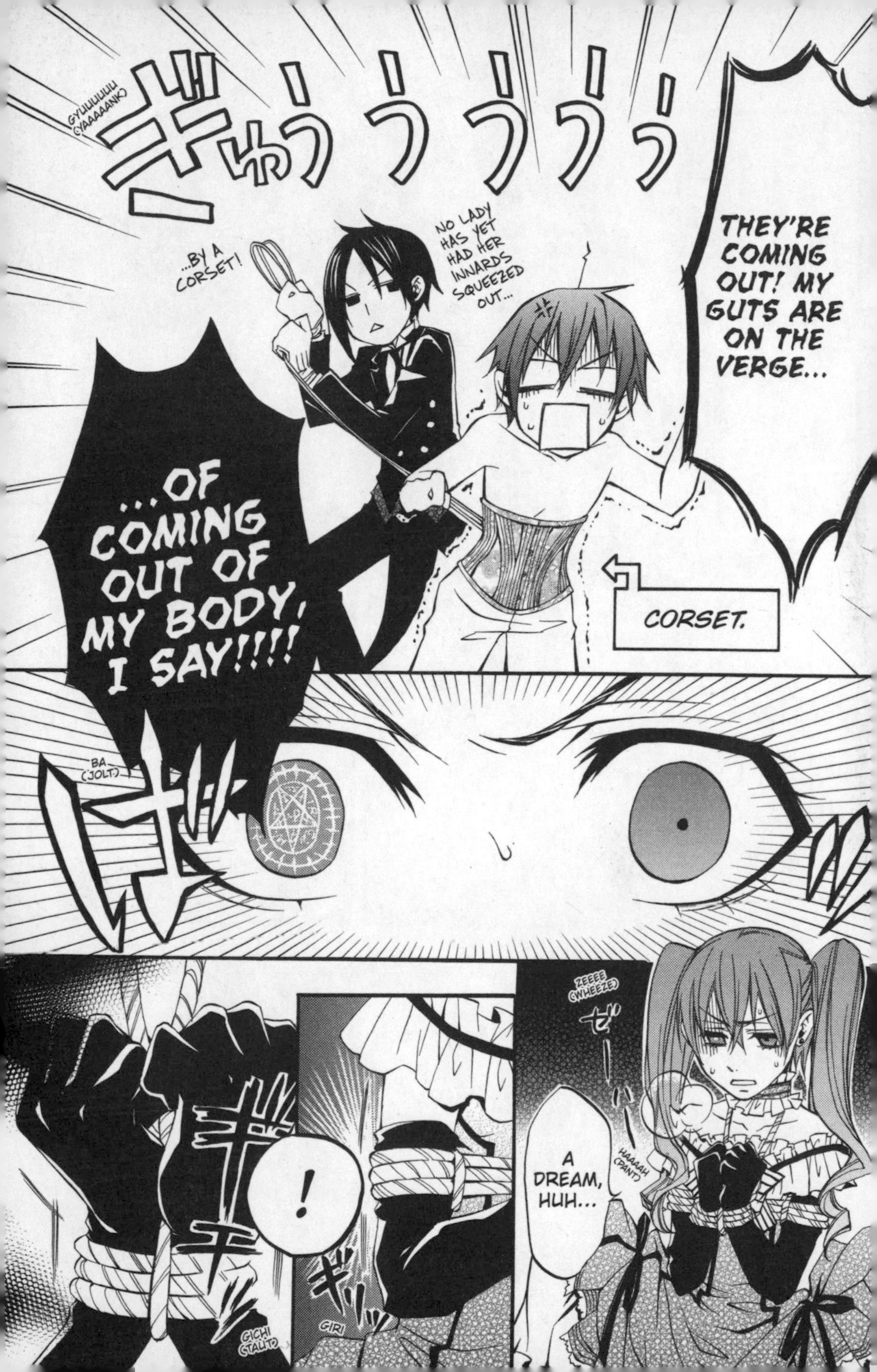
GYUUUUUU (YAAAAANK)
THEY'RE COMING OUT! MY GUTS ARE ON THE VERGE...
NO LADY HAS YET HAD HER INNARDS SQUEEZED OUT...
...BY A CORSET!
...OF COMING OUT OF MY BODY, I SAY!!!!!
CORSET.
BA (JOLT)
ZEEEE (WHEEZE)
HAAAAH (PANT)
A DREAM, HUH...
!
GIRI
GICHI (TAUT)

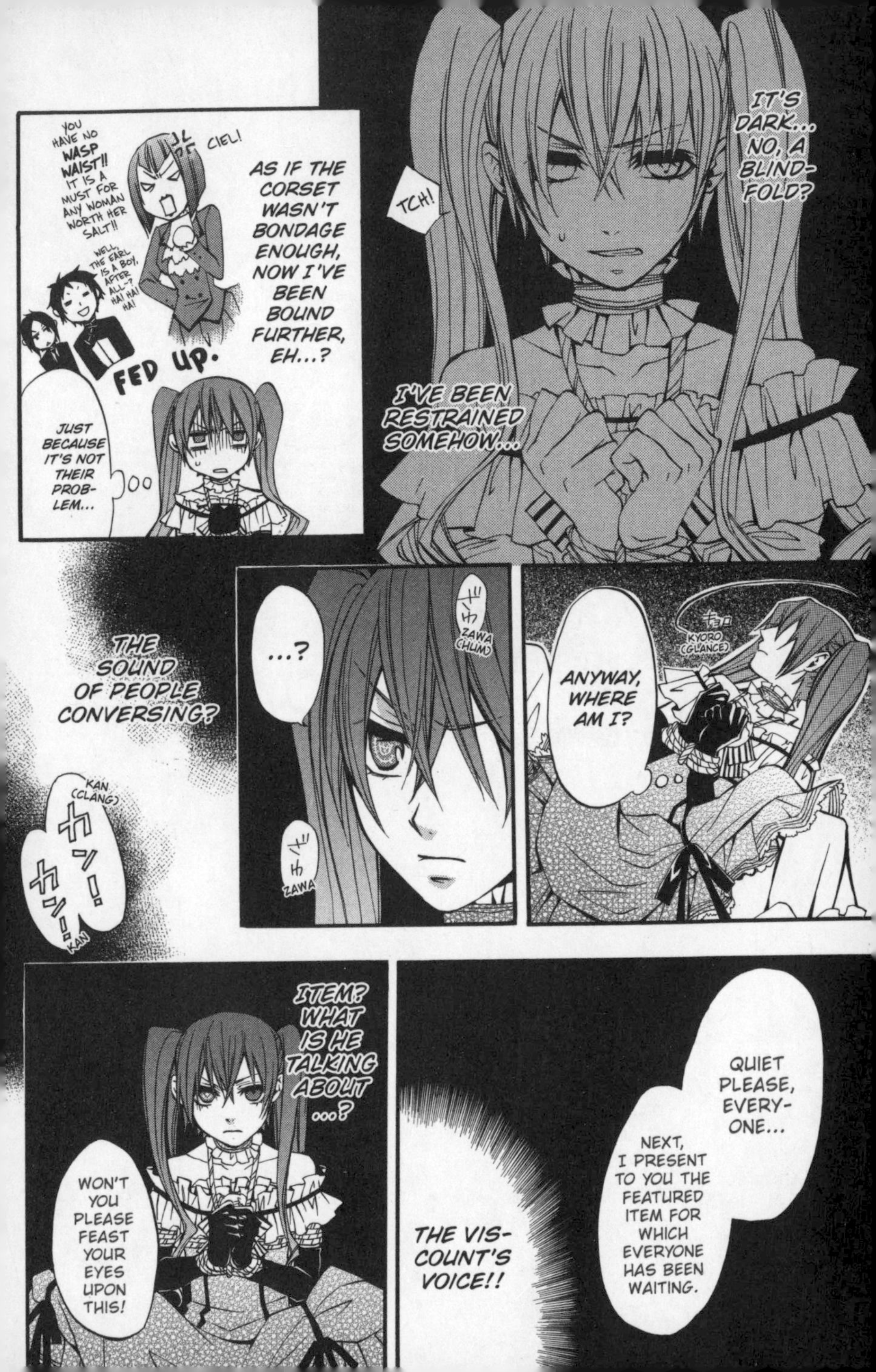
TCH!
IT'S DARK... NO, A BLINDFOLD?
I'VE BEEN RESTRAINED SOMEHOW...
AS IF THE CORSET WASN'T BONDAGE ENOUGH, NOW I'VE BEEN BOUND FURTHER, EH...?
CIEL!
YOU HAVE NO WASP WAIST!! IT IS A MUST FOR ANY WOMAN WORTH HER SALT!!
WELL, THE EARL IS A BOY, AFTER ALL~? HA! HA! HA!
FED UP.
JUST BECAUSE IT'S NOT THEIR PROBLEM...
KYORO (GLANCE)
ANYWAY, WHERE AM I?
ZAWA (HUM)
...?
ZAWA
THE SOUND OF PEOPLE CONVERSING?
KAN (CLANG)
KAN
QUIET PLEASE, EVERYONE...
NEXT, I PRESENT TO YOU THE FEATURED ITEM FOR WHICH EVERYONE HAS BEEN WAITING.
THE VISCOUNT'S VOICE!!
ITEM? WHAT IS HE TALKING ABOUT...?
WON'T YOU PLEASE FEAST YOUR EYES UPON THIS!

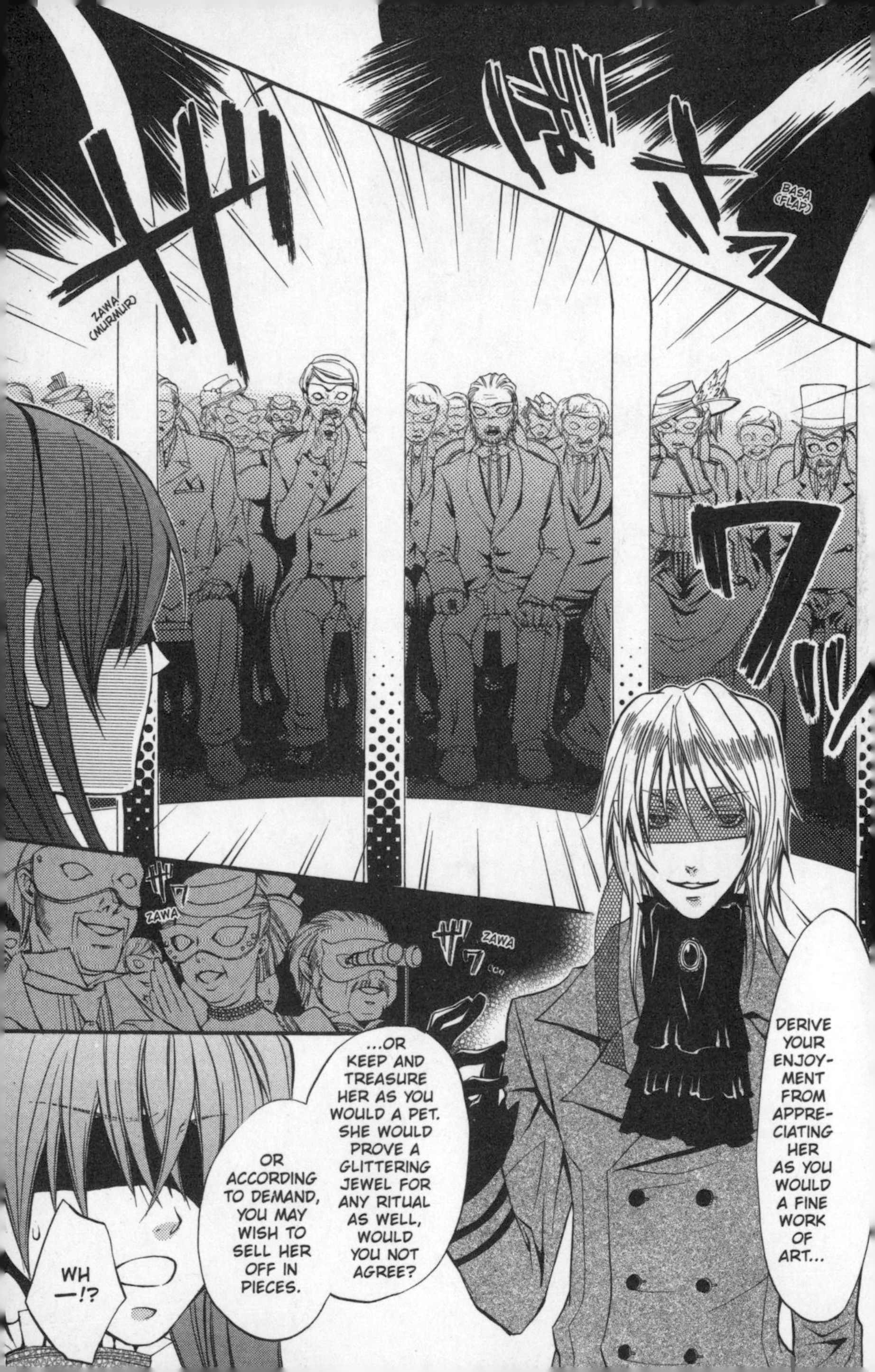
BASA (FLAP)
ZAWA (MURMUR)
ZAWA
ZAWA
DERIVE YOUR ENJOYMENT FROM APPRECIATING HER AS YOU WOULD A FINE WORK OF ART...
...OR KEEP AND TREASURE HER AS YOU WOULD A PET. SHE WOULD PROVE A GLITTERING JEWEL FOR ANY RITUAL AS WELL, WOULD YOU NOT AGREE?
OR ACCORDING TO DEMAND, YOU MAY WISH TO SELL HER OFF IN PIECES.
WH—!?

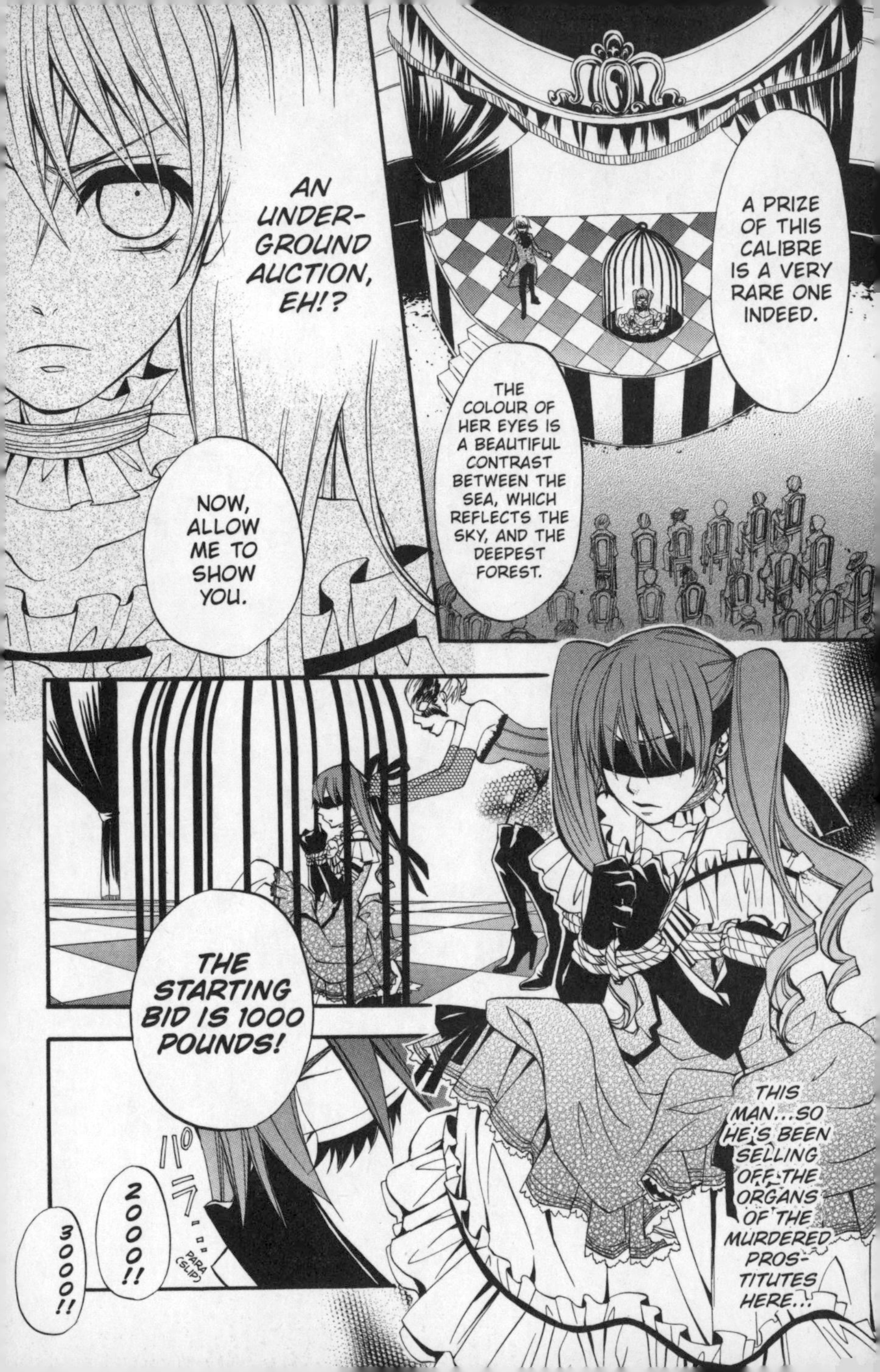
A PRIZE OF THIS CALIBRE IS A VERY RARE ONE INDEED.
THE COLOUR OF HER EYES IS A BEAUTIFUL CONTRAST BETWEEN THE SEA, WHICH REFLECTS THE SKY, AND THE DEEPEST FOREST.
AN UNDER-GROUND AUCTION, EH!?
NOW, ALLOW ME TO SHOW YOU.
THE STARTING BID IS 1000 POUNDS!
THIS MAN...SO HE'S BEEN SELLING OFF THE ORGANS OF THE MURDERED PROS-TITUTES HERE...
2000!!
PARA (SLIP)
3000!!

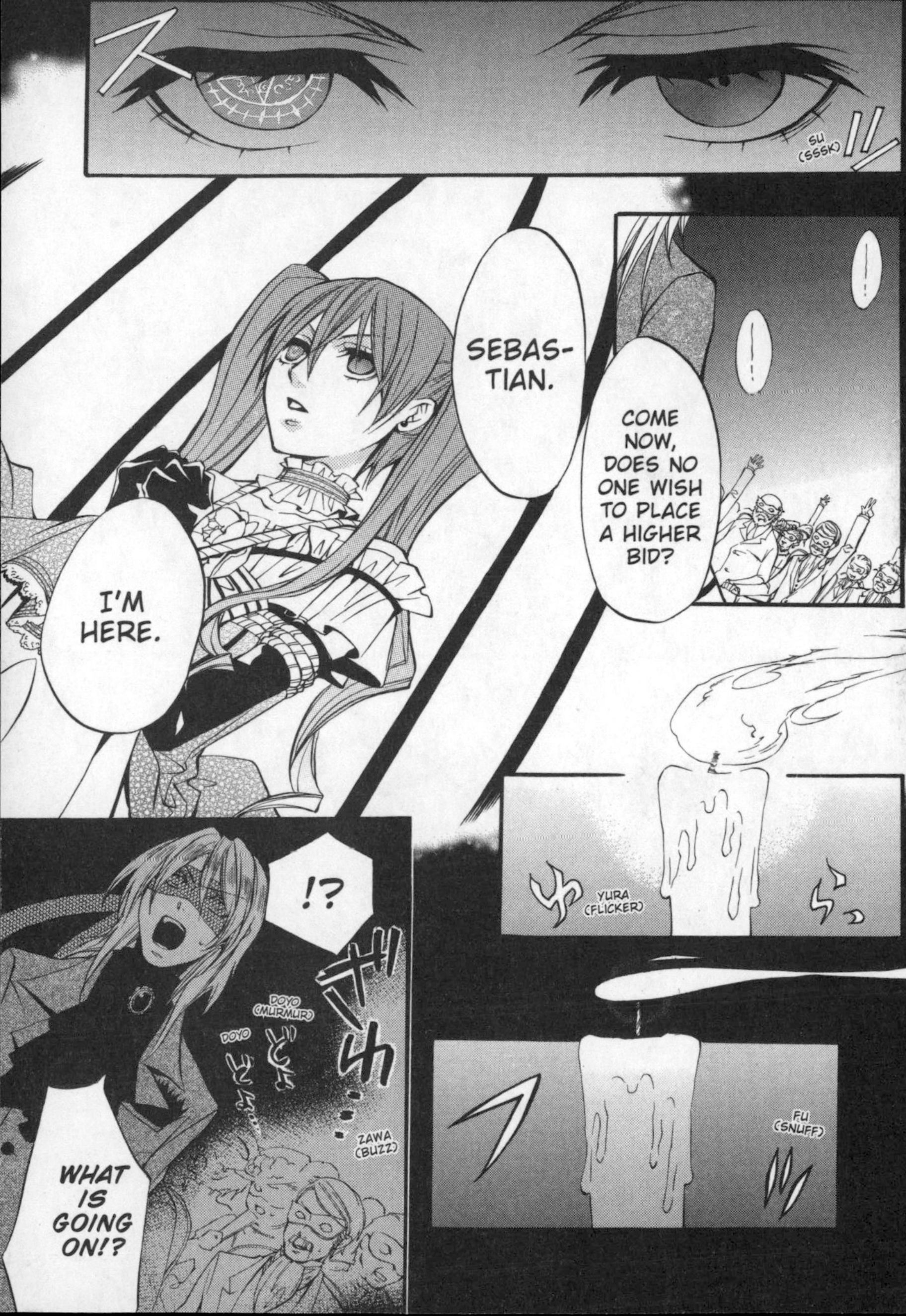
SU (SSSK)
!
!
COME NOW, DOES NO ONE WISH TO PLACE A HIGHER BID?
YURA (FLICKER)
SEBAS-TIAN.
I'M HERE.
FU (SNUFF)
!?
DOYO (MURMUR)
DOYO
ZAWA (BUZZ)
WHAT IS GOING ON!?

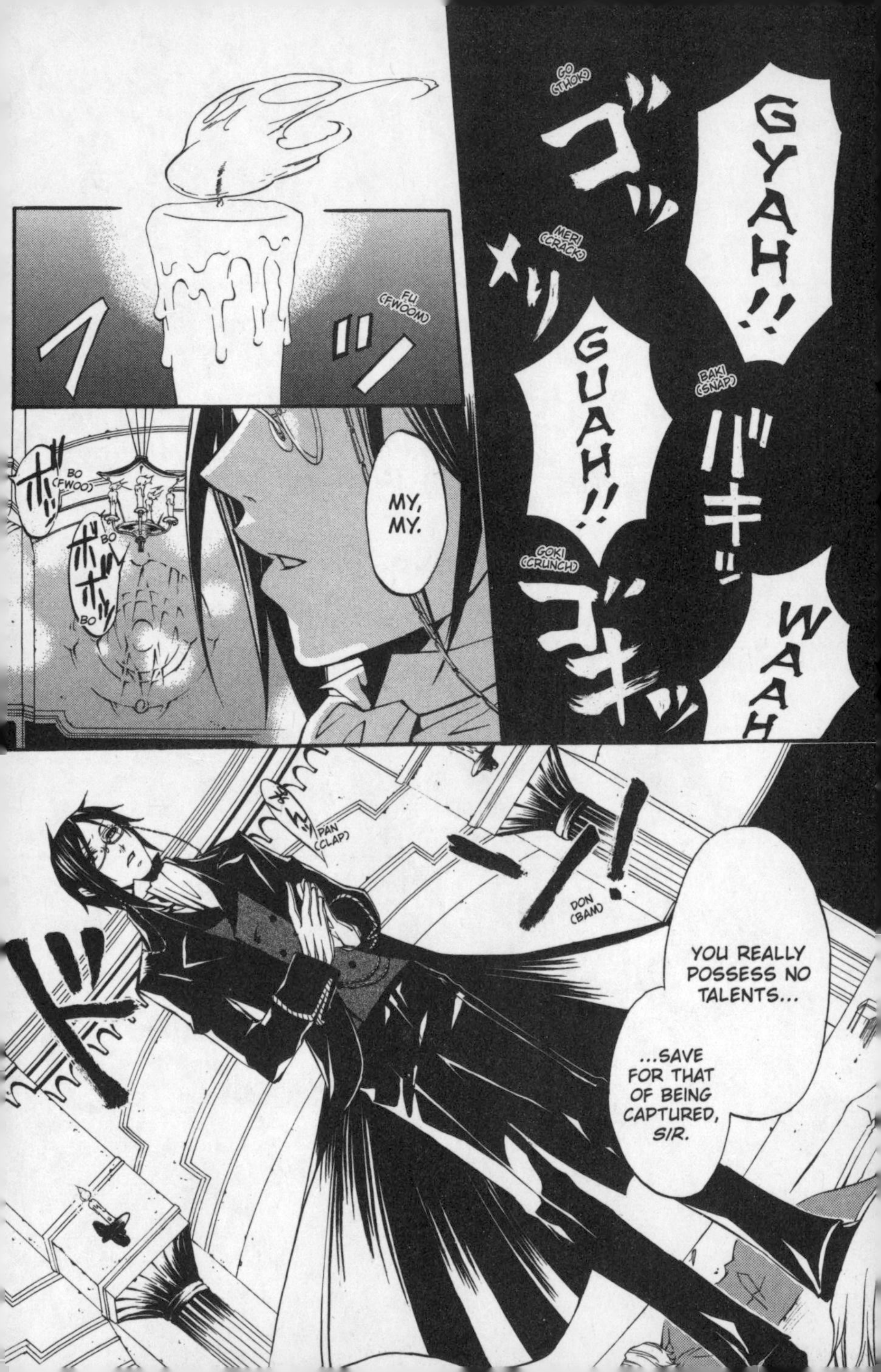
GO (THOK)
GYAH!!
MERI (CRACK)
GUAH!!
BAKI (SNAP)
GOKI (CRUNCH)
WAAH
FU (FWOOM)
MY, MY.
BO (FWOO)
BO
BO
PAN (CLAP)
DON (BAM)
YOU REALLY POSSESS NO TALENTS...
...SAVE FOR THAT OF BEING CAPTURED, SIR.

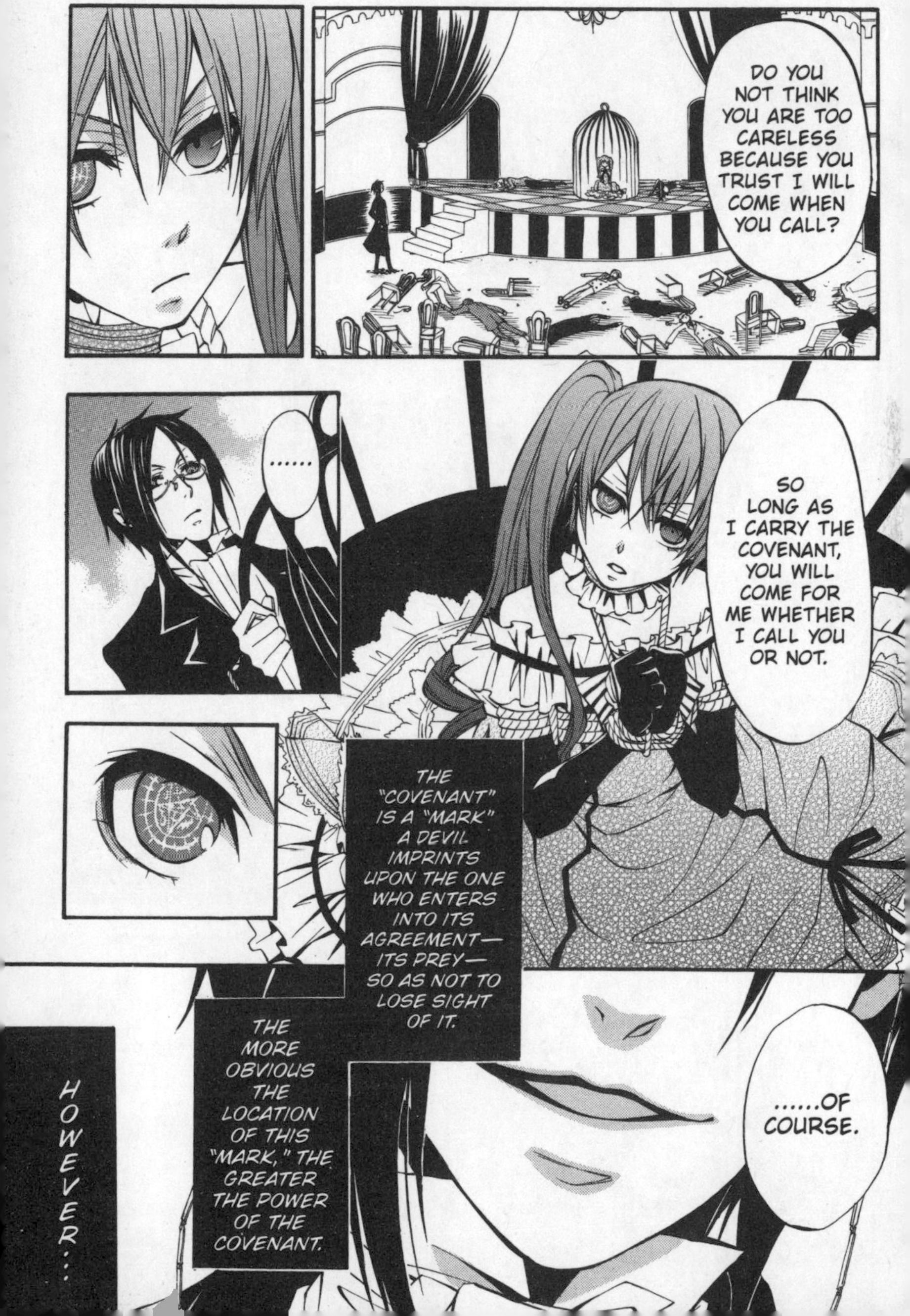
DO YOU NOT THINK YOU ARE TOO CARELESS BECAUSE YOU TRUST I WILL COME WHEN YOU CALL?
SO LONG AS I CARRY THE COVENANT, YOU WILL COME FOR ME WHETHER I CALL YOU OR NOT.
......
THE "COVENANT" IS A "MARK" A DEVIL IMPRINTS UPON THE ONE WHO ENTERS INTO ITS AGREEMENT—ITS PREY—SO AS NOT TO LOSE SIGHT OF IT.
......OF COURSE.
THE MORE OBVIOUS THE LOCATION OF THIS "MARK," THE GREATER THE POWER OF THE COVENANT.
HOWEVER...

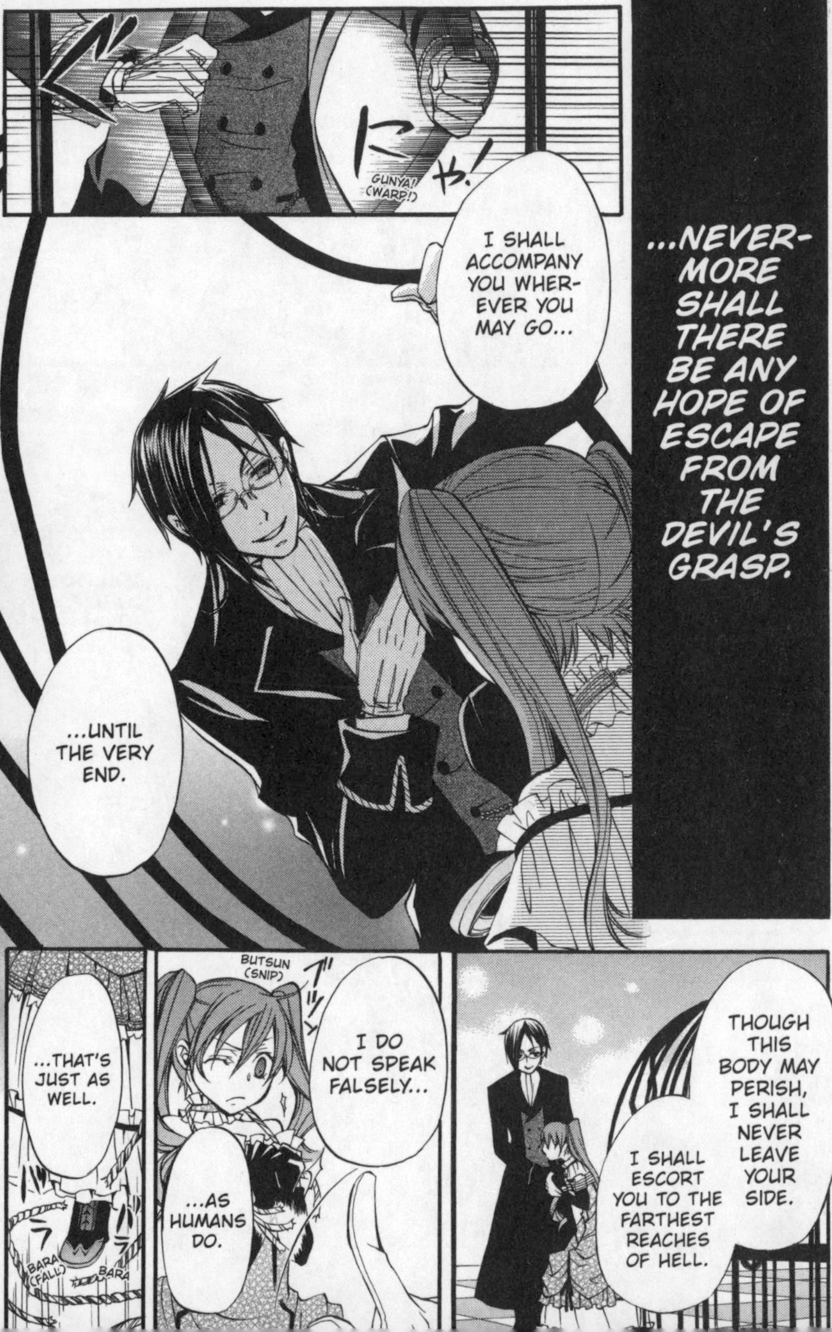
...NEVERMORE SHALL THERE BE ANY HOPE OF ESCAPE FROM THE DEVIL'S GRASP.
GUNYA! (WARP!)
I SHALL ACCOMPANY YOU WHEREVER YOU MAY GO...
...UNTIL THE VERY END.
THOUGH THIS BODY MAY PERISH, I SHALL NEVER LEAVE YOUR SIDE.
I SHALL ESCORT YOU TO THE FARTHEST REACHES OF HELL.
BUTSUN (SNIP)
I DO NOT SPEAK FALSELY...
...AS HUMANS DO.
...THAT'S JUST AS WELL.
BARA (FALL)
BARA

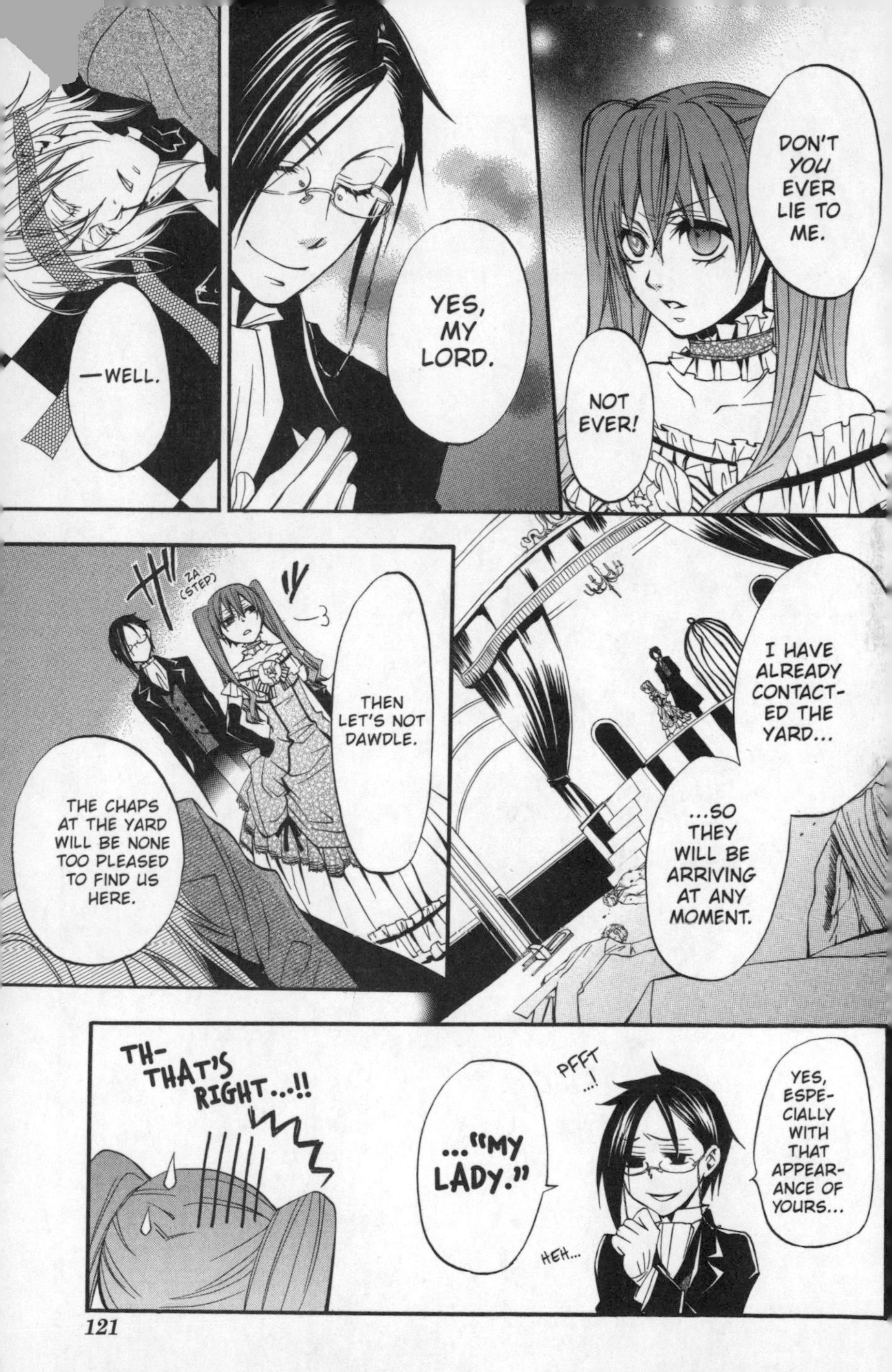
DON'T YOU EVER LIE TO ME.
NOT EVER!
YES, MY LORD.
—WELL.
I HAVE ALREADY CONTACTED THE YARD...
...SO THEY WILL BE ARRIVING AT ANY MOMENT.
ZA (STEP)
THEN LET'S NOT DAWDLE.
THE CHAPS AT THE YARD WILL BE NONE TOO PLEASED TO FIND US HERE.
YES, ESPECIALLY WITH THAT APPEARANCE OF YOURS...
PFFT ..!
HEH...
..."MY LADY."
TH-THAT'S RIGHT...!!

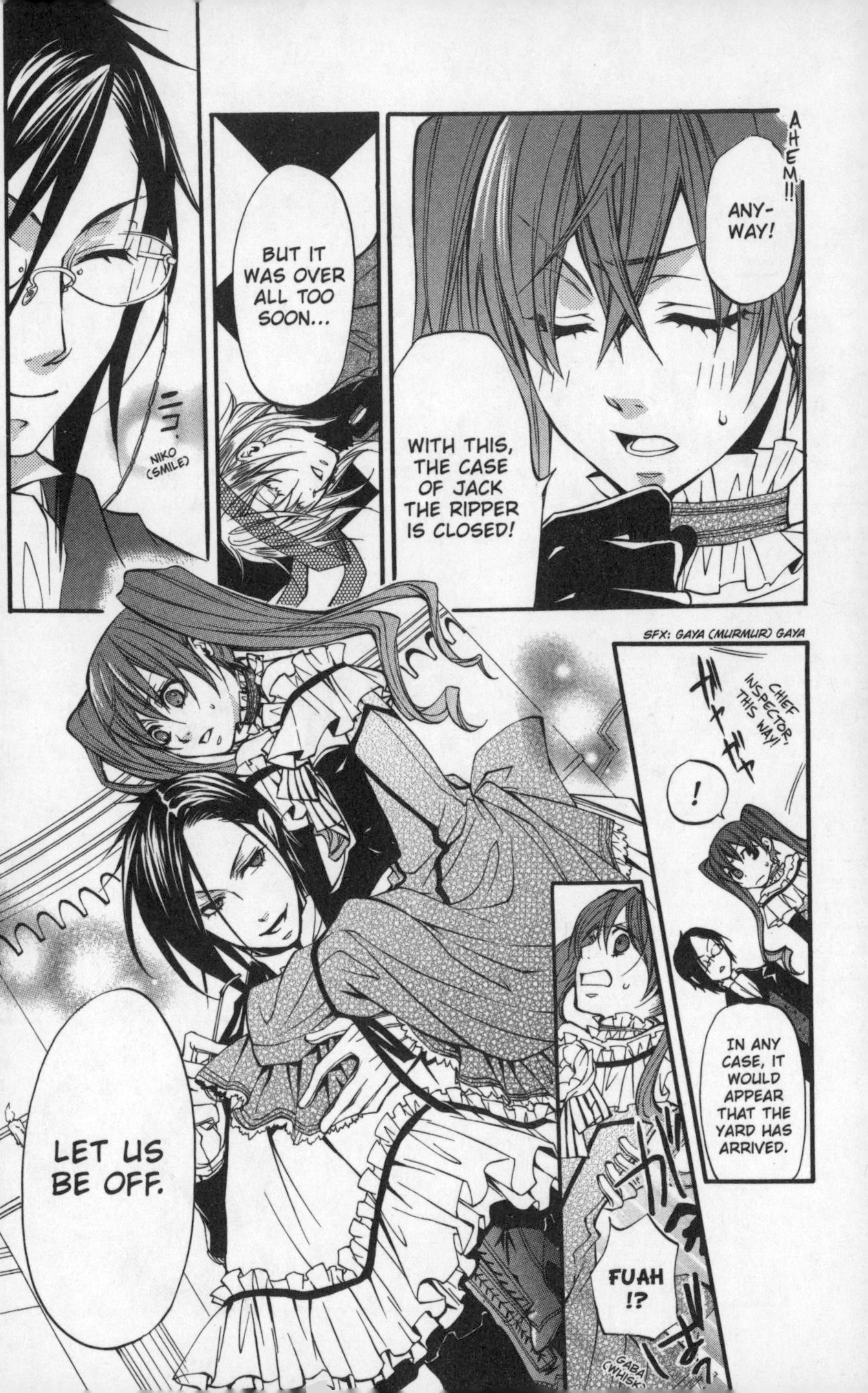
AHEM!!
ANY-WAY!
WITH THIS, THE CASE OF JACK THE RIPPER IS CLOSED!
BUT IT WAS OVER ALL TOO SOON...
NIKO (SMILE)
SFX: GAYA (MURMUR) GAYA
CHIEF INSPECTOR, THIS WAY!
!
IN ANY CASE, IT WOULD APPEAR THAT THE YARD HAS ARRIVED.
FUAH !?
GABA (WHISK)
LET US BE OFF.

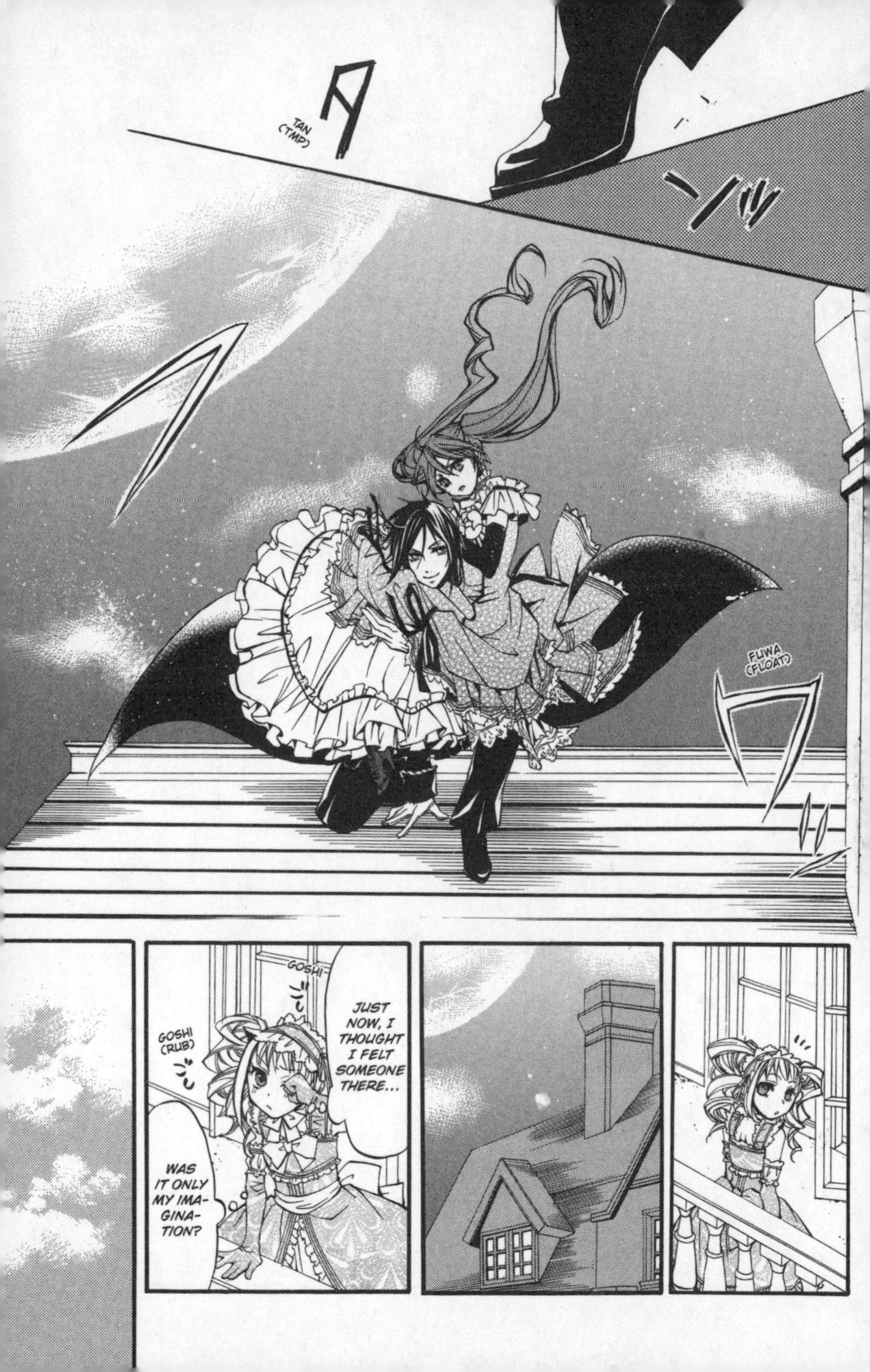
TAN (TMP)
FUWA (FLOAT)
JUST NOW, I THOUGHT I FELT SOMEONE THERE...
GOSHI
GOSHI (RUB)
WAS IT ONLY MY IMAGINATION?

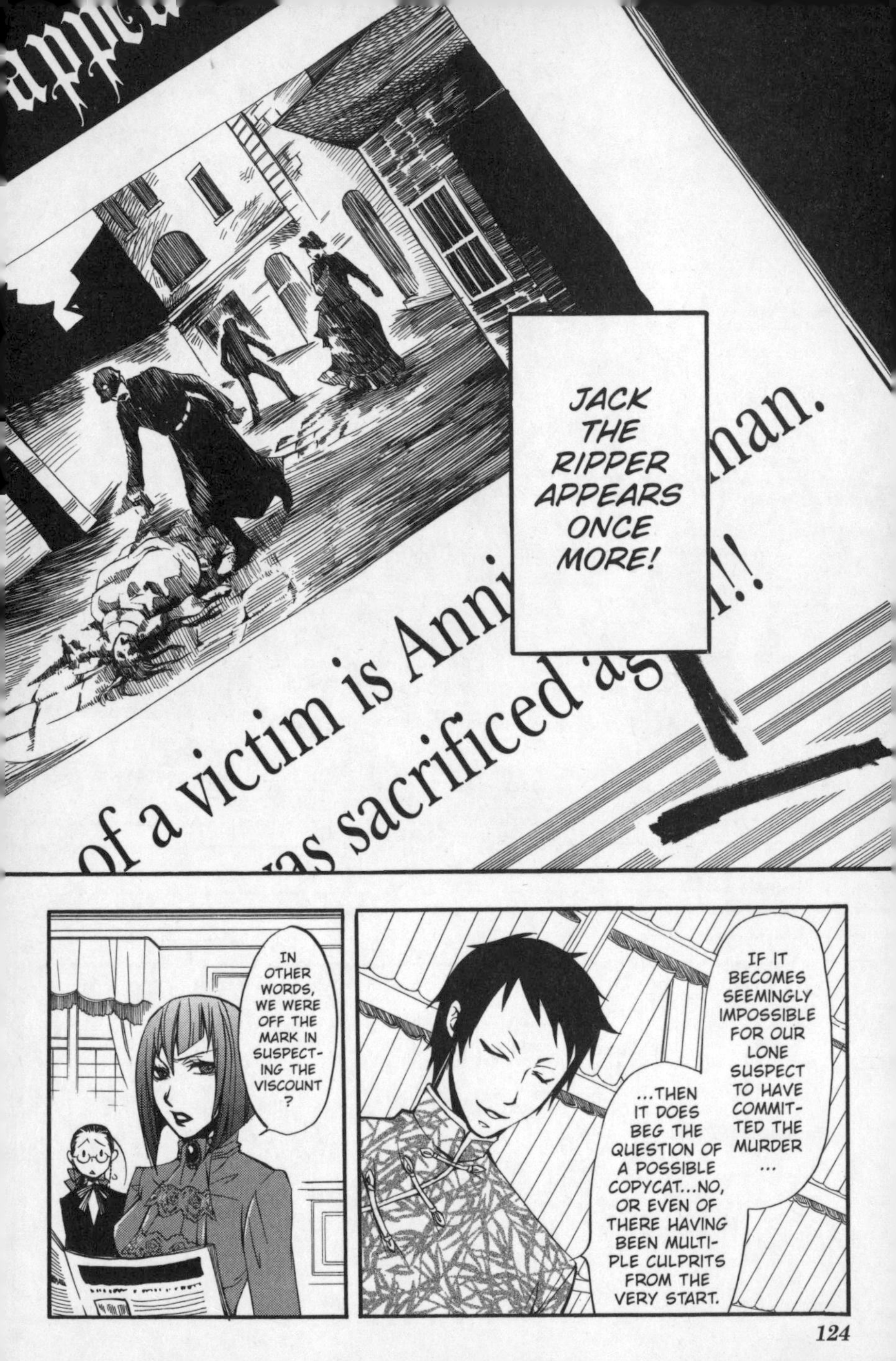
appe
of a victim is Anni
man.
was sacrificed as
!!
JACK THE RIPPER APPEARS ONCE MORE!
IF IT BECOMES SEEMINGLY IMPOSSIBLE FOR OUR LONE SUSPECT TO HAVE COMMITTED THE MURDER...
...THEN IT DOES BEG THE QUESTION OF A POSSIBLE COPYCAT...NO, OR EVEN OF THERE HAVING BEEN MULTIPLE CULPRITS FROM THE VERY START.
IN OTHER WORDS, WE WERE OFF THE MARK IN SUSPECTING THE VISCOUNT?

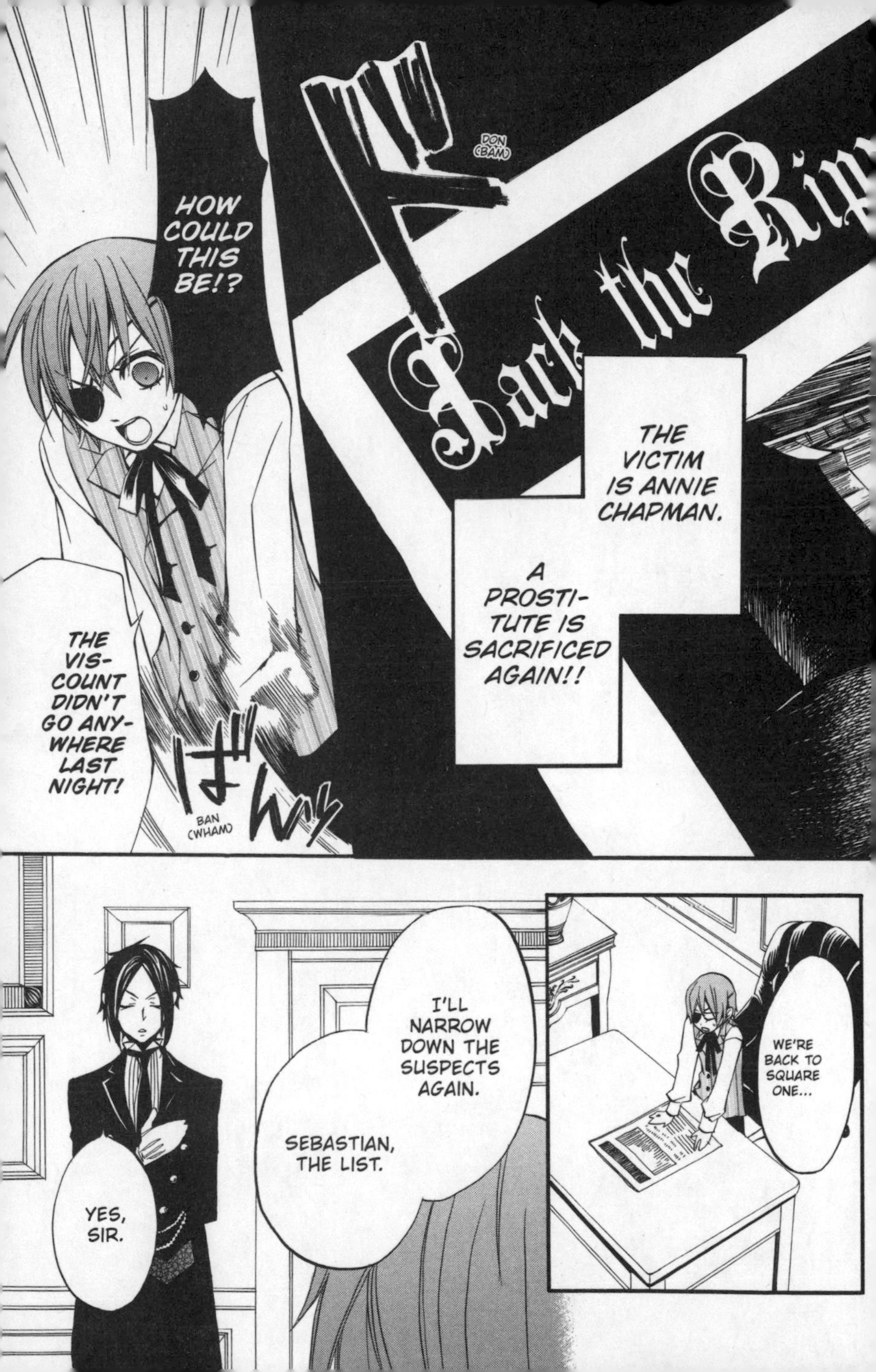

DON (BAM)
Jack the Rip
THE VICTIM IS ANNIE CHAPMAN.
A PROSTITUTE IS SACRIFICED AGAIN!!
HOW COULD THIS BE!?
THE VISCOUNT DIDN'T GO ANYWHERE LAST NIGHT!
BAN (WHAM)
WE'RE BACK TO SQUARE ONE...
I'LL NARROW DOWN THE SUSPECTS AGAIN.
SEBASTIAN, THE LIST.
YES, SIR.

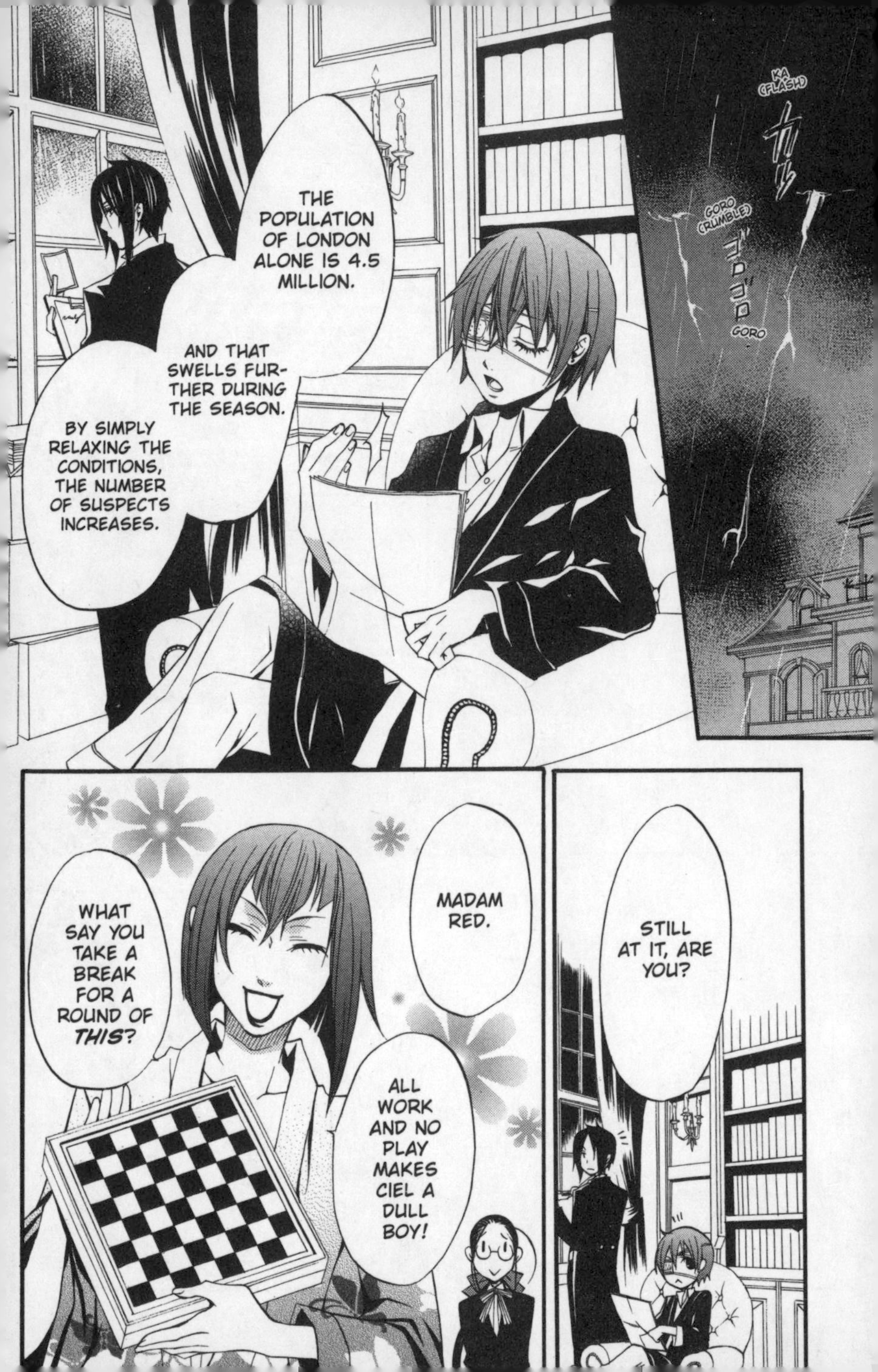

KA (FLASH)
カッ
GORO (RUMBLE)
ゴロゴロ
GORO
THE POPULATION OF LONDON ALONE IS 4.5 MILLION.
AND THAT SWELLS FUR-THER DURING THE SEASON.
BY SIMPLY RELAXING THE CONDITIONS, THE NUMBER OF SUSPECTS INCREASES.
STILL AT IT, ARE YOU?
MADAM RED.
WHAT SAY YOU TAKE A BREAK FOR A ROUND OF *THIS*?
ALL WORK AND NO PLAY MAKES CIEL A DULL BOY!

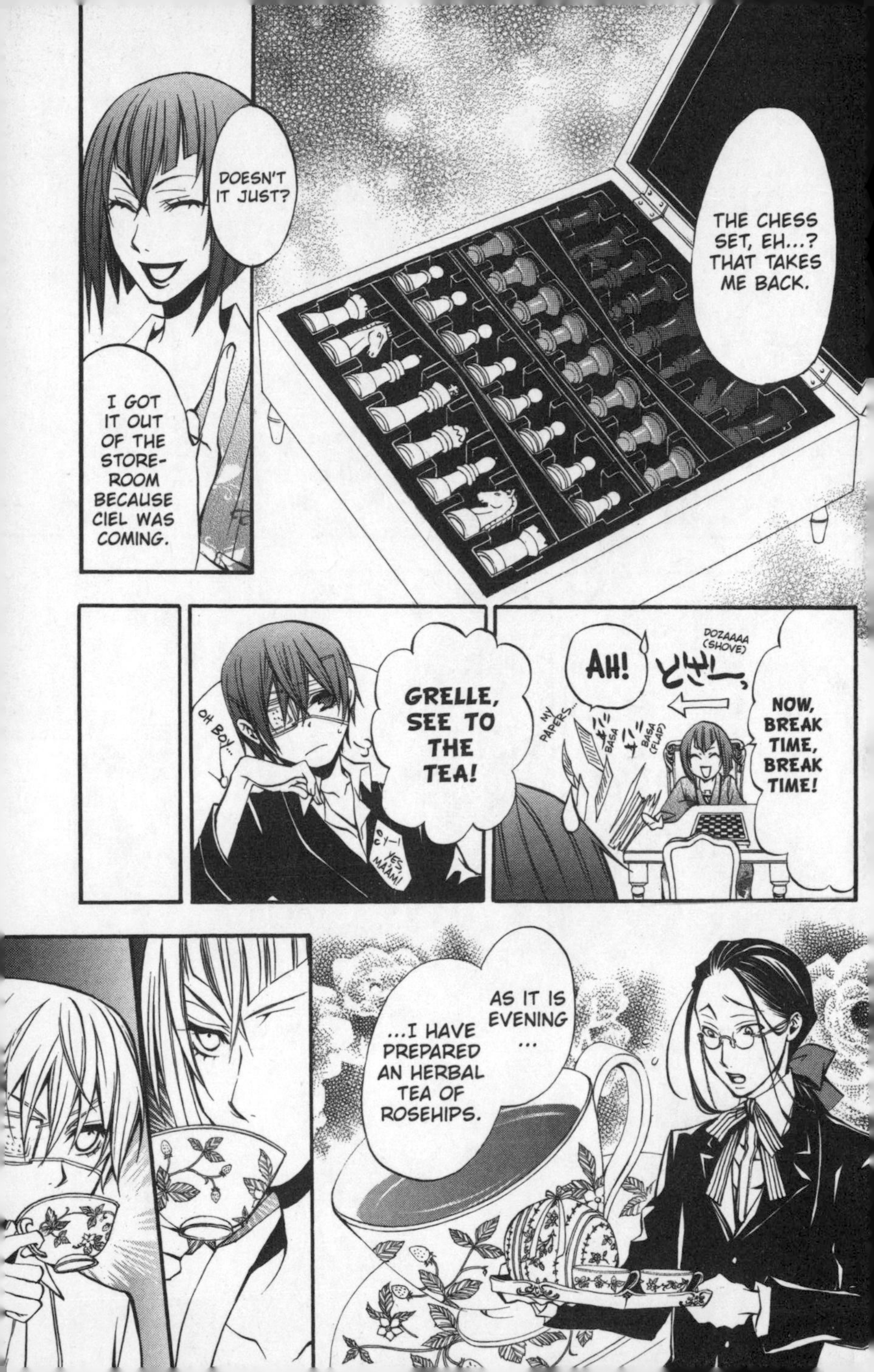
THE CHESS SET, EH...? THAT TAKES ME BACK.
DOESN'T IT JUST?
I GOT IT OUT OF THE STORE-ROOM BECAUSE CIEL WAS COMING.
DOZAAAA (SHOVE)
NOW, BREAK TIME, BREAK TIME!
AH!
BASA (FLAP)
BASA
MY PAPERS...
GRELLE, SEE TO THE TEA!
OH BOY...
YES, MA'AM!
AS IT IS EVENING ...
...I HAVE PREPARED AN HERBAL TEA OF ROSEHIPS.

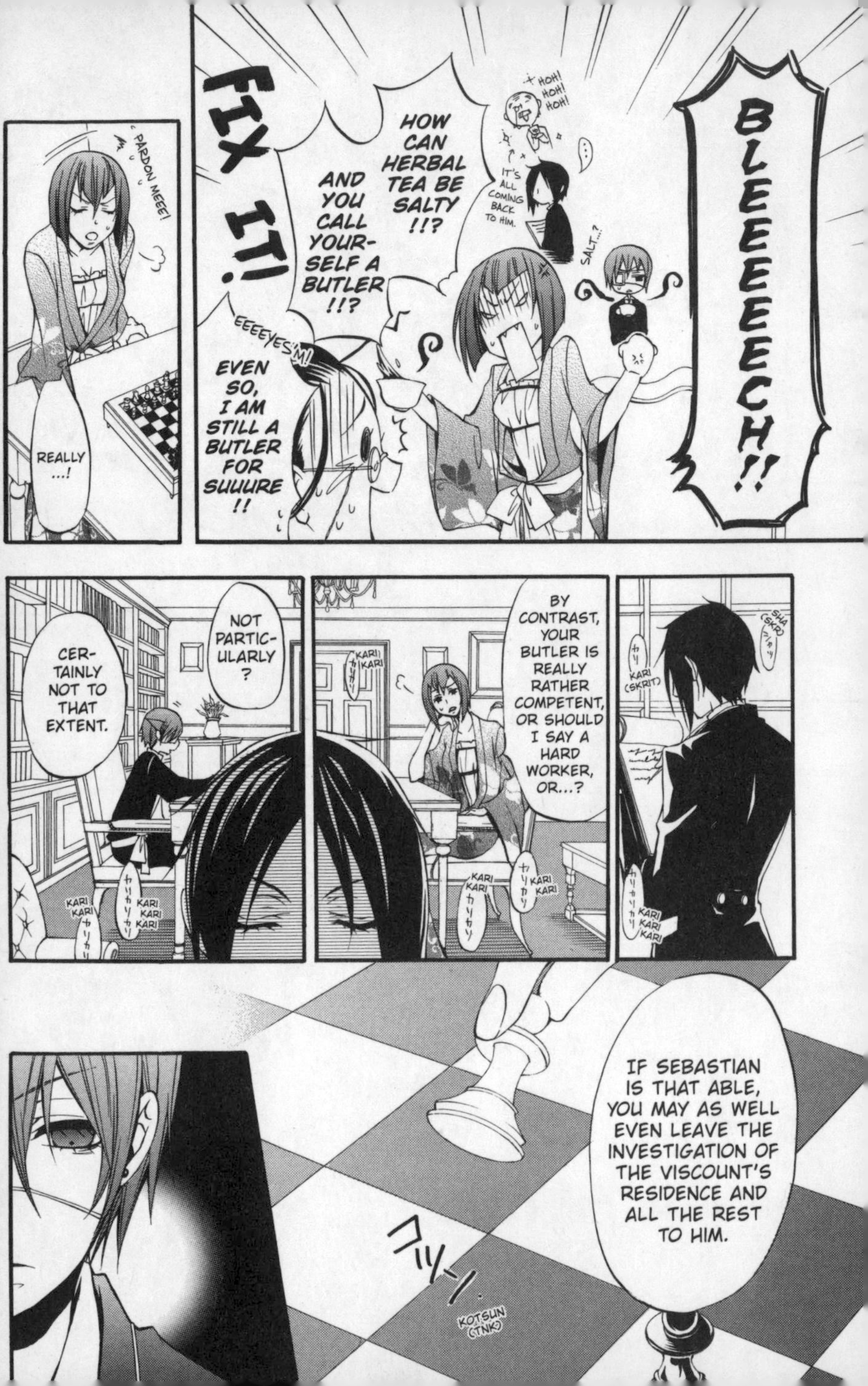
BLEEEEEECH!!
HOH! HOH! HOH!
...
IT'S ALL COMING BACK TO HIM.
SALT...?
HOW CAN HERBAL TEA BE SALTY!!?
AND YOU CALL YOUR-SELF A BUTLER!!?
FIX IT!!
EEEEYES'M!
EVEN SO, I AM STILL A BUTLER FOR SUUURE!!
PARDON MEEE!
REALLY...!
SHA (SKR)
KARI (SKRIT)
KARI KARI KARI
BY CONTRAST, YOUR BUTLER IS REALLY RATHER COMPETENT, OR SHOULD I SAY A HARD WORKER, OR...?
NOT PARTIC-ULARLY?
KARI KARI
KARI KARI
KARI KARI
CER-TAINLY NOT TO THAT EXTENT.
KARI KARI KARI
KARI KARI
IF SEBASTIAN IS THAT ABLE, YOU MAY AS WELL EVEN LEAVE THE INVESTIGATION OF THE VISCOUNT'S RESIDENCE AND ALL THE REST TO HIM.
KOTSUN (TNK)

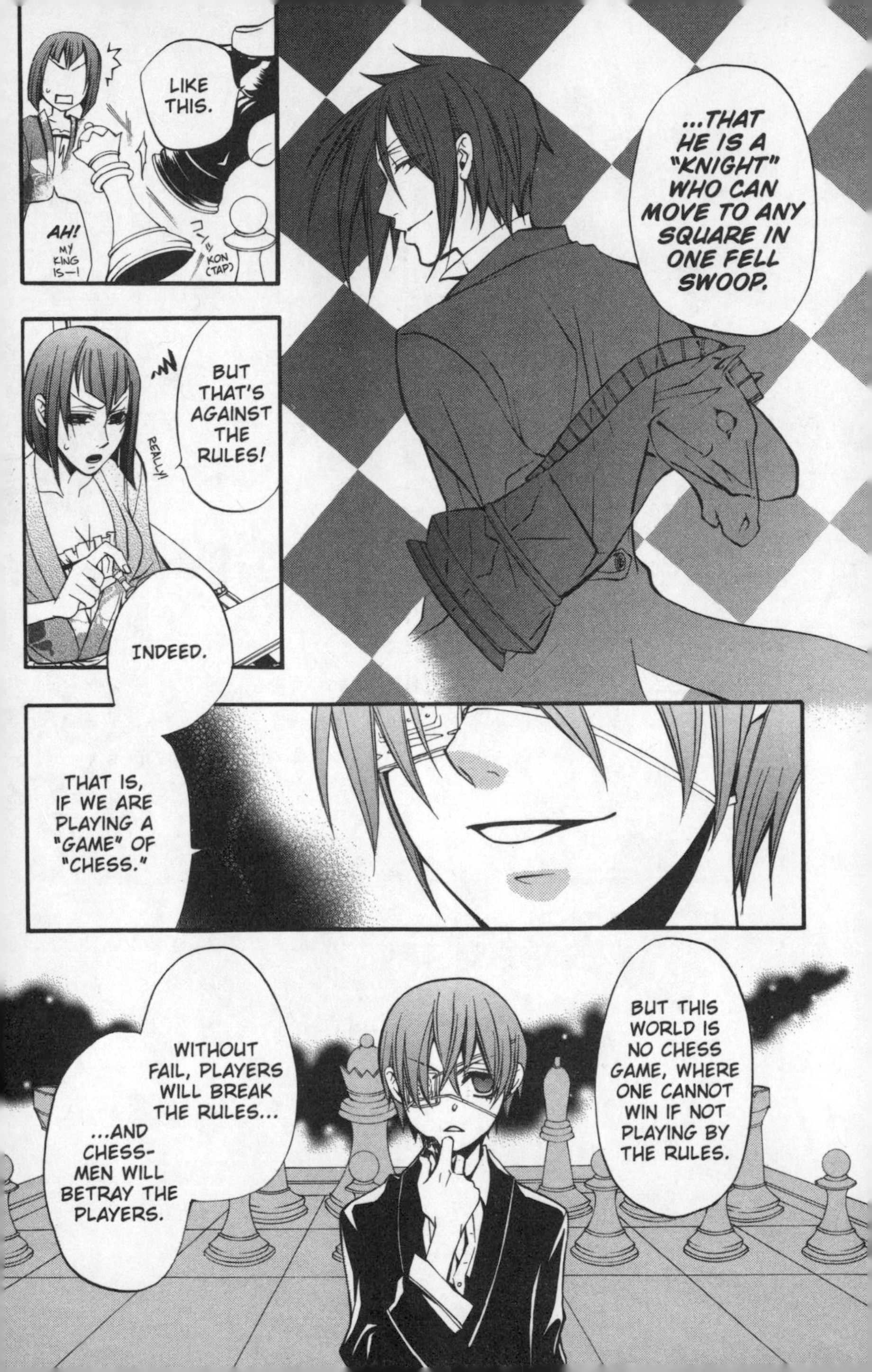
...THAT HE IS A "KNIGHT" WHO CAN MOVE TO ANY SQUARE IN ONE FELL SWOOP.
LIKE THIS.
KON (TAP)
AH! MY KING IS—!
BUT THAT'S AGAINST THE RULES!
REALLY!
INDEED.
THAT IS, IF WE ARE PLAYING A "GAME" OF "CHESS."
BUT THIS WORLD IS NO CHESS GAME, WHERE ONE CANNOT WIN IF NOT PLAYING BY THE RULES.
WITHOUT FAIL, PLAYERS WILL BREAK THE RULES...
...AND CHESS-MEN WILL BETRAY THE PLAYERS.

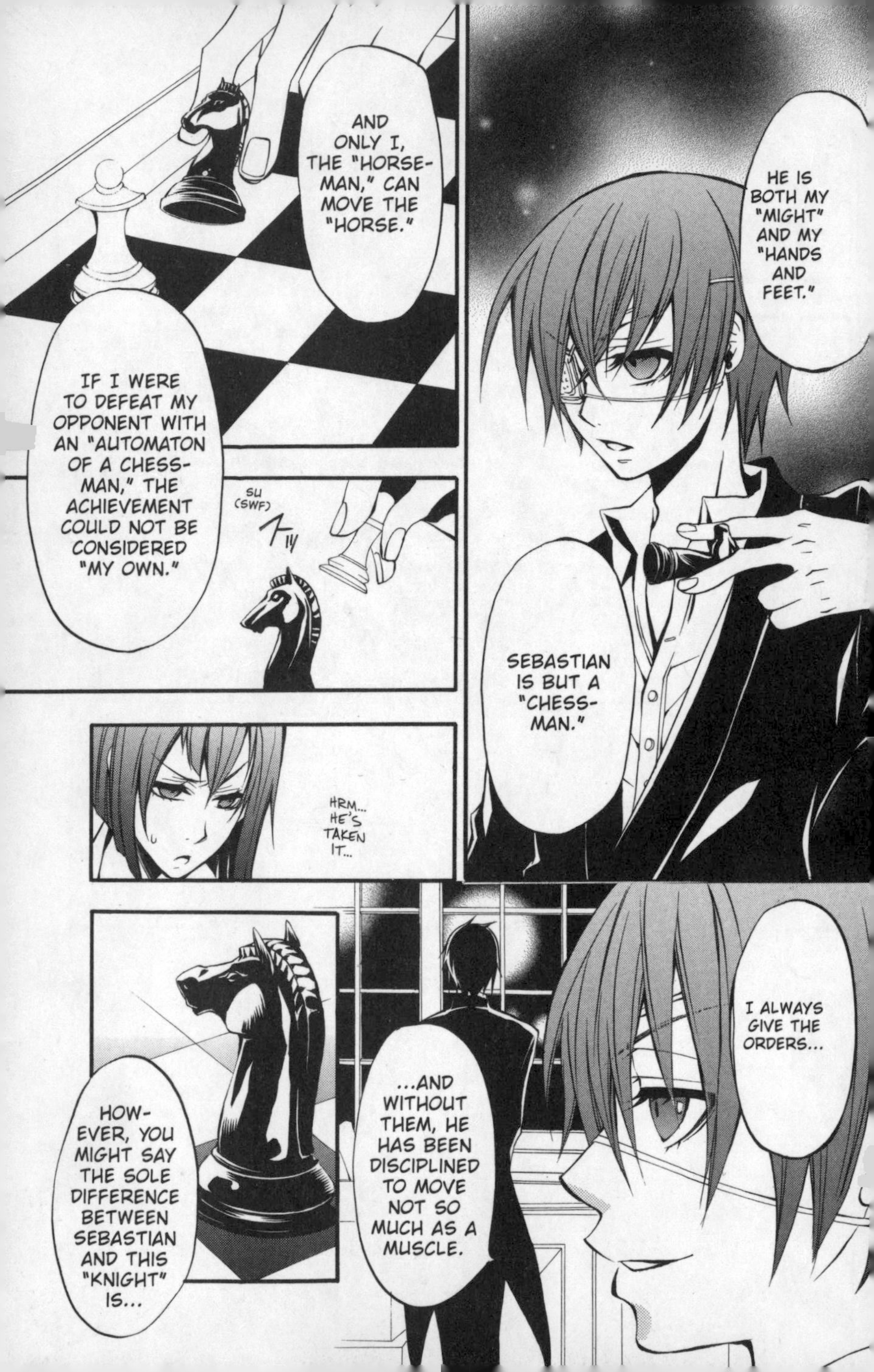
HE IS BOTH MY "MIGHT" AND MY "HANDS AND FEET."
SEBASTIAN IS BUT A "CHESS-MAN."
AND ONLY I, THE "HORSE-MAN," CAN MOVE THE "HORSE."
IF I WERE TO DEFEAT MY OPPONENT WITH AN "AUTOMATON OF A CHESS-MAN," THE ACHIEVEMENT COULD NOT BE CONSIDERED "MY OWN."
SU (SWF)
HRM... HE'S TAKEN IT...
I ALWAYS GIVE THE ORDERS...
...AND WITHOUT THEM, HE HAS BEEN DISCIPLINED TO MOVE NOT SO MUCH AS A MUSCLE.
HOW-EVER, YOU MIGHT SAY THE SOLE DIFFERENCE BETWEEN SEBASTIAN AND THIS "KNIGHT" IS...

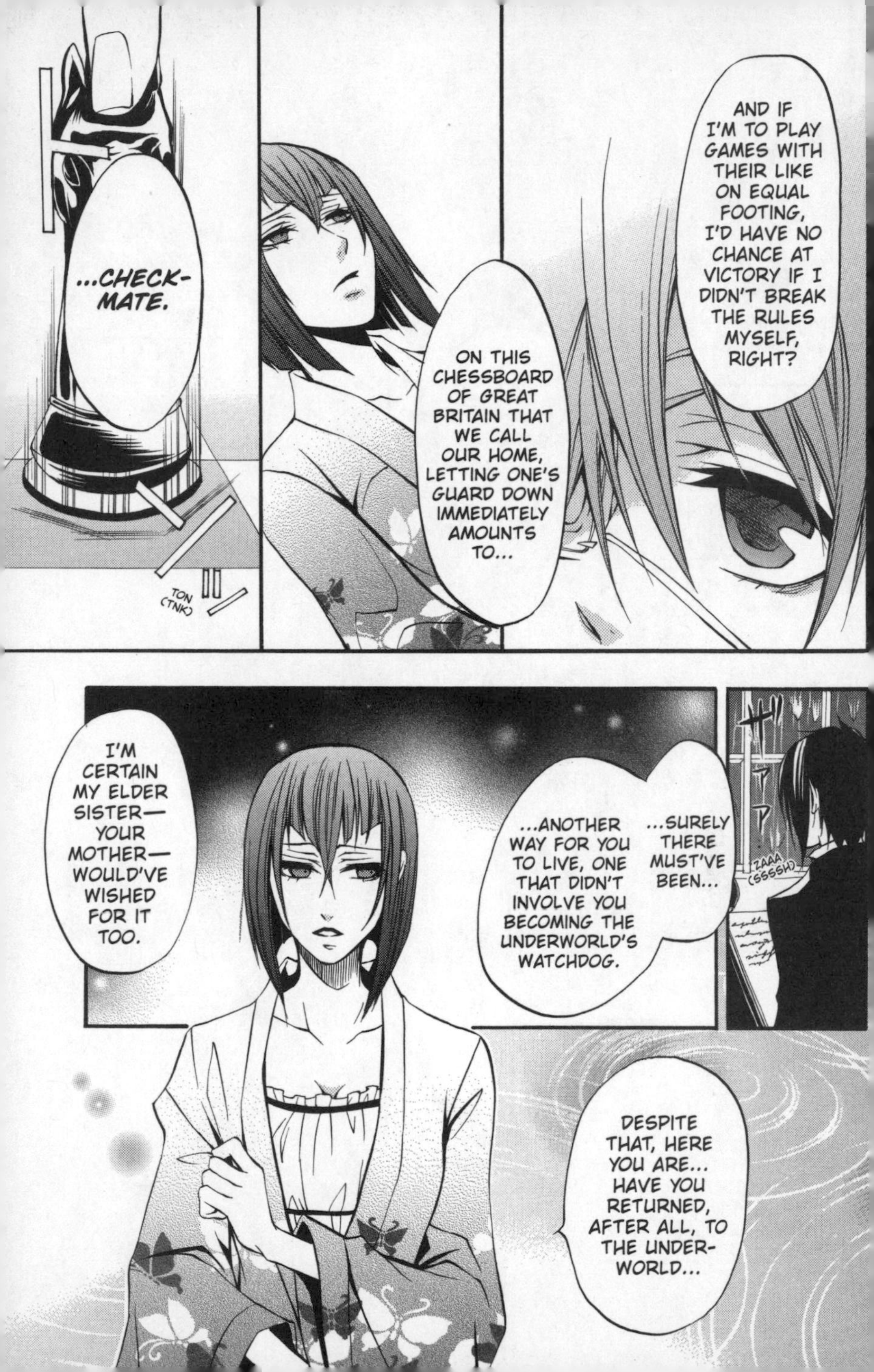
AND IF I'M TO PLAY GAMES WITH THEIR LIKE ON EQUAL FOOTING, I'D HAVE NO CHANCE AT VICTORY IF I DIDN'T BREAK THE RULES MYSELF, RIGHT?
ON THIS CHESSBOARD OF GREAT BRITAIN THAT WE CALL OUR HOME, LETTING ONE'S GUARD DOWN IMMEDIATELY AMOUNTS TO...
...CHECK-MATE.
TON (TNK)
ZAAA (SSSSH)
...SURELY THERE MUST'VE BEEN...
...ANOTHER WAY FOR YOU TO LIVE, ONE THAT DIDN'T INVOLVE YOU BECOMING THE UNDERWORLD'S WATCHDOG.
I'M CERTAIN MY ELDER SISTER—YOUR MOTHER—WOULD'VE WISHED FOR IT TOO.
DESPITE THAT, HERE YOU ARE... HAVE YOU RETURNED, AFTER ALL, TO THE UNDER-WORLD...

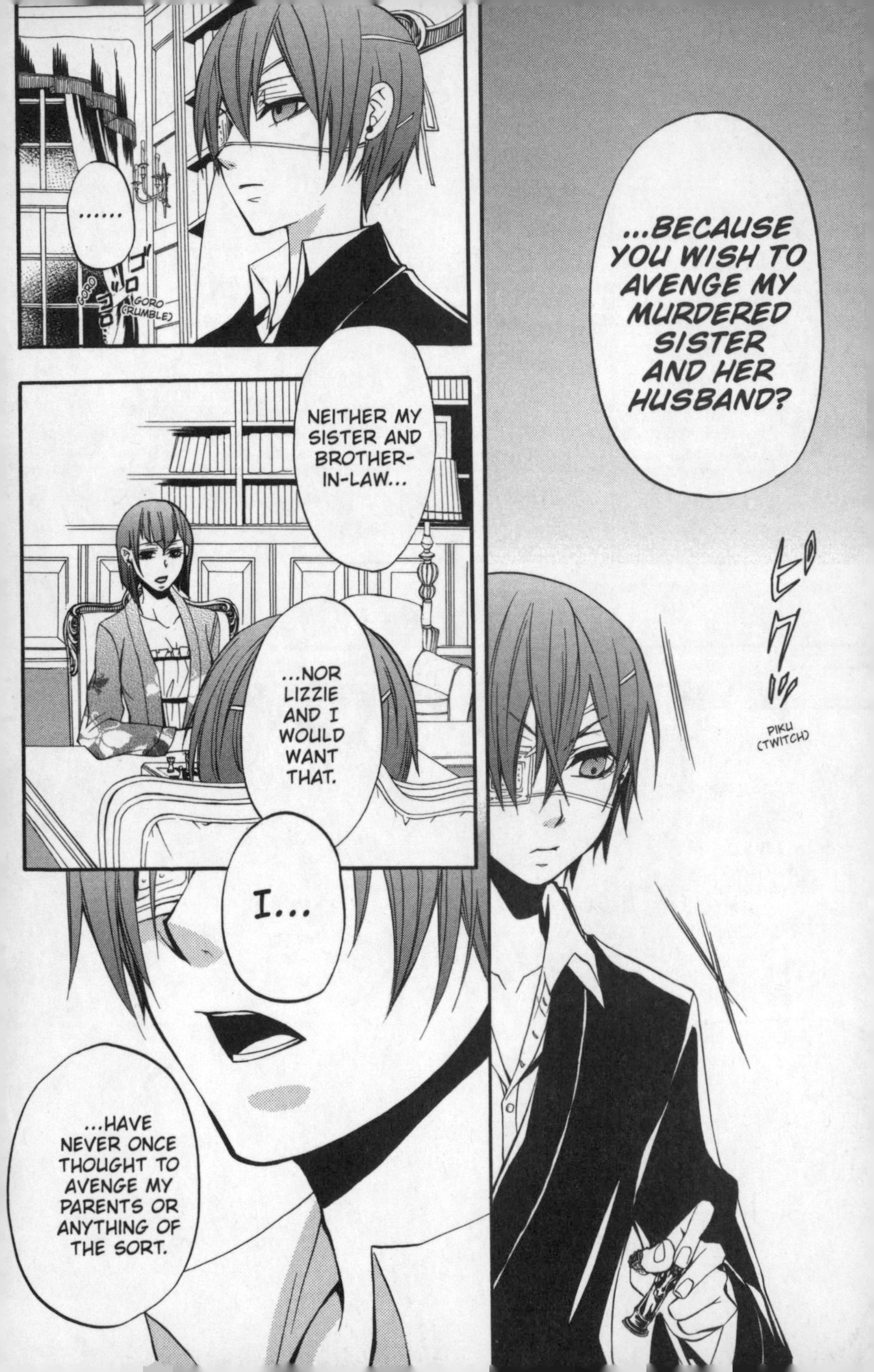
...BECAUSE YOU WISH TO AVENGE MY MURDERED SISTER AND HER HUSBAND?
PIKU (TWITCH)
......
GORO GORO (RUMBLE)
NEITHER MY SISTER AND BROTHER-IN-LAW...
...NOR LIZZIE AND I WOULD WANT THAT.
I...
...HAVE NEVER ONCE THOUGHT TO AVENGE MY PARENTS OR ANYTHING OF THE SORT.

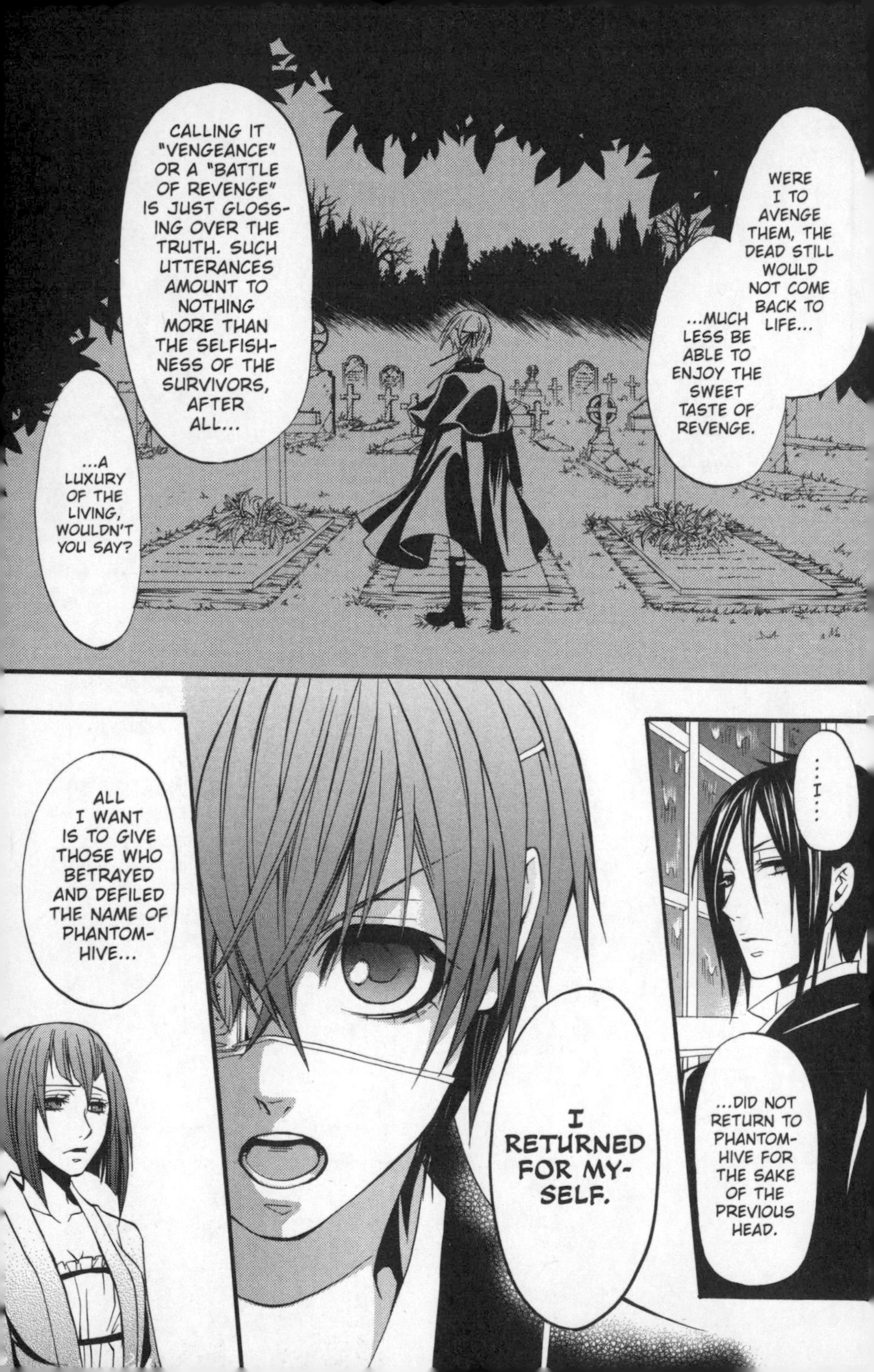
WERE I TO AVENGE THEM, THE DEAD STILL WOULD NOT COME BACK TO LIFE...
...MUCH LESS BE ABLE TO ENJOY THE SWEET TASTE OF REVENGE.
CALLING IT "VENGEANCE" OR A "BATTLE OF REVENGE" IS JUST GLOSSING OVER THE TRUTH. SUCH UTTERANCES AMOUNT TO NOTHING MORE THAN THE SELFISHNESS OF THE SURVIVORS, AFTER ALL...
...A LUXURY OF THE LIVING, WOULDN'T YOU SAY?
...I...
...DID NOT RETURN TO PHANTOMHIVE FOR THE SAKE OF THE PREVIOUS HEAD.
I RETURNED FOR MYSELF.
ALL I WANT IS TO GIVE THOSE WHO BETRAYED AND DEFILED THE NAME OF PHANTOMHIVE...

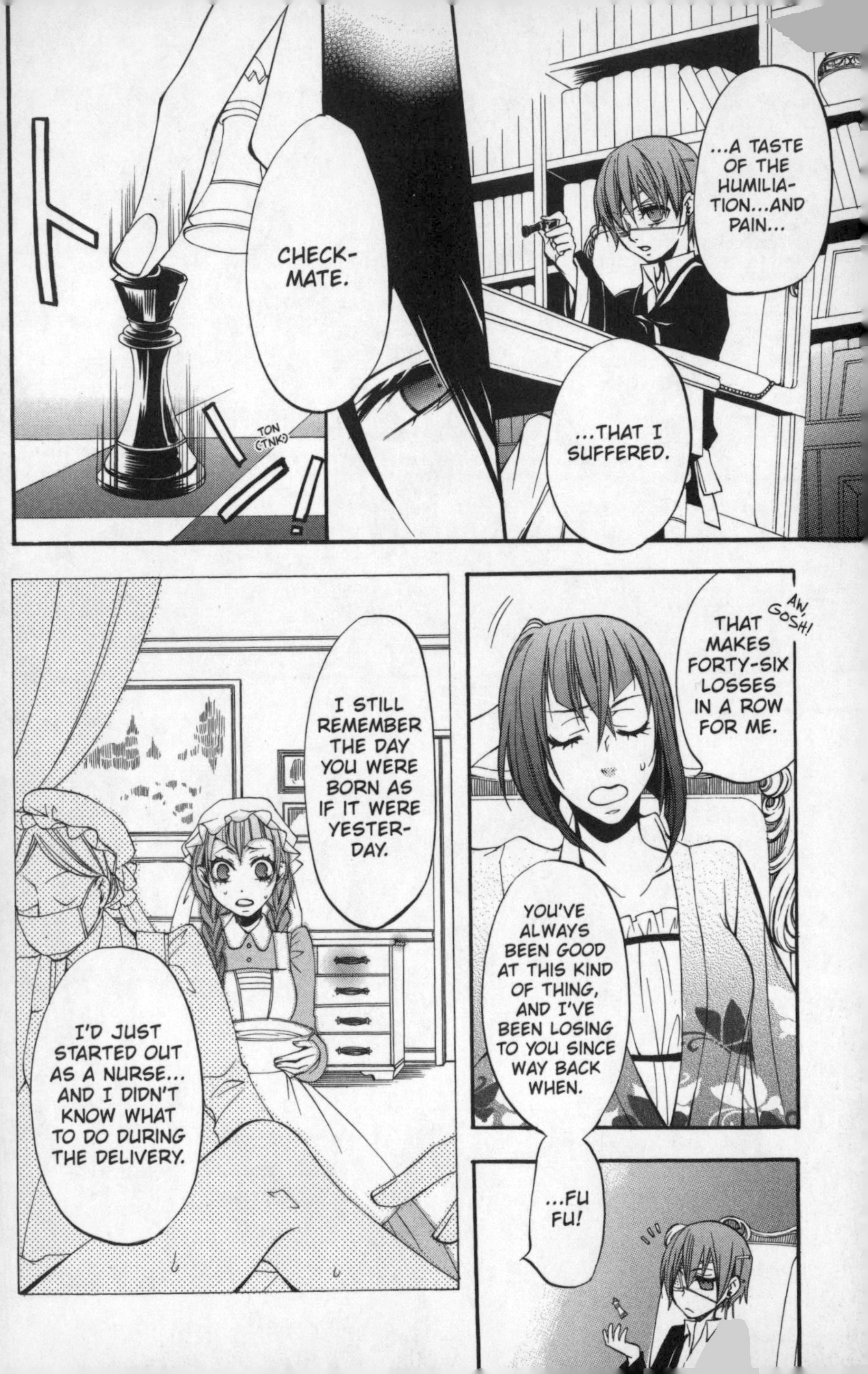
...A TASTE OF THE HUMILIATION...AND PAIN...
...THAT I SUFFERED.
CHECK-MATE.
TON (TNK)
AW, GOSH!
THAT MAKES FORTY-SIX LOSSES IN A ROW FOR ME.
YOU'VE ALWAYS BEEN GOOD AT THIS KIND OF THING, AND I'VE BEEN LOSING TO YOU SINCE WAY BACK WHEN.
...FU FU!
I STILL REMEMBER THE DAY YOU WERE BORN AS IF IT WERE YESTER-DAY.
I'D JUST STARTED OUT AS A NURSE... AND I DIDN'T KNOW WHAT TO DO DURING THE DELIVERY.

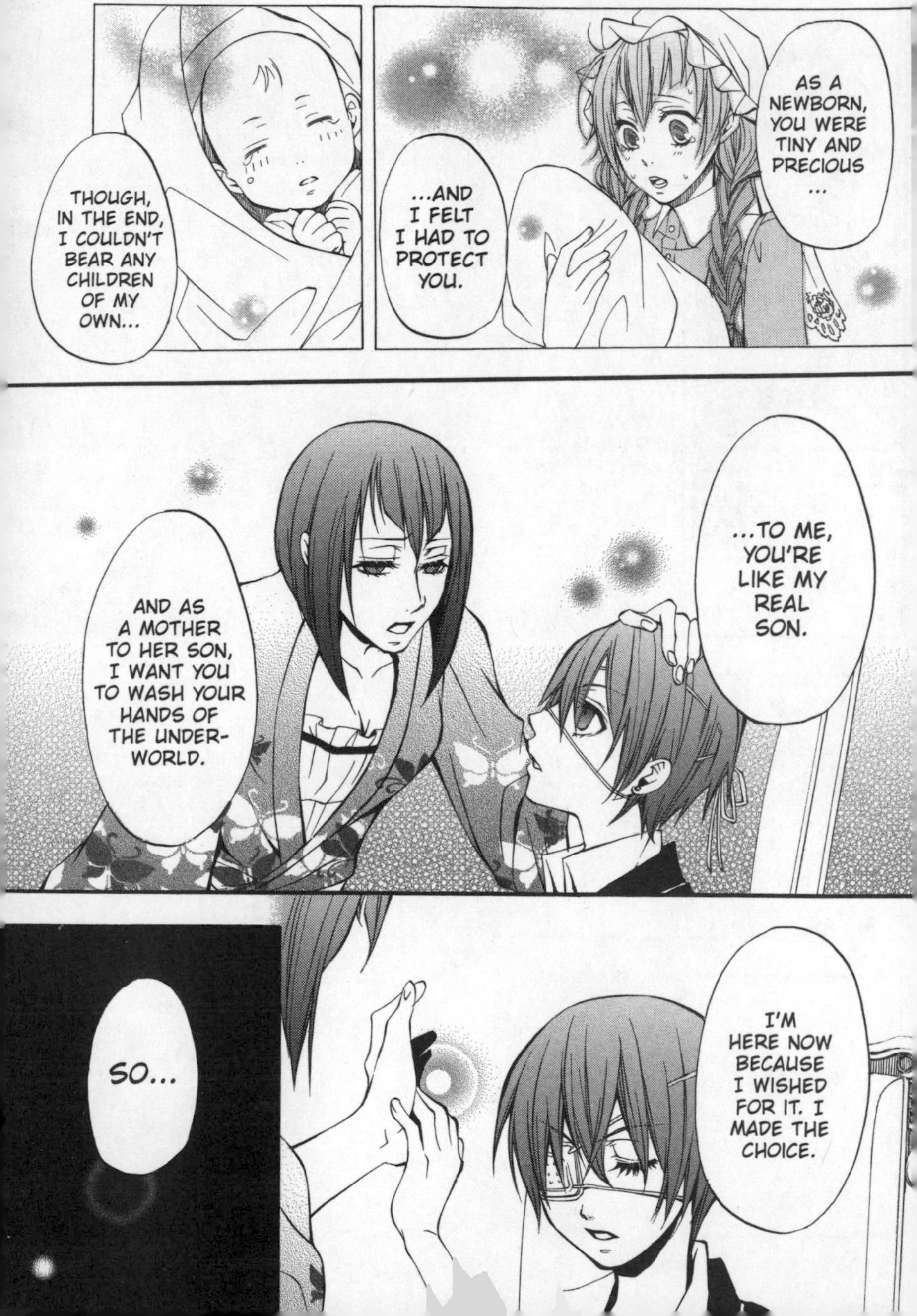
AS A NEWBORN, YOU WERE TINY AND PRECIOUS...
...AND I FELT I HAD TO PROTECT YOU.
THOUGH, IN THE END, I COULDN'T BEAR ANY CHILDREN OF MY OWN...
...TO ME, YOU'RE LIKE MY REAL SON.
AND AS A MOTHER TO HER SON, I WANT YOU TO WASH YOUR HANDS OF THE UNDER-WORLD.
I'M HERE NOW BECAUSE I WISHED FOR IT. I MADE THE CHOICE.
SO...

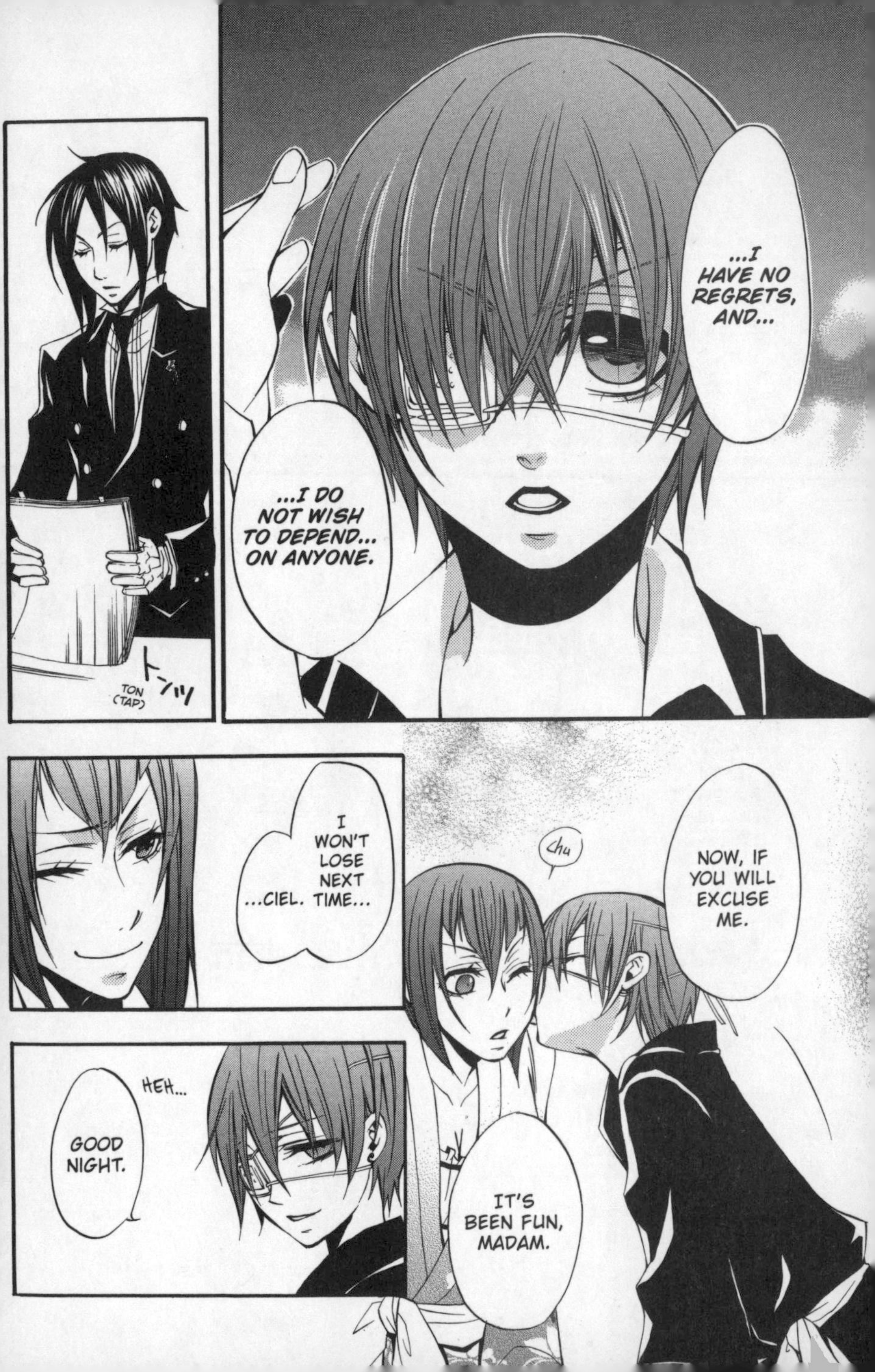
...I HAVE NO REGRETS, AND...
...I DO NOT WISH TO DEPEND... ON ANYONE.
TON (TAP)
NOW, IF YOU WILL EXCUSE ME.
Chu
IT'S BEEN FUN, MADAM.
I WON'T LOSE NEXT TIME...
...CIEL.
HEH...
GOOD NIGHT.

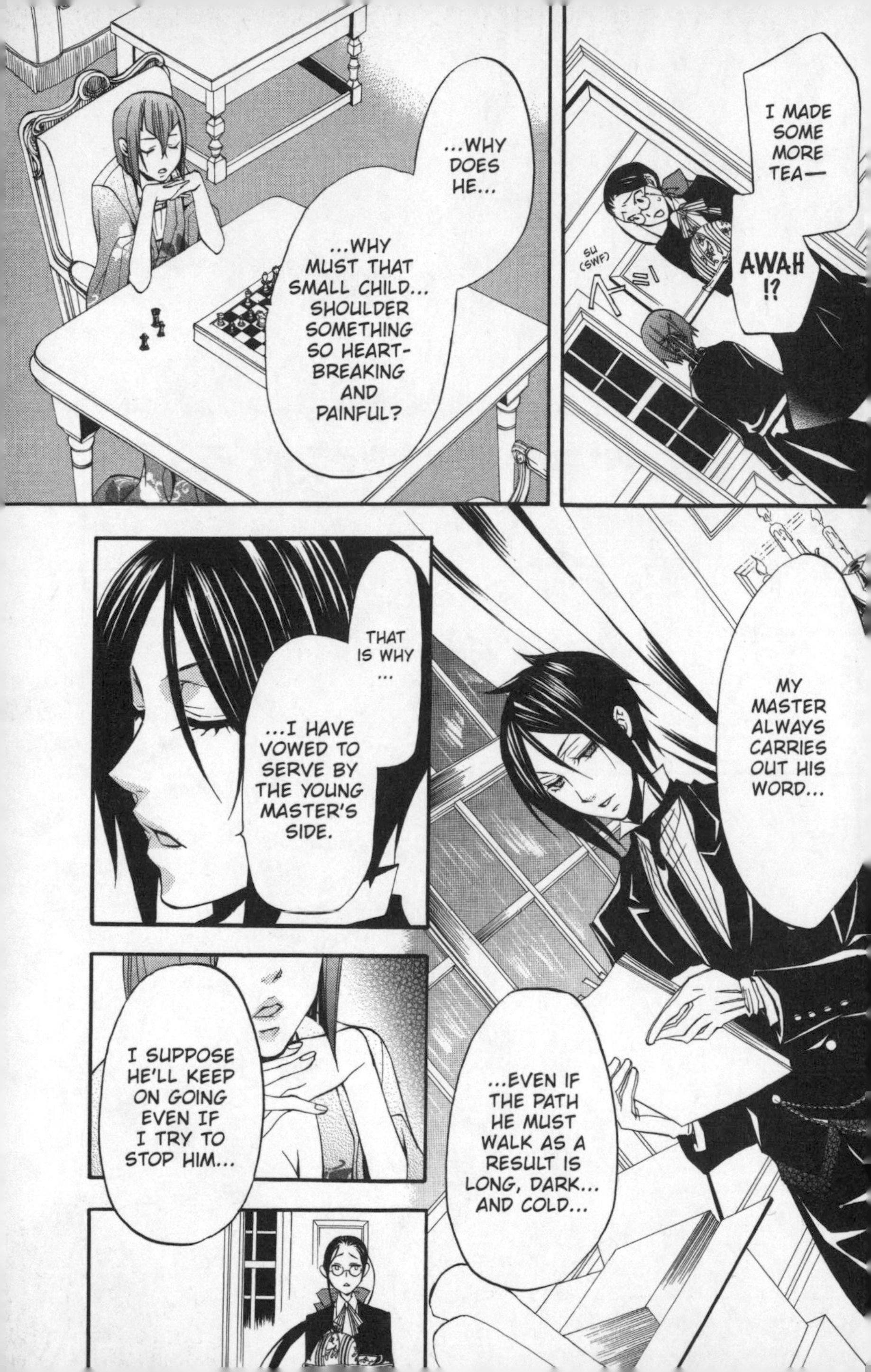
I MADE SOME MORE TEA—
SU (SWF)
AWAH !?
...WHY DOES HE...
...WHY MUST THAT SMALL CHILD... SHOULDER SOMETHING SO HEART-BREAKING AND PAINFUL?
MY MASTER ALWAYS CARRIES OUT HIS WORD...
...EVEN IF THE PATH HE MUST WALK AS A RESULT IS LONG, DARK... AND COLD...
THAT IS WHY ...
...I HAVE VOWED TO SERVE BY THE YOUNG MASTER'S SIDE.
I SUPPOSE HE'LL KEEP ON GOING EVEN IF I TRY TO STOP HIM...

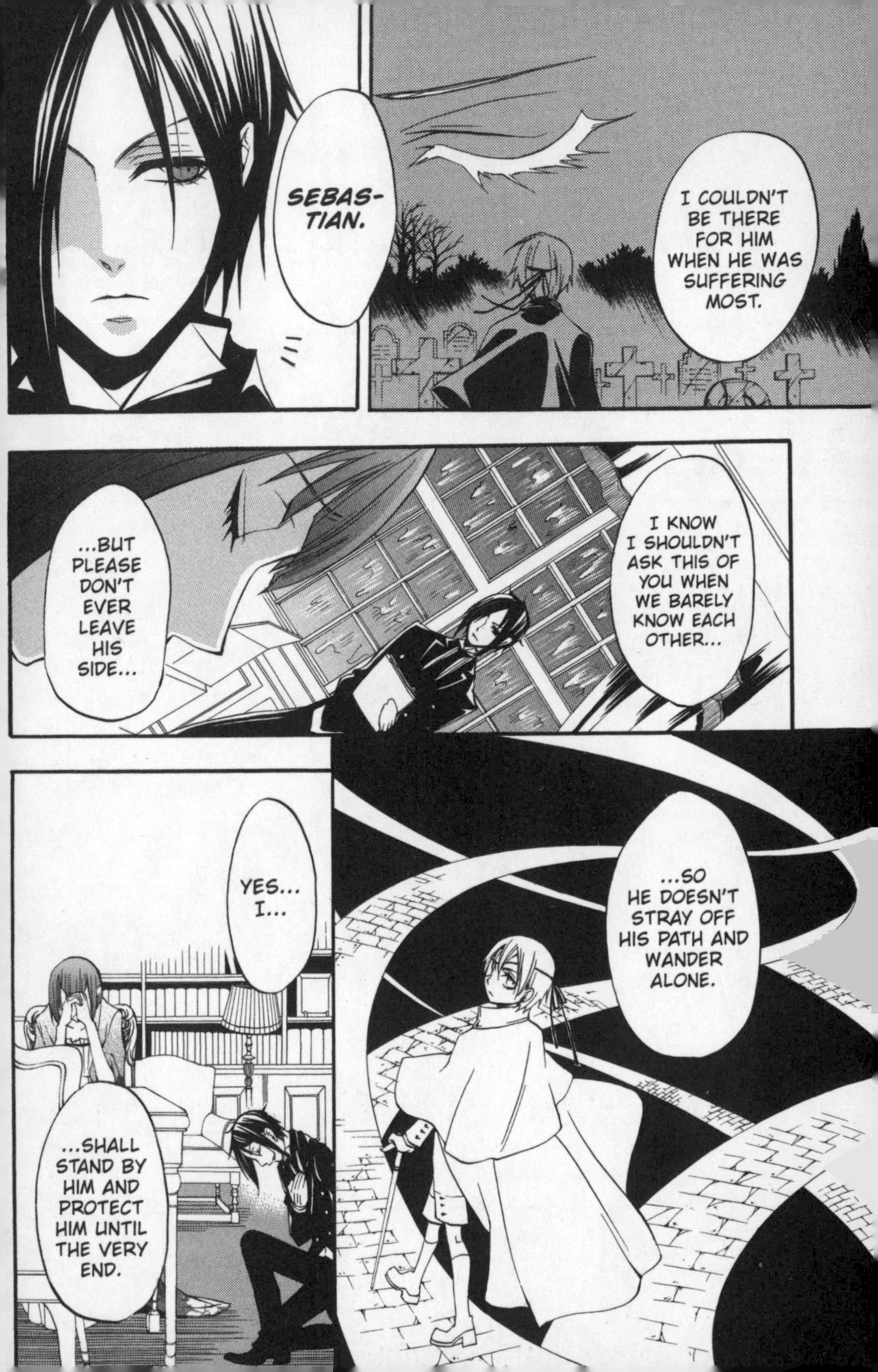
I COULDN'T BE THERE FOR HIM WHEN HE WAS SUFFERING MOST.
SEBAS-TIAN.
I KNOW I SHOULDN'T ASK THIS OF YOU WHEN WE BARELY KNOW EACH OTHER...
...BUT PLEASE DON'T EVER LEAVE HIS SIDE...
...SO HE DOESN'T STRAY OFF HIS PATH AND WANDER ALONE.
YES... I...
...SHALL STAND BY HIM AND PROTECT HIM UNTIL THE VERY END.

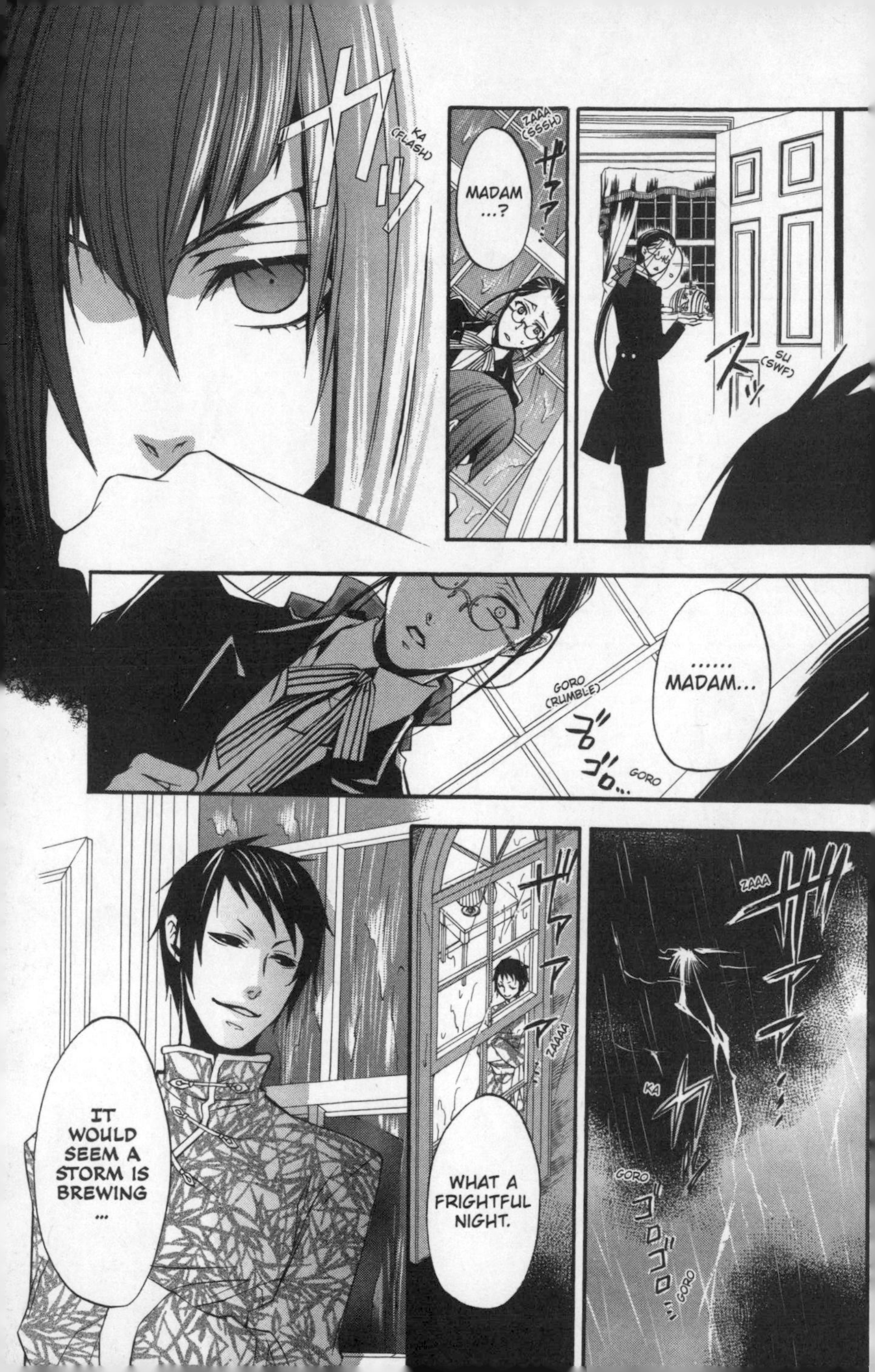
SU (SWF)
ZAAA (SSSH)
MADAM ...?
KA (FLASH)
...... MADAM...
GORO (RUMBLE)
GORO
ZAAA
KA
GORO
GORO
ZAAAA
WHAT A FRIGHTFUL NIGHT.
IT WOULD SEEM A STORM IS BREWING ...

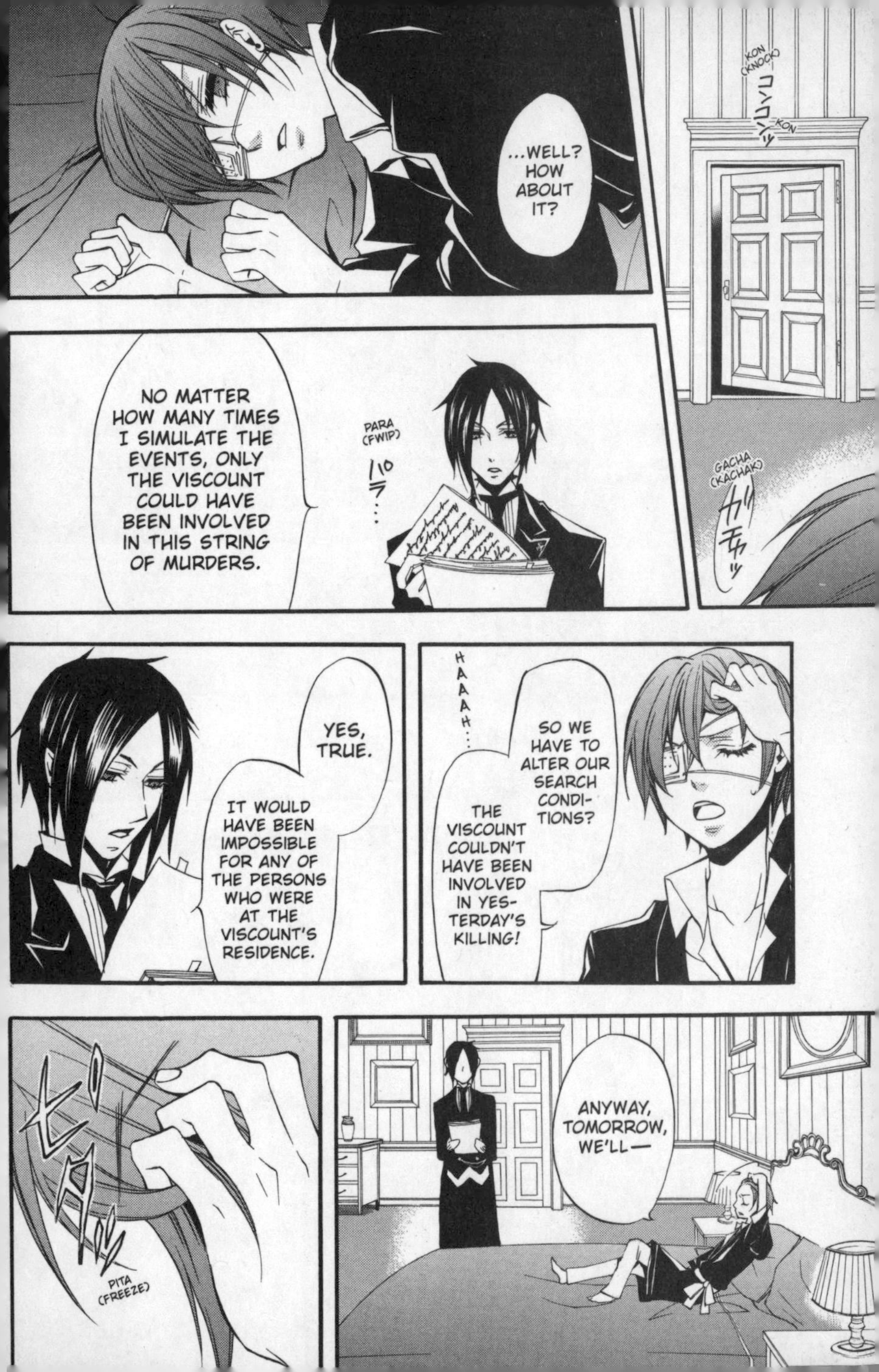
KON (KNOCK)
KON
GACHA (KACHAK)
...WELL? HOW ABOUT IT?
NO MATTER HOW MANY TIMES I SIMULATE THE EVENTS, ONLY THE VISCOUNT COULD HAVE BEEN INVOLVED IN THIS STRING OF MURDERS.
PARA (FWIP)
HAAAH...
SO WE HAVE TO ALTER OUR SEARCH CONDI-TIONS?
THE VISCOUNT COULDN'T HAVE BEEN INVOLVED IN YES-TERDAY'S KILLING!
YES, TRUE.
IT WOULD HAVE BEEN IMPOSSIBLE FOR ANY OF THE PERSONS WHO WERE AT THE VISCOUNT'S RESIDENCE.
ANYWAY, TOMORROW, WE'LL—
PITA (FREEZE)

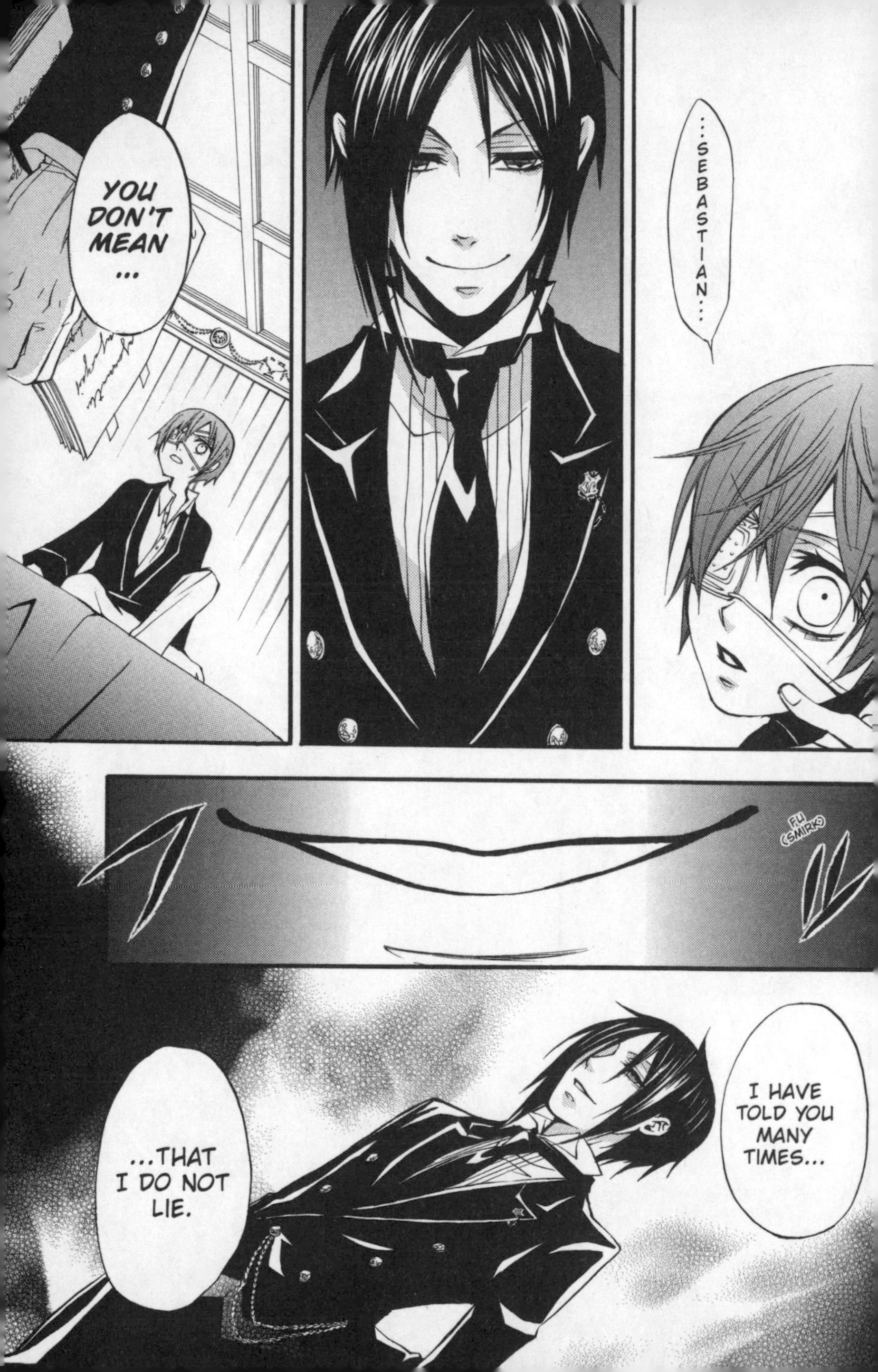
...SEBASTIAN...
YOU DON'T MEAN ...
FU (SMIRK)
I HAVE TOLD YOU MANY TIMES...
...THAT I DO NOT LIE.

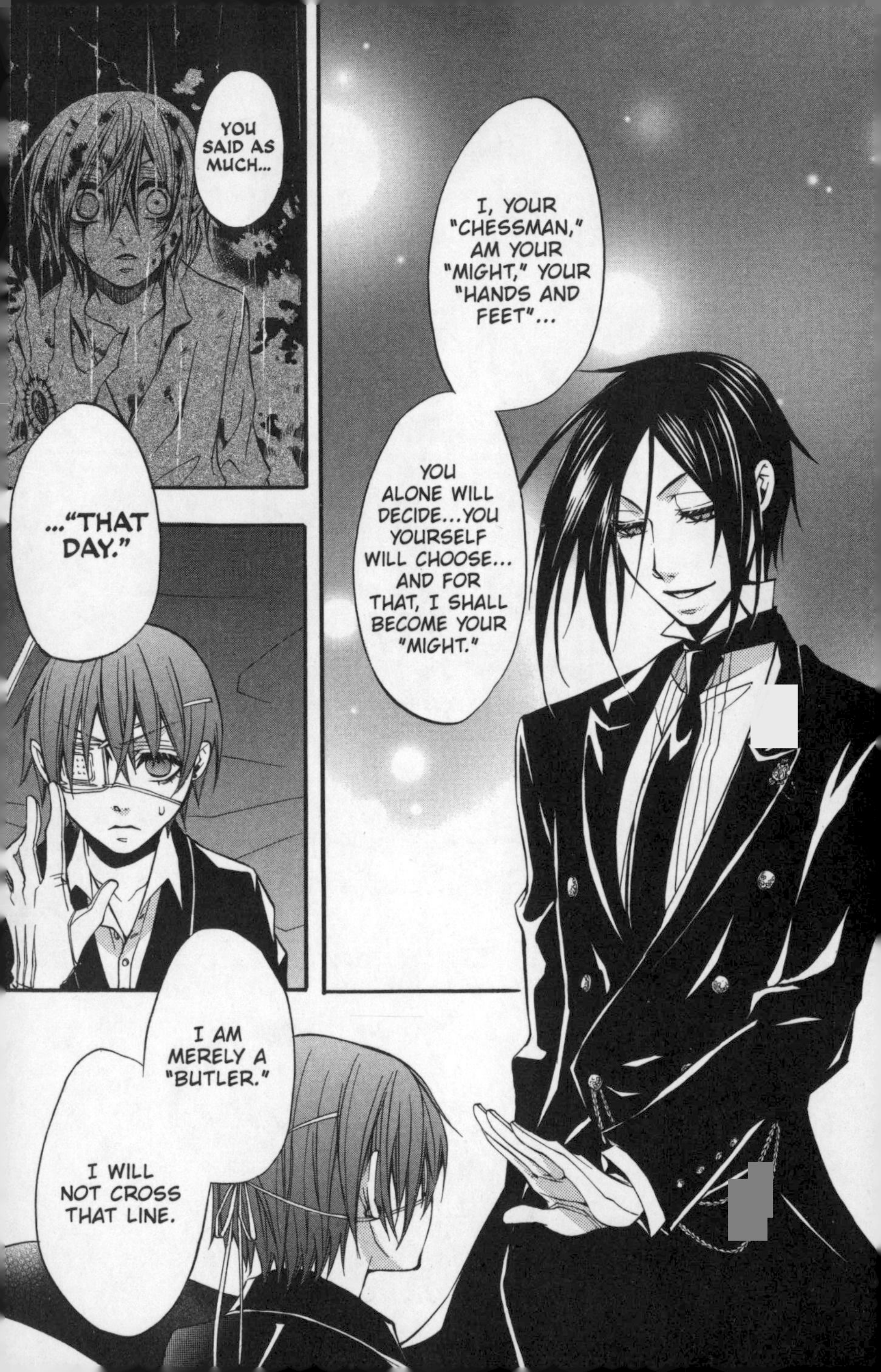
I, YOUR "CHESSMAN," AM YOUR "MIGHT," YOUR "HANDS AND FEET"...
YOU ALONE WILL DECIDE...YOU YOURSELF WILL CHOOSE... AND FOR THAT, I SHALL BECOME YOUR "MIGHT."
YOU SAID AS MUCH...
..."THAT DAY."
I AM MERELY A "BUTLER."
I WILL NOT CROSS THAT LINE.

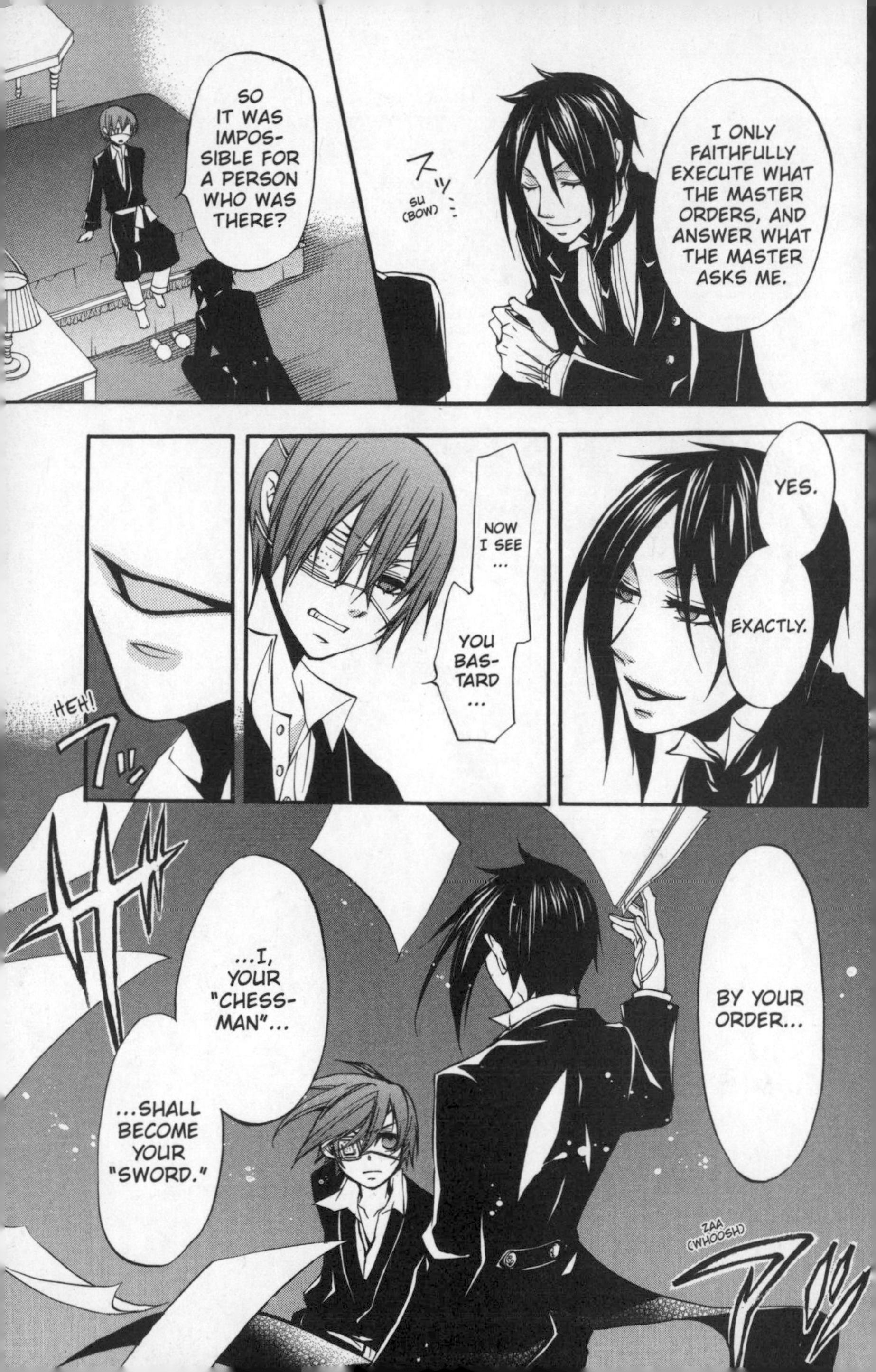
I ONLY FAITHFULLY EXECUTE WHAT THE MASTER ORDERS, AND ANSWER WHAT THE MASTER ASKS ME.
SU (BOW)
SO IT WAS IMPOSSIBLE FOR A PERSON WHO WAS THERE?
YES.
EXACTLY.
NOW I SEE...
YOU BASTARD...
HEH!
BY YOUR ORDER...
...I, YOUR "CHESS-MAN"...
...SHALL BECOME YOUR "SWORD."
ZAA (WHOOSH)

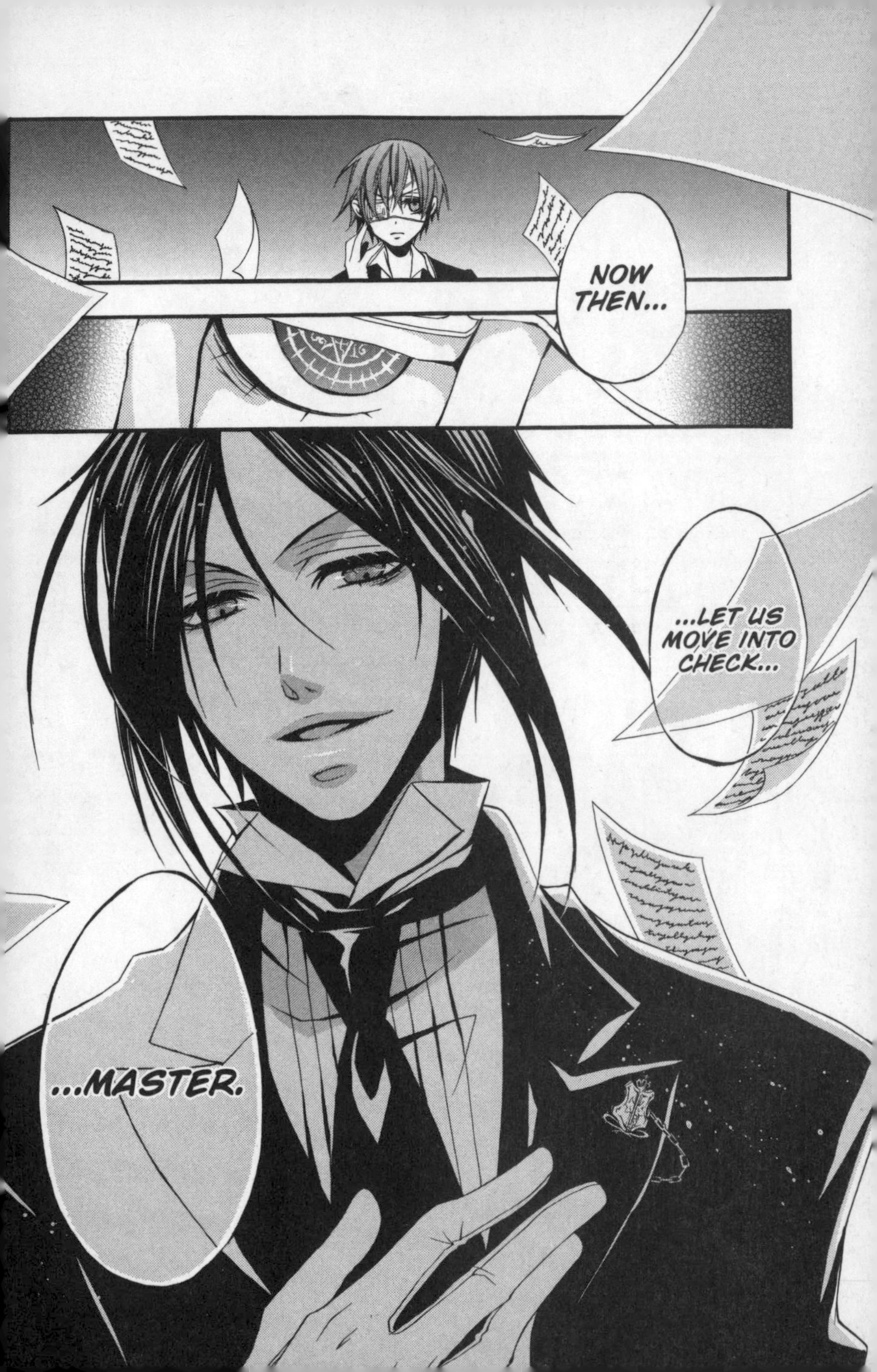
NOW THEN...
...LET US MOVE INTO CHECK...
...MASTER.

Black Butler

Black Butler

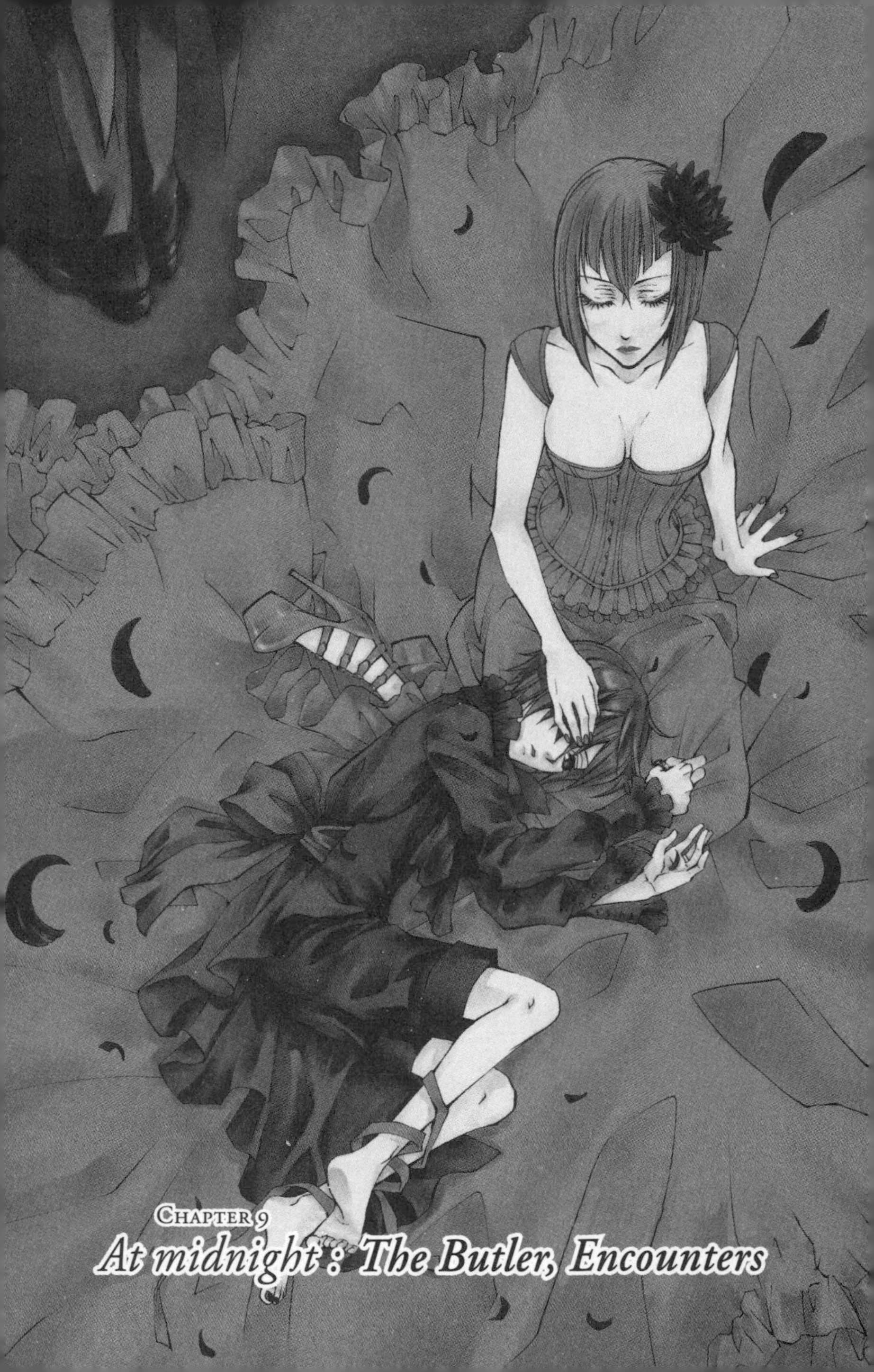
Chapter 9
At midnight : The Butler, Encounters

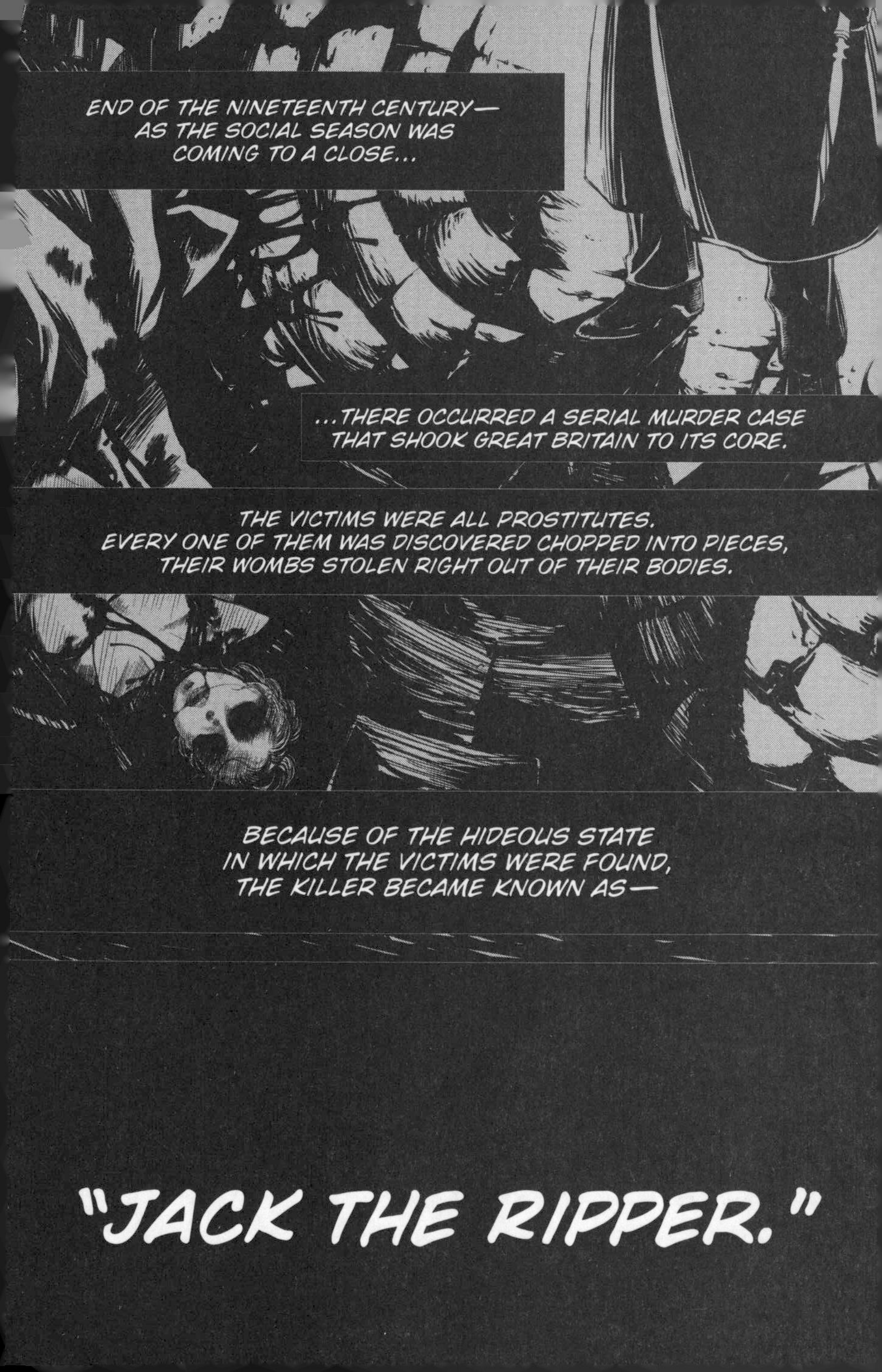
END OF THE NINETEENTH CENTURY— AS THE SOCIAL SEASON WAS COMING TO A CLOSE...
...THERE OCCURRED A SERIAL MURDER CASE THAT SHOOK GREAT BRITAIN TO ITS CORE.
THE VICTIMS WERE ALL PROSTITUTES. EVERY ONE OF THEM WAS DISCOVERED CHOPPED INTO PIECES, THEIR WOMBS STOLEN RIGHT OUT OF THEIR BODIES.
BECAUSE OF THE HIDEOUS STATE IN WHICH THE VICTIMS WERE FOUND, THE KILLER BECAME KNOWN AS—
"JACK THE RIPPER."

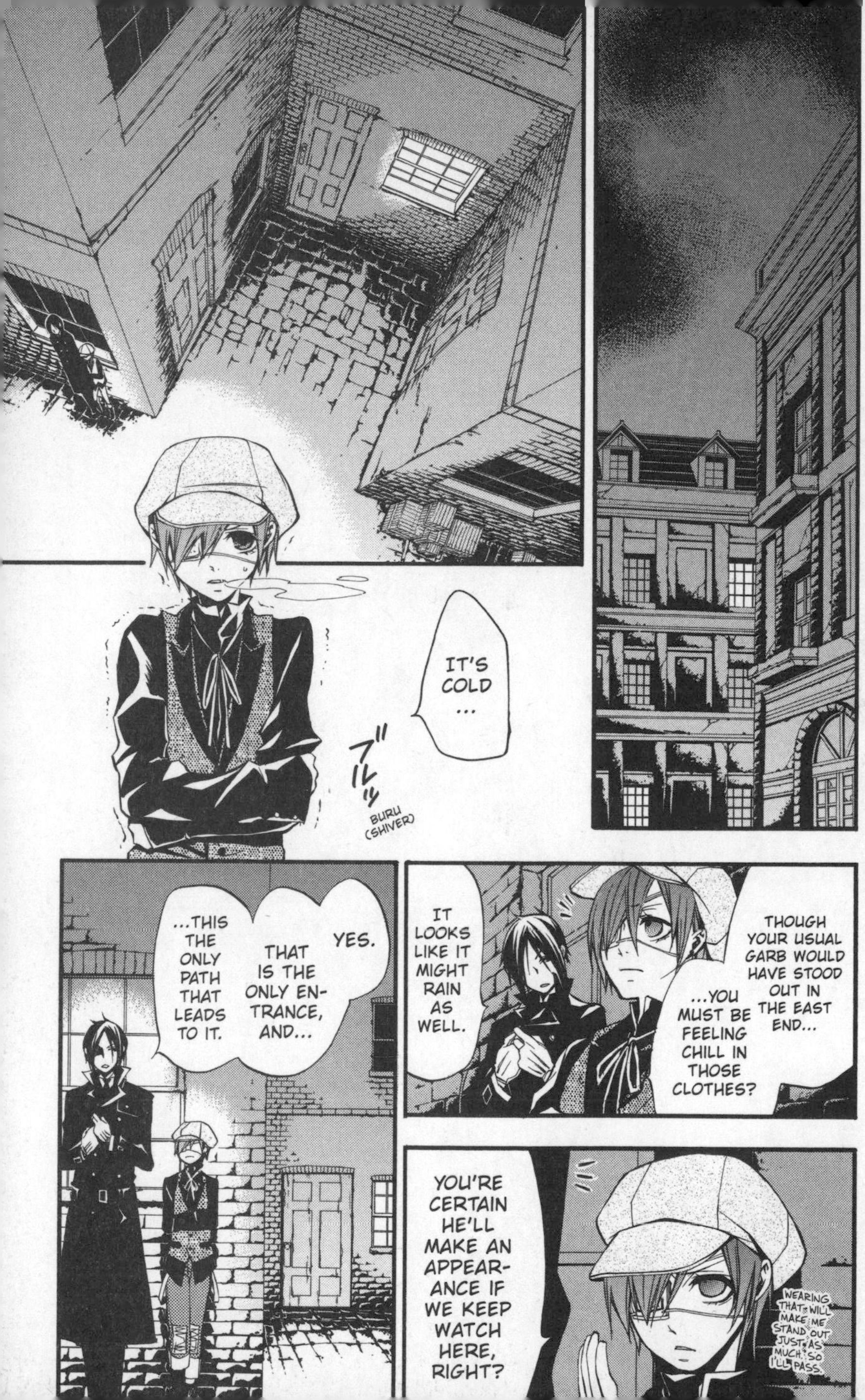
IT'S COLD ...
ブルッ
BURU (SHIVER)
THOUGH YOUR USUAL GARB WOULD HAVE STOOD OUT IN THE EAST END...
...YOU MUST BE FEELING CHILL IN THOSE CLOTHES?
IT LOOKS LIKE IT MIGHT RAIN AS WELL.
WEARING THAT WILL MAKE ME STAND OUT JUST AS MUCH. SO I'LL PASS.
YOU'RE CERTAIN HE'LL MAKE AN APPEARANCE IF WE KEEP WATCH HERE, RIGHT?
YES.
THAT IS THE ONLY EN-TRANCE, AND...
...THIS THE ONLY PATH THAT LEADS TO IT.

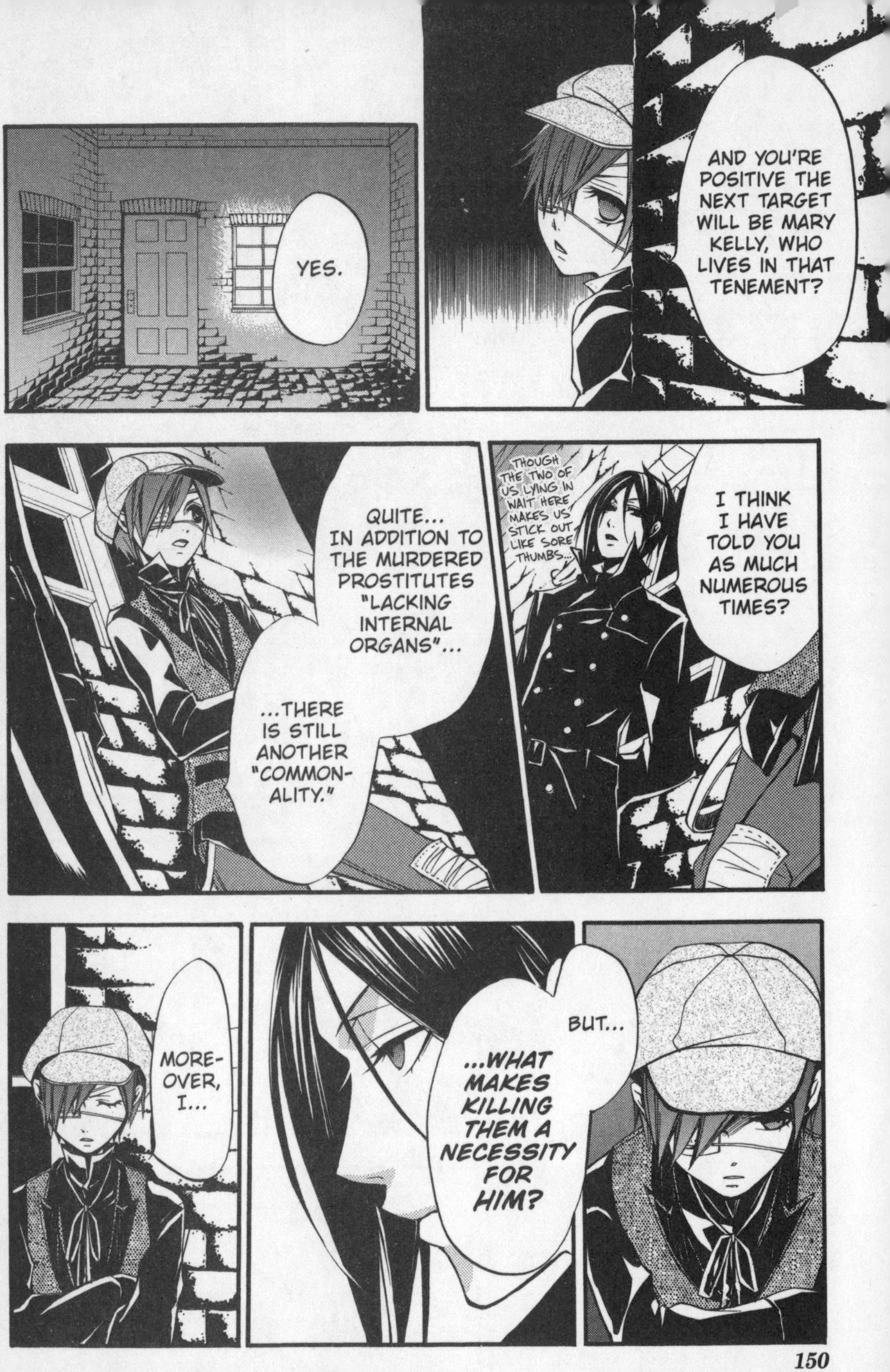
AND YOU'RE POSITIVE THE NEXT TARGET WILL BE MARY KELLY, WHO LIVES IN THAT TENEMENT?
YES.
I THINK I HAVE TOLD YOU AS MUCH NUMEROUS TIMES?
THOUGH THE TWO OF US LYING IN WAIT HERE MAKES US STICK OUT LIKE SORE THUMBS...
QUITE... IN ADDITION TO THE MURDERED PROSTITUTES "LACKING INTERNAL ORGANS"...
...THERE IS STILL ANOTHER "COMMON-ALITY."
BUT...
...WHAT MAKES KILLING THEM A NECESSITY FOR HIM?
MORE-OVER, I...

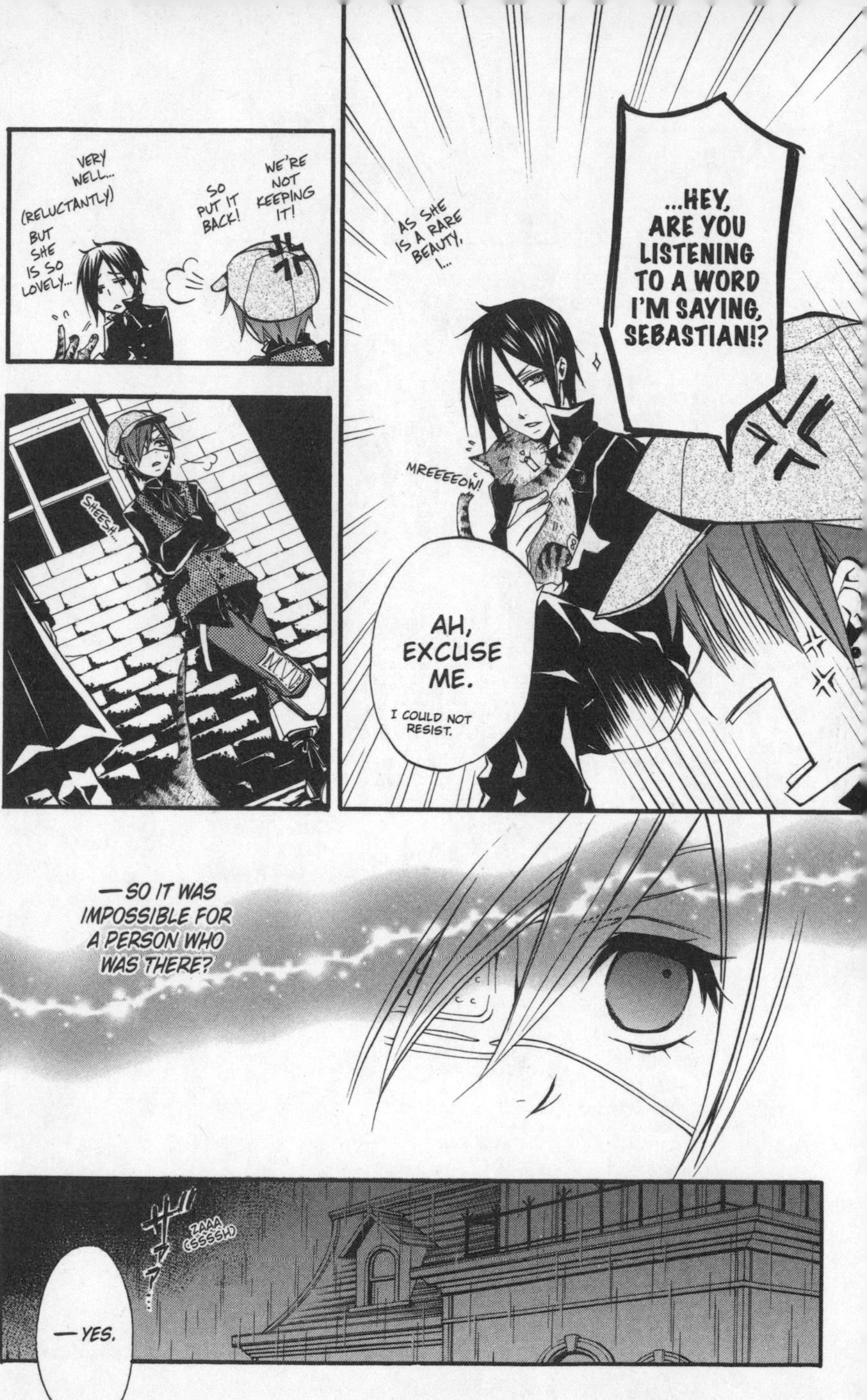
...HEY, ARE YOU LISTENING TO A WORD I'M SAYING, SEBASTIAN!?
AS SHE IS A RARE BEAUTY, I...
MREEEEOW!
AH, EXCUSE ME.
I COULD NOT RESIST.
WE'RE NOT KEEPING IT!
SO PUT IT BACK!
VERY WELL... (RELUCTANTLY)
BUT SHE IS SO LOVELY...
SHEESH...
—SO IT WAS IMPOSSIBLE FOR A PERSON WHO WAS THERE?
ZAAA (SSSSH)
—YES.

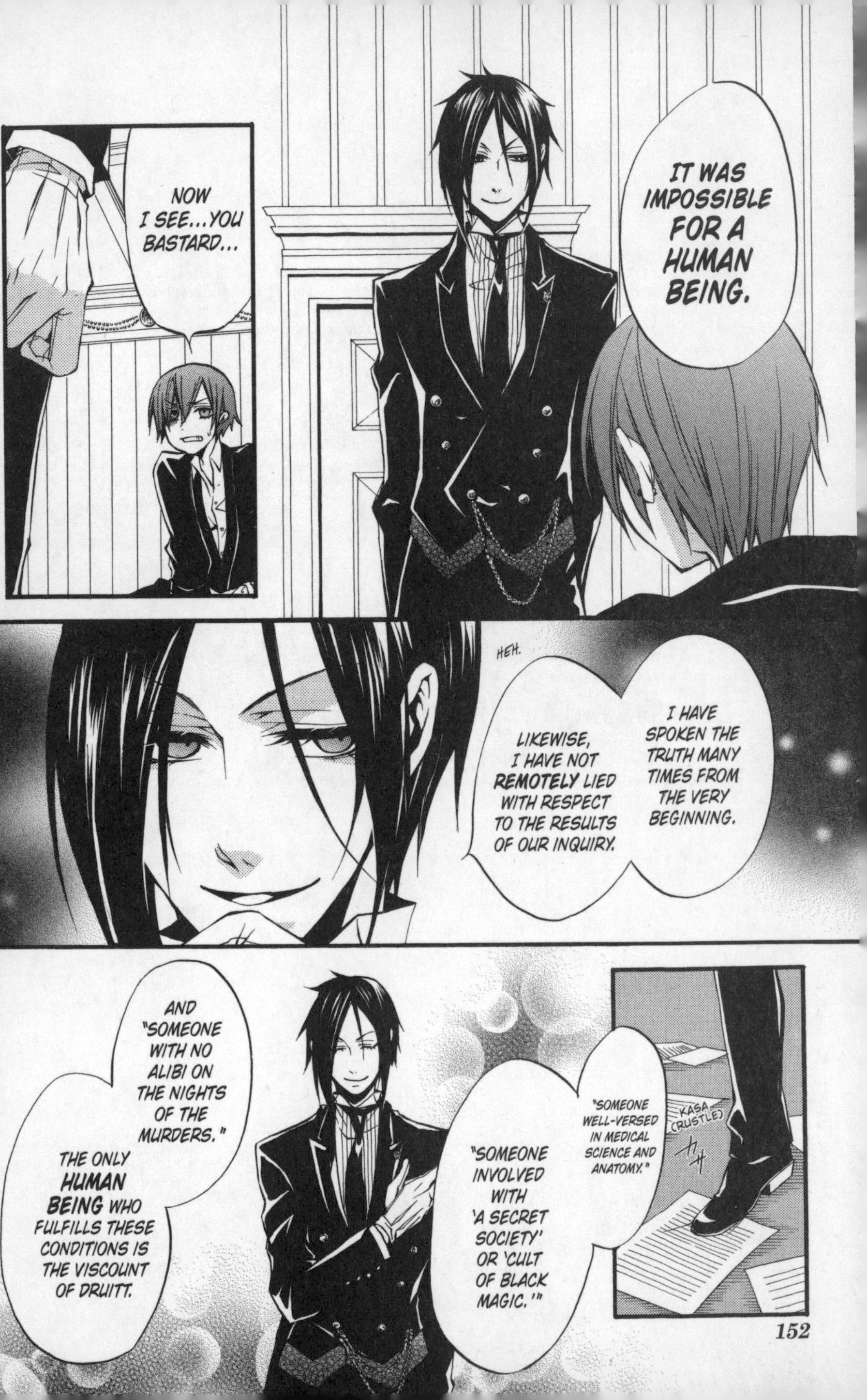
IT WAS IMPOSSIBLE FOR A HUMAN BEING.
NOW I SEE...YOU BASTARD...
HEH.
I HAVE SPOKEN THE TRUTH MANY TIMES FROM THE VERY BEGINNING.
LIKEWISE, I HAVE NOT REMOTELY LIED WITH RESPECT TO THE RESULTS OF OUR INQUIRY.
KASA (RUSTLE)
"SOMEONE WELL-VERSED IN MEDICAL SCIENCE AND ANATOMY."
"SOMEONE INVOLVED WITH 'A SECRET SOCIETY' OR 'CULT OF BLACK MAGIC.'"
AND "SOMEONE WITH NO ALIBI ON THE NIGHTS OF THE MURDERS."
THE ONLY HUMAN BEING WHO FULFILLS THESE CONDITIONS IS THE VISCOUNT OF DRUITT.

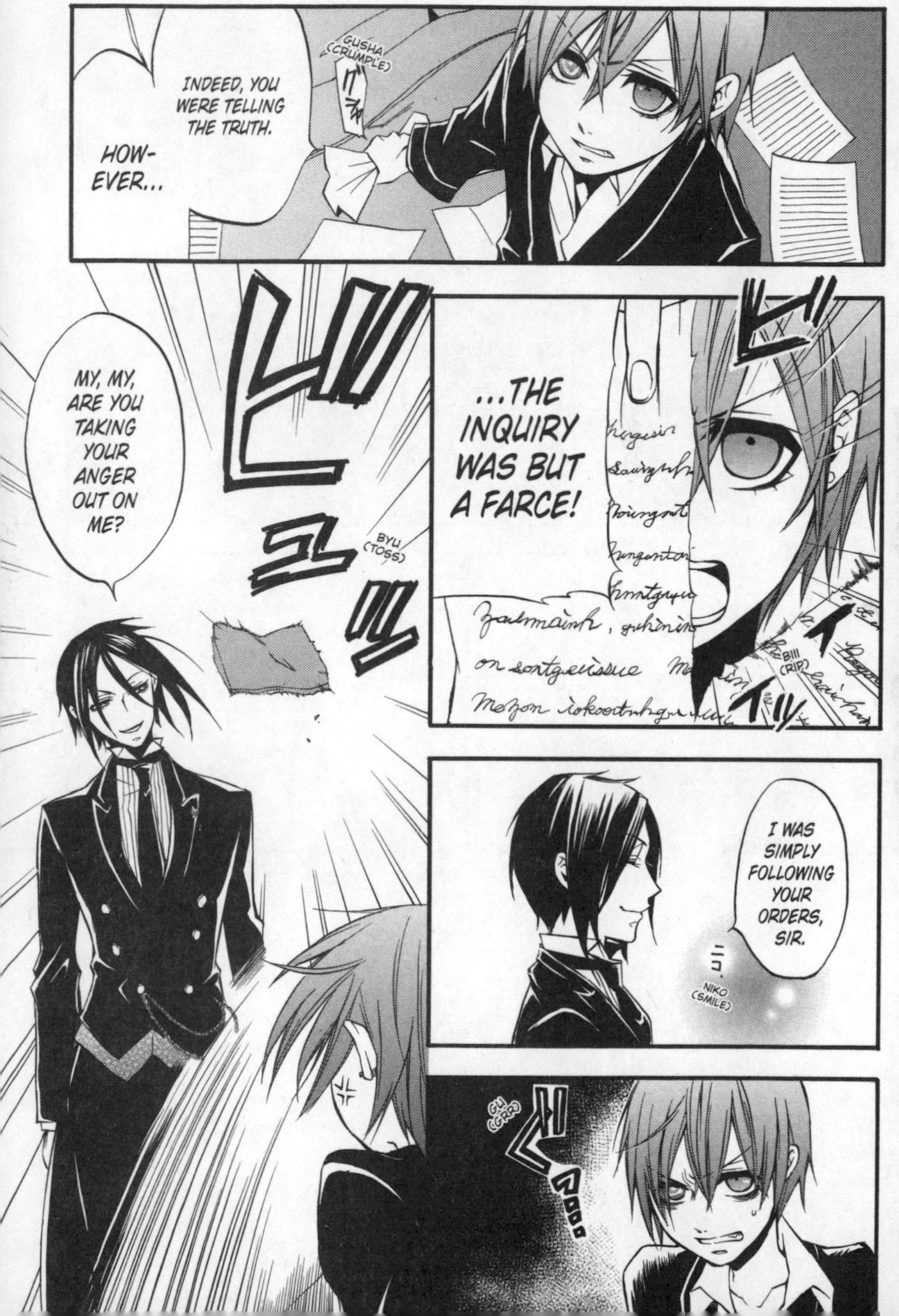
GUSHA (CRUMPLE)
INDEED, YOU WERE TELLING THE TRUTH.
HOW-EVER...
...THE INQUIRY WAS BUT A FARCE!
BIII (RIP)
I WAS SIMPLY FOLLOWING YOUR ORDERS, SIR.
NIKO (SMILE)
GU (GRR)
BYU (TOSS)
MY, MY, ARE YOU TAKING YOUR ANGER OUT ON ME?

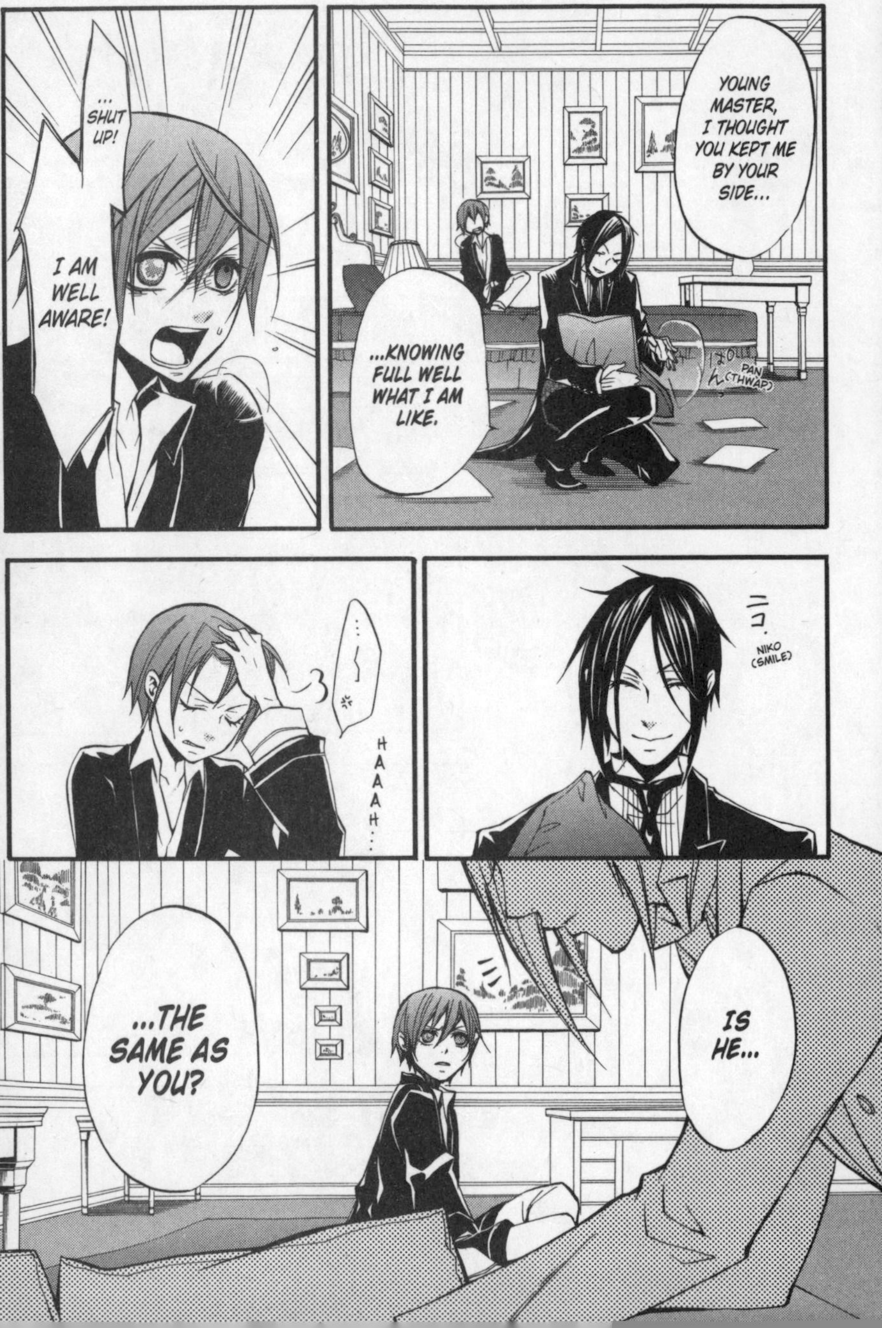
YOUNG MASTER, I THOUGHT YOU KEPT ME BY YOUR SIDE...
...KNOWING FULL WELL WHAT I AM LIKE.
ぱん
PAN (THWAP)
...SHUT UP!
I AM WELL AWARE!
ニコ
NIKO (SMILE)
HAAAAH...
IS HE...
...THE SAME AS YOU?

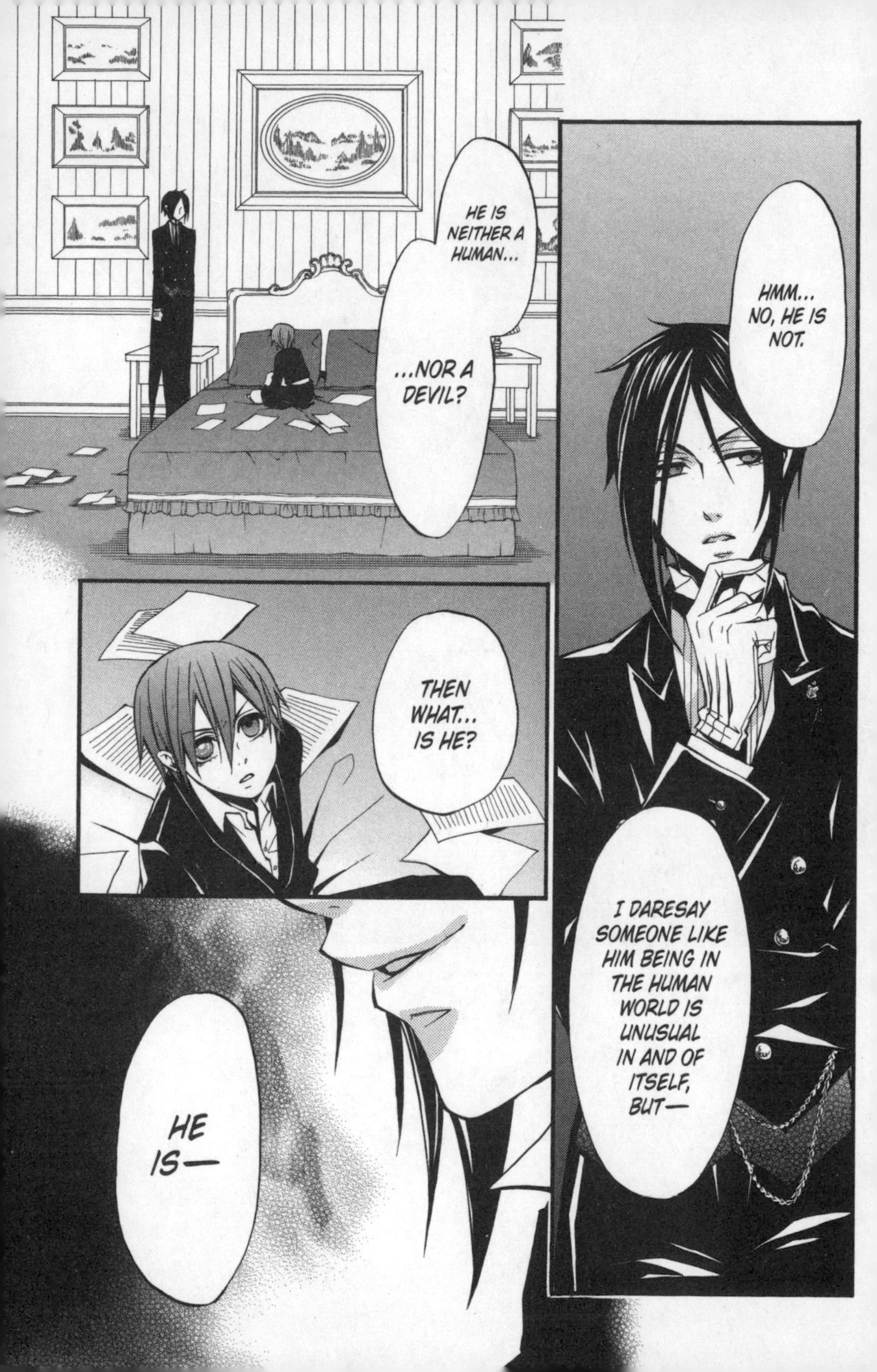
HE IS NEITHER A HUMAN...
...NOR A DEVIL?
HMM... NO, HE IS NOT.
I DARESAY SOMEONE LIKE HIM BEING IN THE HUMAN WORLD IS UNUSUAL IN AND OF ITSELF, BUT—
THEN WHAT... IS HE?
HE IS—

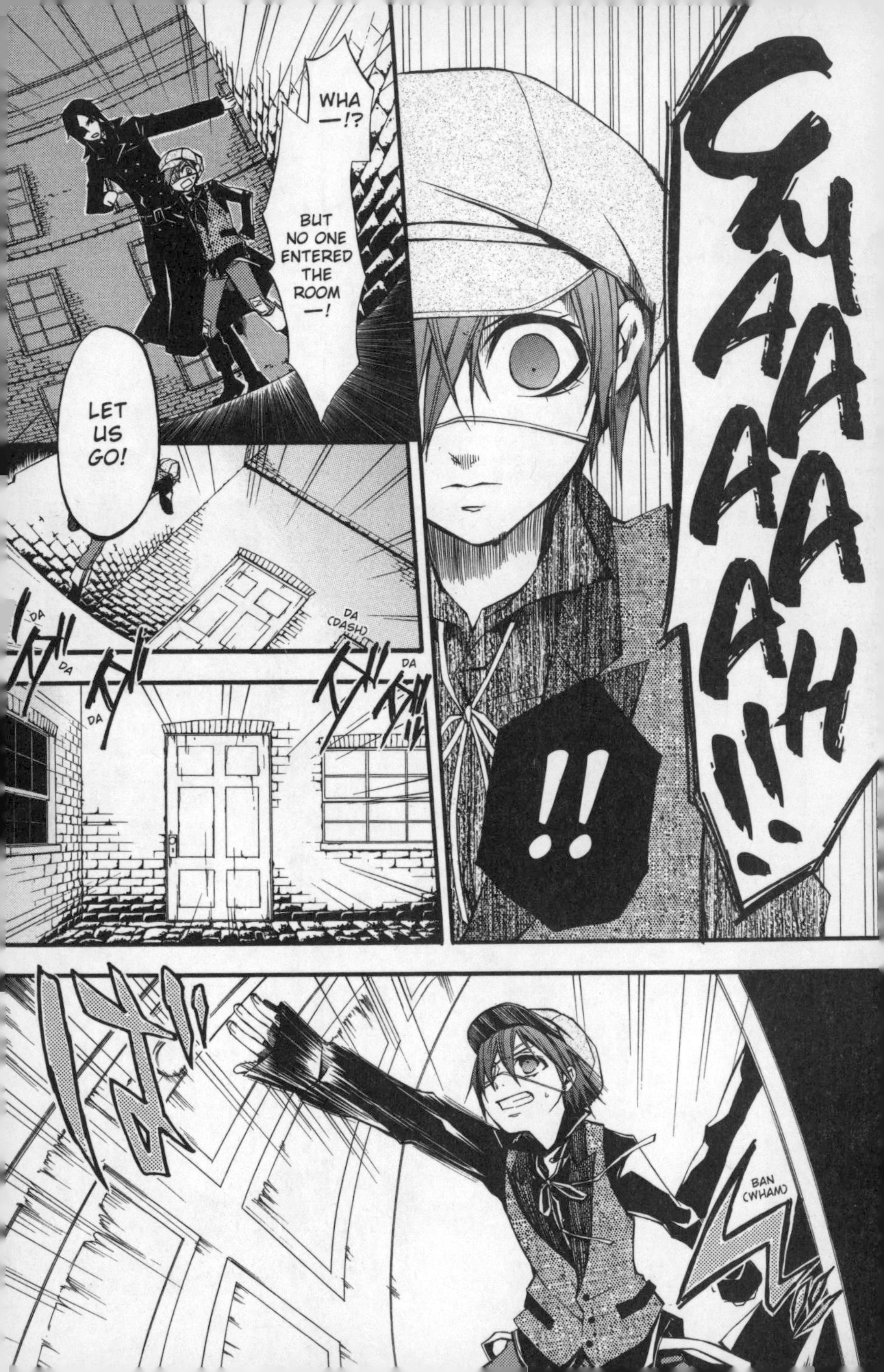
GYAAAAAAH!!
!!
WHA—!?
BUT NO ONE ENTERED THE ROOM—!
LET US GO!
DA (DASH)
DA
DA
DA
DA
BAN (WHAM)

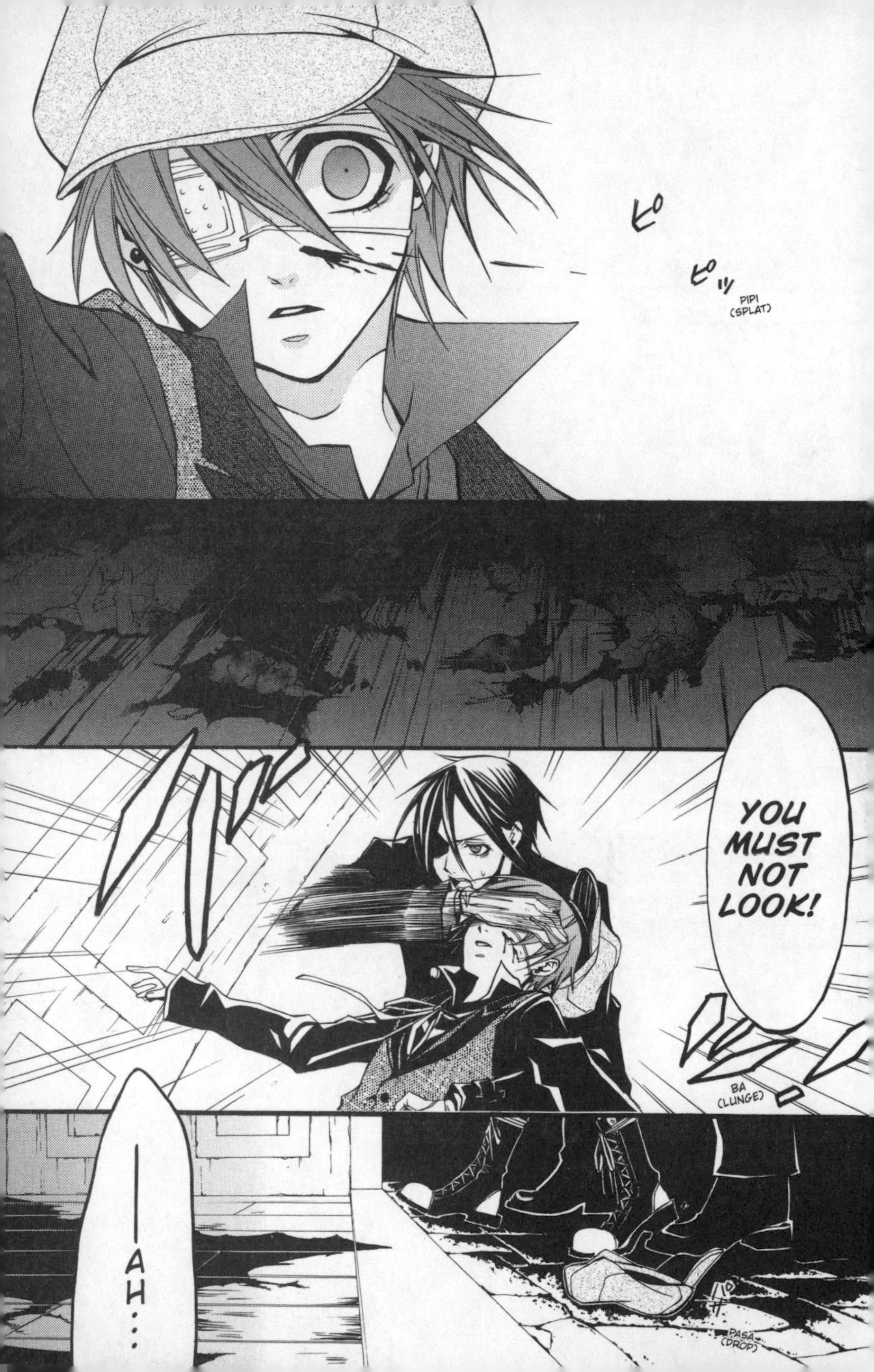
ピ
ピッ
PIPI
(SPLAT)
YOU MUST NOT LOOK!
BA
(LUNGE)
パサ
PASA
(DROP)
—AH...

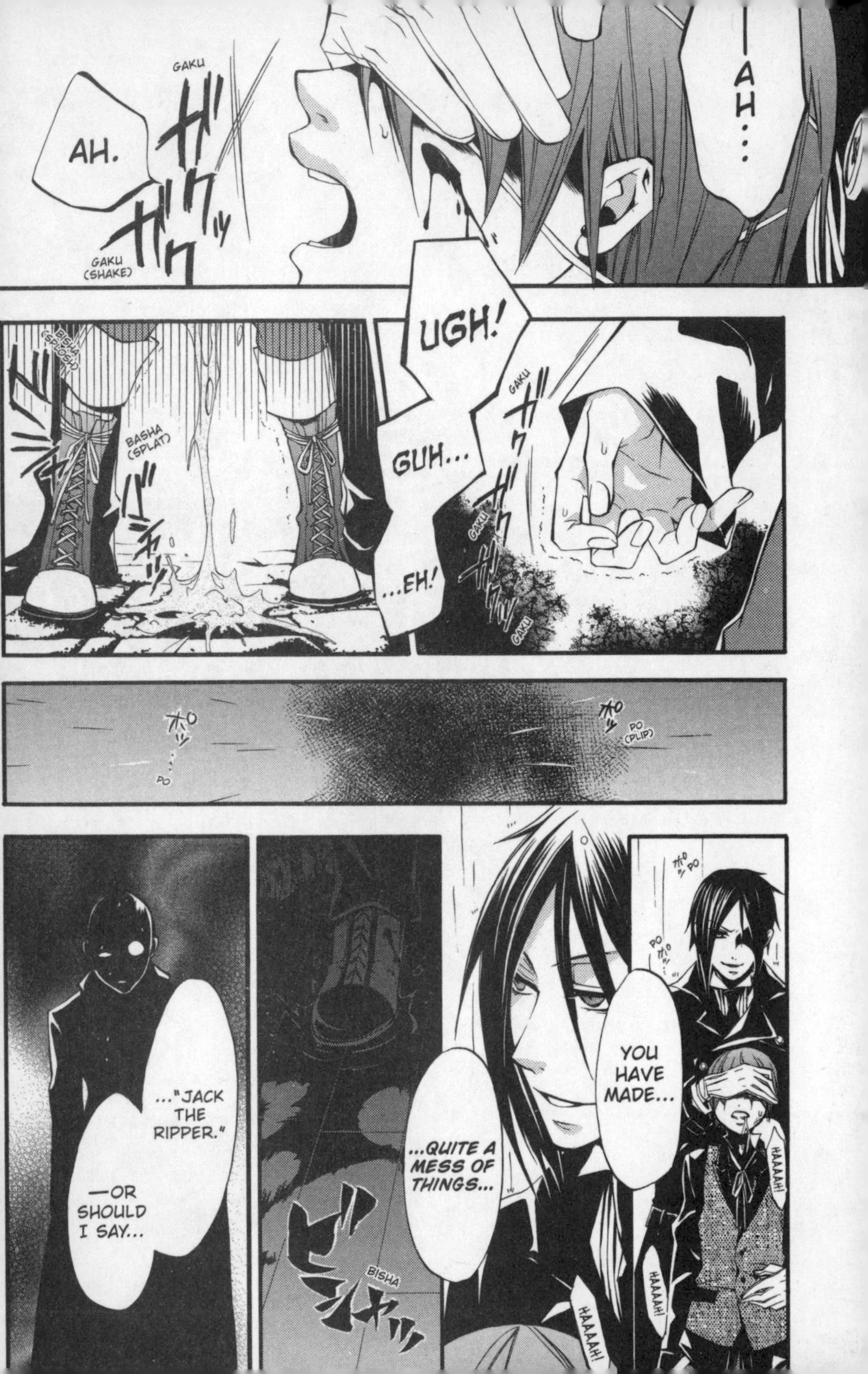

AH...
GAKU
AH.
GAKU (SHAKE)
UGH!
GAKU
GUH...
GAKU
...EH!
GAKU
BISHA (SPLOSH)
BASHA (SPLAT)
PO (PLIP)
PO
PO
PO
HAAAAH!
HAAAAH!
HAAAAH!
YOU HAVE MADE...
...QUITE A MESS OF THINGS...
BISHA
..."JACK THE RIPPER."
—OR SHOULD I SAY...

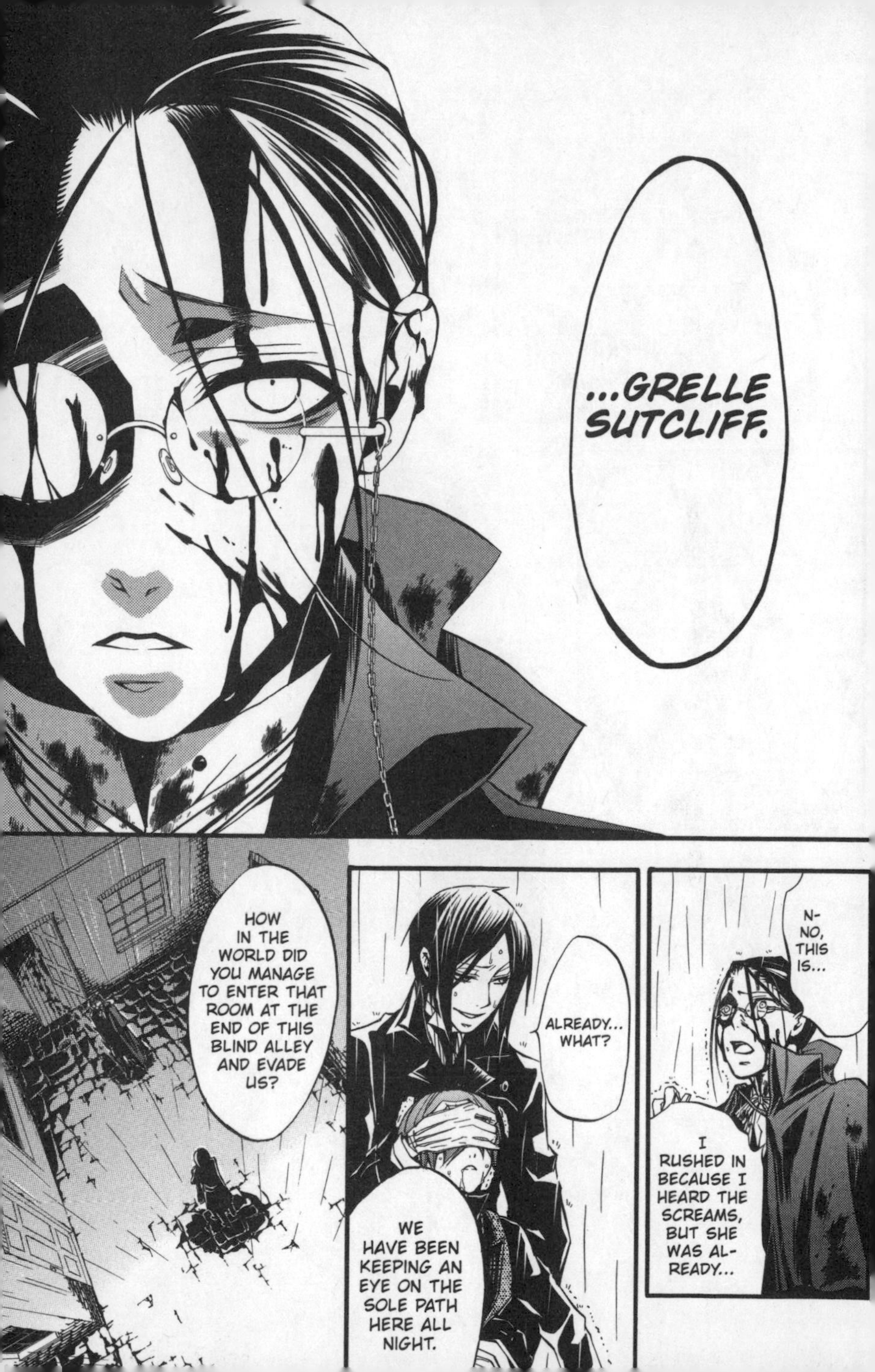
...GRELLE SUTCLIFF.
N-NO, THIS IS...
I RUSHED IN BECAUSE I HEARD THE SCREAMS, BUT SHE WAS AL-READY...
ALREADY... WHAT?
WE HAVE BEEN KEEPING AN EYE ON THE SOLE PATH HERE ALL NIGHT.
HOW IN THE WORLD DID YOU MANAGE TO ENTER THAT ROOM AT THE END OF THIS BLIND ALLEY AND EVADE US?

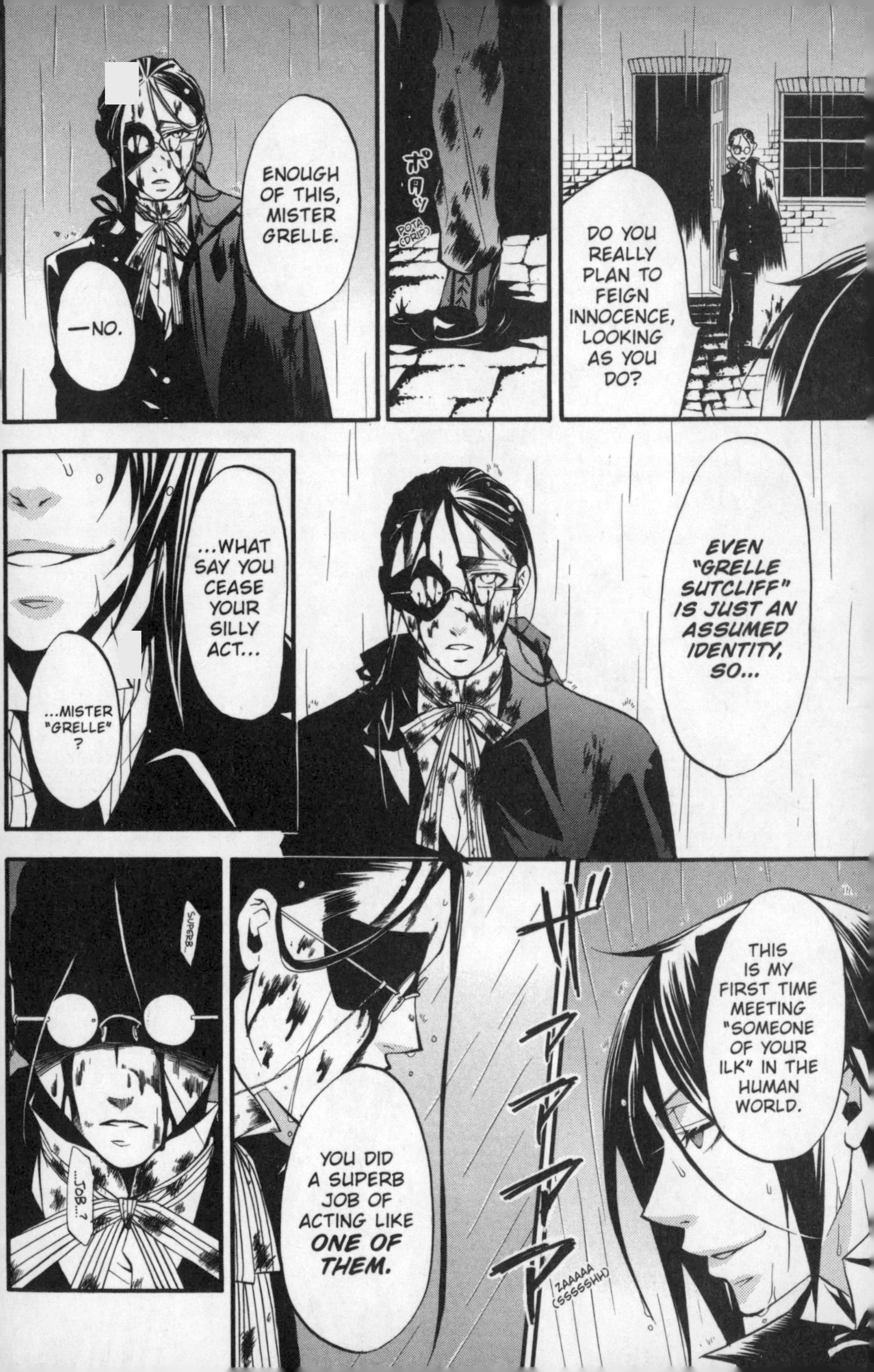
DO YOU REALLY PLAN TO FEIGN INNOCENCE, LOOKING AS YOU DO?
ポタッ
POTA (DRIP)
ENOUGH OF THIS, MISTER GRELLE.
—NO.
EVEN "GRELLE SUTCLIFF" IS JUST AN ASSUMED IDENTITY, SO...
...WHAT SAY YOU CEASE YOUR SILLY ACT...
...MISTER "GRELLE"?
THIS IS MY FIRST TIME MEETING "SOMEONE OF YOUR ILK" IN THE HUMAN WORLD.
ZAAAAA (SSSSSHH)
YOU DID A SUPERB JOB OF ACTING LIKE ONE OF THEM.
SUPERB...
...JOB...?

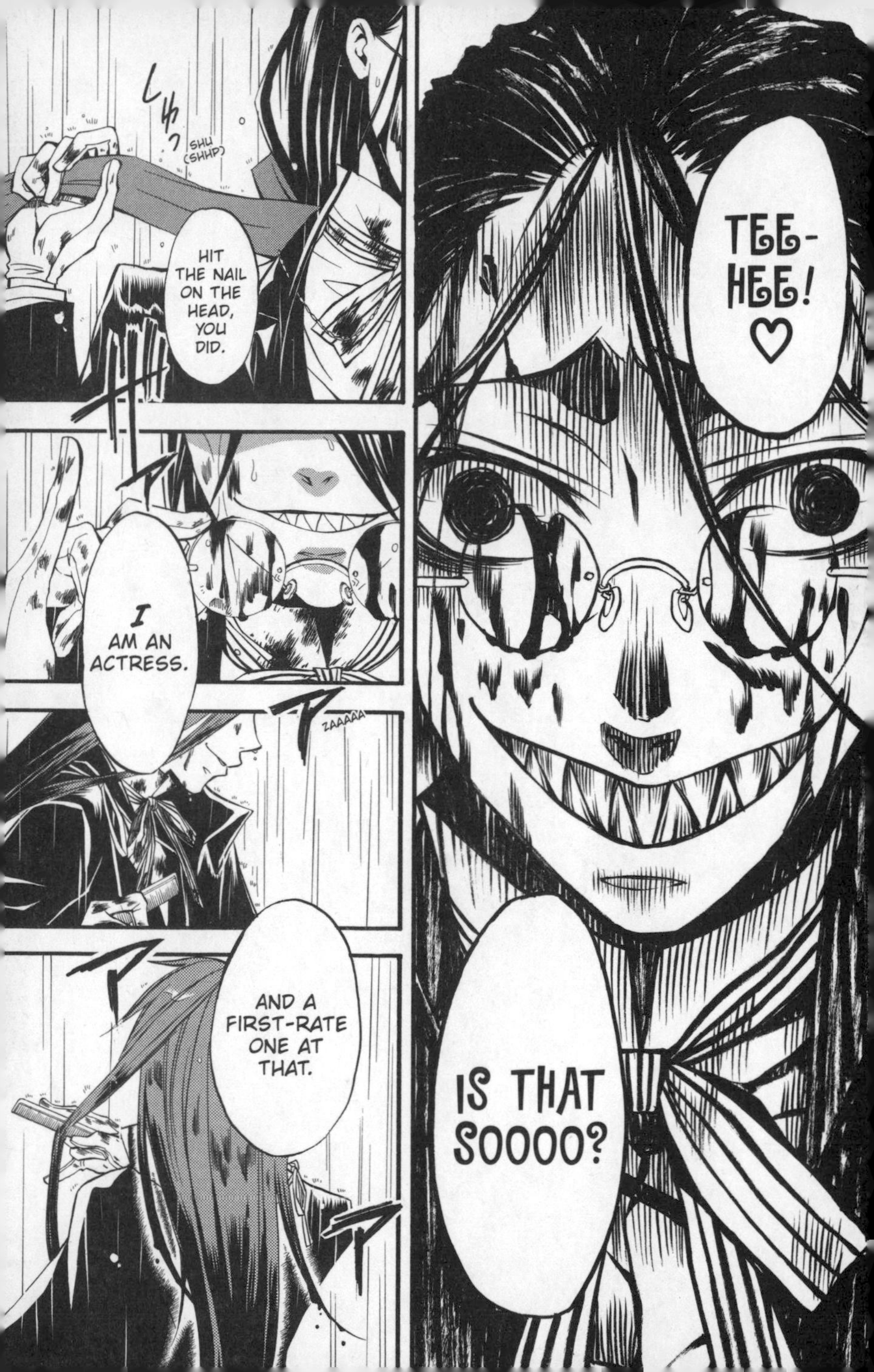

TEE-HEE! ♥
IS THAT SOOOO?
SHU (SHHP)
HIT THE NAIL ON THE HEAD, YOU DID.
I AM AN ACTRESS.
ZAAAAA
AND A FIRST-RATE ONE AT THAT.

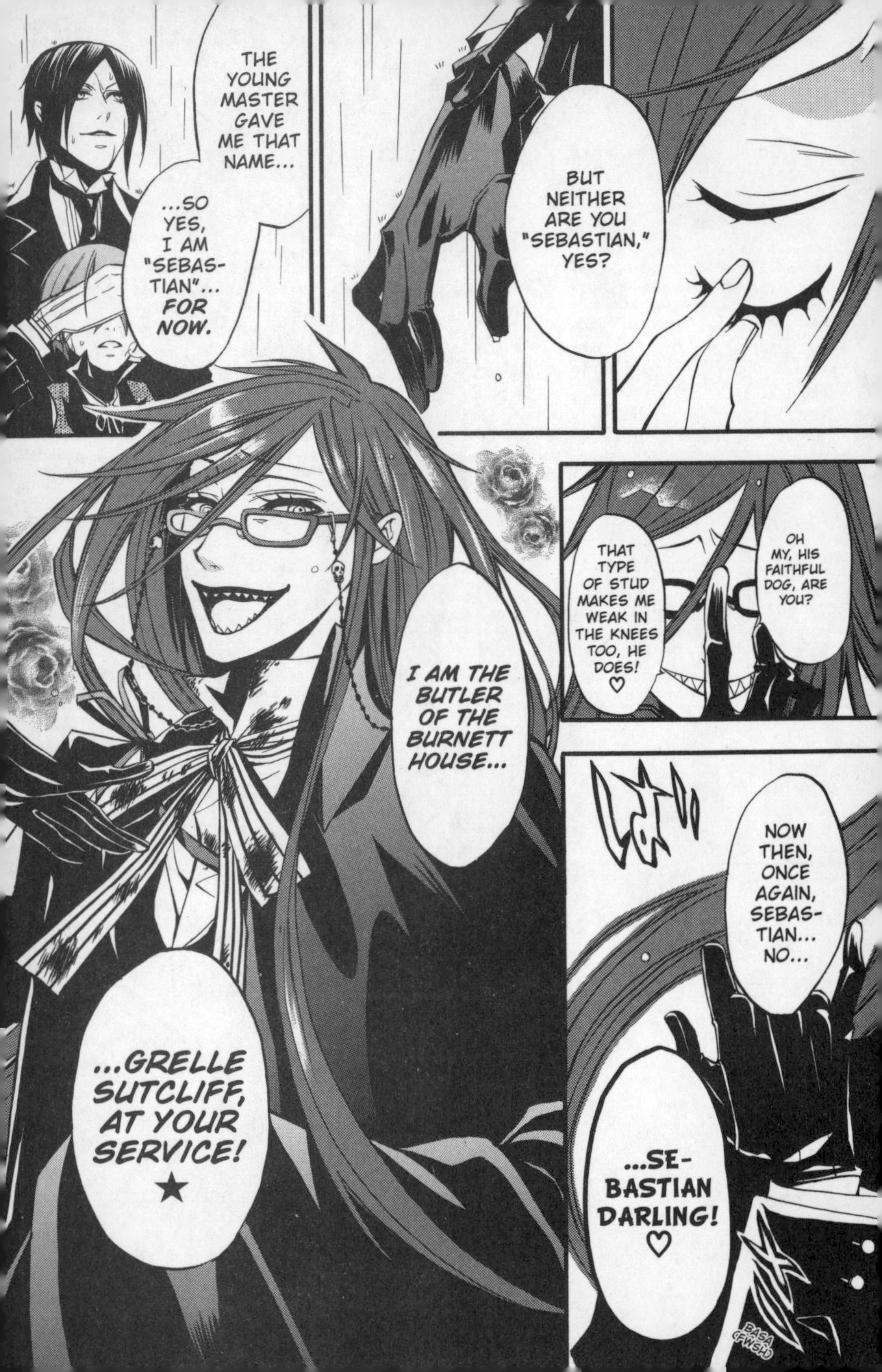
BUT NEITHER ARE YOU "SEBASTIAN," YES?
THE YOUNG MASTER GAVE ME THAT NAME...
...SO YES, I AM "SEBAS-TIAN"... FOR NOW.
OH MY, HIS FAITHFUL DOG, ARE YOU?
THAT TYPE OF STUD MAKES ME WEAK IN THE KNEES TOO, HE DOES! ♡
NOW THEN, ONCE AGAIN, SEBAS-TIAN... NO...
...SE-BASTIAN DARLING! ♡
BASA (FWSH)
I AM THE BUTLER OF THE BURNETT HOUSE...
...GRELLE SUTCLIFF, AT YOUR SERVICE! ★

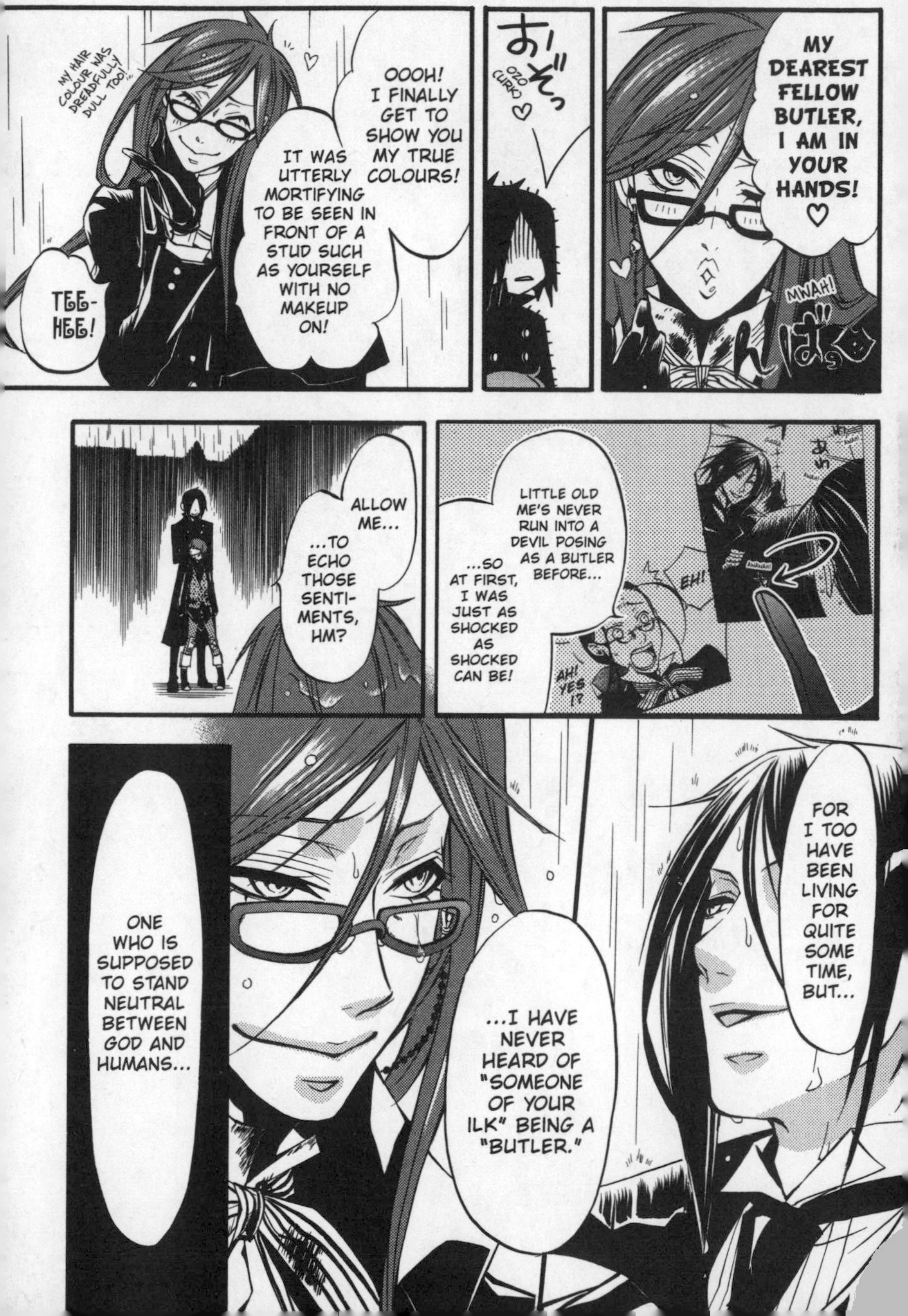
MY DEAREST FELLOW BUTLER, I AM IN YOUR HANDS! ♥
MWAH!
OZO (URK) ♥
OOOH! I FINALLY GET TO SHOW YOU MY TRUE COLOURS!
IT WAS UTTERLY MORTIFYING TO BE SEEN IN FRONT OF A STUD SUCH AS YOURSELF WITH NO MAKEUP ON!
MY HAIR COLOUR WAS DREADFULLY DULL TOO!
TEE-HEE!
LITTLE OLD ME'S NEVER RUN INTO A DEVIL POSING AS A BUTLER BEFORE...
...SO AT FIRST, I WAS JUST AS SHOCKED AS SHOCKED CAN BE!
AH!AH!AH!
EH!
AH! YES!?
ALLOW ME...
...TO ECHO THOSE SENTIMENTS, HM?
FOR I TOO HAVE BEEN LIVING FOR QUITE SOME TIME, BUT...
...I HAVE NEVER HEARD OF "SOMEONE OF YOUR ILK" BEING A "BUTLER."
ONE WHO IS SUPPOSED TO STAND NEUTRAL BETWEEN GOD AND HUMANS...

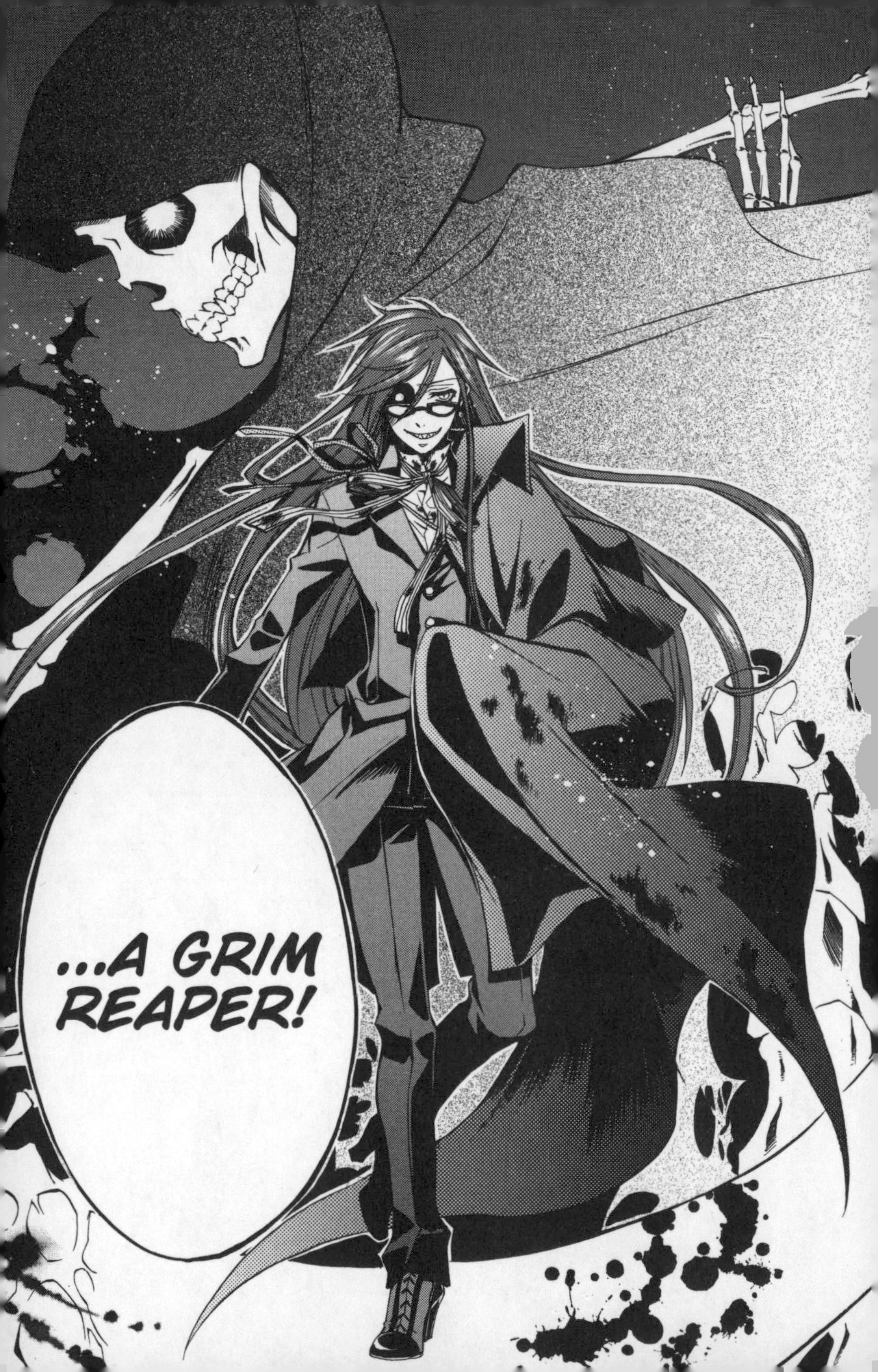
...A GRIM REAPER!

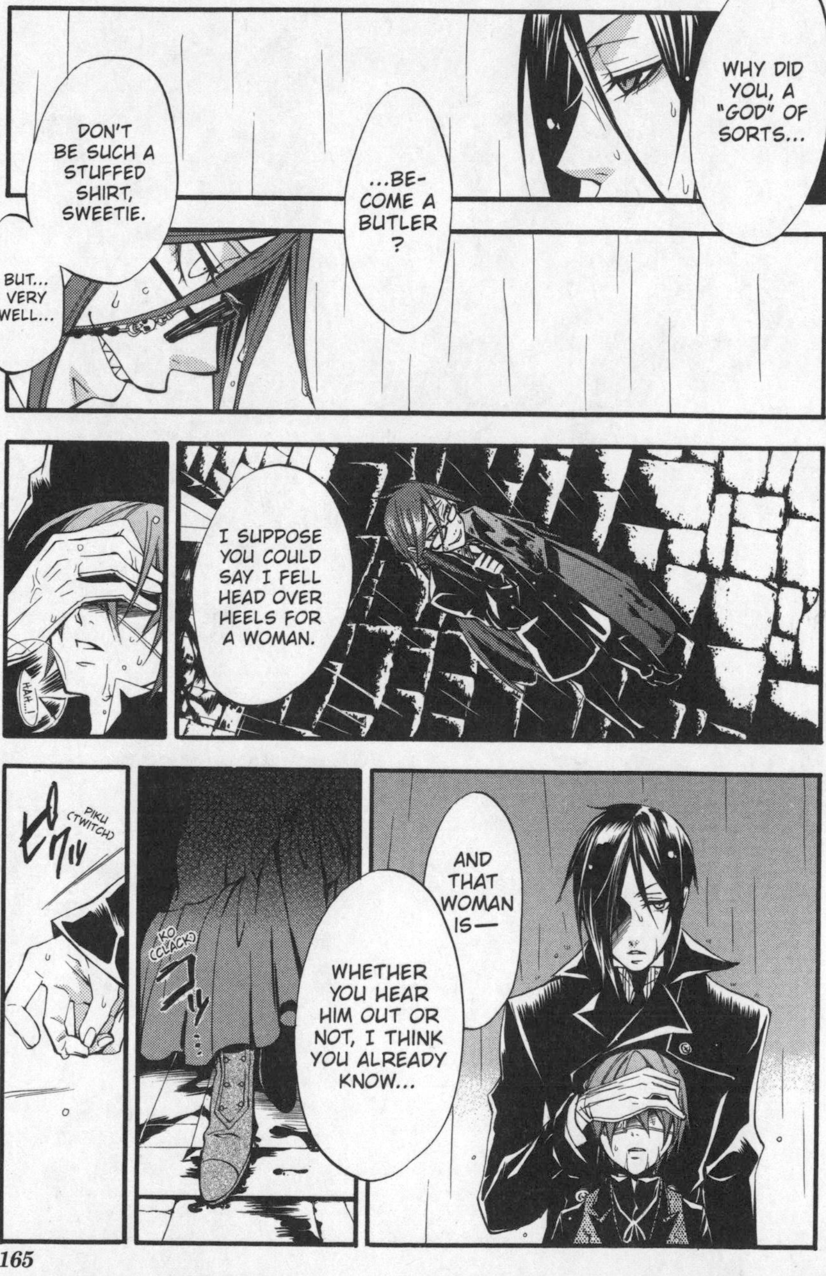
WHY DID YOU, A "GOD" OF SORTS...
...BE-COME A BUTLER?
DON'T BE SUCH A STUFFED SHIRT, SWEETIE.
BUT... VERY WELL...
I SUPPOSE YOU COULD SAY I FELL HEAD OVER HEELS FOR A WOMAN.
HAH...!
AND THAT WOMAN IS—
WHETHER YOU HEAR HIM OUT OR NOT, I THINK YOU ALREADY KNOW...
KO (CLACK)
PIKU (TWITCH)

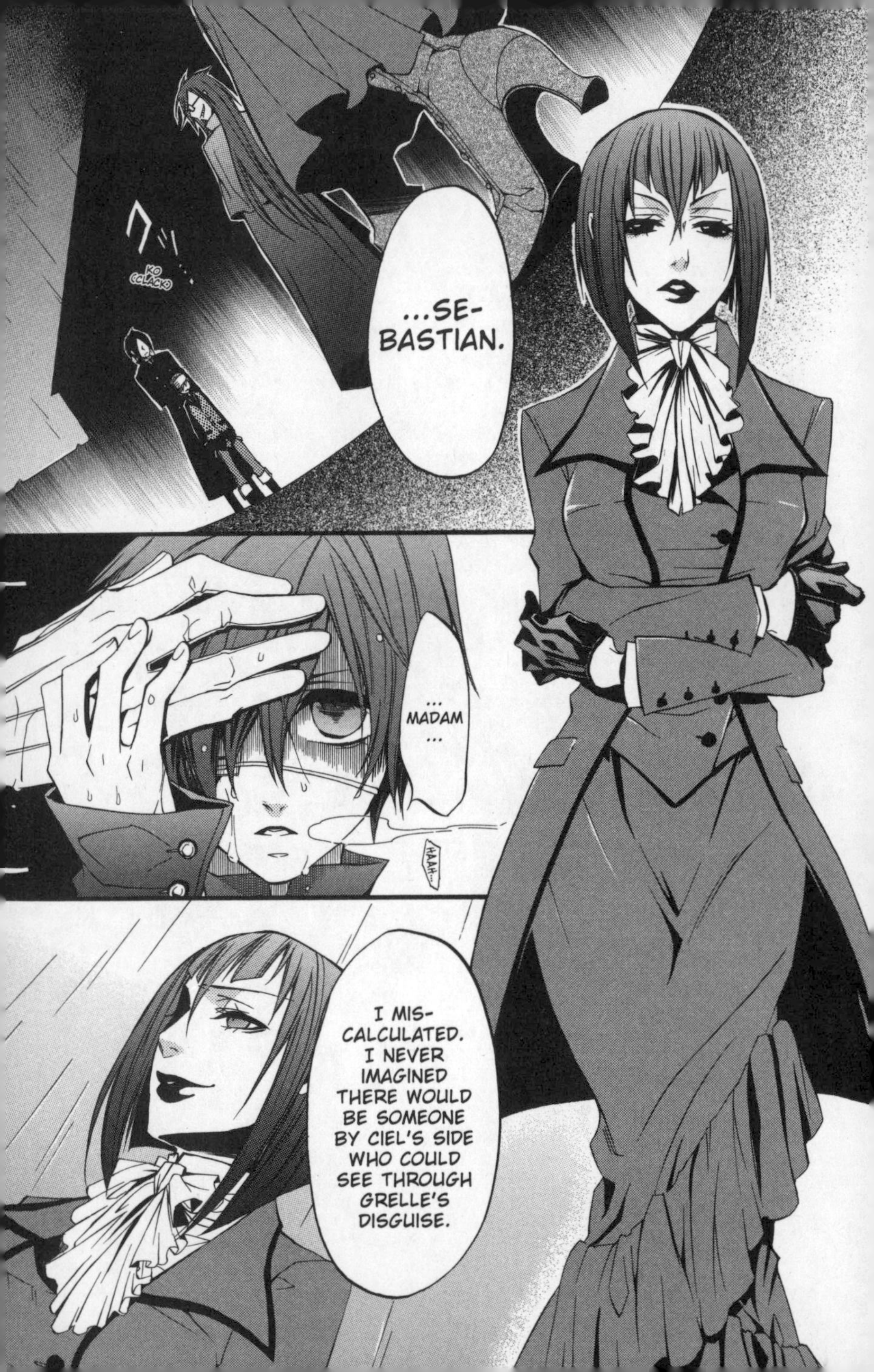
...SE-BASTIAN.
KO (CLACK)
...MADAM...
HAAH...
I MIS-CALCULATED. I NEVER IMAGINED THERE WOULD BE SOMEONE BY CIEL'S SIDE WHO COULD SEE THROUGH GRELLE'S DISGUISE.

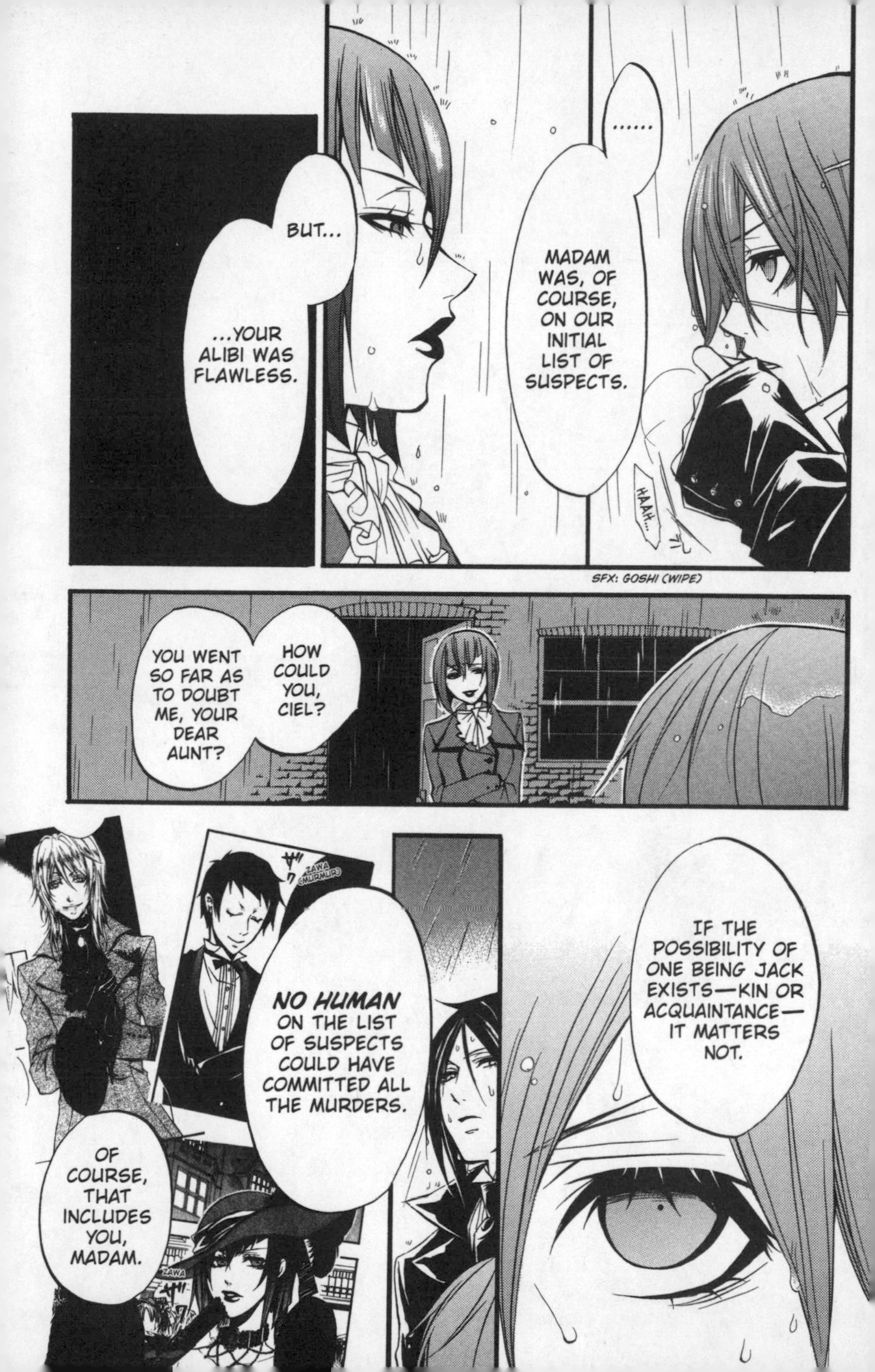
......
MADAM WAS, OF COURSE, ON OUR INITIAL LIST OF SUSPECTS.
HAAH...
BUT...
...YOUR ALIBI WAS FLAWLESS.
SFX: GOSHI (WIPE)
HOW COULD YOU, CIEL?
YOU WENT SO FAR AS TO DOUBT ME, YOUR DEAR AUNT?
IF THE POSSIBILITY OF ONE BEING JACK EXISTS—KIN OR ACQUAINTANCE—IT MATTERS NOT.
NO HUMAN ON THE LIST OF SUSPECTS COULD HAVE COMMITTED ALL THE MURDERS.
ZAWA (MURMUR)
OF COURSE, THAT INCLUDES YOU, MADAM.
ZAWA

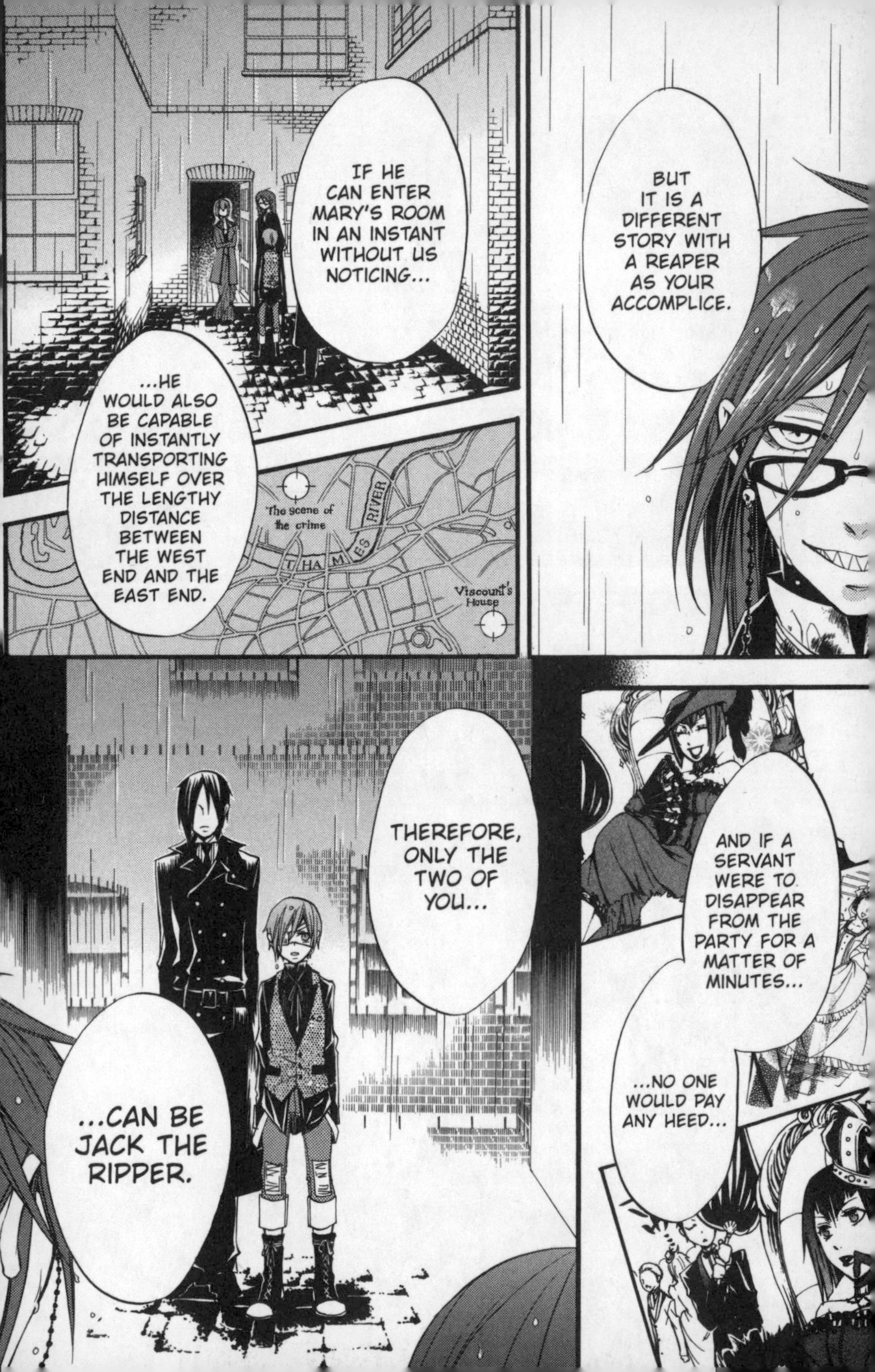
BUT IT IS A DIFFERENT STORY WITH A REAPER AS YOUR ACCOMPLICE.
IF HE CAN ENTER MARY'S ROOM IN AN INSTANT WITHOUT US NOTICING...
...HE WOULD ALSO BE CAPABLE OF INSTANTLY TRANSPORTING HIMSELF OVER THE LENGTHY DISTANCE BETWEEN THE WEST END AND THE EAST END.
The scene of the crime
THAMES RIVER
Viscount's House
AND IF A SERVANT WERE TO DISAPPEAR FROM THE PARTY FOR A MATTER OF MINUTES...
...NO ONE WOULD PAY ANY HEED...
THEREFORE, ONLY THE TWO OF YOU...
...CAN BE JACK THE RIPPER.

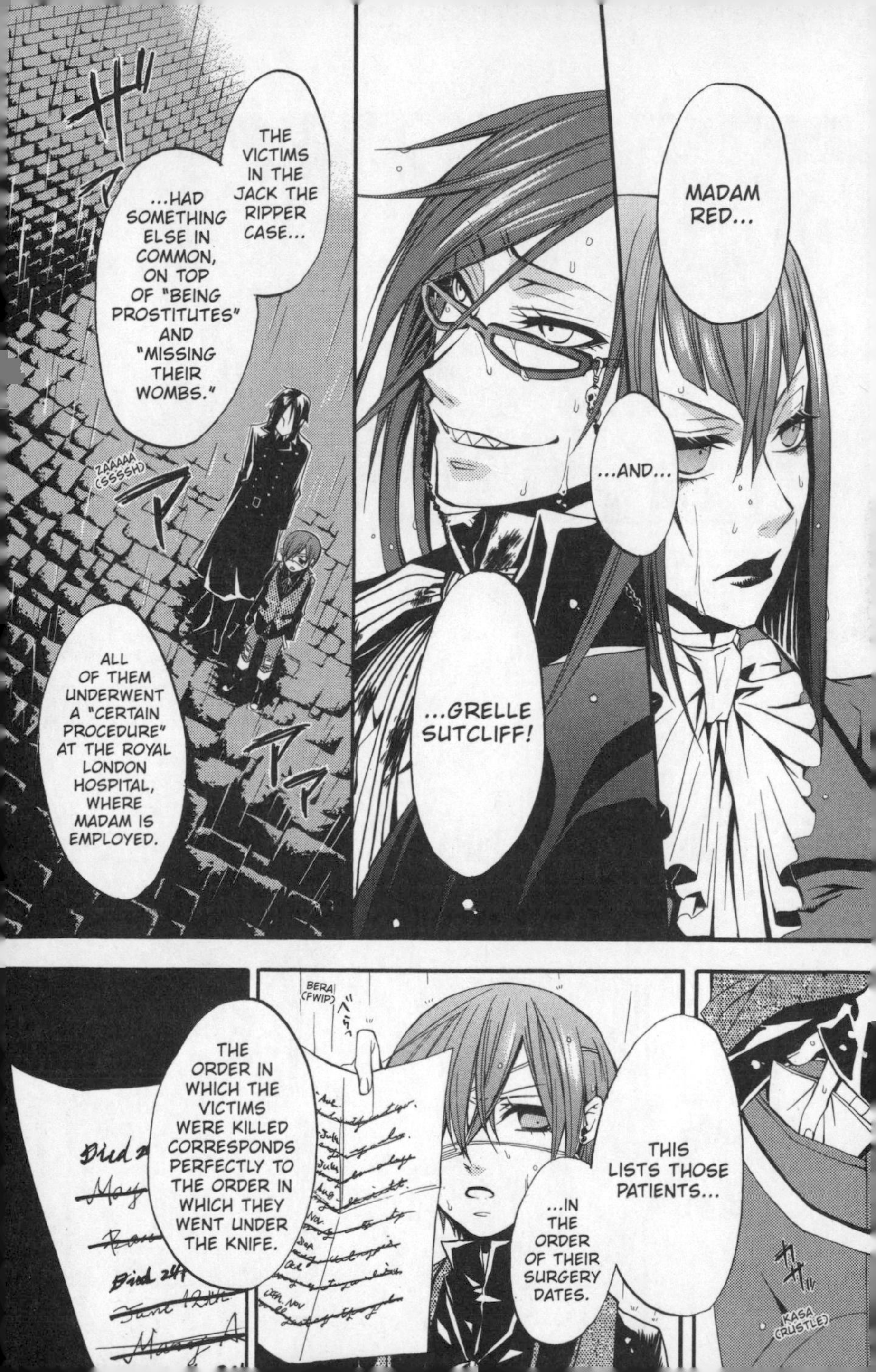
MADAM RED...
...AND...
...GRELLE SUTCLIFF!
THE VICTIMS IN THE JACK THE RIPPER CASE...
...HAD SOMETHING ELSE IN COMMON, ON TOP OF "BEING PROSTITUTES" AND "MISSING THEIR WOMBS."
ZAAAAA (SSSSH)
ALL OF THEM UNDERWENT A "CERTAIN PROCEDURE" AT THE ROYAL LONDON HOSPITAL, WHERE MADAM IS EMPLOYED.
KASA (RUSTLE)
THIS LISTS THOSE PATIENTS...
...IN THE ORDER OF THEIR SURGERY DATES.
BERA (FWIP)
THE ORDER IN WHICH THE VICTIMS WERE KILLED CORRESPONDS PERFECTLY TO THE ORDER IN WHICH THEY WENT UNDER THE KNIFE.

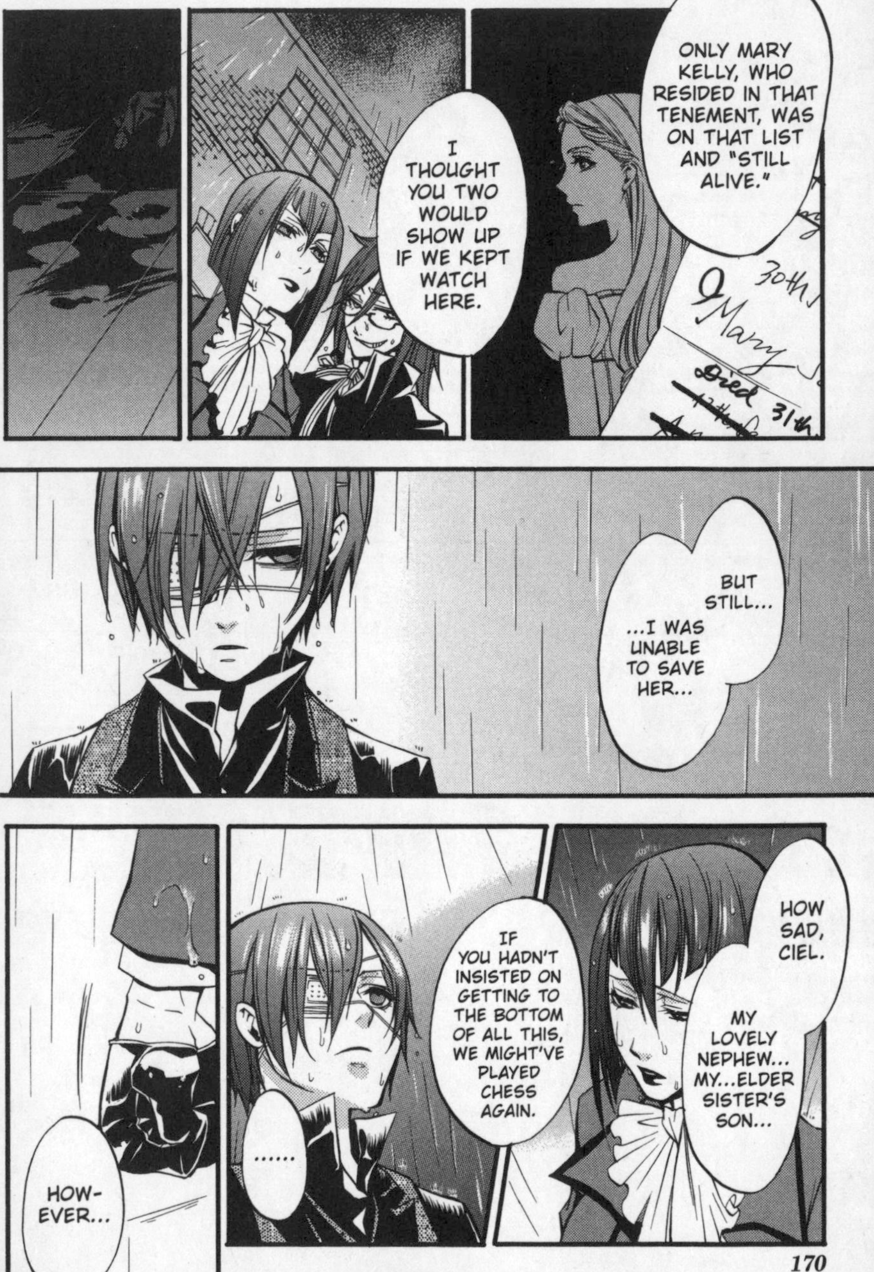
ONLY MARY KELLY, WHO RESIDED IN THAT TENEMENT, WAS ON THAT LIST AND "STILL ALIVE."
I THOUGHT YOU TWO WOULD SHOW UP IF WE KEPT WATCH HERE.
BUT STILL...
...I WAS UNABLE TO SAVE HER...
HOW SAD, CIEL.
MY LOVELY NEPHEW... MY...ELDER SISTER'S SON...
IF YOU HADN'T INSISTED ON GETTING TO THE BOTTOM OF ALL THIS, WE MIGHT'VE PLAYED CHESS AGAIN.
......
HOW-EVER...

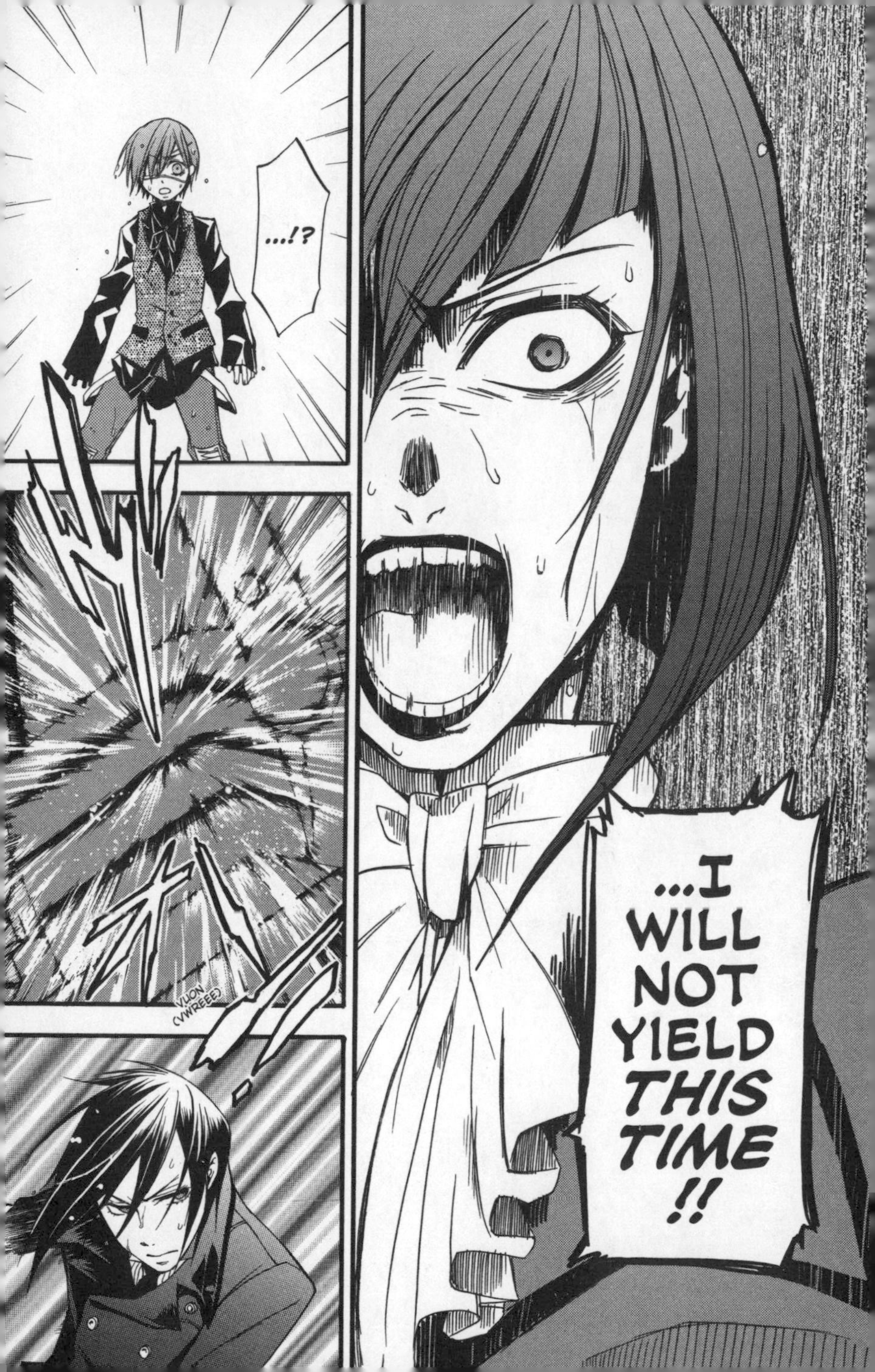
...I WILL NOT YIELD THIS TIME!!
...!?
VUON (VWREEE)

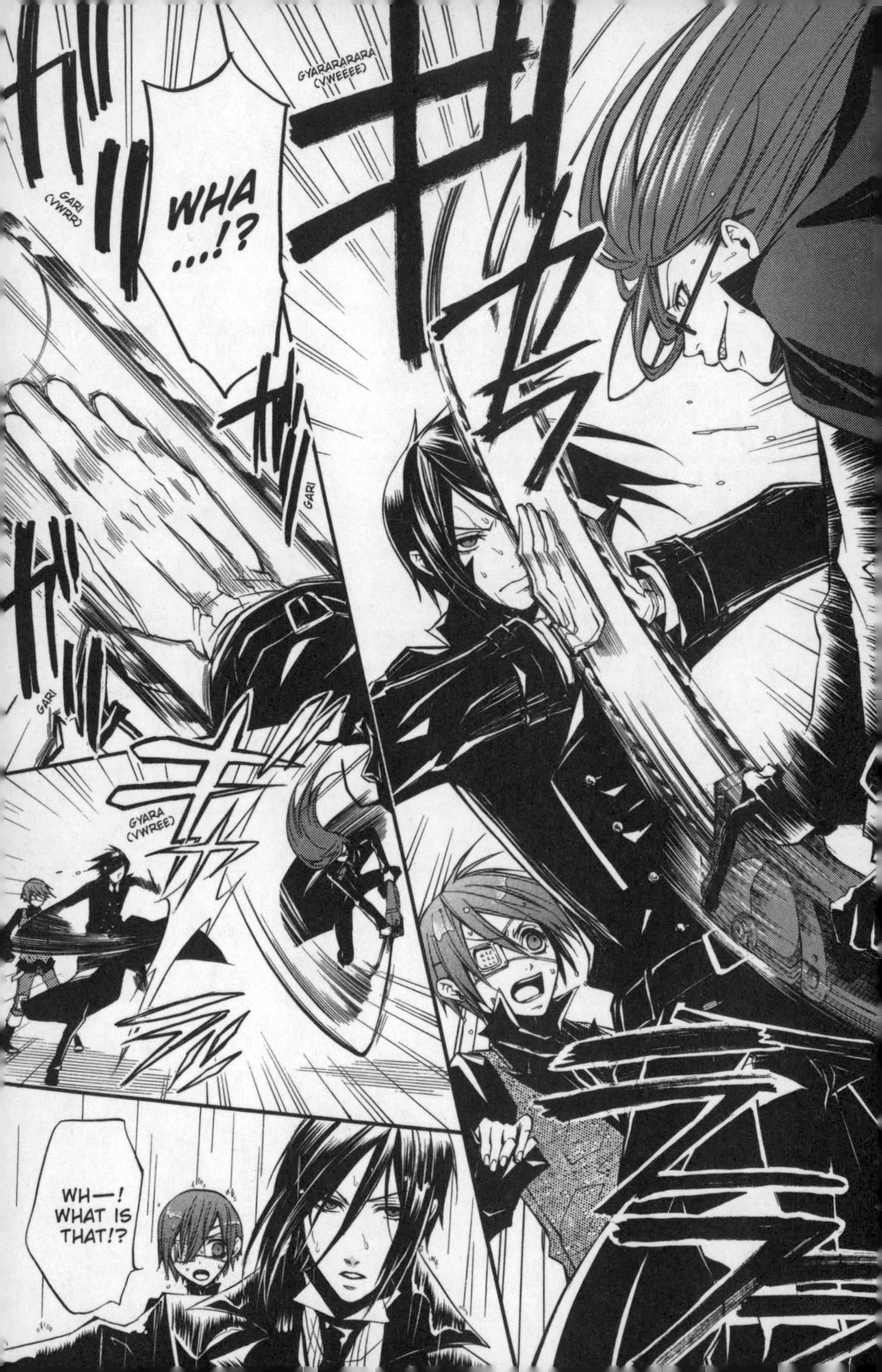
GYARARARARA (VWEEEE)
WHA ...!?
GARI (VWRR)
GARI
GARI
GYARA (VWREE)
WH—! WHAT IS THAT!?

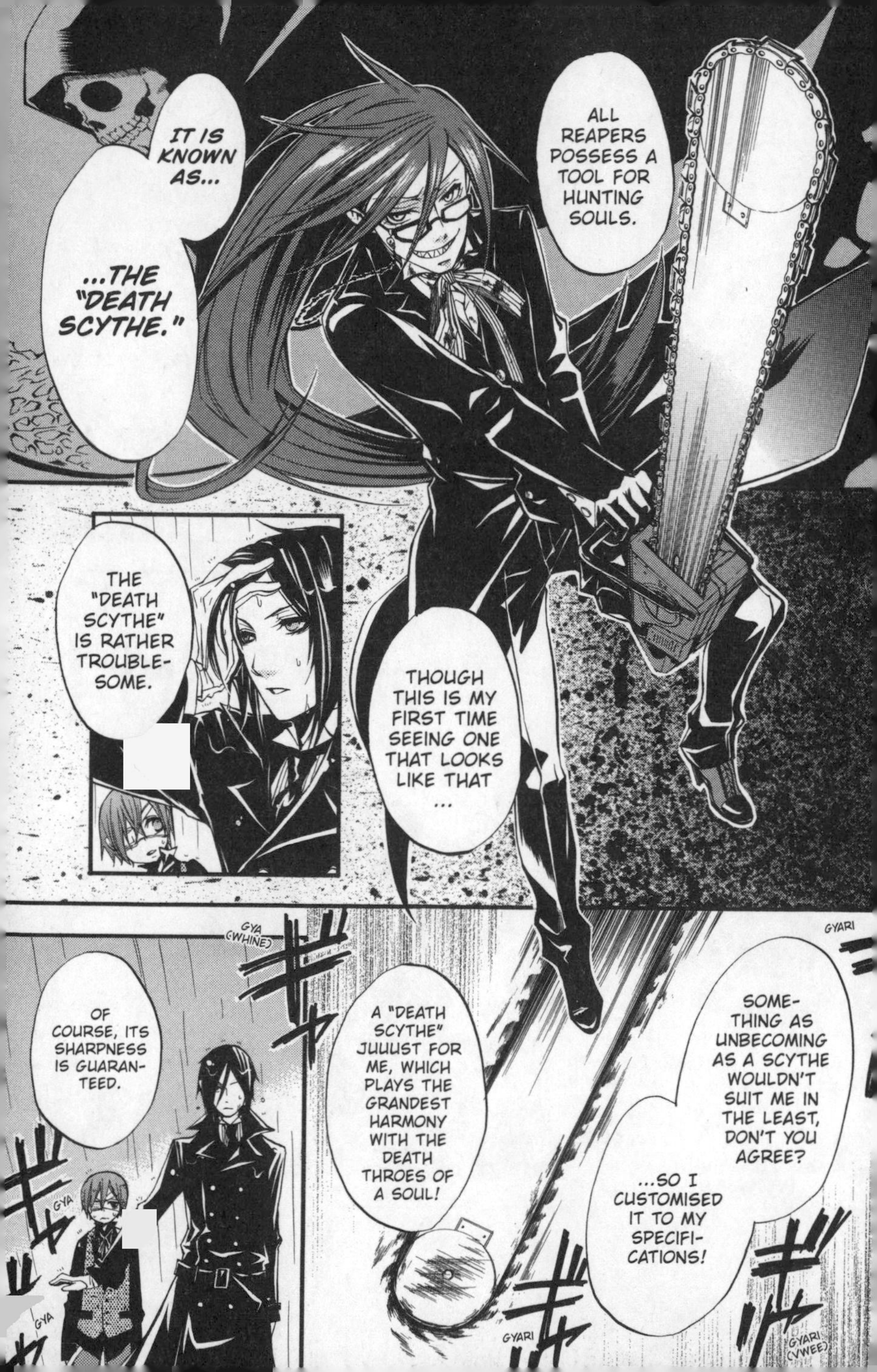
ALL REAPERS POSSESS A TOOL FOR HUNTING SOULS.
IT IS KNOWN AS...
...THE "DEATH SCYTHE."
THE "DEATH SCYTHE" IS RATHER TROUBLE-SOME.
THOUGH THIS IS MY FIRST TIME SEEING ONE THAT LOOKS LIKE THAT ...
GYARI
SOME-THING AS UNBECOMING AS A SCYTHE WOULDN'T SUIT ME IN THE LEAST, DON'T YOU AGREE?
...SO I CUSTOMISED IT TO MY SPECIFI-CATIONS!
GYARI (VWEE)
GYARI
A "DEATH SCYTHE" JUUUST FOR ME, WHICH PLAYS THE GRANDEST HARMONY WITH THE DEATH THROES OF A SOUL!
GYA (WHINE)
OF COURSE, ITS SHARPNESS IS GUARAN-TEED.
GYA
GYA

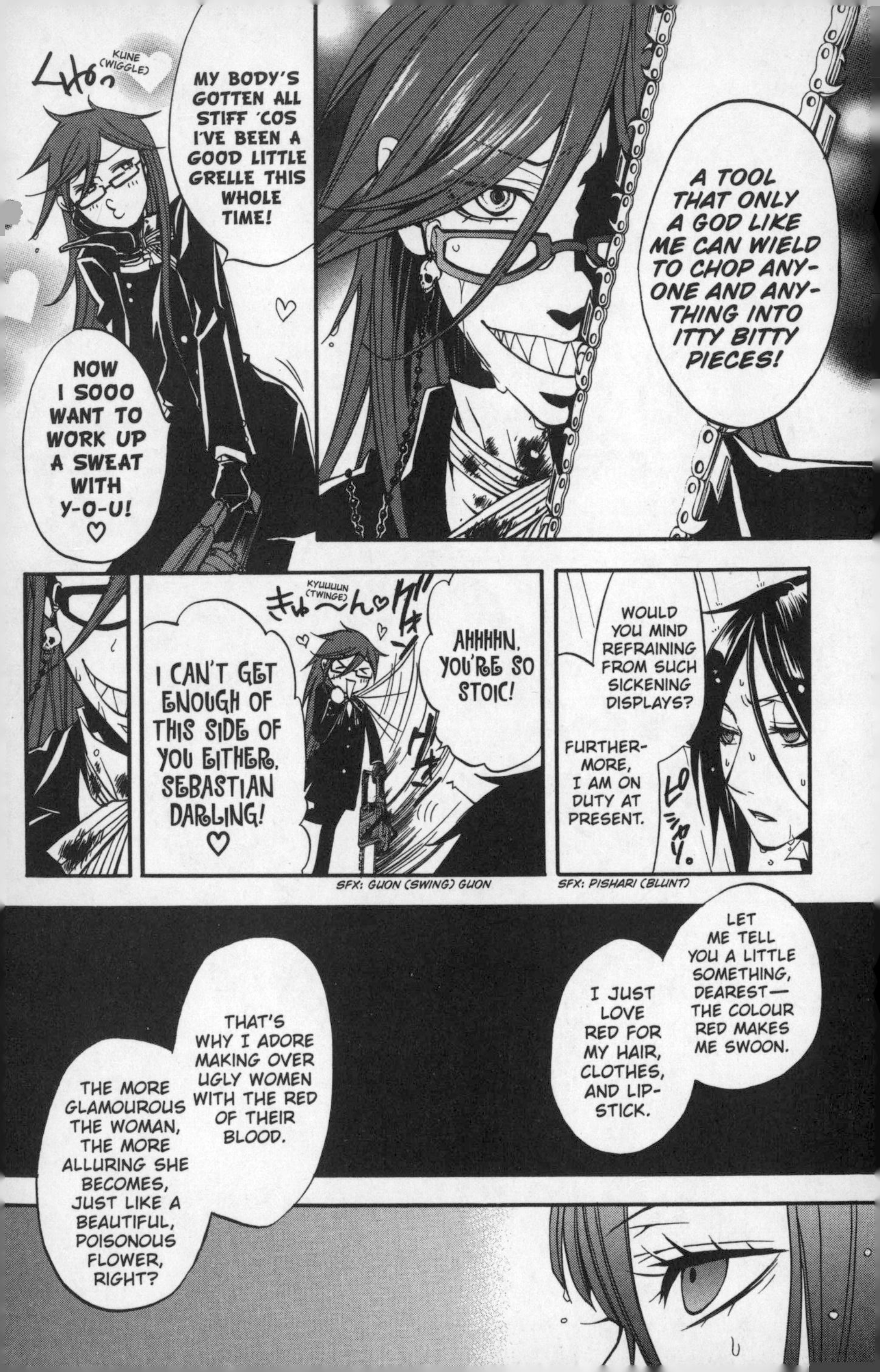
A TOOL THAT ONLY A GOD LIKE ME CAN WIELD TO CHOP ANYONE AND ANYTHING INTO ITTY BITTY PIECES!
MY BODY'S GOTTEN ALL STIFF 'COS I'VE BEEN A GOOD LITTLE GRELLE THIS WHOLE TIME! ♡
KUNE (WIGGLE)
NOW I SOOO WANT TO WORK UP A SWEAT WITH Y-O-U! ♡
WOULD YOU MIND REFRAINING FROM SUCH SICKENING DISPLAYS?
FURTHERMORE, I AM ON DUTY AT PRESENT.
SFX: PISHARI (BLUNT)
AHHHHN. YOU'RE SO STOIC!
KYUUUUN (TWINGE)
I CAN'T GET ENOUGH OF THIS SIDE OF YOU EITHER, SEBASTIAN DARLING! ♡
SFX: GUON (SWING) GUON
LET ME TELL YOU A LITTLE SOMETHING, DEAREST—THE COLOUR RED MAKES ME SWOON.
I JUST LOVE RED FOR MY HAIR, CLOTHES, AND LIPSTICK.
THAT'S WHY I ADORE MAKING OVER UGLY WOMEN WITH THE RED OF THEIR BLOOD.
THE MORE GLAMOUROUS THE WOMAN, THE MORE ALLURING SHE BECOMES, JUST LIKE A BEAUTIFUL, POISONOUS FLOWER, RIGHT?

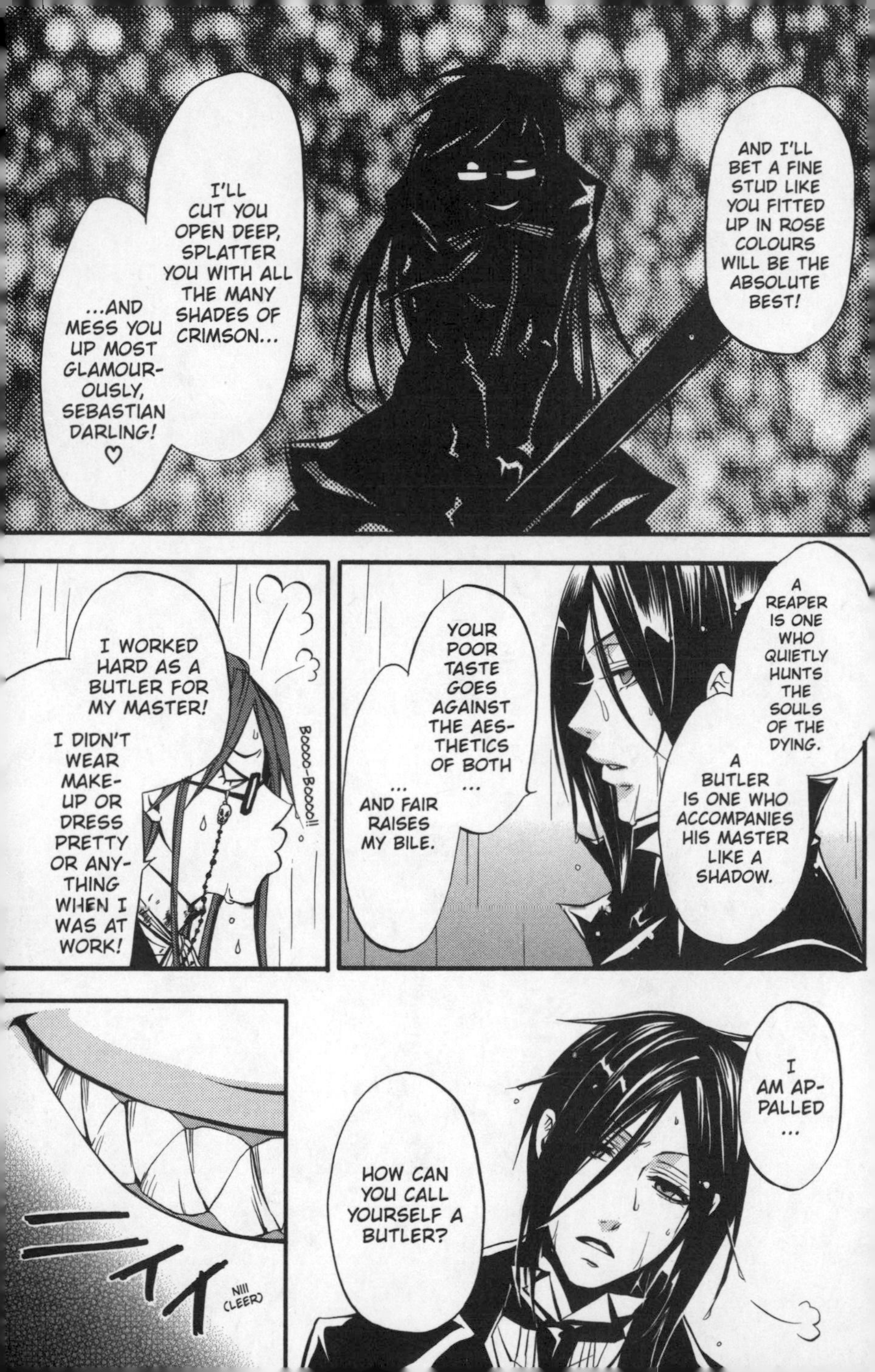
AND I'LL BET A FINE STUD LIKE YOU FITTED UP IN ROSE COLOURS WILL BE THE ABSOLUTE BEST!
I'LL CUT YOU OPEN DEEP, SPLATTER YOU WITH ALL THE MANY SHADES OF CRIMSON...
...AND MESS YOU UP MOST GLAMOUR-OUSLY, SEBASTIAN DARLING! ♡
A REAPER IS ONE WHO QUIETLY HUNTS THE SOULS OF THE DYING.
A BUTLER IS ONE WHO ACCOMPANIES HIS MASTER LIKE A SHADOW.
YOUR POOR TASTE GOES AGAINST THE AES-THETICS OF BOTH...
...AND FAIR RAISES MY BILE.
I WORKED HARD AS A BUTLER FOR MY MASTER!
I DIDN'T WEAR MAKE-UP OR DRESS PRETTY OR ANY-THING WHEN I WAS AT WORK!
Boooo-Boooo!!
I AM AP-PALLED...
HOW CAN YOU CALL YOURSELF A BUTLER?
NIII (LEER)

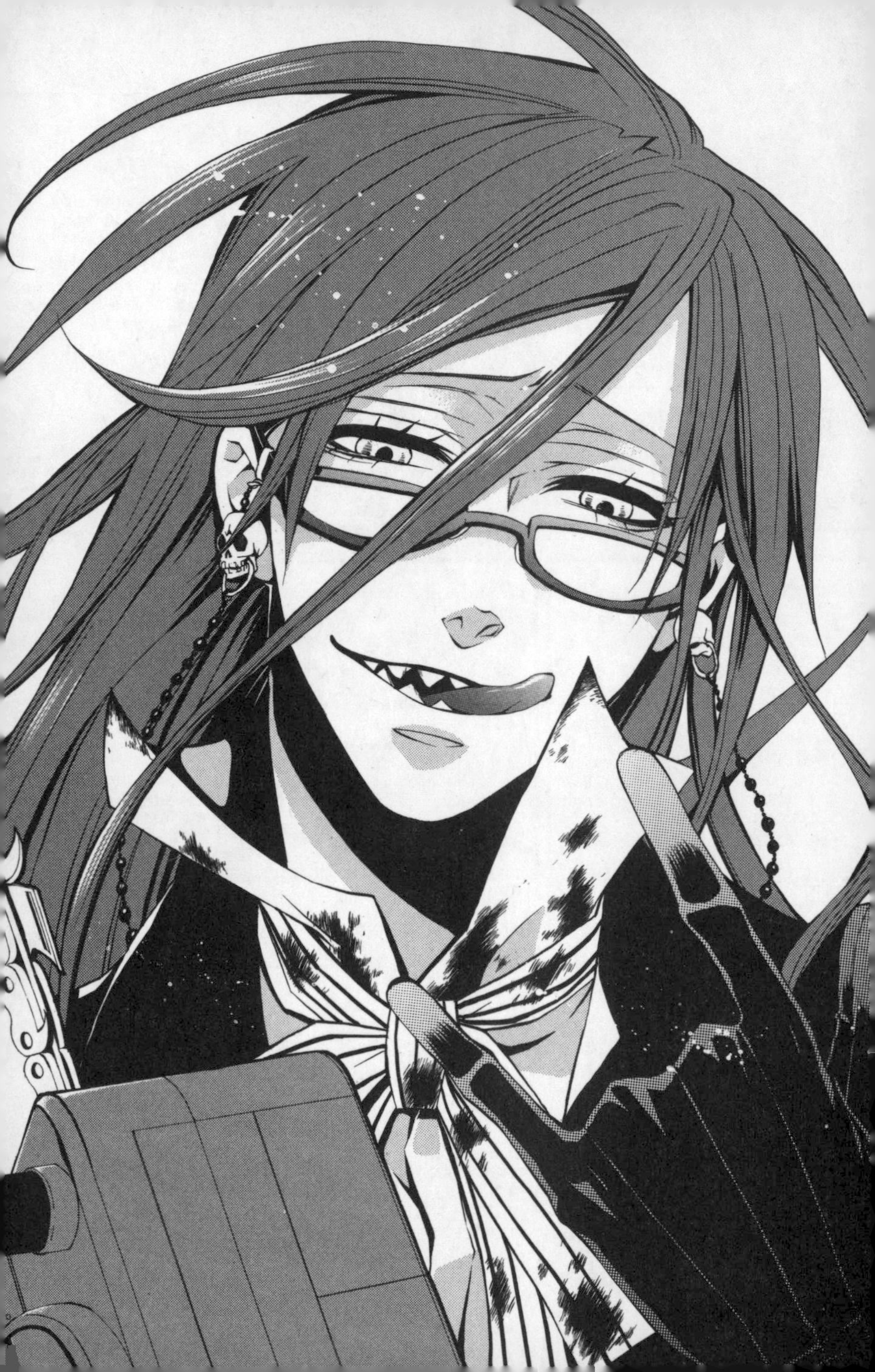

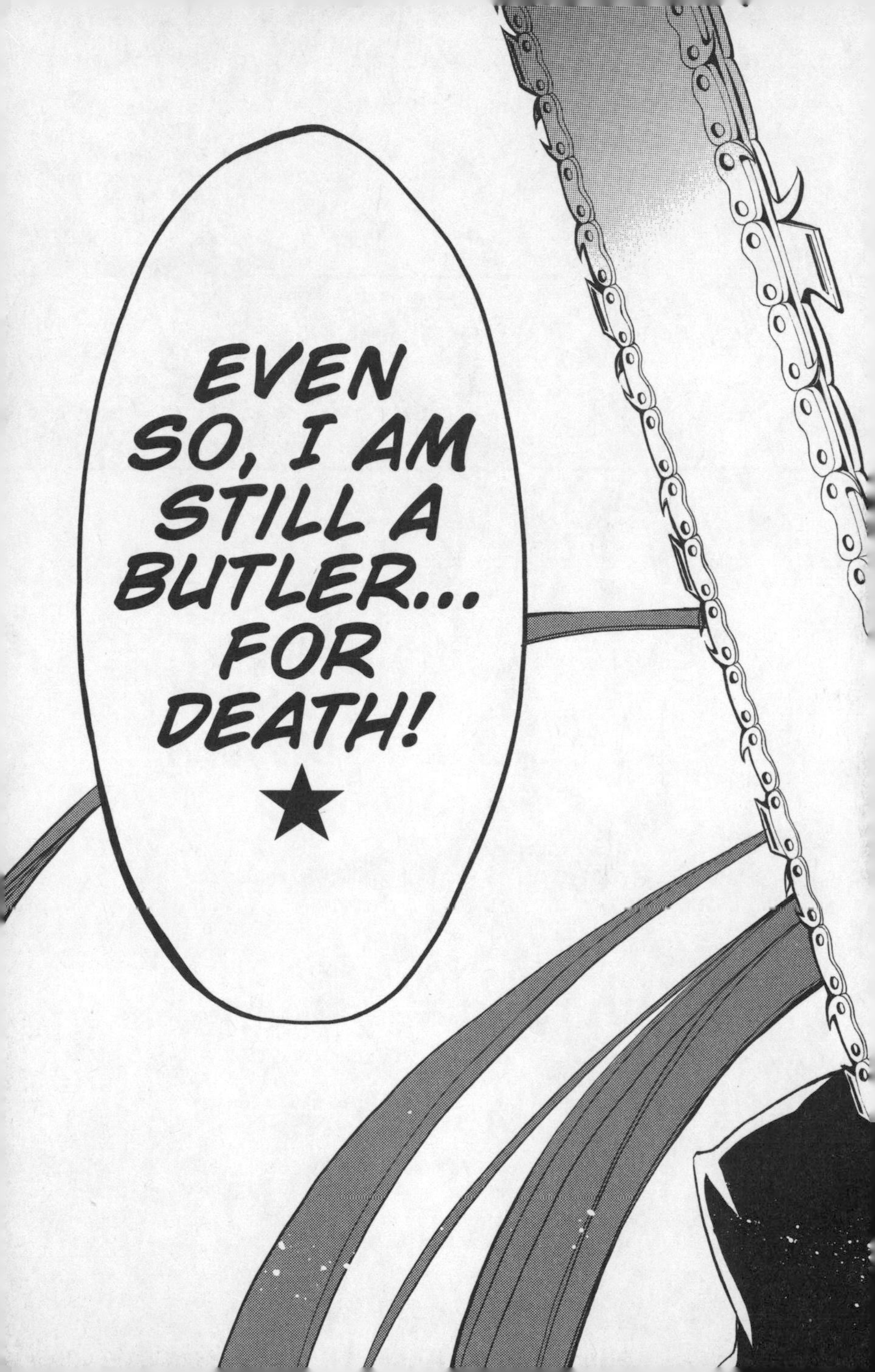
EVEN SO, I AM STILL A BUTLER... FOR DEATH! ★

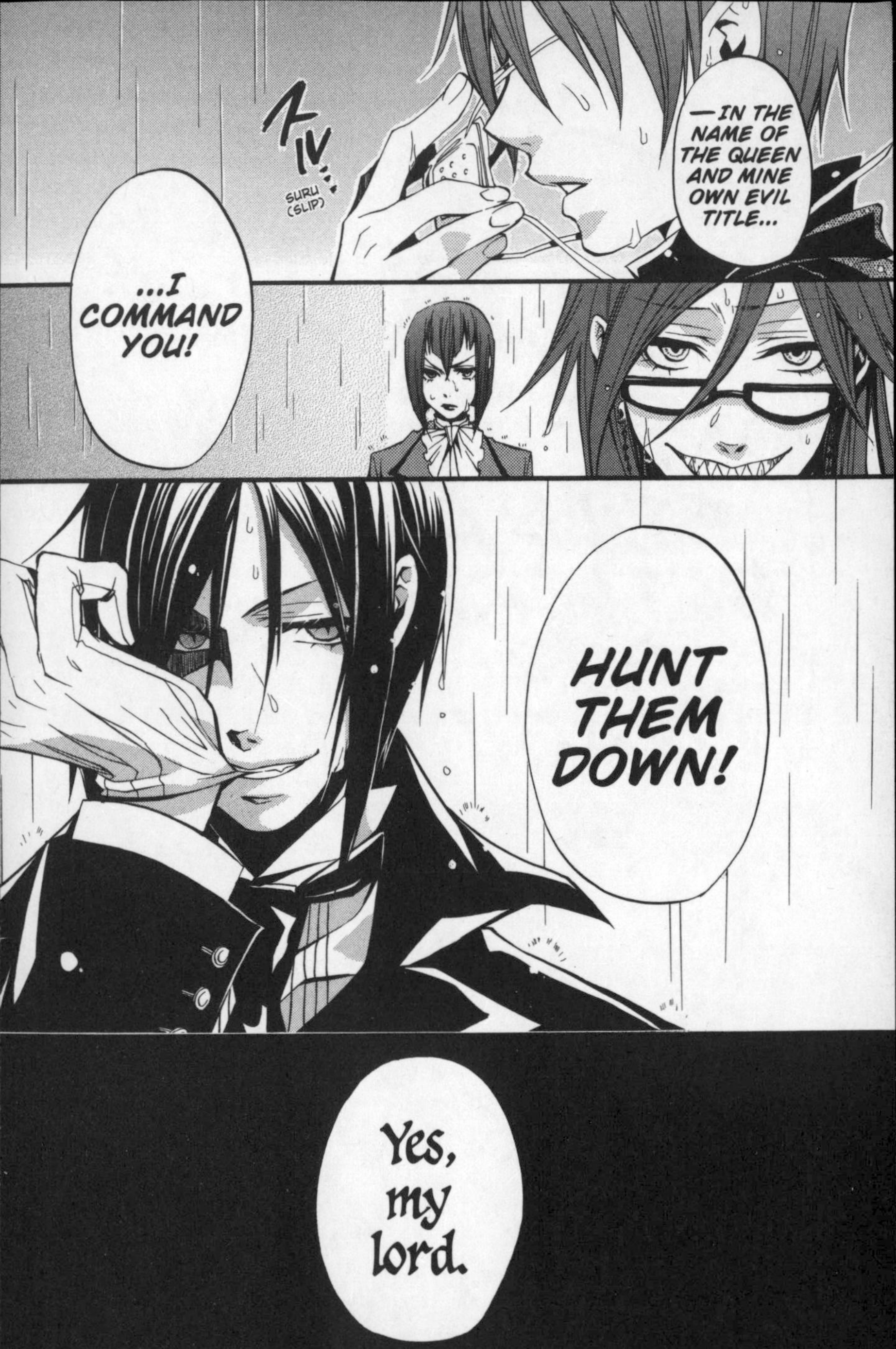
—IN THE NAME OF THE QUEEN AND MINE OWN EVIL TITLE...
SURU (SLIP)
...I COMMAND YOU!
HUNT THEM DOWN!
Yes, my lord.

➤Black Butler➤

黒執事

Downstairs

KiYo

MiNe

Wakana Haduki

Akiyo Satorigi

Be sama

Kirito

Yana's Mother

*

Takeshi Kuma

*

Yana Toboso

SpecialThanks

to You!

BONUS MANGA

Madam Red's ★ LESSON ON HOW TO BE A PROPER ENGLISH LADY

(THIS TOOK PLACE BEFORE THEY WENT TO THE VISCOUNT'S RESIDENCE.)

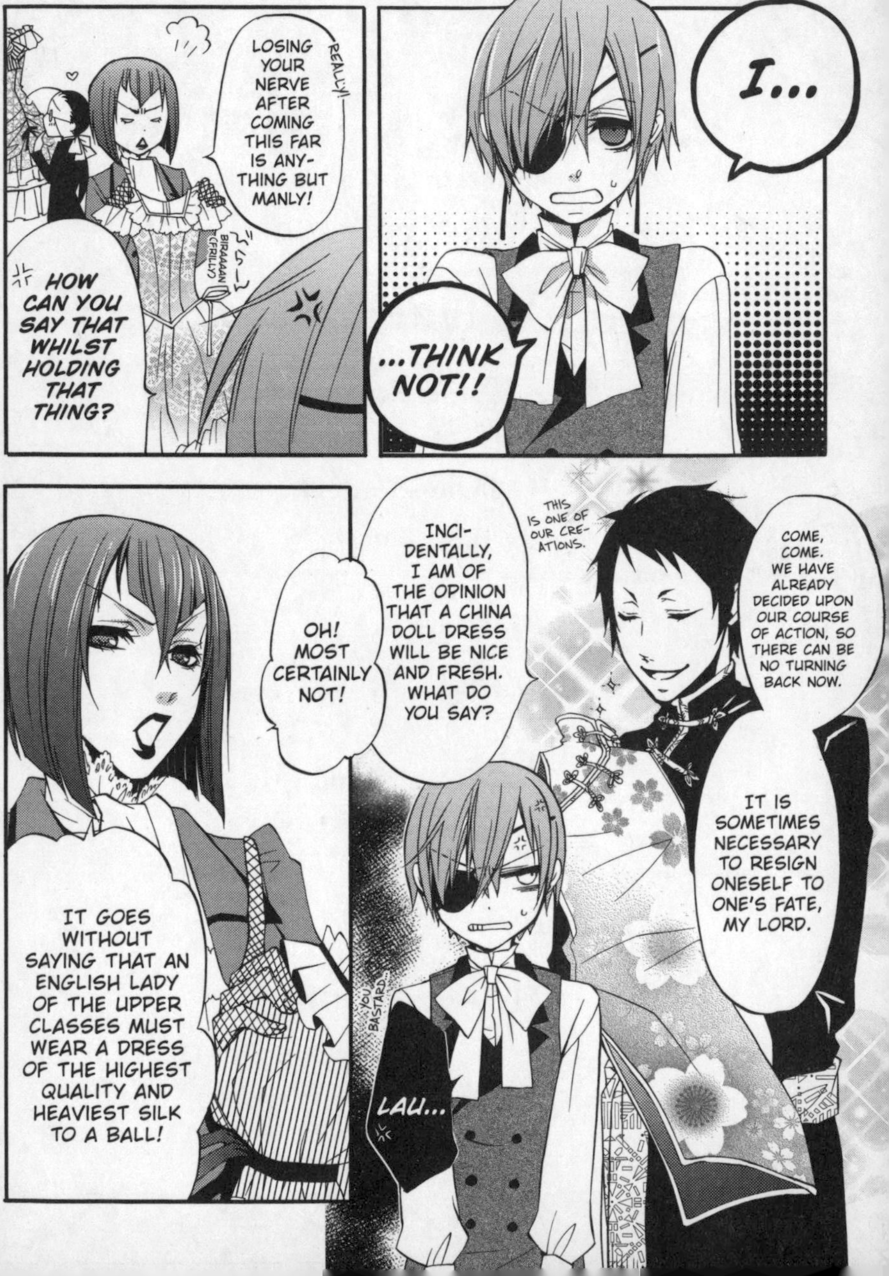
I...
...THINK NOT!!
LOSING YOUR NERVE AFTER COMING THIS FAR IS ANYTHING BUT MANLY!
REALLY!
BIRAAAN (FRILLY)
HOW CAN YOU SAY THAT WHILST HOLDING THAT THING?
COME, COME. WE HAVE ALREADY DECIDED UPON OUR COURSE OF ACTION, SO THERE CAN BE NO TURNING BACK NOW.
THIS IS ONE OF OUR CREATIONS.
INCIDENTALLY, I AM OF THE OPINION THAT A CHINA DOLL DRESS WILL BE NICE AND FRESH. WHAT DO YOU SAY?
OH! MOST CERTAINLY NOT!
IT IS SOMETIMES NECESSARY TO RESIGN ONESELF TO ONE'S FATE, MY LORD.
YOU BASTARD...
LAU...
IT GOES WITHOUT SAYING THAT AN ENGLISH LADY OF THE UPPER CLASSES MUST WEAR A DRESS OF THE HIGHEST QUALITY AND HEAVIEST SILK TO A BALL!

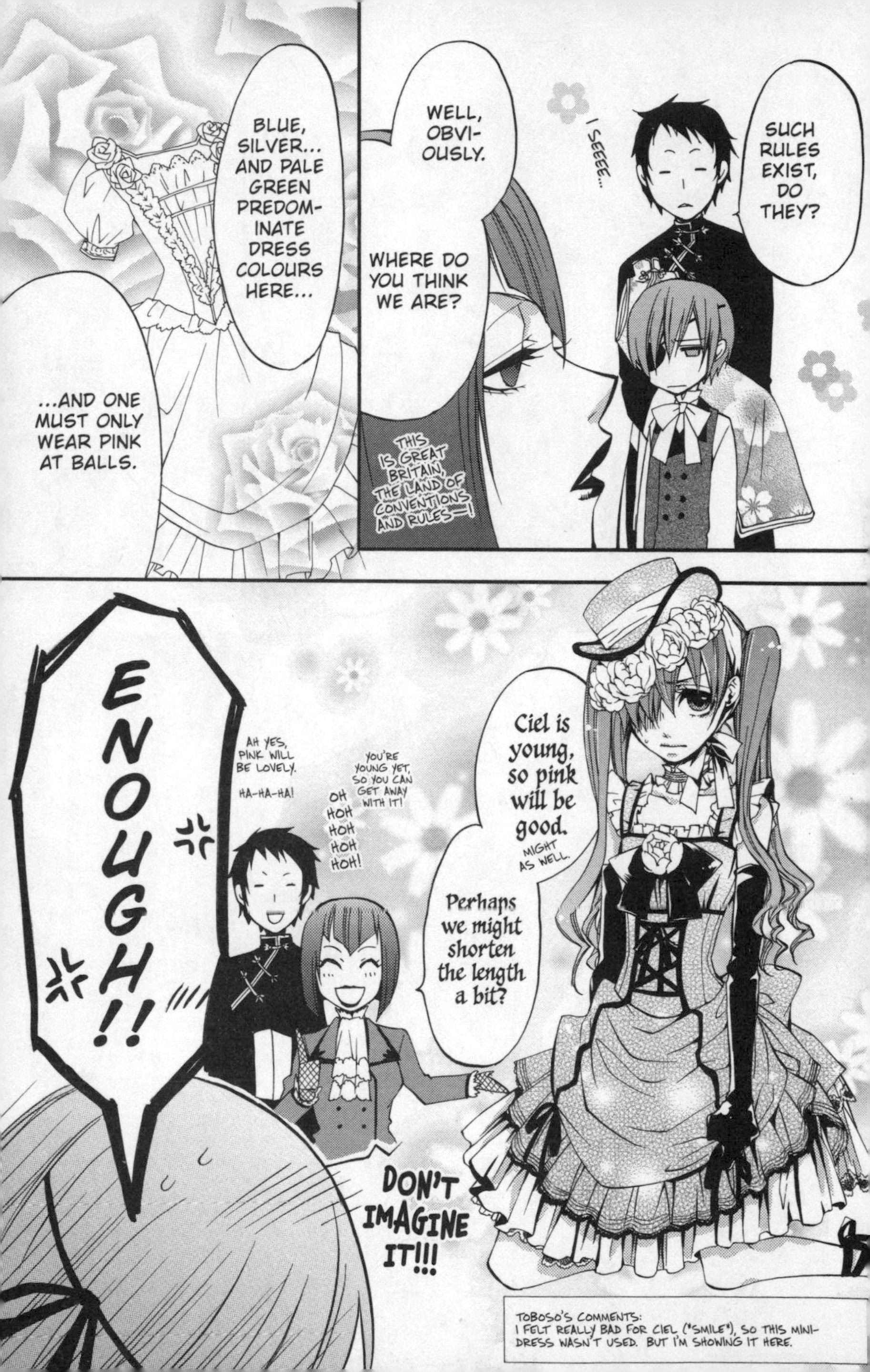
SUCH RULES EXIST, DO THEY?
I SEEEE...
WELL, OBVIOUSLY.
WHERE DO YOU THINK WE ARE?
THIS IS GREAT BRITAIN, THE LAND OF CONVENTIONS AND RULES—!
BLUE, SILVER... AND PALE GREEN PREDOMINATE DRESS COLOURS HERE...
...AND ONE MUST ONLY WEAR PINK AT BALLS.
Ciel is young, so pink will be good.
MIGHT AS WELL.
Perhaps we might shorten the length a bit?
YOU'RE YOUNG YET, SO YOU CAN GET AWAY WITH IT!
OH HOH HOH HOH HOH!
AH YES, PINK WILL BE LOVELY.
HA-HA-HA!
ENOUGH!!
DON'T IMAGINE IT!!!
TOBOSO'S COMMENTS:
I FELT REALLY BAD FOR CIEL (*SMILE*), SO THIS MINI-DRESS WASN'T USED. BUT I'M SHOWING IT HERE.

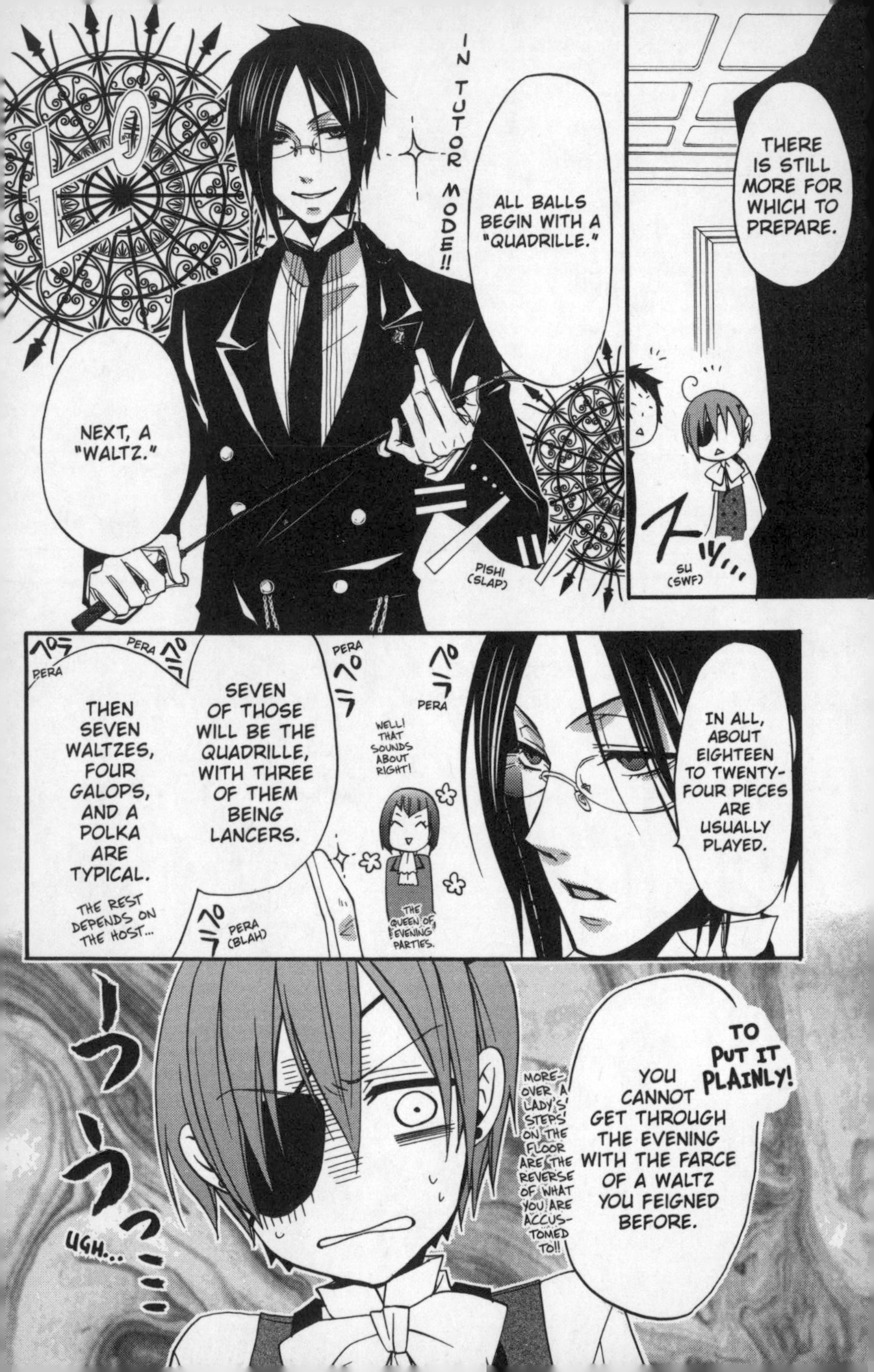
THERE IS STILL MORE FOR WHICH TO PREPARE.
SU (SWF)
IN TUTOR MODE!!
ALL BALLS BEGIN WITH A "QUADRILLE."
NEXT, A "WALTZ."
PISHI (SLAP)
IN ALL, ABOUT EIGHTEEN TO TWENTY-FOUR PIECES ARE USUALLY PLAYED.
PERA
PERA
SEVEN OF THOSE WILL BE THE QUADRILLE, WITH THREE OF THEM BEING LANCERS.
WELL! THAT SOUNDS ABOUT RIGHT!
THE QUEEN OF EVENING PARTIES.
PERA
PERA
THEN SEVEN WALTZES, FOUR GALOPS, AND A POLKA ARE TYPICAL.
THE REST DEPENDS ON THE HOST...
PERA (BLAH)
TO PUT IT PLAINLY!
YOU CANNOT GET THROUGH THE EVENING WITH THE FARCE OF A WALTZ YOU FEIGNED BEFORE.
MORE-OVER A LADY'S STEPS ON THE FLOOR ARE THE REVERSE OF WHAT YOU ARE ACCUS-TOMED TO!!
UGH...

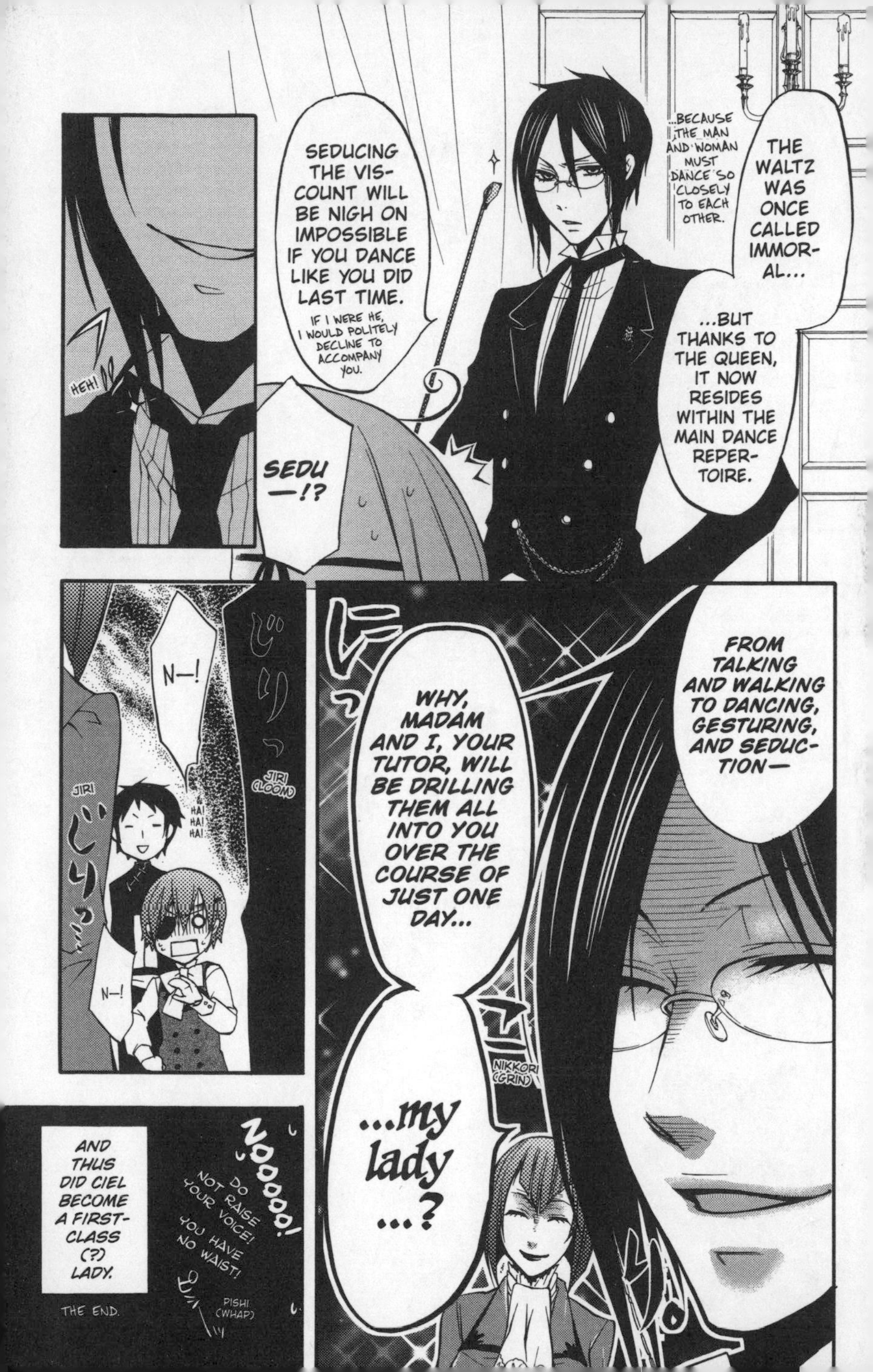
THE WALTZ WAS ONCE CALLED IMMORAL...
...BECAUSE THE MAN AND WOMAN MUST DANCE SO CLOSELY TO EACH OTHER.
...BUT THANKS TO THE QUEEN, IT NOW RESIDES WITHIN THE MAIN DANCE REPERTOIRE.
SEDUCING THE VISCOUNT WILL BE NIGH ON IMPOSSIBLE IF YOU DANCE LIKE YOU DID LAST TIME.
IF I WERE HE, I WOULD POLITELY DECLINE TO ACCOMPANY YOU.
SEDU—!?
HEH!
FROM TALKING AND WALKING TO DANCING, GESTURING, AND SEDUCTION—
WHY, MADAM AND I, YOUR TUTOR, WILL BE DRILLING THEM ALL INTO YOU OVER THE COURSE OF JUST ONE DAY...
NIKKORI (GRIN)
...my lady ...?
N—!
JIRI (GLOOM)
HA! HA! HA!
JIRI
N—!
NOOOOO!
DO NOT RAISE YOUR VOICE! YOU HAVE NO WAIST!
PISHI (WHAP)
AND THUS DID CIEL BECOME A FIRST-CLASS (?) LADY.
THE END.

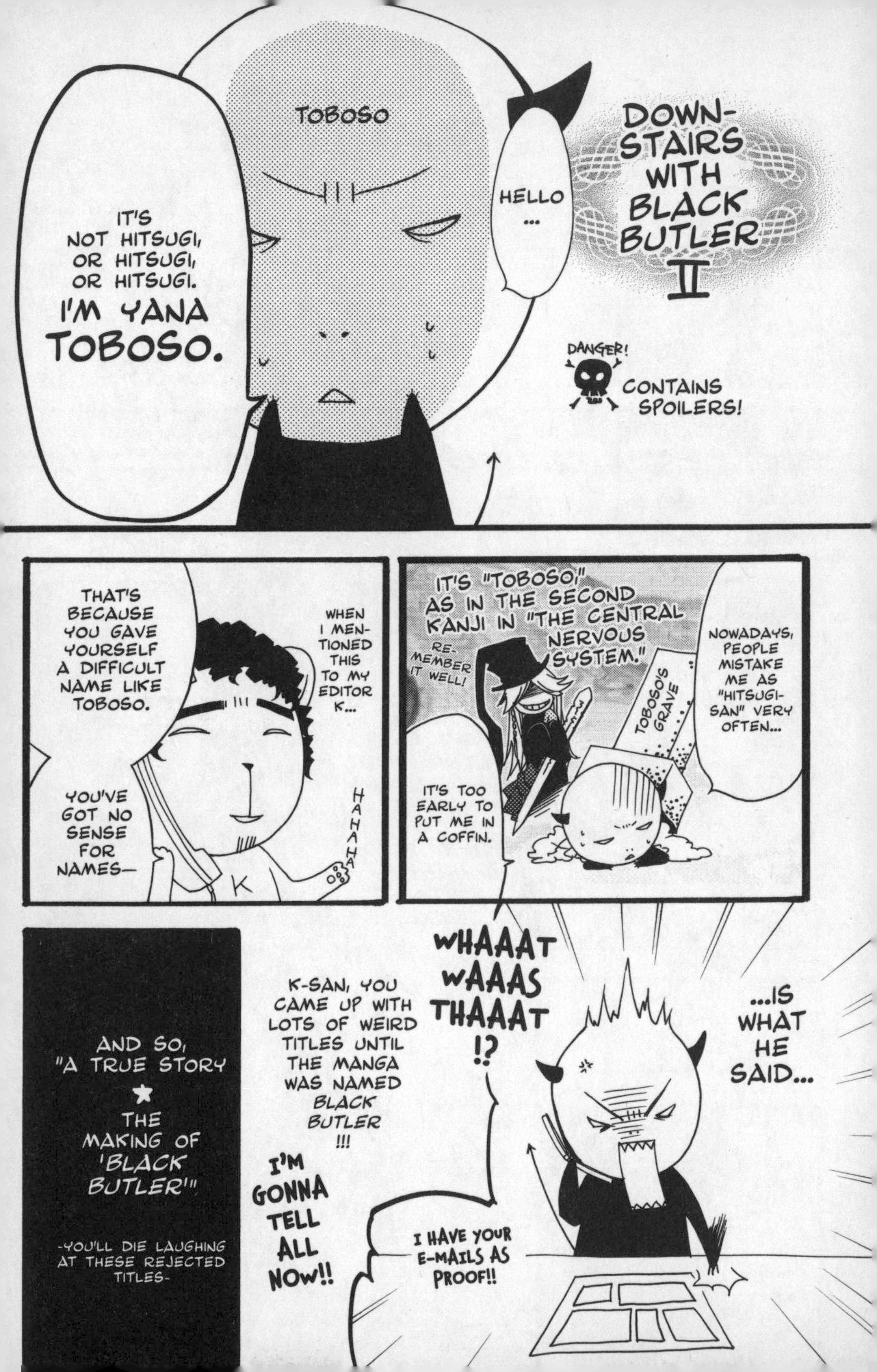
DOWN-STAIRS WITH BLACK BUTLER II
DANGER!
CONTAINS SPOILERS!
HELLO...
TOBOSO
IT'S NOT HITSUGI, OR HITSUGI, OR HITSUGI. I'M YANA TOBOSO.
NOWADAYS, PEOPLE MISTAKE ME AS "HITSUGI-SAN" VERY OFTEN...
IT'S "TOBOSO," AS IN THE SECOND KANJI IN "THE CENTRAL NERVOUS SYSTEM."
RE-MEMBER IT WELL!
TOBOSO'S GRAVE
IT'S TOO EARLY TO PUT ME IN A COFFIN.
WHEN I MEN-TIONED THIS TO MY EDITOR K...
THAT'S BECAUSE YOU GAVE YOURSELF A DIFFICULT NAME LIKE TOBOSO.
HAHAHAHA
YOU'VE GOT NO SENSE FOR NAMES—
K
...IS WHAT HE SAID...
WHAAAT WAAAS THAAAT !?
K-SAN, YOU CAME UP WITH LOTS OF WEIRD TITLES UNTIL THE MANGA WAS NAMED BLACK BUTLER !!!
I HAVE YOUR E-MAILS AS PROOF!!
I'M GONNA TELL ALL NOW!!
AND SO, "A TRUE STORY ★ THE MAKING OF 'BLACK BUTLER'"
-YOU'LL DIE LAUGHING AT THESE REJECTED TITLES-

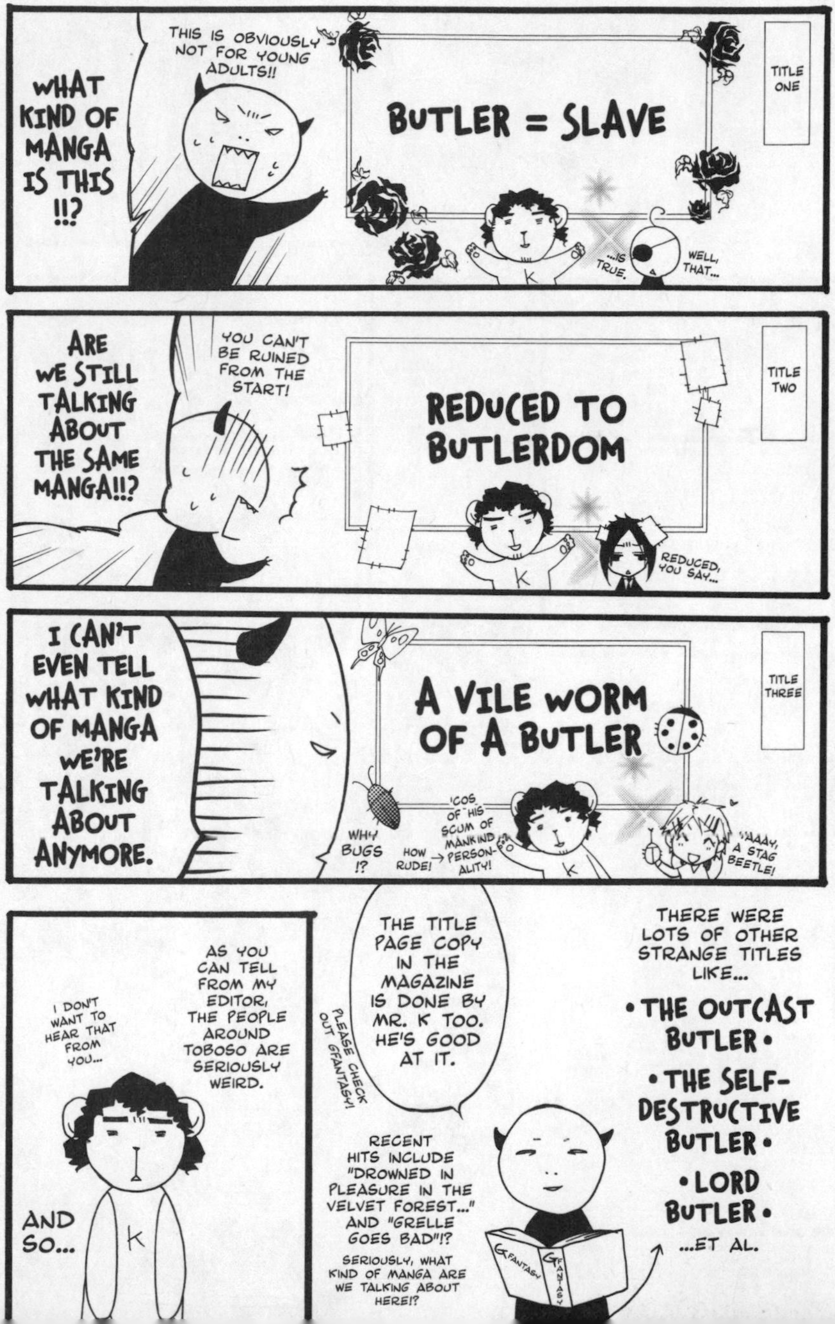

TITLE ONE
BUTLER = SLAVE
WELL, THAT...
...IS TRUE.
THIS IS OBVIOUSLY NOT FOR YOUNG ADULTS!!
WHAT KIND OF MANGA IS THIS !!?
TITLE TWO
REDUCED TO BUTLERDOM
REDUCED, YOU SAY...
YOU CAN'T BE RUINED FROM THE START!
ARE WE STILL TALKING ABOUT THE SAME MANGA!!?
TITLE THREE
A VILE WORM OF A BUTLER
YAAAY, A STAG BEETLE!
'COS OF HIS SCUM OF MANKIND PERSON-ALITY!
HOW RUDE!
WHY BUGS !?
I CAN'T EVEN TELL WHAT KIND OF MANGA WE'RE TALKING ABOUT ANYMORE.
THERE WERE LOTS OF OTHER STRANGE TITLES LIKE...
• THE OUTCAST BUTLER •
• THE SELF-DESTRUCTIVE BUTLER •
• LORD BUTLER •
...ET AL.
THE TITLE PAGE COPY IN THE MAGAZINE IS DONE BY MR. K TOO. HE'S GOOD AT IT.
PLEASE CHECK OUT GFANTASY!
RECENT HITS INCLUDE "DROWNED IN PLEASURE IN THE VELVET FOREST..." AND "GRELLE GOES BAD"!?
SERIOUSLY, WHAT KIND OF MANGA ARE WE TALKING ABOUT HERE!?
GFANTASY
GFANTASY
AS YOU CAN TELL FROM MY EDITOR, THE PEOPLE AROUND TOBOSO ARE SERIOUSLY WEIRD.
I DON'T WANT TO HEAR THAT FROM YOU...
AND SO...

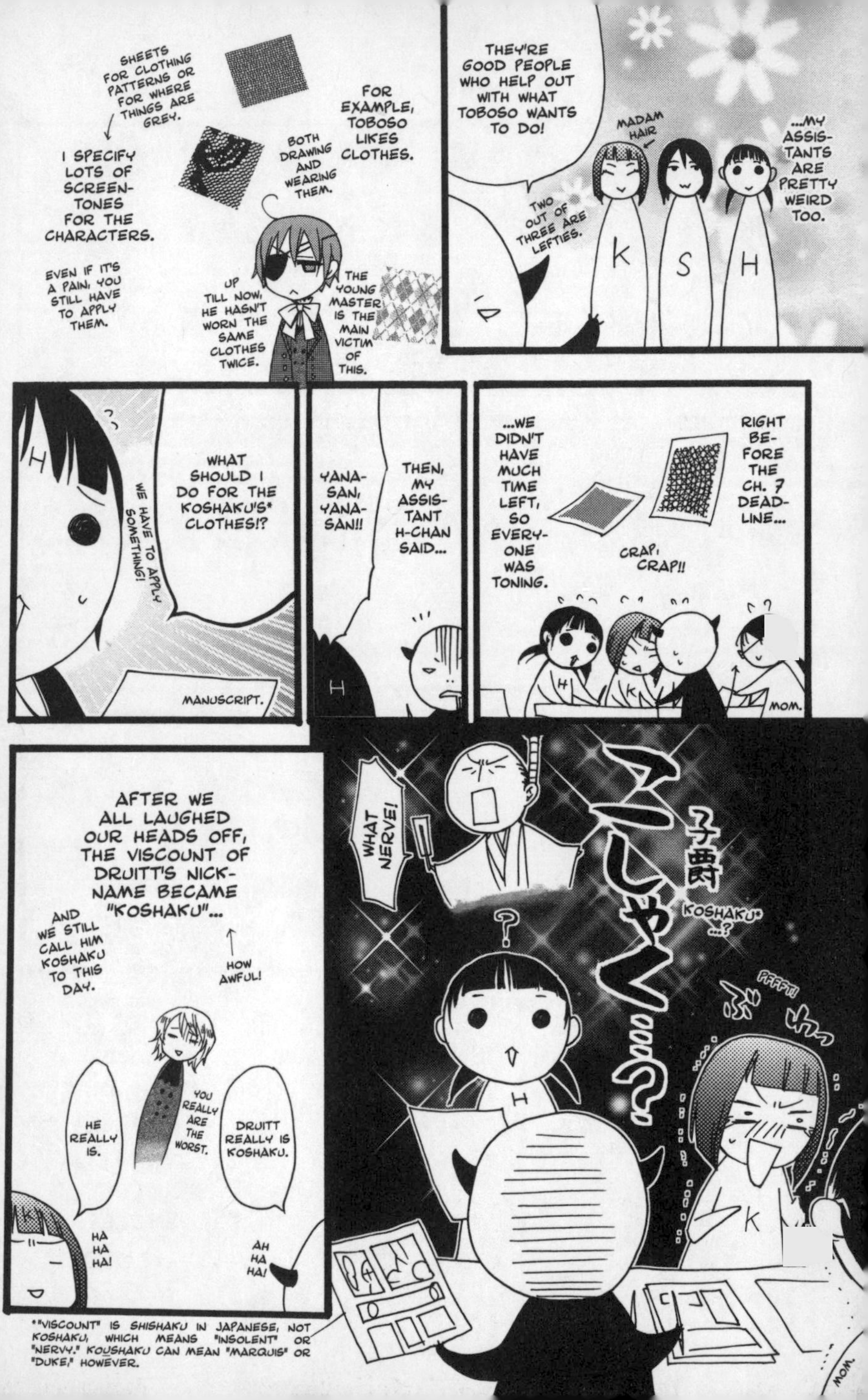
THEY'RE GOOD PEOPLE WHO HELP OUT WITH WHAT TOBOSO WANTS TO DO!
...MY ASSISTANTS ARE PRETTY WEIRD TOO.
MADAM HAIR
TWO OUT OF THREE ARE LEFTIES.
K
S
H
FOR EXAMPLE, TOBOSO LIKES CLOTHES.
BOTH DRAWING AND WEARING THEM.
SHEETS FOR CLOTHING PATTERNS OR FOR WHERE THINGS ARE GREY.
I SPECIFY LOTS OF SCREEN-TONES FOR THE CHARACTERS.
EVEN IF IT'S A PAIN, YOU STILL HAVE TO APPLY THEM.
UP TILL NOW, HE HASN'T WORN THE SAME CLOTHES TWICE.
THE YOUNG MASTER IS THE MAIN VICTIM OF THIS.
RIGHT BEFORE THE CH. 7 DEAD-LINE...
...WE DIDN'T HAVE MUCH TIME LEFT, SO EVERY-ONE WAS TONING.
CRAP, CRAP!!
H
K
MOM.
THEN, MY ASSIS-TANT H-CHAN SAID...
YANA-SAN, YANA-SAN!!
H
WHAT SHOULD I DO FOR THE KOSHAKU'S* CLOTHES!?
WE HAVE TO APPLY SOMETHING!
H
MANUSCRIPT.
子爵
KOSHAKU* ...?
こしゃくぅ?
WHAT NERVE!
?
H
PFFFT!!
ぶわっ
K
MOM.
AFTER WE ALL LAUGHED OUR HEADS OFF, THE VISCOUNT OF DRUITT'S NICK-NAME BECAME "KOSHAKU"...
AND WE STILL CALL HIM KOSHAKU TO THIS DAY.
HOW AWFUL!
DRUITT REALLY IS KOSHAKU.
YOU REALLY ARE THE WORST.
HE REALLY IS.
K
HA HA HA!
AH HA HA!

*"VISCOUNT" IS SHISHAKU IN JAPANESE, NOT KOSHAKU, WHICH MEANS "INSOLENT" OR "NERVY." KOUSHAKU CAN MEAN "MARQUIS" OR "DUKE," HOWEVER.

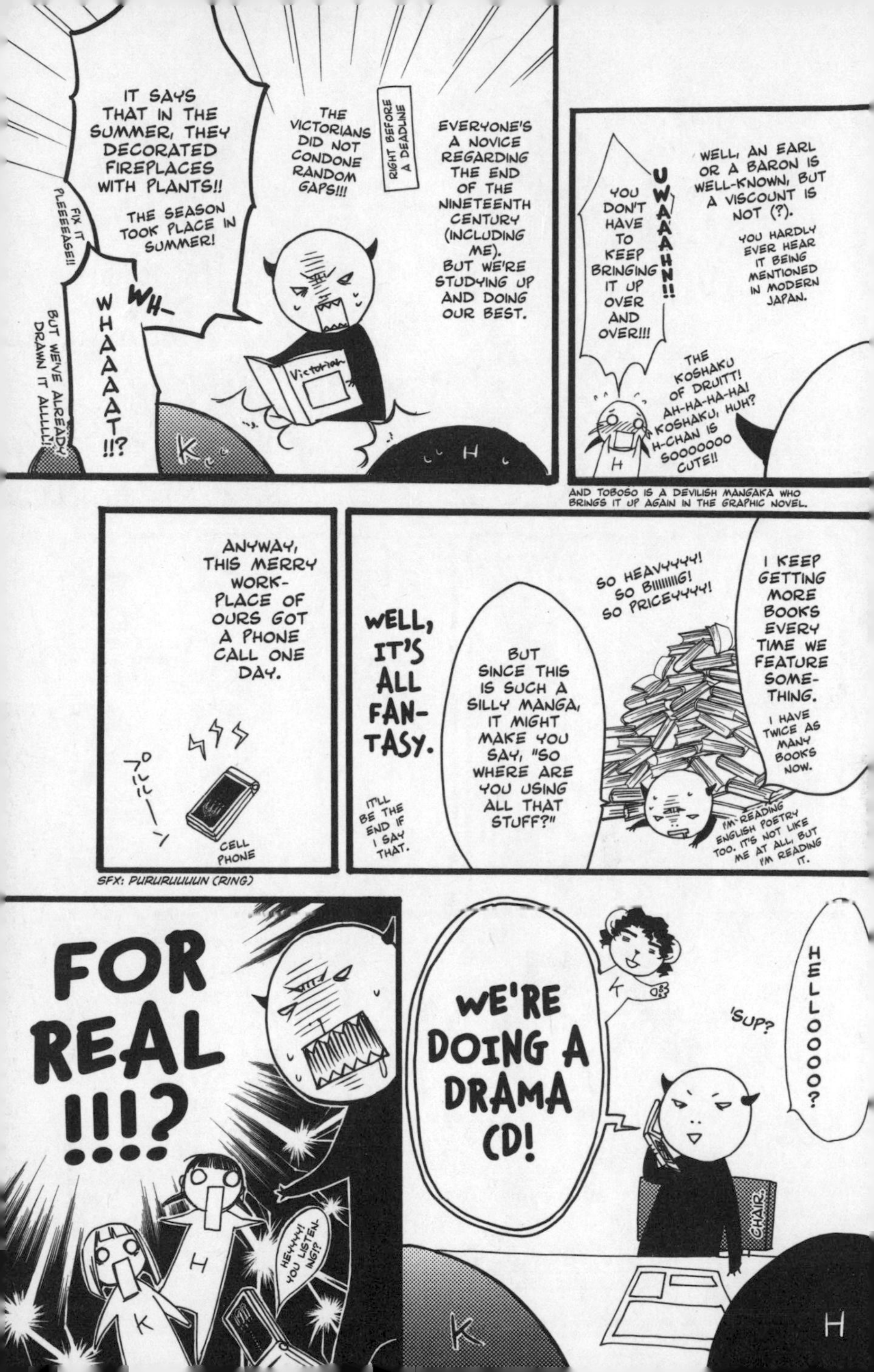
WELL, AN EARL OR A BARON IS WELL-KNOWN, BUT A VISCOUNT IS NOT (?).
YOU HARDLY EVER HEAR IT BEING MENTIONED IN MODERN JAPAN.
UWAAAHN!!
YOU DON'T HAVE TO KEEP BRINGING IT UP OVER AND OVER!!!
THE KOSHAKU OF DRUITT! AH-HA-HA-HA! KOSHAKU, HUH? H-CHAN IS SOOOOOOO CUTE!!
H
AND TOBOSO IS A DEVILISH MANGAKA WHO BRINGS IT UP AGAIN IN THE GRAPHIC NOVEL.
EVERYONE'S A NOVICE REGARDING THE END OF THE NINETEENTH CENTURY (INCLUDING ME). BUT WE'RE STUDYING UP AND DOING OUR BEST.
RIGHT BEFORE A DEADLINE
THE VICTORIANS DID NOT CONDONE RANDOM GAPS!!!
IT SAYS THAT IN THE SUMMER, THEY DECORATED FIREPLACES WITH PLANTS!!
THE SEASON TOOK PLACE IN SUMMER!
FIX IT PLEEEEASE!!
WH-
WHAAAAAT!!?
BUT WE'VE ALREADY DRAWN IT ALLLL!
Victorian
H
K
I KEEP GETTING MORE BOOKS EVERY TIME WE FEATURE SOME-THING.
I HAVE TWICE AS MANY BOOKS NOW.
SO HEAVYYYY! SO BIIIIIIIG! SO PRICEYYYY!
I'M READING ENGLISH POETRY TOO. IT'S NOT LIKE ME AT ALL, BUT I'M READING IT.
BUT SINCE THIS IS SUCH A SILLY MANGA, IT MIGHT MAKE YOU SAY, "SO WHERE ARE YOU USING ALL THAT STUFF?"
WELL, IT'S ALL FAN-TASY.
IT'LL BE THE END IF I SAY THAT.
ANYWAY, THIS MERRY WORK-PLACE OF OURS GOT A PHONE CALL ONE DAY.
CELL PHONE
SFX: PURURULUUUN (RING)
HELLOOOO?
'SUP?
K
WE'RE DOING A DRAMA CD!
CHAIR.
H
K
FOR REAL!!!?
H
HEYYYY! YOU LISTEN-ING!?
K

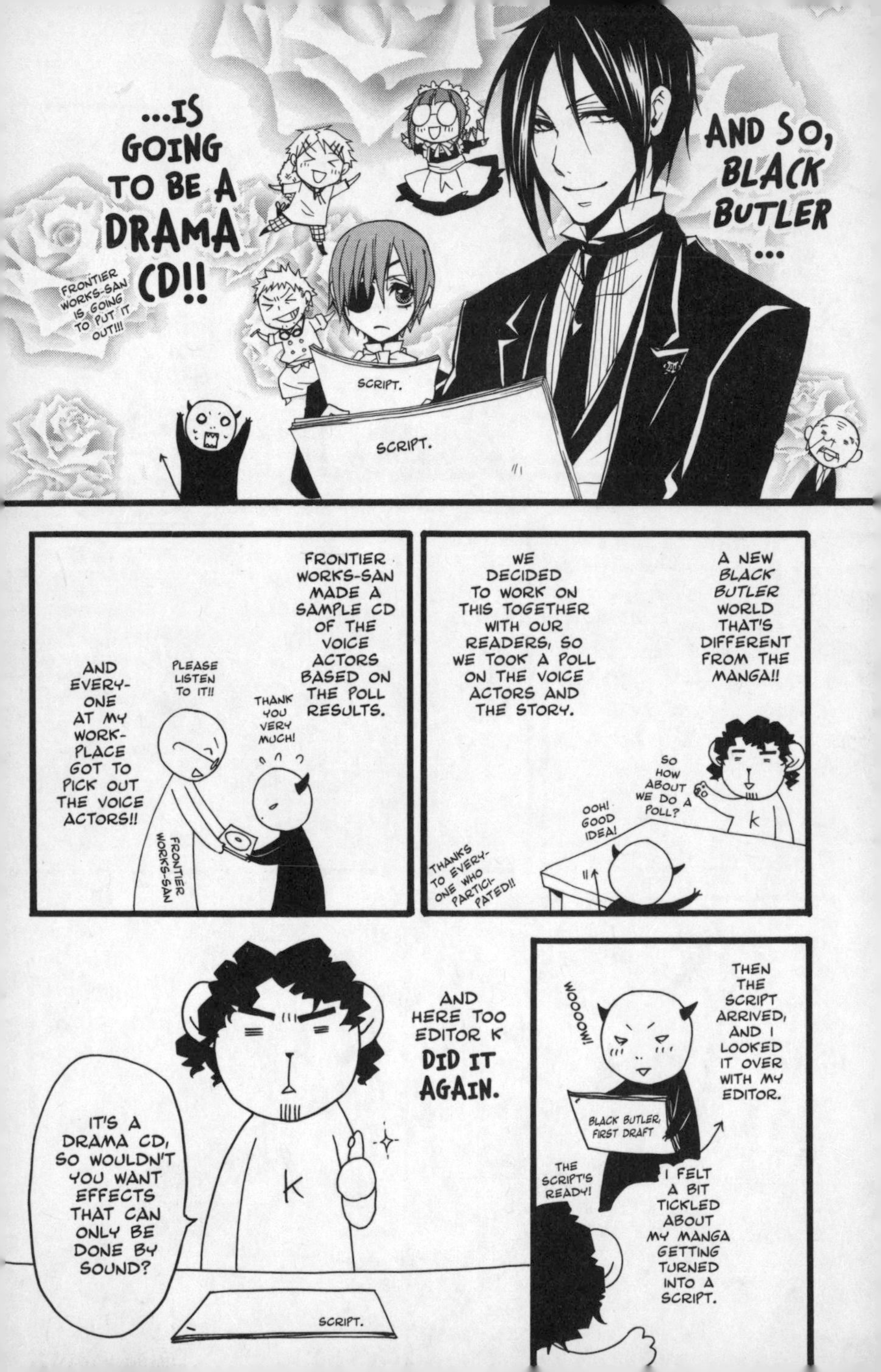

AND SO, BLACK BUTLER ...
...IS GOING TO BE A DRAMA CD!!
FRONTIER WORKS-SAN IS GOING TO PUT IT OUT!!!
SCRIPT.
SCRIPT.
A NEW BLACK BUTLER WORLD THAT'S DIFFERENT FROM THE MANGA!!
WE DECIDED TO WORK ON THIS TOGETHER WITH OUR READERS, SO WE TOOK A POLL ON THE VOICE ACTORS AND THE STORY.
SO HOW ABOUT WE DO A POLL?
OOH! GOOD IDEA!
THANKS TO EVERYONE WHO PARTICIPATED!!
FRONTIER WORKS-SAN MADE A SAMPLE CD OF THE VOICE ACTORS BASED ON THE POLL RESULTS.
THANK YOU VERY MUCH!
PLEASE LISTEN TO IT!!
AND EVERYONE AT MY WORKPLACE GOT TO PICK OUT THE VOICE ACTORS!!
FRONTIER WORKS-SAN
THEN THE SCRIPT ARRIVED, AND I LOOKED IT OVER WITH MY EDITOR.
WOOOOW!
BLACK BUTLER, FIRST DRAFT
THE SCRIPT'S READY!
I FELT A BIT TICKLED ABOUT MY MANGA GETTING TURNED INTO A SCRIPT.
AND HERE TOO EDITOR K DID IT AGAIN.
IT'S A DRAMA CD, SO WOULDN'T YOU WANT EFFECTS THAT CAN ONLY BE DONE BY SOUND?
SCRIPT.

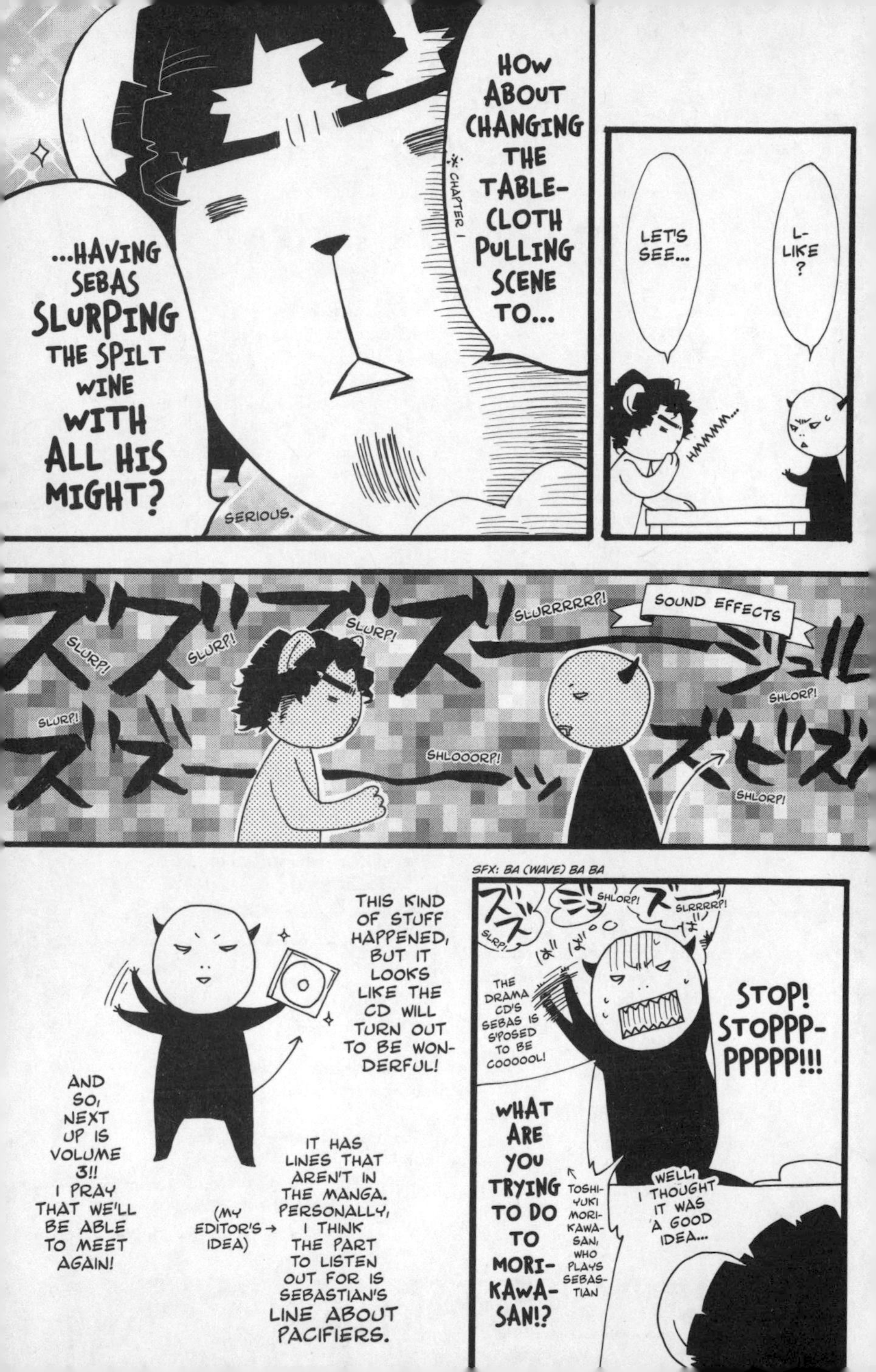
L-LIKE?
LET'S SEE...
HMMMM...
HOW ABOUT CHANGING THE TABLE-CLOTH PULLING SCENE TO...
※CHAPTER 1
...HAVING SEBAS SLURPING THE SPILT WINE WITH ALL HIS MIGHT?
SERIOUS.
SOUND EFFECTS
SLURRRRRP!
SLURP!
SLURP!
SLURP!
SLURP!
SHLOOORP!
SHLORP!
SHLORP!
SFX: BA (WAVE) BA BA
SHLORP!
SLRRRRP!
SLRP!
STOP! STOPPP-PPPPP!!!
THE DRAMA CD'S SEBAS IS S'POSED TO BE COOOOOL!
WHAT ARE YOU TRYING TO DO TO MORI-KAWA-SAN!?
TOSHI-YUKI MORI-KAWA-SAN, WHO PLAYS SEBAS-TIAN
WELL, I THOUGHT IT WAS A GOOD IDEA...
THIS KIND OF STUFF HAPPENED, BUT IT LOOKS LIKE THE CD WILL TURN OUT TO BE WON-DERFUL!
IT HAS LINES THAT AREN'T IN THE MANGA. PERSONALLY, I THINK THE PART TO LISTEN OUT FOR IS SEBASTIAN'S LINE ABOUT PACIFIERS.
(MY EDITOR'S IDEA)
AND SO, NEXT UP IS VOLUME 3!! I PRAY THAT WE'LL BE ABLE TO MEET AGAIN!

Translation Notes

PAGE 7
Assam tea
A rich, full-bodied black tea grown in Assam, India which is often used in breakfast tea blends such as English Breakfast Tea.

PAGE 8
Herend Chinoiserie
This is arguably Herend Porcelain's most famous pattern and was debuted in 1851 at the first World's Fair in London, where it caught the eye of Queen Victoria and was later renamed for her. Herend Porcelain is a Hungarian manufacturer of luxury porcelain goods that was popular with European aristocrats during the Victorian era.

PAGE 9
Keemun tea
An aromatic black tea of Chinese origin that has a fruity taste. It was first produced in 1875.

PAGE 10
Couverture
High-grade chocolate that contains a greater percentage of cocoa butter, producing a creamier flavor and extra sheen when tempered. These characteristics are especially valuable to professional chocolate makers.

Cointreau
A triple-distilled French liqueur made from the peels of bitter oranges.

PAGE 14
"Art is an explosion!"
A reference to the Japanese painter and sculptor Taro Okamoto, who was known for his avant-garde works; "Art is explosion!" was a catchphrase of his.

PAGE 39
Elevenses
A light, mid-morning snack similar to afternoon tea, but for the time at which it is consumed.

Jackson's Earl Grey
Earl Grey is a fragrant, citrusy bergamot-flavoured black tea that was named for the second Earl Grey, who is said to have gotten the blend from China. Jackson's of Piccadilly Earl Grey is still available today; you should try it!

PAGE 41
Jack the Ripper
A serial killer who stalked the streets of Whitechapel in East London in late 1888. Though hotly contested, Mary Ann "Polly" Nichols was one of the Ripper's first victims.

PAGE 50
"What the heck?"
A typical *tsukkomi* ("straight man") line and gesture in a *manzai* (two-person stand-up comedy) act.

"The next performer seems to be good."
A typical way to end a performance in *rakugo*, a Japanese storytelling tra-

dition featuring one storyteller who uses few props and vocal and physical gestures to tell lengthy, comical stories involving multiple characters.

PAGE 51
"A fool on the futon."
Originally, *futon ga futtonda* ("The futon blew away"; a bad pun in Japanese).

PAGE 55
"Sell off yer kidney or liver to make the money!"
An example of what yakuza loan sharks are thought to say when collecting on loans.

PAGE 87
Ciel's dialogue while in drag
In the original edition, Ciel employs certain speech patterns and turns of phrase that are particular to women when he is speaking to the Viscount of Druitt at the party.

PAGE 114
Wasp waist
A fashion silhouette that was popular in the nineteenth century, where a woman's waist was cinched even more tightly than in an average corset, creating a tiny waist that was considered essential for any woman who wanted to be the picture of feminine beauty.

PAGE 125
Annie Chapman
Often recognised as Jack the Ripper's second confirmed victim, Annie Chapman was killed and her uterus removed in September 1888 in East London.

PAGE 150
Mary Kelly
Often thought to be the final victim of the actual Jack the Ripper, Mary Kelly was a prostitute who was killed in November 1888 in East London.

PAGE 161
Grelle's mode of speech (aka *onee kotoba*)
Once Grelle's true identity is revealed, he begins speaking in *onee kotoba* (literally, "older sister speech"). This is a rough, effeminate form of spoken Japanese often employed by gay and male-to-female transgendered individuals in which feminine pronouns, word endings, and intonation are used. For example, instead of using *watashi* (a common, polite, neutral pronoun meaning "I"), he refers to himself as *atashi*, which is a colloquial pronoun that a young woman might use to refer to herself.

PAGE 162
Sebastian darling/Sebastian
In the Japanese edition, Grelle uses "Sebas-*chan*" as his nickname for Sebastian. This is essentially a homophone for the Phantomhive butler's name, but the way it's written shows that Grelle is shortening Sebastian's given name and adding -*chan* to it. -*chan* is a diminutive honourific used for little girls and cute persons or creatures of either gender that indicates familiarity. Grelle's getting a little intimate here, and Sebastian might well take it as an insult if he's so inclined!

Speaking of Sebastian's given name, did you know that in anime and manga, the name "Sebastian" is sort of the Japanese equivalent of "Jeeves"? In other words, it's the most popular/ stereotypical name for a butler. This has a lot to do with the popular 1970s anime classic *Heidi, Girl of the Alps* and the butler character in it — Sebastian, of course.

PAGE 169
Royal London Hospital
An actual institution in Whitechapel, this was known as the London Hospital until 1990, when its name was changed to the Royal London Hospital.

PAGE 177
"Even so, I am still a butler . . . for DEATH!"
Grelle too seems to be fond of puns. In Japanese, he says, "*Kore demo shitsuji DEATH!*" *DEATH* in Japanese is a homophone for *desu*, a linking verb that typically means "to be" and is found at the end of sentences.

PAGE 182
Quadrille, Lancers quadrille, galop, polka
The dances Sebastian mentions were all very popular during the social season in Victorian England. Introduced in England in the nineteenth century, the quadrille is a brisk, traditional dance involving intricate figures (or movements) performed by four couples organised in the shape of a square who face inward toward each other on the floor. The Lancers quadrille was another set of movements introduced later that were said to be more complicated than its predecessor. The galop is a fast, popular, closed-hold country dance. And the polka was a dance that originated in Central Europe and involved small half-steps to a light, airy tune.

PAGE 183
"It's not Hitsugi . . ."
The single kanji character that makes up Toboso-sensei's last name is easily confused with the kanji for "coffin."

PAGE 184
"Grelle Goes Bad"
The Japanese for this chapter description is "Gureru • Gureru!?" which is a play on words. Grelle is pronounced "Gureru" in Japanese and is a homophone for *gureru*, which means "to stray from the right path."

JAPANESE HONOURIFICS

-san: The Japanese equivalent of Mr./ Mrs./Miss. If a situation calls for politeness, this is the fail-safe honourific.

-kun: Used most often when referring to boys (though it can be applied to girls as well), this indicates affection or familiarity. Occasionally used by older men among their peers, but it may also be used by anyone referring to a person of lower standing.

-chan: An affectionate honourific indicating familiarity used mostly in reference to girls; also used in reference to cute persons or animals of either gender.

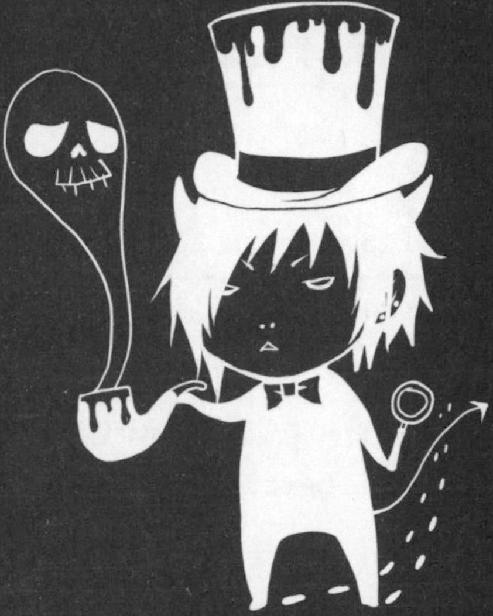

Yana Toboso

AUTHOR'S NOTE

Nowadays, I really feel that nothing goes right unless I make up my mind and am ready.

Working, playing, doing good things, and doing bad things won't go the way I want them to unless I brace myself in advance.

Even doing silly things isn't fun unless I'm prepared for it.

Well then.

I felt like that with ***Black Butler*** 2.

BLACK BUTLER ❷

YANA TOBOSO

Translation: Tomo Kimura • **Lettering: Tania Biswas**

KUROSHITSUJI Vol. 2 ©2007 Yana Toboso/SQUARE ENIX CO., LTD. First published in Japan in 2007 by SQUARE ENIX CO., LTD. English translation rights arranged with SQUARE ENIX CO., LTD. and Yen Press, LLC through Tuttle-Mori Agency, Inc.

English translation © 2010 by SQUARE ENIX CO., LTD.

Yen Press
1290 Avenue of the Americas
New York, NY 10104

Visit us at yenpress.com
facebook.com/yenpress
twitter.com/yenpress
yenpress.tumblr.com
instagram.com/yenpress

First Yen Press Edition: May 2010

Yen Press is an imprint of Yen Press, LLC.
The Yen Press name and logo are trademarks of Yen Press, LLC.

ISBN: 978-0-316-08425-3

30 29 28 27

WOR

Printed in the United States of America